Published by Scarecrow Press, Inc.
A wholly owned subsidiary of The Rowman & Littlefield Publishing Group, Inc.
4501 Forbes Boulevard, Suite 200, Lanham, Maryland 20706
http://www.scarecrowpress.com

Estover Road, Plymouth PL6 7PY, United Kingdom

British Library Cataloguing in Publication Information Available

Library of Congress Cataloging-in-Publication Data

Phillips, Gene D.
  Out of the shadows : expanding the canon of classic film noir / Gene D. Phillips.
    p. cm.
  Includes bibliographical references and index.
  Includes filmography.
  ISBN 978-0-8108-8189-1 (cloth : alk. paper) — ISBN 978-0-8108-8190-7 (ebook)
 1. Film noir—History and criticism. I. Title.
  PN1995.9.F54P475 2012
  791.43'655—dc23   2011023510

∞™ The paper used in this publication meets the minimum requirements of American
National Standard for Information Sciences—Permanence of Paper for Printed Library
Materials, ANSI/NISO Z39.48-1992.

Printed in the United States of America

For
George Cukor

The younger generation of directors still hasn't
learned some things about filmmaking that
George Cukor forgot in 1941.

Dashiell Hammett took murder out of the vicar's rose garden and dropped it in the alley.

—Raymond Chandler

CONTENTS

Acknowledgments vii
Prologue: Overlooked Noir ix

PART ONE   CITY OF NIGHT: THE ADVENT OF FILM NOIR

CHAPTER ONE   *Black Mask* Brigade: Dashiell Hammett,
Hard-Boiled Fiction, and Film Noir 3

CHAPTER TWO   Exploring Film Noir: *Stranger on the Third
Floor* and Other Films .13

**PART TWO   NIGHTMARE TOWN: DASHIELL HAMMETT'S
FICTION AS FILM NOIR**

CHAPTER THREE   John Huston: *The Maltese Falcon* 29

CHAPTER FOUR   Stuart Heisler: *The Glass Key*
Edward Buzzell: *Song of the Thin Man* 45

**PART THREE   DARKNESS AT NOON: REPRESENTATIVE
NOIR FILMS**

CHAPTER FIVE   Fritz Lang: *Ministry of Fear* and *Scarlet Street* 69

CHAPTER SIX   Alfred Hitchcock: *Spellbound* and *Strangers
on a Train*. 87

CONTENTS

CHAPTER SEVEN   George Cukor: *A Double Life*
Billy Wilder: *Sunset Boulevard* 111

CHAPTER EIGHT   Robert Siodmak: *The Killers* (1946)
Don Siegel: *The Killers* (1964) 131

CHAPTER NINE   Otto Preminger: *Laura* and *Anatomy of a Murder* 151

CHAPTER TEN   Fred Zinnemann: *Act of Violence*
Stanley Kubrick: *The Killing* 177

CHAPTER ELEVEN   Orson Welles: *The Stranger* and *Touch of Evil* 197

PART FOUR   THE LOWER DEPTHS: THE RISE OF NEO-NOIR

CHAPTER TWELVE   Dashiell Hammett and Neo-Noir:
The Dain Curse and *Hammett* 225

CHAPTER THIRTEEN   Anthony Minghella: *The Talented Mr. Ripley*
Liliana Cavani: *Ripley's Game* 247

Afterword by Jim Welsh 265
Filmography 275
Selected Bibliography 287
Index 295
About the Author 307

ACKNOWLEDGMENTS

First of all, I am grateful to the filmmakers who discussed their noir films with me in the course of the long period in which I was engaged in remote preparation for this study. I interviewed Fritz Lang, George Cukor, and Billy Wilder in Hollywood; Sir Alfred Hitchcock, John Huston, and Otto Preminger in New York City; and Fred Zinnemann and Stanley Kubrick in London. I also talked with Don Siegel at the Chicago International Film Festival.

In addition, I would also like to single out the following for their assistance: Patricia Hitchcock O'Connell, who played a supporting role in *Strangers on a Train*, for examining an early draft of the material on the film directed by her father; and Garson Kanin and Ruth Gordon, who wrote the screenplay for Cukor's *A Double Life*.

Many institutions and individuals provided me with research materials. I would like specifically to single out the following: the staff of the Film Study Center of the Museum of Modern Art in New York; the staff of the Motion Picture Section of the Library of Congress in Washington; the staff of the National Film Archive of the Library of the British Film Institute in London; and the staff of the Department of Special Collections, the Newberry Research Library in Chicago.

Research materials were also provided by the Paramount Collection of the Margaret Herrick Library of the Academy of Motion Picture Arts and Sciences in Hollywood; the Department of Special Collections of the Research Library of the University of California at Los Angeles; the Billy Rose Collection of the Theater and Film Collection of the New York

ACKNOWLEDGMENTS

Public Library at Lincoln Center; the Film Archive of George Eastman House in Rochester, New York; the Warner Bros. Collection in the Archive of the Library of the University of Southern California.

As well as the Script Repositories of Columbia Pictures, Metro-Goldwyn-Mayer, Warner Bros., Paramount, United Artists, Twentieth Century Fox, and Universal Studios; film historian and documentary filmmaker Kevin Brownlow, movie critic and film historian Andrew Sarris, film scholar Bernard Dick of Fairleigh Dickinson University; film historian Charles Higham.

Some materials in this book appeared in a completely different form in the following publications: "Stanley Kubrick," in *The Movie Makers: Artists in an Industry* (Chicago: Nelson-Hall, 1973), copyright by Gene D. Phillips; "Billy Wilder: An Interview," *Literature/Film Quarterly* 4, no. 1 (Winter 1976), 2–12, copyright 1976 by Salisbury University; *Exiles in Hollywood: Major European Film Directors in America* (Cranbury, N.J.: Associated University Presses, 1998), copyright by Associated University Presses (it includes Billy Wilder); *Creatures of Darkness: Raymond Chandler, Detective Fiction, and Film Noir* (Lexington: University Press of Kentucky, 2000), copyright 2000 by the University Press of Kentucky. This material is used with permission.

PROLOGUE

OVERLOOKED NOIR

Film historians generally agree that the classic period of film noir lasted roughly from 1940 to 1960. Specifically, film noir was a cycle in American cinema that first came into prominence during World War II, peaked in the 1950s, and began to taper off as a definable trend by 1960. Throughout the 1940s and 1950s the American screen was riddled with films that reflected the dark underside of American life, writes Andrew Dickos. The directors of these films "fashioned this noir landscape in the city and peopled it with troubled and desperate characters."[1]

Over the years a canon of films from the period has emerged that film historians consider the standard group of films of the classic noir cycle, ranging from *The Naked City* (1948), for example, to *The Big Combo* (1955)—movies that clearly depicted the haunted world of film noir. Nevertheless, film noir cannot be kept within the narrow limits of the official canon of films that have been established by film historians—it is too wide ranging for that.

As Bernard Dick explains, the elements of film noir "are applicable to a wide range of plots: the whodunit, the old dark house, the cover-up, the murderous couple, the murderous lover, and so on."[2] Consequently, there is still a number of neglected movies made during the classic noir period that need to be reevaluated as noir films. "We all agree that there is a core set of films in the noir canon," Mark Conrad states. "But the boundary is so fuzzy that we disagree about whether a great many others . . . belong there as well."[3] Accordingly, this book is designed to be a mix of major noir films like Wilder's *Sunset Boulevard* (1950) and films not often associated with film noir like Cukor's *A Double Life* (1947).

It is generally agreed that Dashiell Hammett invented hard-boiled detective fiction—which became the basis of film noir—with the novels and stories he wrote in the 1920s and 1930s. So Hammett is featured in this book, which includes the films *The Maltese Falcon* (1941), a recognized noir, and *The Glass Key* (1942), an overlooked noir. The latter movie is unfamiliar as far as being considered a classic noir, but it is well known as one of the crime films of the 1940s in which Alan Ladd and Veronica Lake costarred (along with *This Gun for Hire* and *The Blue Dahlia*). I shall also treat *Song of the Thin Man* (1934), the film version of Hammett's novel of that name. Although it falls within the period of classic noir, *Song of the Thin Man* is a neglected noir.

My book *Creatures of the Darkness: Raymond Chandler, Detective Fiction, and Film Noir* (2000) focused on the noir films made from the hard-boiled fiction of Raymond Chandler. But Hammett's career as a writer of hard-boiled fiction was shorter than Chandler's. After his fifth novel, Hammett ceased writing novels in 1934, whereas Chandler continued writing fiction until 1958. So I cannot devote a whole book to Hammett, as I did to Chandler. But Hammett is featured in this book, since he was not focused on in my Chandler book.

In short, I wish to emphasize that my present book on film noir is not merely a revision of my Chandler book on film noir. (Foster Hirsch and James Naremore have published revised editions of their noir books.) As a matter of fact, Chandler appears in this book as the coauthor of the screenplay for Hitchcock's *Strangers on a Train* (1951); I do not include any of the films based on Chandler's fiction in the present volume. I do include two films derived from Hammett's novels, as mentioned already. That Hammett is still very much associated with hard-boiled fiction is verified by Joe Gores's novel *Spade and Archer*, a 2009 spin-off from *The Maltese Falcon*, which provides a backstory for Hammett's celebrated novel.

That some important works have appeared on film noir indicates the continued interest in the topic over the years. But I am confident that I am bringing a new twist to the topic by expanding the canon of classic film noir.

In surveying the previous books on film noir I note that Dickos's *Street with No Name: A History of Classic Film Noir* (2009) sticks to the "official canon" of film noir movies of the classic period. Dickos also deals with the French antecedents of American film noir in great detail (Renoir, etc.); and there is no need to repeat which he has done in this regard. Books like Foster Hirsch's *The Dark Side of the Screen: Film Noir* (1981; revised 2009) and James Naremore's *More Than Night: Film Noir in Its Contexts* (1998; revised 2008) present a survey of noir films, but with in-depth commentary on a few selected films. Mayer and McDonnell's *Encyclopedia of Film Noir* (2007) is likewise a survey of noir films. It is a reference book with entries arranged in alphabetical order.

At the other end of the spectrum books like William Hare's *Early Film Noir* (2002) and John Irwin's *Unless the Threat of Death Is behind Them: Hard-Boiled Fiction and Film Noir* (2006) cover only a few major noir films like *Double Indemnity*. A series of four volumes edited by Alain Silver and James Ursini under the title of *Film Noir Reader* (1996–2003) are collections of essays by various authors, which are in general more theoretical than my present study.

In sum, I present an in-depth examination of several key noir films, some of which are in the canon of noir films of the classic period, like Otto Preminger's *Laura* (1944), and some that deserve to be in the canon, like Preminger's *Anatomy of a Murder* (1959). Thus I aim to widen the scope of the discussion of film noir with some films hitherto not usually considered as noirs, such as Hitchcock's *Spellbound* (1945).

Still I have avoided the trap of operating on the notion that once you start looking for noir you see it everywhere. One must be aware that a film must meet certain standards to be considered among the classic film noirs. Otherwise one can nominate biker movies and slasher movies as film noirs—as Wheeler Dixon does in *Film Noir and Cinema of Paranoia* (2009).

My book coincides with a resurgence of critical interest in film noir, and that makes it all the more timely. Among the notable directors represented in the book are Billy Wilder, Orson Welles, and Stanley Kubrick, all of whom made superior noir films. During the long period in which this author was researching this book, he interviewed many of the important directors represented here, such as Alfred Hitchcock, Fritz Lang, John Huston, and others. This interview material is a highlight of the book.

Moreover, the present study makes use of material not previously available: A comparison of the British release version of *Strangers on a Train*, which has been found, with the American release version. A comparison of the prereleased version of Welles's *Touch of Evil* (1958), which has been brought to light, with the version released in the theaters.

Fred Zinnemann's *Act of Violence* (1949) has been a neglected noir simply because it was inexplicably unavailable for nearly fifty years—until it came to light in recent years on DVD. By the same token, the TV adaptation of Hammett's *Dain Curse* disappeared without a trace after it premiered on CBS-TV as a five-hour miniseries in 1978. It is now available on DVD and can be examined as the longest screen adaptation of a Hammett novel.

My procedure is the same one that I employed in my earlier volumes on film history. I interviewed directors and others connected with their films; I have read the screenplays whenever they are available. All of this increases the book's merit as a work of original scholarship. Moreover, I have weighed the evaluations of other commentators on the films, to achieve an in-depth examination of all of the films. I focus not only on the most celebrated noir films like Stanley Kubrick's *The Killing*, but I give equal time to other noirs—some of which are given short shrift in other books on noir, like Zinnemann's *Act of Violence*. Surely these underrated noir films deserve the reconsideration that I offer here. As film historian Brandon Linden puts it, "These films offer a wonderful chance to unearth and examine some compelling, virulent films from the dark side of life."[4]

In the final chapters I examine neo-noir—noir films that have appeared since the classic period of noir, like Roman Polanski's *Chinatown* (1974) and Curtis Hanson's *L.A. Confidential* (1997). I focus particularly on Anthony Minghella's *The Talented Mr. Ripley* (1999) and its neglected sequel, Liliana Cavani's *Ripley's Game* (2003). These films bring into relief that film noir is still with us in the neo-noirs that continue to be made since the classic period of noir.

Notes

Any direct quotations in this book that are undocumented are derived from the author's personal interviews with the subjects.

1. Andrew Dickos, *Street with No Name: A History of Classic Film Noir* (Lexington: University Press of Kentucky, 2002), xi.

2. Bernard Dick, *Anatomy of Film*, rev. ed. (New York: Bedford/St. Martin's, 2010), 150.

3. Mark Conrad, "The Meaning and Definition of Noir," in *The Philosophy of Film Noir*, ed. Mark Conrad (Lexington: University Press of Kentucky, 2006), 14.

4. Brandon Linden, "Unknown Noir," *Facets Film Studies* (Chicago: Facets Multimedia, 2006), 2.

Part One

CITY OF NIGHT: THE ADVENT OF FILM NOIR

BLACK MASK BRIGADE: DASHIELL HAMMETT, HARD-BOILED FICTION, AND FILM NOIR

In the annals of detective fiction Sir Arthur Conan Doyle was one of the foremost writers of classic British mystery stories. Conan Doyle's Sherlock Holmes, with his "science of deduction," could unravel the threads of a mystery and cleverly arrive at an astonishing solution. Conan Doyle published the first of his Sherlock Holmes stories, *A Study in Scarlet*, in 1887. Holmes became the world's first consulting detective.[1]

"Holmes seemed so real, so magnificently life-like," writes Jeremy McCarter, "that some readers thought he really existed."[2] Indeed, Conan Doyle regularly received letters addressed to Holmes till the end of his days. The popularity of Holmes was such that William Gillette wrote a play, *Sherlock Holmes* (1899), in which he played Holmes on tour for three decades. It was Gillette, by the way, who coined the celebrated phrase, "Elementary, my dear Watson," in his play.[3]

Nevertheless, Dashiell Hammett dismissed Conan Doyle's stories as exercises in mere puzzle solving. Still Conan Doyle, whose last volume of Holmes stories, *The Case-Book of Sherlock Holmes*, published in 1927, ushered in "the so-called Golden Age of British detective fiction" in the 1920s and 1930s. "Writers became known for their expert refinements of the puzzle."[4] The most famous of these authors was Dame Agatha Christie, whose stories were usually set in the baronial country estates of upper-class society. Her first novel, *The Mysterious Affair at Styles* (1920), introduced the Belgian private detective Hercule Poirot, whose fictional career endured until his last appearance in *Curtain* (1975), which was the occasion of Christie's celebrated detective receiving an obituary in the

London Times (!), Poirot, Christie's armchair sleuth, could find the solution to any mystery with his ingenious faculties of deduction.

British mystery writer P. D. James, the creator of detective Adam Dalgliesh, writes off both Conan Doyle and Christie as "overrated relics of the English crime story's much-vaunted Golden Age." She simply dismisses Conan Doyle's Sherlock Holmes as an implausible figure. Christie she blasts because "she wasn't an innovator and had no interest in exploring the possibilities of the genre," as did Dashiell Hammett.[5]

Satirizing the mystery fiction of Agatha Christie, Raymond Chandler (*The Big Sleep*) wrote, "Heigh ho, I think I'll write an English detective story, one about Superintendent Jones and the two elderly ladies in the thatched cottage." After the case is solved, Chandler concluded, "everyone breathes a sigh of relief while the butler pours a round of sherry."[6] Chandler believed that Dashiell Hammett's tough, hard-boiled crime fiction, which he began publishing in the early 1920s, was the first significant departure from the more refined, genteel British school of detective stories.

The Boys in the Back Room

Chandler was aware that literary critic Edmund Wilson called the practitioners of hard-boiled fiction "the boys in the back room" because they churned out mystery stories for cut-rate pulp magazines at a penny a word. For his part, Chandler paid tribute to Dashiell Hammett by declaring that Hammett, in his hard-boiled fiction, had taken murder out of "the vicar's rose garden," where Christie had placed it, "and dropped it in the alley."[7]

Chandler explained, "Hammett gave murder back to the kind of people who commit it for reasons," not just to provide a gentleman detective with a mystery to puzzle over. "He put these people down on paper as they are, and he made them talk and think in the language they customarily used for these purposes."[8]

The British school of detective fiction, epitomized by Conan Doyle and Agatha Christie, presented an optimistic view of the world. The British mystery story "upheld a moral code that crime must not pay; yet we all know it can and does."[9] Hammett biographer William Nolan, in his brilliant essay on Hammett, writes that, with the arrival of Dashiell Hammett on the literary scene, "the staid English tradition of the tweedy gentleman detective was shattered. . . . The polite British sleuth gave way to a hard-boiled man of action, who didn't mind bending some rules to get the job done."[10]

Perhaps Hammett himself described the typical private eye best when he wrote, "Your private detective does not want to be an erudite solver of riddles in the Sherlock Holmes manner; he wants to be a hard and shifty fellow, able to take care of himself in any situation, able to get the best of anybody he comes in contact with, whether criminal, innocent bystander, or client."[11]

Hammett is less interested in the solution of a mystery than in portraying his detective hero's encounters with the evils of modern society in a vivid and compelling fashion. As Chandler put it, "The solution of the mystery is only the olive in the martini."[12] Chandler freely acknowledged his debt to Hammett: "I did not invent the hard-boiled murder story," he wrote to fellow writer Cleve Adams; "I have never made any secret of my opinion that Hammett deserves most or all of the credit."[13]

Like F. Scott Fitzgerald, Dashiell Hammett came out of the Maryland Catholic tradition; he was raised a Catholic but drifted away from practicing the faith in his adult life. Nevertheless, despite the fact that Hammett never pretended to present a coherent religious philosophy in his work, his characters operate in a Judeo-Christian environment; and many of them—regardless of their personal shortcomings—represent a genuine concern for ethical and moral values. It is precisely by striving to live up to their ideals that Hammett's characters can redeem themselves. "In everything that can be called art there is a quality of redemption," Chandler affirmed in "The Simple Art of Murder"; and this is certainly true of Hammett's work.[14] His fiction reflects the interlocking Catholic themes of sin, repentance, and redemption.

Hammett's stories may imply the hope of a better day to come for some of his characters, but not for society at large. He frankly believed that society itself was corrupt. His disheveled gumshoe may solve the mystery at hand, but the story inevitably concludes with an abiding sense of dissatisfaction. For the detective-protagonist is aware that his best efforts are ultimately futile, to the extent that the corrupt urban environment will inevitably undercut and outlast his heroic attempts to see justice done. When the case is closed, the city remains essentially lawless.

With the emergence of hard-boiled detective fiction in the 1920s, the mystery story shed its refined English manners and went native. Indeed, detective fiction grew more pessimistic, hard, and cynical, according to

Chandler. He once said that when the author of a hard-boiled mystery story is in doubt about what to do next, he should have "a man come through a door with a gun in his hand."[15] Hammett did in fact employ that solution to the plot complications of a story at times. (Hard-boiled fiction was so named because the tough detective-hero developed a shell like a hard-boiled egg in order to protect his feelings from being bruised by the calloused and cruel criminal types he often encountered.)

In general Hammett endorsed Chandler's analysis of Hammett's work in his essay "The Simple Art of Murder." In a letter to his daughter Mary, dated December 28, 1944, Hammett wrote, "There's an article about detective stories (and me) in the December *Atlantic Monthly* by Raymond Chandler. He did a pretty good job."[16]

Hard-boiled detective fiction flourished in the 1920s and 1930s with the work of Dashiell Hammett, Raymond Chandler, and James M. Cain (*Double Indemnity*). This trio is considered the pantheon of hard-boiled fiction, as they not only helped make detective fiction respectable, but helped raise it to the lofty level of literature.

Edmund Wilson was one of the first literary critics to note that Chandler, Hammett, and Cain all "stemmed originally from Hemingway."[17] And rightly so. Ernest Hemingway's terse, brittle, vernacular prose, which was similar to that of a journalist's on-the-spot reportage, plus his economical, colloquial dialogue, impressed the writers of hard-boiled fiction, and they honed their own writing styles to achieve a similar effect.

Foster Hirsch affirms that the triumvirate of Hammett, Chandler, and Cain admired Hemingway because he pioneered the hard-boiled style of fiction. "Hemingway did more than any other single writer to legitimate the colloquial mode in American prose"; he perfected a lean, spare style, with no frills.[18]

While Chandler praised Hammett as "the ace performer" among writers of hard-boiled fiction, he added, "There is nothing in his work that is not implicit in the early novels and short stories of Hemingway."[19] More than one reviewer of Hammett's novel *The Maltese Falcon* (1930), for example, likened Hammett's crisp, clean-cut language to that of Hemingway's hard-boiled short story "The Killers" (1927). Indeed, in 1931 Hammett himself stated that he "especially admired the fiction of Hemingway."[20]

James M. Cain did not mind being compared to Hemingway: "Each of us shudders at the least hint of the highfalutin, the pompous, or the literary.

We have people talk as they do talk; and, as some of them are of a low station in life, no doubt they often say things in a similar way." Such resemblances between Hemingway and himself, Cain conceded, suggest that "I had in some part walked in his footsteps." But Cain decidedly denied that he could be compared to Hammett. After reading twenty pages of Hammett (the first chapter of *The Glass Key*), "I said, forget this goddamned book." Yet, Cain complained, critics referred to his "'hammett-and-tongs' style."[21]

The hard-boiled detective story first began appearing in the pages of the pulp detective magazine *Black Mask* in the spring of 1923. (Pulp fiction got its name from the "cheap, rough, wood-pulp paper" on which it was printed, a paper far less costly than the smooth paper typical of slick magazines like the *Saturday Evening Post*.)[22]

While Joseph "Captain" Shaw was editor of *Black Mask* (1926–1936) the magazine defined the best of American hard-boiled detective fiction by its departure from the older, conventional British detective stories. "We meditated on the possibility of creating a new type of detective story," Shaw later wrote, different from the mystery stories of Conan Doyle; that is, "the crossword puzzle sort, lacking—deliberately—all other human emotional values."[23]

Dashiell Hammett's detective stories were first published in *Black Mask* in the fall of 1923. Hammett was a literate and polished writer. He had himself been an operative for the Pinkerton Agency, the first private detective agency in the United States, which had been established in 1850. In fact, Pinkerton's trademark, an all-seeing eye coupled with the motto "We never sleep," was the genesis of the term *private eye*.[24]

Dashiell Hammett and *Black Mask*

Samuel Dashiell Hammett signed on as an agent of the Baltimore office of the Pinkerton Detective Bureau in 1915. He was known as Sam Hammett for his seven-year stint with the Pinkerton Agency—with time off to serve in World War I. (He would later give his first name to private eye Sam Spade in *The Maltese Falcon*.) In 1921 Hammett's work as a private eye took him to San Francisco, where he worked as a private detective until he left the Pinkerton Agency for good in 1922 at the age of twenty-seven. San Francisco, where he lived throughout the Roaring Twenties, would become in his fiction a symbol of mystery, duplicity, and corruption,

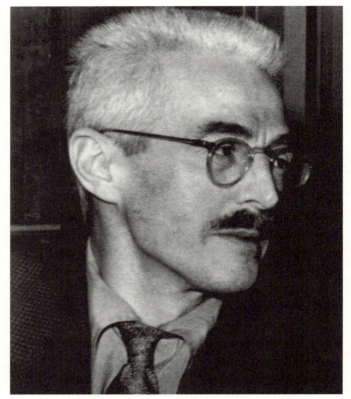

Novelist Dashiell Hammett, whose hard-boiled detective fiction inspired the rise of film noir.

especially in *The Maltese Falcon*. He had traveled widely as a private detective and had become convinced by his experiences that society was venal and corrupt.

With a stroke of genius Hammett saw that he could dramatize his accumulated experiences as a private eye. He began to write about the kind of lowlifes he had come to know while he was a Pinkerton agent. Stories began to pour out of him for the next decade. Nolan writes, "His stint as a working operative with Pinkerton provided a rock-solid base for his fiction," which no other pulp fiction writer could match.[25]

Many of his fictional characters were drawn from life. For example, Hammett recalled that the prototype of Joel Cairo, one of the petty criminals in *The Maltese Falcon*, was a crook "I picked up on a forgery charge in Pasco, Washington, in 1920." The original for "Wilmer, the boy gunman, was picked up in Stockton, California. He was a neat, small, smooth-faced, quiet boy of twenty-one. . . . He had robbed a Stockton filling station the previous week."[26]

In the stories he wrote for *Black Mask* Hammett portrays private detectives who are not supersleuths like Sherlock Holmes. "They are three-dimensional characters who bleed, suffer, make mistakes—in fact, human beings."[27]

Hammett's fiction was far removed from the sort of routine thrillers with wafer-thin plots devoted to solving a mystery, which are little more than "private eye-wash." He was convinced that it is not the solution to the mystery that really matters, but the finely wrought characterizations and human conflicts that make for a gripping detective story.

After Hammett published his first novel, *Red Harvest* (1929), in *Black Mask* in installments, it was clear that he was a serious writer, one who could "go the distance" and compose a complete novel, not just short stories. The Alfred Knopf Company published *Red Harvest*, a violent tale of labor disputes in a small Western town, as a novel shortly after its serialization in *Black Mask*.

Hammett's classic hard-boiled novel *The Maltese Falcon*, which featured his celebrated gumshoe Sam Spade, was serialized in *Black Mask* before its book publication in 1930. In the novel, Hammett minted the prototypical private investigator, a cynical, tough individual who maintains his code of honor in a world tarnished by deception and betrayal at all levels of society. It was this pivotal novel that firmly established the vogue of hard-boiled detective fiction.

British novelist Somerset Maugham, in his renowned essay "The Decline and Fall of the Detective Story," called Hammett "an inventive and original writer" and termed his antihero, Sam Spade, "a nasty bit of goods, but admirably depicted."[28] Hammett was the mentor of playwright Lillian Hellman, his companion for the last thirty years of his life. She would observe him while he was writing *The Thin Man*. "I had never seen anybody work that way," she recalled, "the care for every word."[29]

When Hammett was asked about his literary aspirations by his publisher, he replied, "I'm one of the few—if there are any more—people moderately literate who takes the detective story seriously. Some day somebody's going to make 'literature' of it."[30] By the time Hammett had published his third novel, *The Maltese Falcon*, Raymond Chandler did not hesitate to declare that "Hammett's work missed being literature, if at all, by the narrowest margin."[31] More recently, crime novelist Ross Macdonald named Hammett the number one writer of crime fiction: "We all came out from under Hammett's black mask."[32]

The Knopf Company gave its imprimatur to hard-boiled fiction by publishing novels by Cain and Chandler, as well as by Hammett, thereby attracting the interest of the Hollywood studios. Hammett's fiction was central to the development of the trend in American cinema in the 1940s known as film noir (dark cinema). Because the novels of Hammett and other writers of hard-boiled fiction influenced the development of film noir, their work became known as American noir fiction.

As a matter of fact, the widespread popularity of hard-boiled fiction in the 1930s prepared the American public for film noir. Readers of hard-boiled detective novels were fascinated by the dark world they depicted: bourbon for breakfast, bloody corpses, and shadowy streets lit by garish neon signs. Nevertheless, Chandler warned that serious novels could be transformed by the movie studios into "cheap, gun-in-the-kidney melo-dramas with wooden plots, and stock characters."[33]

Be that as it may, there was hope that hard-boiled novels could be made into movies that were reasonably faithful to their literary sources, as Paul Schrader writes in one of the most influential essays on film noir in English. The hard-boiled school of novelists "had a style made to order for film noir, and in turn they influenced noir screenwriting."[34]

Writers on the order of Hammett, "brandishing incredibly laconic prose and razor-sharp dialogue, wrote books that had almost the skeletal structure and style of a script." Movies like *The Maltese Falcon* capitalized on the filmic qualities of Hammett's tough detective fiction: "Crisp, clever plotting; locales where light and shadow could disport themselves; characters short on talk and big on action."[35]

Hammett, Cain, and Chandler all tried their hands at writing screenplays, with varying degrees of success. For the most part, however, it was as the authors of hard-boiled novels that were adapted to the screen that they left their lasting mark on film noir, "from lightning-quick dialogue to labyrinthine plots."[36]

Notes

1. Allen Eyles, *Sherlock Holmes: A Centenary Celebration* (New York: Harper & Row, 1986), 111.

2. Jeremy McCarter, "Arthur Conan Doyle and Sherlock Holmes," *New York Times Book Review*, December 20, 2007, 15.

3. Eyles, *Sherlock Holmes*, 39.

4. "Detective Fiction," in *Cambridge Guide to Literature in English*, ed. Dominic Head, rev. ed. (New York: Cambridge University Press, 2006), 296.

5. Janet Maslin, "P. D. James Is on the Case," *New York Times*, December 7, 2009, sec. C:1.

6. Roger Schatzkin, "Doubled Indemnity: Raymond Chandler, Popular Fiction, and Film" (Ph.D. diss., Rutgers University, 1984), 113.

7. Woody Haut, *Heartbreak and Vine: Hard-Boiled Writers in Hollywood* (London: Serpent's Tail, 2002), 17.

8. Raymond Chandler, "The Simple Art of Murder," in Raymond Chandler, *Later Novels and Other Writings*, ed. Frank MacShane (New York: Library of America, 1995), 989. This essay originally appeared in *Atlantic Monthly*, December 1944. It is not to be confused with the Introduction to *The Simple Art of Murder*, a volume of Chandler's short stories, cited below.

9. Mike Ripley and Maxim Jakubowski, "Fresh Blood: British Neo-Noir," in *The Big Book of Noir*, ed. Ed Gorman, Lee Server, and Martin Greenberg (New York: Carroll and Graf, 1998), 320.

10. William Nolan, "Introduction," in Dashiell Hammett, *Nightmare Town: Stories*, ed. Kirby McCauley, Martin Greenberg, and Ed Gorman (New York: Vintage Books, 2000), xii.

11. Dashiell Hammett, "Introduction," in *The Maltese Falcon* (New York: Modern Library, 1934), viii.

12. Jerry Speir, *Raymond Chandler* (New York: Unger, 1981), 10.

13. Letter from Raymond Chandler to Cleve Adams. Dated September 4, 1948, in Philip Kiszely, *Hollywood through Private Eyes: The Hard-Boiled Novel in the Studio Era* (New York: Lang, 2006), 35.

14. Chandler, "The Simple Art of Murder," 991.

15. Raymond Chandler, "Introduction," in *The Simple Art of Murder*, in Raymond Chandler, *Later Novels and Other Writings*, 1017.

16. Dashiell Hammett, *Selected Letters of Dashiell Hammett*, ed. Richard Layman and Julie Rivett (Washington, D.C.: Counterpoint, 2001), 396.

17. Edmund Wilson, "The Boys in the Back Room," in Edmund Wilson, *Classics and Commercials: A Literary Chronicle of the Forties* (New York: Noonday Press, 1967), 21.

18. Foster Hirsch, *The Dark Side of the Screen: Film Noir*, rev. ed. (New York: Da Capo Press, 2009), 28–29.

19. Chandler, "The Simple Art of Murder," 988.

20. Robert Gale, *A Dashiell Hammett Companion* (Westport, Conn.: Greenwood Press, 2000), 115.

21. James M. Cain, "Preface," in James M. Cain, *Three by Cain* (New York: Vintage Books, 1984), 352–54.

22. Marilyn Yaquinto, *Pump 'Em Full of Lead: Gangsters on Film* (New York: Twayne, 1998), 75.

23. Joseph Shaw, "Introduction," in *The Hard-Boiled Omnibus: Early Stories from* Black Mask, ed. Joseph Shaw (New York: Simon and Schuster, 1946), v.

24. Clifford May, "The Private Eye in Fact and Fiction," *Atlantic Monthly* 236, no. 2 (August 1975): 30.

25. Nolan, "Introduction," in Dashiell Hammett, *Nightmare Town*, xiii.

26. Hammett, "Introduction," in *The Maltese Falcon*, vii–viii.

27. Julian Symons, *Dashiell Hammett* (New York: Harcourt, Brace, and Jovanovich, 1985), 3.

28. Somerset Maugham, "The Decline and Fall of the Detective Story," in Somerset Maugham, *The Vagrant Mood: Six Essays* (Garden City, N.Y.: Doubleday, 1953), 126.

29. Lillian Hellman, "Introduction," in Dashiell Hammett, *The Big Knockover: Selected Stories and Short Novels* (New York: Vintage Books, 1989), xvi.

30. Diane Johnson, *Dashiell Hammett: A Life* (New York: Random House, 1983), 72.

31. Christopher Metress, "Introduction," in *The Critical Response to Dashiell Hammett*, ed. Christopher Metress (New York: Greenwood Press, 1994), xxi.

32. Nolan, "Introduction," in Dashiell Hammett, *Nightmare Town*, vii.

33. Raymond Chandler, "Writers in Hollywood," in Raymond Chandler, *Later Novels and Other Writings*, 995.

34. Paul Schrader, "Notes on Film Noir," in *American Movie Critics*, ed. Phillip Lopate, rev. ed. (New York: Library of America, 2008), 460.

35. Lawrence O'Toole, "Now Read the Movie," *Film Comment* 18, no. 8 (November–December 1982): 37.

36. James Monaco, ed., *Encyclopedia of Films* (New York: Putnam, 1990), 107.

CHAPTER TWO

EXPLORING FILM NOIR: *STRANGER ON THE THIRD FLOOR* AND OTHER FILMS

In attempting to explain the sudden emergence of film noir in the early 1940s, Philip Hanson points out that Joseph Breen, the industry censor, had become more liberal in approving projects in the 1940s that he would have turned down during the previous decade. This is perhaps because Breen was conscious that, as Raymond Chandler remarked in 1945, "People can take the hard-boiled stuff nowadays."[1]

For example, when Metro-Goldwyn-Mayer submitted James M. Cain's novella *Double Indemnity* to Breen's office in 1935, the censor decreed that "the sordid flavor of this story makes it thoroughly unacceptable for screen production."[2] When Paramount submitted a screen treatment (detailed synopsis) of *Double Indemnity* to Breen in 1943, however, Breen approved the project, commenting that, after all, "adultery is no longer quite as objectionable" as it once had been in films.[3]

The Rise of Film Noir

It has been said that film noir has lived in greater intimacy with its literary sources than any comparable trend in cinema. Hard-boiled fiction, especially the works by "its most respectable figures such as Dashiell Hammett and Raymond Chandler," had a great impact on the movies "by maintaining a constant supply of subject matter for the film noirs of the 1940s and 1950s." Thus, just as Dashiell Hammett's *Maltese Falcon* was the founding novel of hard-boiled detective fiction, so John Huston's film version

13

of *The Maltese Falcon* (1941) was a milestone in the development of film noir. With *Falcon*, a new kind of detective film had arrived—leaner, tougher, and darker than the crime movies of the 1930s.[4]

Noir films were frequently shot on the double and on the cheap; that is, on a tight shooting schedule and a stringent budget. Because a typical noir took place in a contemporary setting, no period sets or costumes were needed. "Since the action often occurred at night and was shot in low-key light, whatever sets were necessary could be minimal."[5] For example, the director would cast a heavy shadow across a room to hide the small set and its sparse furniture.

Still many superior examples of film noir, including Billy Wilder's *Double Indemnity* (1944), were turned out under these conditions. Furthermore, the low-budget, high-quality thrillers that surfaced in the 1940s had a profound influence on the crime film throughout the 1940s and 1950s. Indeed, the term *film noir* has continued to be applied to a body of films that has been influenced by the noir tradition in succeeding decades.

This trend in American cinema flourished during World War II. French critics christened films that fit this category film noir in 1946, when they were at last able to view the backlog of American movies made during World War II, which the war had prevented them from seeing. The French reviewers noticed "the new mood of cynicism, pessimism, and darkness that had crept into American cinema," writes Paul Schrader in one of the most influential essays on film noir in English. Never before had Hollywood films "dared to take such a harsh, uncomplimentary look at American life."[6]

A seminal essay on film noir was written for *French Screen* (*L'Ecran Français*), August 28, 1946, by French critic Nino Frank, who coined the term *film noir* and was the first critic to use it in print. In the essay Frank singles out *Double Indemnity*, *Laura*, and *The Maltese Falcon* as being in the vanguard of the new movement. These films, says Frank, have followed in the path of the revolution in the detective novel spearheaded by Dashiell Hammett.[7]

The very phrase *film noir* is a variation on the French term *roman noir* (dark novel), which referred to a tough sort of fiction dealing with lowlife criminals turned out by certain French novelists. This term, in turn, was related to the phrase *série noire* (dark series), which denoted the Parisian publisher Gaston Gallimard's new collection of contemporary crime fiction, most of them of American origin. The concept of the editor of the series, Marcel Duhamel, was to produce French translations of the works of such writers of hard-boiled fiction as Hammett, Chandler, and Cain, which were easily identifiable by their standard black covers. The initial directors of noir films were derived from these grimly naturalistic stories, such as Hammett's *Maltese Falcon*, "with its roots in the American pulps."[8] Film noir, then, was the cinematic extension of hard-boiled fiction. The work of Hammett, Cain, and Chandler became the source of some of the most trenchant films of the next decade.

The term *film noir* was not in common use in the film industry itself at the time. None of the directors who made these movies would have known the term; they would have described these pictures as thrillers or crime dramas. It was not until the 1960s that *film noir* became an accepted critical term.

Schrader rightly maintains that "film noir is not a genre," since it depends on the conventions of established genres, such as the gangster film and the murder mystery.[9] Similarly, Christopher Orr maintains that film noir is rather a "cycle of films" that are "expressions of pre-existing genres."[10]

Stephen Holden describes the standard ingredients of film noir in a nutshell: "A world-weary private eye finds himself trapped in a decadent, crime-ridden society. Even when he solves a case," good doesn't necessarily triumph over evil. "The evil is simply mopped up."[11] The milieu of film noir is a stark night world of dark angles and elongated shadows, where rain glistens on windows and windshields and faces are barred with shadows that suggest some imprisonment of body or soul. This dark, brooding atmosphere, coupled with an equally somber view of life, marks a movie as film noir.

The pessimistic view of the human condition exhibited in such movies was an outgrowth of the disillusionment spawned by World War II, with its "massive casualties, genocide, and torture." Moreover, this "post–World War II disillusionment" would continue into the cold war, that period of uncertainty that was the war's aftermath.[12] Indeed, the cold war, which followed the hot war, spawned Senator Joseph McCarthy's witch hunt for communists, which was carried on by the hearings of the House Un-American Activities Committee. "The world was gloomier and more complicated than it had been before."[13]

Also in keeping with the conventions of film noir is an air of spare, unvarnished realism, typified by the stark, documentary-like quality of the cinematography, especially in the grim scenes that take place at night. In essence, the sinister nightmare world of film noir is one of seedy motels, boardinghouses, roadside diners, shabby bars, and fly-specked cafés.

It is a world in which a woman with a past can encounter a man with no future in the insulated atmosphere of a tawdry cocktail lounge. The heroine is usually discovered "propped against a piano, singing an insolent dirge. The hero is a cynic who has been pushed around once too often" by life.[14]

In his film adaptation of *The Maltese Falcon*, writer-director Huston presents two prominent character types that would become staples of film noir: the noirish lone wolf private detective, Sam Spade, and the crafty, malevolent femme fatale Brigid O'Shaughnessy. The femme fatale is a seductive siren, a double-dealing, heartless woman who uses men and then discards them. Admittedly, the femme fatale is a deadly dragon lady, but she is also "a fascinating creature," Dickos writes. She exists in a posture of defiance, precisely because she does not acquiesce to "the traditionally imposed subordinate function in a male-dominated society."[15] Hence men regard her as a challenge.

German Expressionism

"It might be said that Hollywood's most generous benefactor was Adolf Hitler," film historian Tony Thomas has written. "The Nazi regime forced numerous . . . directors to find their way to California."[16] When Hitler came to power in 1933, he "put into action policies of extreme nationalism. As a scapegoat for Germany's political, military, and economic troubles of the previous fifteen years, Hitler targeted Jews," Giannetti and Eyman point out. "After May, 1933, when he became chancellor, prescient Jewish Germans began packing their bags, for under the Nazis no Jew could be employed in any branch of the film industry."[17]

Since the German film industry was the foremost center of filmmaking in Europe, Austrians like Fritz Lang, Billy Wilder, and Fred Zinnemann worked in the studios in Berlin, along with native Germans like Robert Siodmak. In 1929 Siodmak, Wilder, and Zinnemann joined forces on a semidocumentary entitled *Menschen am Sonntag* (*People on Sunday*). The film was directed by Siodmak, written by Wilder, and Zinnemann was the assistant cameraman. All three of them would migrate to Hollywood eventually and become directors there—and all three, along with Lang, are represented in this book. Lang, Wilder, and Zinnemann joined the exodus to Hollywood after Hitler nationalized the German film industry in 1933.[18] Siodmak chose to make films in France throughout the 1930s and decamped for Hollywood in 1939, when the war broke out in Europe.

They were all working in Germany when the movement known as expressionism had a significant impact on both stage and screen. It is not my purpose to dwell in detail on the influence of expressionism on the films of the directors who immigrated to Hollywood from Germany in the wake of the rise of Hitler, but the following observations are in order.

Lotte Eisner, in *The Haunted Screen: Expressionism in the German Cinema*, describes the movement in the following terms: "Expressionism sets itself against Naturalism, with its mania for recording mere facts"; instead, the expressionistic artist seeks the symbolic meaning that underlies the facts.[19] German expressionistic films were shot on claustrophobic studio sets, where physical reality could be distorted. To be precise, expressionism exaggerated surface reality in order to make a symbolic point.

For example, the outer world may be distorted "in order to better express the anxious, tormented inner world of the characters."[20] As early as 1919 Robert Wiene directed *Das Kabinett des Dr. Caligari* (*The Cabinet of Dr. Caligari*), a key expressionistic film. In the film Francis, a student, denounces Dr. Caligari, the head of a mental institution, as a madman. But the epilogue reveals that it is Francis who is insane. Consequently, the foregoing tale is a lunatic's hallucination, as seen through the eyes of the demented Francis. Accordingly, Wiene made use of expressionistic lighting throughout the film.

A sinister atmosphere is created in certain interiors by infusing them with menacing shadows looming on walls and ceilings, which give a Gothic quality to the doom-laden characters and serve to convey the angular, warped world of Francis's deranged mind. Similarly expressionistic lighting lends itself readily to the moody atmosphere of film noir. Thus in Fritz Lang's *Scarlet Street*: chiaroscuro cinematography depicts eerie, night-shrouded streets and alleys, ominous corridors, and dark archways, which contribute to the stark atmosphere of film noir.

It has been said that immigrant filmmakers from Germany like Fritz Lang avoided implementing expressionism in their American films altogether. That is not really the case. Actually Fritz Lang insisted that he employed expressionism in only a few key scenes in his American thrillers.

After all, excessive use of expressionistic techniques in a commercial Hollywood picture would have seemed heavy handed and pretentious.[21]

Hirsch also notes that directors like Billy Wilder, who began their careers in Europe, became masters of film noir in Hollywood. For their American films often reflected the characteristics of film noir enumerated earlier; for example, a predilection for dark, gloomy settings and for stories that portray the perilous plights of doom-ridden characters. "The best noir directors" were German or Austrian expatriates who shared a worldview "that was shaped by their bitter personal experiences of . . . escaping from a nation that had lost its mind." They brought to their American films a taste for "stories about man's uncertain fate, and about psychological obsession and derangement."[22] Noir films like Lang's *Scarlet Street* or Wilder's *Double Indemnity* displayed a German influence, from their fatalism to their claustrophobic sets and brooding shadows.

French Naturalism

Jean Renoir declared that *La Chienne* (*The Bitch*, 1931) was "an attempt to make a naturalistic film."[23] Naturalism emphasizes realistic detail, in order to build up an authentic atmosphere that would make a story seem more true to life. As a matter of fact, the release of *La Chienne* coincided with the movement toward greater realism in French cinema in the 1930s. Avoiding studio glamour, now movies were frequently shot on location in order to lend them a stronger sense of realism. Hence films were often acted out in realistic surroundings, which dictated that the actors give performances for the most part free of theatrical mannerisms and that the camera employ a newsreel-like style to photograph the action. These films gave screen fiction a new kind of verisimilitude.

Renoir was in the front rank of French directors employing the new naturalism. According to André Bazin, Renoir was "one of the masters of photographic realism. He was also the heir of the tradition of the naturalistic novel," represented by Emile Zola's novels like *La Bete Humaine* (*The Human Beast*), which Renoir filmed in 1938.[24]

After they had fled Germany in 1933, Fritz Lang and Billy Wilder spent a year in Paris, where each of them made a film, before moving on to Hollywood in 1934. They were both working in Paris when the movement called naturalism took hold in the French film industry. By then Renoir had released *Boudu Saved from Drowning* (1932), with Michel Simon as a scruffy tramp. Like *La Chienne*, *Boudu* was shot on the streets of Paris.

The cinematographer for *La Chienne* was Theodor Sparkuhl, yet another refugee from the German film industry, who worked in Paris for a while before heading for Hollywood—as did Lang and Wilder. *La Chienne* was a powerful naturalistic drama that painted a vivid, unvarnished picture of life in the bohemian Montmartre district of Paris, where Renoir shot the film on location. Fritz Lang remade *La Chienne* as an American film noir, *Scarlet Street*, which is examined in chapter 5. Hence I shall take the occasion to discuss *La Chienne* at this point.

The films in the cycle of French naturalism in the 1930s focused on the troubled lives of haunted characters and emphasized doom and despair. *La Chienne* is a dark drama about Maurice (Michel Simon), a hapless bookkeeper who is infatuated with Lulu (Janie Mareze), a greedy harlot. Maurice is crushed when he discovers that she is having an affair with another man.

As Renoir describes the scene in which Maurice confronts Lulu, "Suddenly he understands she does not love him, has never loved him. He tells her so, and it makes her laugh; that laughter is so exasperating" that Maurice snatches a letter opener that is lying nearby "and stabs her to death."[25]

Sometimes Renoir places his camera outside a room where a scene is taking place, and photographs the action going on inside the room through a doorway or a window. The viewer accordingly feels as if they are observing a scene that is really taking place—it is not merely a scene staged for the camera. Thus, after Maurice murders Lulu in her apartment, Sparkuhl's camera pans up to the apartment window from the street below and peers into the room. We then see Maurice gazing silently at the dead girl for the last time, before he flees the scene of the crime.

At the same time we can hear some street musicians as they sing a romantic ballad outside Lulu's apartment building. The love song is an ironic comment on the romantic illusions that Maurice had earlier nurtured about the faithless Lulu.

When I spoke with Michel Simon in June 1967, at the Berlin Film Festival, he said that he was pleasantly surprised that *La Chienne* had turned out so well, since it was Renoir's first major sound picture. He noted that it was fortunate that he possessed a deep voice that was perfectly suited for sound films. Sadly, he added, Janie Mareze, who played

Lulu, was killed in an auto accident only two weeks after shooting was completed.

Renoir's later film, *La Bete Humaine*, was also remade as a film noir by Fritz Lang, entitled *Human Desire* (1954). Renoir's movie centers on Jacques (Jean Gabin), a train engineer. He is also a psychopath who kills his mistress Severine (Simone Simon) in a fit of madness after she abandons him for a younger man.

Once more Renoir made excellent use of actual locations. As Jacques drives his steam engine along the railroad track the day after the murder, "the charging train becomes a portent of an unstoppable fate: His despair is mounting in unison with the accelerating train; the engineer jumps to his death." In sum, in *La Bete Humaine* Renoir again "constructs a world in which sex and violence are fused inextricably," thereby paving the way for film noir.[26]

Billy Wilder's crime film *Double Indemnity* (1944) highlighted the movement toward naturalism in American cinema that harkened back to the French naturalism of the 1930s. Films like *Double Indemnity* had the same kind of documentary realism that had characterized naturalistic French films like Renoir's *La Chienne*. Wilder shot *Double Indemnity* on location in some of the seedier sections of downtown Los Angeles. The iconography of naturalism was reflected in the shadowy nighttime streets, the tawdry nightspots, and the haunted faces of the actors.[27]

Foster Hirsch, in his exhaustive study of film noir, writes that the trend prospered between the early 1940s and the late 1950s. To be more precise, Paul Schrader states that the outer limits of the cycle stretch from *The Maltese Falcon* (1941) to *Touch of Evil* (1958), which Orson Welles adapted from Whit Masterson's hard-boiled novel *Badge of Evil*.[28] Welles's grim study of the ignominious downfall of a corrupt cop named Quinlan (played by Welles) appeared just when film noir was on the wane. Hirsch told the *New York Times* that Welles's film "gathered many of the noir trademarks" (paranoia, double-dealing, darkness, and danger) into a summary statement of the genre's conventions and thus serves as a "convenient demarcation" for the end of the classic noir cycle. Nevertheless, he adds that the impulse that fueled noir "did not suddenly stop after *Touch of Evil*."[29]

Although film noir has ceased to exist as a distinct movement in American cinema, its influence survives in the tough, uncompromising crime movies that Hollywood continues to turn out from time to time. These films, known as neo-noir, retain the qualities of film noir as it existed in the classic period. For example, films made from Patricia Highsmith's fiction, like *The Talented Mr. Ripley* (1999), still bear the unmistakable earmarks of classic film noir (see chapter 13).

Although *The Maltese Falcon* is usually deemed the first full-fledged film noir, *Stranger on the Third Floor*, released a year before *Falcon*, can be considered a proto-noir, that is, a film that anticipates film noir. Consequently, I shall discuss it before turning to *The Maltese Falcon* in the next chapter.

Stranger on the Third Floor (1940)

RKO approved Frank Partos's original screenplay of *Stranger on the Third Floor* for production in May 1940. Before shooting started, however, Nathanael West, a struggling novelist (*Day of the Locust*), did an uncredited revision of the script. West was forced to earn his living by serving as a hotel night clerk and by working on screenplays for low-budget movies. (When Dashiell Hammett, a friend of West's, was broke while he was writing *The Thin Man*, West allowed him to stay at the rundown hotel where he was working.)

While he was revising the script for *Stranger*, the broken and broken-hearted characters who populate the tawdry rooming house in the film reminded West of the pathetic figures whom he observed during his night duty as a hotel clerk. So he added some authentic touches to the funny and touching losers who are denizens of the rooming house where the stranger of the title lives, while polishing Partos's screenplay.

Peter Lorre, who had played Hans Beckert, a psychopathic child murderer, in Fritz Lang's German film *M* (1931), was chosen to play the title role in the present film. Lorre's Beckert possesses bulging, anxious eyes and contorted, fearful facial expressions that suggest genuine terror. Like Beckert, the unnamed "stranger" is a mysterious, menacing, sad-eyed creature. Lorre modeled his performance as the deranged killer in *Stranger on the Third Floor* on his portrayal of Beckert in *M*. *Stranger on the Third Floor*, which was shot during the month of June 1940, was the first directorial effort of Boris Ingster, a former screenwriter. Ingster began his film career in his native Russia, working for Sergei Eisenstein (*Potemkin*). He would not have been familiar with German expressionism.

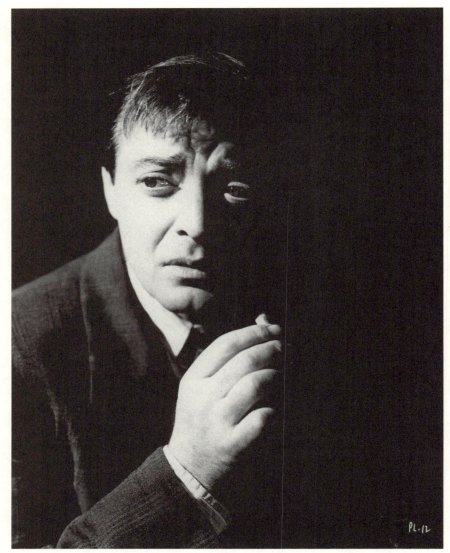

Peter Lorre in the title role of *Stranger on the Third Floor*, now considered the precursor of film noir.

Director of photography Nicholas Musuraca, on the other hand, was an experienced lighting cameraman; he had picked up on the Germanic style of cinematography during the silent period in Hollywood from directors like Josef von Sternberg. Musuraca's shadowy camerawork for *Stranger on the Third Floor* "owed a major debt to German Expressionism, and codified the visual conventions of film noir."[30] For example, Musuraca suggested a jail cell in the present film by merely a bed with barred shadows on the wall. Indeed, Musuraca would become a leading director of photography during the period of classic noir, with movies like Lang's *Clash by Night* (1952) to his credit.

In *Stranger on the Third Floor* cab driver Joe Briggs (Elisha Cook, Jr.) is convicted of slitting the throat of Nick, the manager of a neighborhood diner, largely on circumstantial evidence and the testimony of the key witness, newspaperman Michael Ward (John McGuire), who saw Briggs running from the scene of the crime. But Michael soon begins to suspect that the sinister stranger who lives near him in a seedy rooming house is the real culprit.

Michael suffers gnawing misgivings that Briggs may be innocent. He has a weird nightmare in which his next-door neighbor, Albert Meng, an obnoxious busybody, is slain, and Michael is accused of the murder. Among the images that materialize in Michael's nightmare: "A forest of oblique lines silhouette Michael's cell wall; the figure of blindfolded justice hangs over the courtroom; an electric chair casts its giant shadow against a wall, barred by diagonal lines."[31]

The bizarre, six-and-a-half-minute nightmare sequence was, of course, photographed by Nicholas Musuraca; it was the first of many such stark sequences the cinematographer would contribute to noir films. The strongly expressionistic dream sequence reflects the overt influence of German films like *The Cabinet of Dr. Caligari* on Musuraca's work.

Michael awakens from his grotesque nightmare, only to discover that Meng really has had his throat slashed; he suspects the phantom stranger on the third floor. Ironically, Michael is incriminated in Meng's death by the same sort of circumstantial evidence that served to convict Briggs, and he is railroaded into jail.

While Michael languishes in a jail cell, Jane, his fiancée (Margaret Tallichet), is determined to track down the elusive stranger. Michael had described him to her as a sullen foreigner, at once sinister and pathetic, with bulging eyes, and wearing a shabby overcoat and a grimy silk scarf. Late one night, when Jane, weary of searching the area for the stranger, steps into the diner where Nick was killed, she spies a man who fits Michael's description of the stranger. He is ordering two raw hamburger patties, with which to feed a stray dog.

Recalling the old adage that the murderer returns to the scene of the crime, Jane strikes up a conversation with the lonely man. They go for a walk as darkness encroaches on the deserted street. The stranger admits to Jane that he has escaped from a mental institution and is afraid that he will be captured and locked up there again. Suddenly he turns on her: "They sent *you* to take me back, because they knew I would trust a woman!"

The maniac goes berserk and attempts to strangle Jane, but she breaks free. He chases her into the street, where he is run down by a truck. As he lies dying, he confesses that he killed both Nick and Meng, because they had each threatened to report him as an escaped lunatic. "But I'm *not* going back," he murmurs as he expires. . . .

Lorre's biographer perceptively states that his characterization of the stranger "is an updated version of the murderer in *M*, Hans Beckert. "Feeding stray animals and killing people evokes the ugly memory of the childlike Beckert, who kindheartedly offered his young female victims candy before murdering them."[32]

Jason Holt writes that the first film noir is not *The Maltese Falcon* but "the little known *Stranger on the Third Floor*, in the inception of the classic period."[33] But it is precisely because the latter film is little known that it qualifies as a precursor of film noir, not as the first film noir. After all, Musuraca's brilliant use of expressionistic photography went almost unnoticed at the time, with critics dismissing the movie as pretentious and confusing, mostly because of the nightmare sequence. *Variety* carped, "It's a film too arty for average audiences," freighted with "fancy camera effects and lighting."[34]

Without Nicholas Musuraca as his lighting cameraman, Boris Ingster "never again directed anything nearly as interesting as this neglected demi-classic."[35] The more widely known *Maltese Falcon* was much more influential in initiating the film noir cycle. (Interestingly enough, Peter Lorre and Elisha Cook, Jr., appeared in both *Stranger on the Third Floor* and *The Maltese Falcon*.) In short, *The Maltese Falcon* remains the "official" beginning of the film noir cycle.

Notes

1. Philip Hanson, *This Side of Despair: The Movies and the Great Depression* (Madison, N.J.: Fairleigh Dickinson University Press, 2008), 154.

2. Murray Schumach, *The Face on the Cutting Room Floor* (New York: Da Capo, 1975), 64.

3. Frank Walsh, *Sin and Censorship* (New Haven, Conn.: Yale University Press, 1996), 187.

4. Andrew Sarris, *You Ain't Heard Nothin' Yet: The American Talking Film, 1927–49* (New York: Oxford University Press, 1995), 108.

5. J. P. Tolette, "Film Noir at Columbia," in *Columbia Pictures: Portrait of a Studio*, ed. Bernard Dick (Lexington: University Press of Kentucky, 1992), 107.

6. Schrader, "Notes on Film Noir," 456.

7. Nino Frank, "The Crime Adventure Story: A New Kind of Detective Film," trans. Barton Palmer, in *Perspectives on Film Noir*, ed. Barton Palmer (New York: G. K. Hall, 1996), 21.

8. Etienne Borgers, "Série Noire," in *The Big Book of Noir*, 232.

9. Schrader, "Notes on Film Noir," 457.

10. Christopher Orr, "Genre Theory in the Context of Film Noir," *Film Criticism* 22, no. 1 (Fall 1997): 24; see also Dickos, *Street with No Name*, 2.

11. Stephen Holden, "Neo-Noir's a Fashion That Fits Only a Few," *New York Times*, March 8, 1998, sec. 2:15.

12. Ronald Schwartz, *Neo-Noir* (Lanham, Md.: Scarecrow Press, 2005), x.

13. Sarris, *You Ain't Heard Nothin' Yet*, 119.

14. Penelope Houston, *Contemporary Cinema* (Baltimore: Penguin, 1969), 66.

15. Dickos, *Street with No Name*, 156; see also Bernard Dick, "The Femmes Fatales of Film Noir," in *Literature/Film Quarterly* 23, no. 3 (Summer 1993): 136.

16. Tony Thomas, *The Films of the Forties* (New York: Carol, 1993), 136.

17. Louis Giannetti and Scott Eyman, *Flashback: A Brief History of Film*, rev. ed. (Boston: Allyn and Bacon, 2010), 119.

18. See Amos Vogel, "You Have to Survive Even If It Kills You," *Film Comment* 30, no. 2 (March–April, 1994): 31–36.

19. Lotte Eisner, *The Haunted Screen: Expressionism in German Cinema*, rev. ed., trans. Roger Greaves (Los Angeles: University of California Press, 1994), 10.

20. Brian McDonnell, "Film Noir Style," in *Encyclopedia of Film Noir*, ed. Geoff Mayer and Brian McDonnell (Westport, Conn.: Greenwood Press, 2007), 72.

21. Fritz Lang, interview by the author, Beverly Hills, June 9, 1974. See Jim Hillier and Alastair Phillips, *100 Film Noirs* (London: British Film Institute, 2009), 244.

22. Hirsch, *The Dark Side of the Screen*, 115.

23. David Thomson, *Have You Seen . . . ?: 1,000 Films* (New York: Knopf, 2008), 163.

24. William Verone, "Jean Renoir," in *The Encyclopedia of Filmmakers*, ed. John Tibbetts and James Welsh (New York: Facts on File, 2002), vol. 2, 324.

25. Thomson, *Have You Seen . . . ?*, 163.

26. Foster Hirsch, *Detours and Lost Highways: A Map of Neo-Noir* (New York: Limelight, 1999), 73.

27. See Dickos, *Street with No Name*, 17–18.

28. Schrader, "Notes on Film Noir," 457.

29. David Everitt, "The New Noir: In the Daylight, but Still Deadly," *New York Times*, January 23, 2000, sec. 2:28.

30. Eric Shaefer, "Nicholas Musuraca," in *International Dictionary of Films and Filmmakers*, ed. Nicolet Elert, Andrew Sarris, and Grace Jeromski, rev. ed. (New York: St. James Press, 2000), vol. 4, 604.

31. Stephen Youngkin, *The Lost One: Peter Lorre* (Lexington: University Press of Kentucky, 2005), 168–69.

32. Youngkin, *The Lost One*, 169.

33. Jason Holt, "A Darker Shade," in *The Philosophy of Film Noir*, 27.

34. *Variety Film Reviews* (New Providence, N.J.: Bowker, 1997), vol. 8. This collection of reviews is unpaginated.

35. Jay Nash and Stanley Ross, eds., *Motion Picture Guide* (Chicago: Cinebooks, 1987), vol. 7, 3164. Pagination is consecutive throughout all twelve volumes.

Part Two

NIGHTMARE TOWN: DASHIELL HAMMETT'S FICTION AS FILM NOIR

CHAPTER THREE

JOHN HUSTON: *THE MALTESE FALCON*

Film noir has a closer connection with its literary sources than any other trend in American cinema. This is because writers of hard-boiled fiction like Dashiell Hammett had an impact on the movies by supplying subject matter for noir films. Thus, just as Hammett's *Maltese Falcon* was a milestone in the development of hard-boiled fiction, so John Huston's film adaptation of *The Maltese Falcon* was the founding motion picture of the original film noir cycle.

Be that as it may, *The Maltese Falcon* has not been the subject of scholarly examination to the same degree as other major noir films such as Preminger's *Laura*. The very popularity of *The Maltese Falcon* has been reason enough for some critics to write it off as a mere "crowd pleaser," rather than as an authentic work of cinematic art. There is, of course, no reason why a film cannot be both.

Dashiell Hammett wrote that the inspiration for *The Maltese Falcon* came from his reading about the Knights Hospitallers (Templars) of St. John the Baptist, founded during the Crusades for the care of pilgrims to the Holy Land.[1] A Warner Bros. researcher discovered in the Los Angeles Public Library that after Emperor Charles V ceded Malta to the Knights Hospitallers they became known as the Knights of Malta. In order to acknowledge that Malta was still under Spain, they paid tribute to Charles by presenting him every year with a live falcon on All Saints Day.[2]

Hammett embroidered on the historical facts by writing that in 1539 the Knights sent to Charles the statue of a falcon studded with precious gems. But the falcon was later lost, and no one knows what became of it. Hammett decided to make the efforts of a group of criminals to track down the Maltese falcon, which had been painted black to disguise its value, the center of a novel.

Hammett opted to incorporate into his novel some material from two of the short stories he had published in the pulp magazine *Black Mask* in 1925. "The Whosis Kid" dealt with a shifty crook who was involved in a jewelry store robbery with a shady lady named Ines Almad. Ines attempted to abscond with the jewels she was supposed to share with her partners in crime. So Ines hired a private detective known as the Continental Op (short for Operative of the Continental Detective Agency) to protect her from the criminals she had double-crossed. But the Op eventually turns her and the loot over to the police instead. Ines became Brigid O'Shaughnessy in *The Maltese Falcon*. The Op describes Ines as "appealing and . . . dangerous."[3] That description likewise fits Brigid perfectly.

In "The Gutting of Couffignal" the Op is assigned to guard the wedding presents at a high society wedding. The most expensive gifts are stolen by Princess Sonya Zhukovski, an exiled White Russian aristocrat who fled Russia after the revolution. When the Op catches Sonya with the goods, she employs her feminine wiles to coax him into allowing her to escape. But the Op resists her blandishments, explaining, "You might as well expect a hound to play tiddly-winks with the fox he's caught."[4] In the parallel scene in *The Maltese Falcon* Sam Spade tells Brigid, "Expecting me to run criminals down and then let them go free is like asking a dog to catch a rabbit and let it go."[5] Like the Continental Op, Sam Spade has a professional code, which is never explicitly stated, but which he steadfastly adheres to.

In each of the two stories, Hammett commented, he had "an equally promising denouement, . . . but I had failed to make the most of the situation."[6] Hammett was able to mesh adroitly the recycled material from the two short stories into a unified novel primarily because he amalgamated Ines, the femme fatale in "The Whosis Kid" with Sonya, the femme fatale in "The Gutting of Couffignal," in order to create in *The Maltese Falcon* Brigid O'Shaughnessy, who is a more fully developed character than either Ines or Sonya.

Hammett published *The Maltese Falcon* in serial form in *Black Mask* in five installments, beginning in September 1929, and in book form in 1930. "The actual writing of *The Maltese Falcon* shows the author's determination to move out of the pulp world into that of the genuine novelist,"

Julian Symons points out.[7] Hammett pays more attention to character development in the novel than he did before in his short fiction. Most critics see *The Maltese Falcon* as the peak of Hammett's achievement. As Ross Macdonald puts it, "*The Maltese Falcon* broke the barrier of the genre: it was and is a work of art."[8]

Two Early Films of *The Maltese Falcon*

The Maltese Falcon caused a considerable stir when it was published in 1930. Warner Bros. purchased the exclusive screen rights on June 23, 1930; the rights could be secured at that point for a mere $8,500. (Furthermore, Hammett received no additional compensation from Warner Bros. when the novel was filmed twice more.) Executive vice president Jack Warner assigned Roy Del Ruth to direct *The Maltese Falcon* (1931).

A solid filmmaker, Del Ruth was known in the industry for the brisk pacing of his pictures. Bebe Daniels was picked to play Ruth Wonderly. In this film the femme fatale is inexplicably called by her alias, Ruth Wonderly, rather than by her real name, Brigid O'Shaughnessy. Bebe Daniels was renowned for playing hardened, experienced con artists. Ricardo Cortez became the first Sam Spade, although Warner Bros. had groomed him as a Latin lover. Cortez played Spade as a slick, debonair ladies' man. The movie's pressbook called Cortez's character a "cool, relentless private detective, who refuses to let the dictates of his heart stand in the way of his duty," when he turns Ruth Wonderly over to the cops at the end.[9]

Del Ruth's film was made during the "pre-Code" period in Hollywood, that is, before the industry censor Joseph Breen implemented the Censorship Code in 1934. Hence the film could follow Hammett's novel in depicting Spade's adulterous affair with Iva Archer, his partner's wife (Thelma Todd). Moreover, the homosexual relationship of Kasper Gutman (Casper in the novel) and his baby-faced lackey Wilmer Cook (Dwight Frye) is rather explicit: Gutman (Dudley Digges) fondly pats Wilmer on the cheek, and Wilmer is referred to as Gutman's "boyfriend." Both adultery and homosexuality would be forbidden by the 1934 Code, and therefore would be soft pedaled in both the remakes.

Critics called Del Ruth's *Falcon* a competent, efficiently made movie. Nevertheless, when Warner Bros. submitted the original *Falcon* movie to Joseph Breen, the newly appointed industry censor, in May 1934 on the occasion of its re-release, Breen was appalled at the risqué elements in the film. He later declared that this picture was the final deciding factor in his officially implementing the Censorship Code in July 1934 as an effective measure in raising the moral tone of Hollywood pictures.[10]

Be that as it may, the Del Ruth *Falcon* had been a hit, and Warner Bros. production chief Hal Wallis sent a memo to Warner executive Harry Joe Brown, dated June 27, 1934, suggesting a remake of *The Maltese Falcon*. Wallis maintained that some elements of the novel had been overlooked in the 1931 movie, and that there was still enough material in the book to serve as the basis of another film version of the novel: "I think we can get another screenplay out of it."[11]

The original story, as reworked for the remake, turned out to be something of a romp, foolishly played for laughs. This film was entitled *Satan Met a Lady* (1936). Referring to Spade in the film's title as "Satan" is a reference to Hammett's description of Sam Spade as "a blond Satan."[12] This adaptation of the book was directed by William Dieterle, a German immigrant who was a dependable craftsman; still, his forte was decidedly not comedy.

Warren William was given the role of Spade, now called Ted Shayne, a dapper, wise-cracking private eye, much more of a roguish flirt than was Cortez's Spade. Bette Davis played the femme fatale, now called Valerie Purvis. Davis did so under protest, as she thought the script was clumsy and second rate.

In actual fact, the screenplay was by Brown Holmes, who had collaborated on the script for the 1931 *Falcon*. This time around Holmes altered Hammett's plot beyond recognition in his scenario for *Satan Met a Lady*. The Maltese Falcon itself is transformed into a ram's horn, supposedly stuffed with jewels, that allegedly once belonged to the legendary eighth-century French hero Roland. In addition, Gutman is refashioned into Madame Barabbas (Alison Skipworth), a dowager crook, whose young lover is called Kenneth (Maynard Holmes), rather than Wilmer—their relationship is thus rendered heterosexual to satisfy the censorship code. Furthermore, Ted Shayne's affair with his partner's wife is only hinted at for the same reason. At the fadeout, Warren William's Shayne laughs cynically as he hands over the treacherous Valerie to the police, whereas Cortez's Spade turns over Ruth Wonderly to the cops with wistful resignation.

Critics disliked this low-rent version of Hammett's novel, which had been retooled into a vehicle for Bette Davis, as well as a comedy of sorts.

They called it a slapdash, near parody of the book, and a real snooze. In short, *Satan Met a Lady* squandered a great novel.

Although Del Ruth's film was certainly a better take on the book than Dieterle's, John Huston nevertheless believed that those two pictures only touched the story contained in the Hammett original. For example, Spade's tormented sexual attraction to the "black widow" Brigid O'Shaughnessy was underdeveloped in this movie. Huston whipped up yet another screenplay for *The Maltese Falcon*, with some help from his fellow screenwriter Allen Rivkin (who received no screen credit). Huston hoped to direct the finished product.

The Maltese Falcon (1941)

John Huston told me, "Once I had become established as a screenwriter at Warners I got a clause put into my contract that if I stayed on there they would give me the chance to direct. After Allen Rivkin and I finished the screenplay of *The Maltese Falcon*, I asked to direct it. Dashiell Hammett's book had been filmed twice before, but the previous screen adapters didn't have the faith in the story that we did. Our script simply reduced the book to a screenplay, without any fancy additions of our own."[13]

It was Howard Hawks, for whom Huston had worked on the script of *Sergeant York* (1941), who encouraged Huston to "shoot the book," which Hawks agreed had not been done before. "Always some idiot thought he could write better than Dashiell Hammett," Hawks continued. "You go and make *The Maltese Falcon* exactly the way Hammett wrote it; use the dialogue. Don't change a goddam thing, and you'll have a hell of a picture."[14] Huston summed up: "The *Maltese Falcon* script was done in a very short time, because it was based on a very fine book, and there was very little for me to invent."[15] Huston, of course, had no inkling that he was making a classic film. "I just knew it was a marvelous book, Hammett is one of our great American writers."[16]

"Huston's screenplay is an intelligent editing of the novel, which is mostly dialogue anyway," writes James Naremore. Huston economized by telescoping some scenes, cutting some minor characters, and making "slight changes to get past the censor. . . . The words are mostly Hammett's."[17]

The Maltese Falcon, as we know, is often considered to have inaugurated the original film noir cycle, for Huston's film established many of the elements of film noir: There is, for example, the male protagonist who is characterized by pessimism and "a cold, detached view of the world." The femme fatale is "sexually alluring, but treacherous." A somber urban setting, often photographed at night, "with dark alleyways and sleazy bars, is the common milieu."[18] Indeed, Borde and Chaumeton, in their pioneering 1955 study of film noir, cite film historian George Sadoul as saying, "*The Maltese Falcon* created, in one fell swoop, the conventions of film noir."[19]

Warner Bros. already owned the screen rights to Hammett's book, so they were free to do yet another remake. The studio assigned Huston a tight shooting schedule of six weeks, and allocated him a budget of $381,000. This was a modest sum by the standards of the time. "Since no particularly large sums of money were involved," writes Philip Kiszely, the studio was not risking a great deal on a neophyte director.[20]

Huston remembered, "I was extremely lucky to have such a fine group of actors to work with. I had known Humphrey Bogart, who played detective Sam Spade, for a long time. I had written *High Sierra* for him earlier. George Raft had been approached to play Spade, but he didn't want to work with a director who was a newcomer."

Besides, Raft saw *The Maltese Falcon* as a "low budget whodunit," and, as such, not an important picture. So the role of Sam Spade went to Humphrey Bogart, who defined the quintessential noir gumshoe as worldly-wise, cynical, quick witted, and courageous. "The belted trench coat and the soft-brimmed fedora became a Bogart trademark."[21] Mary Astor, who received an Academy Award for her performance in *The Great Lie* (1941), was suitably cast in the role of Brigid O'Shaughnessy, a pathological liar.

Huston selected Peter Lorre to play the small-time crook Joel Cairo; Lorre had scored a critical success in *Stranger on the Third Floor*, in which he was "the squat, wild-eyed spirit," slyly prowling in and out of the shadows.[22] That description could likewise fit Cairo. Since Cairo is an overt homosexual in the book, Hal Wallis warned Huston, "Don't try to get a nancy quality into him," since homosexuality was still taboo according to the Censorship Code.[23] Huston has Cairo make his first appearance in the picture by presenting Spade with a scented calling card that smells of gardenia; this signals to the audience that the effeminate Cairo is homosexual.

John Huston saw Sydney Greenstreet in the touring company of Robert E. Sherwood's play *There Shall Be No Night* at the Biltmore Theater in Los Angeles. Huston coaxed Greenstreet, who had made a career of playing butlers on the stage, to make his screen debut at age sixty-one as Kasper Gutman (Casper in the novel: Huston, like Del Ruth, wanted the name to have a "foreign" flavor). Greenstreet was very close to Hammett's conception of Gutman, an ostensibly friendly fat man on the surface, but quite devious underneath.

Elisha Cook, Jr., who also appeared in *Stranger on the Third Floor*, was given the part of Wilmer Cook, Gutman's boyish "gunsel"—Breen let the term pass because he assumed that it referred to a gunman. The term, as correctly used by Hammett in the book, is underworld slang for a young man kept by an older man. Cook looks much younger than his thirty-five years, because of his diminutive size. The part of Wilmer was his defining role as one of life's losers. Cook complained later on that, after *The Maltese Falcon*, he was required to play a series of "pimps, informers, and cocksuckers."[24]

"Warner Bros. was indulgent with me," Huston recalled, supplying him with an experienced production crew, including production designer Robert Hass, who had served in the same capacity for the 1931 *Falcon*, and cinematographer Arthur Edeson, who had photographed *Satan Met a Lady*.

The story is set in San Francisco, where Hammett lived throughout the 1920s, a locale that provided him with material for his fiction. The screenplay begins with a new client, Ruth Wonderly, coming to Spade with a tale about her sister Corinne, who has come to San Francisco with a man named Floyd Thursby, with whom Corinne is infatuated. Spade accepts a $200 retainer from Wonderly and arranges to have his partner, Miles Archer, follow Thursby in order to find Corinne. The upshot is that Archer is killed, shortly after Thursby is killed, and Spade learns that Ruth Wonderly has no sister. In fact, Ruth Wonderly is really Brigid O'Shaughnessy, who is fond of employing aliases.

Brigid eventually admits that she lied to Spade in order to have him put a tail on Thursby, her erstwhile cohort, whom she no longer trusted. Spade replies to Brigid's confession, "We didn't exactly believe your story. We believed your two hundred dollars. I mean that you paid us more than if you'd been telling the truth; and enough more to make it alright." This is a salient example of Huston lifting Hammett's dialogue right from the novel for the screenplay.[25]

As for Brigid's being a habitual liar, she admittedly lies constantly, but always with a sprinkling of truth that suggests the illusion of sincerity. Moreover, she tries hard to justify her lies, after they are exposed, so that she can elicit renewed confidence from her victim by her confession. She can then continue deceiving them. The full extent of Brigid's treachery is not revealed until the film's end.

Spade had suspected from the outset that Brigid was a congenital liar. She was telling the truth, however, when she called Thursby a dangerous man. She tells Spade, "He never went to sleep without covering the floor around his bed with crumpled newspapers, so nobody could come silently into his room." Spade infers that Brigid knew Thursby's bedtime habits because she had slept with him. He concludes that Thursby was Brigid's lover as well as her partner in crime. Brigid concealed her real motives for hiring Spade, he later reflects, because "everybody has something to conceal." That statement, says Stephen Cooper, "could well be his working motto."[26]

Spade's unswerving adherence to his professional code of honor and fair play provides the mainspring of the plot. We relate to Sam Spade, writes Roger Ebert, "because he does his job according to the rules he lives by," and because we sense that beneath his rough exterior is a humanity that can be reached.[27]

Spade, as Bogart plays him, is a man of principle who cannot be bought. His cynicism masks his basic integrity. "Don't be too sure I'm as crooked as I'm supposed to be," Spade warns Brigid; "that kind of reputation makes it easier to deal with the enemy." At one point Spade finds it expedient, for example, to convince Gutman that his services are for sale to the highest bidder, and he is therefore not committed to helping Brigid, who hired him in the first place.

Bogart's Sam Spade is an antihero, "a cynical private eye caught in a den of jackals," says Charles Berg; he is at once tough and vulnerable.[28] Spade is willing at times to make moral compromises, wherein he employs deception and even violence in order to reach his goals. Nevertheless, as Ebert contends, he has an ethical code he will not break. Perhaps John Huston said it all when he declared, "Dashiell Hammett was highly moral and adhered strictly to the set of rules that his protagonist has laid down for himself."[29]

Prior to the start of principal photography on June 9, 1941, Huston, as a tyro movie director, took the precaution of storyboarding every scene in the film. "I didn't want to look like a fool on my first picture," he explained. "Before I started shooting I made drawings, set-up by set-up, of the action. I discovered that about half the time the actors automatically fell into the blocking that I had worked out in my drawings, and the rest

Brigid O'Shaughnessy (Mary Astor) watches Sam Spade (Humphrey Bogart) question Joel Cairo (Peter Lorre), a suspicious character, in John Huston's film of Dashiell Hammett's *Maltese Falcon*.

of the time I would either bring them into line with my original conception of the blocking or let them work out something for themselves."

Because of the movie's frugal budget, the stark sets were supplied with plain furnishings by production designer Robert Hass, as, for example, Spade's seedy bachelor flat. Moreover, Huston utilized low-key lighting, which often darkened the sets, thereby creating a sinister, brooding atmosphere. The shadowy sets also kept the rather simple décor from being noticed by the audience. Little wonder that low-key lighting became customary on noir films.

Huston was fortunate to have as director of photography on his first film Arthur Edeson, who had photographed the original *Frankenstein* (1931) for James Whale, which showed that he was familiar with German expressionism; Edeson employed it skillfully in his use of chiaroscuro lighting throughout *Falcon*. Huston collaborated closely with Edeson during the shoot. He had Edeson photograph Greenstreet with low angle shots at times; shooting upward at Greenstreet made him look all the more massive and menacing.

Edeson's camera follows Spade, shadowing him through the night-time streets of San Francisco, producing a threatening, foreboding ambience. M. S. Fonseca contends that Edeson reached the peak of his long career with *Falcon*, the film that "can be said to have invented film noir."[30]

In her autobiography Mary Astor praises Huston for having "the wit to keep Hammett's book intact. His shooting script was a precise map of what went on. Every shot, camera move, entrance, exit was down on paper, leaving nothing to chance, inspiration, and invention."[31] Given Huston's meticulous preplanning, it is no wonder that he brought the movie in ahead of schedule and under budget. The picture wrapped on July 18, 1941, after thirty-four days of filming—two days ahead of schedule. Furthermore, the film was budgeted at $381,000 and Huston brought it in for $327,000.[32]

The Maltese Falcon encountered no serious censorship problems. After all, Huston was careful to play down the illicit affair between Spade and Iva Archer, his partner's wife, to satisfy Joseph Breen, the censor. Moreover, since homosexuality was prohibited by the Censorship Code, Huston muted Cairo's homosexuality so that he came across as a perfumed fop, but not as an obvious pansy. By the same token, Gutman's fancy dressing gown gives a broad hint that he is a classy homosexual; he also subtly places his hand on Sam's knee as they confer. Moreover, Gutman's sly expressions of affection for Wilmer intimate that Wilmer is a kept boy. In sum, it is clear to the cognoscenti who are on the right wavelength when a character in this film is homosexual. So Huston's adaptation of *The Maltese Falcon* passed muster with the censor.

The film opens with a printed prologue that is not in the shooting script. This short statement was actually added to the movie after principal photography had been completed at the request of Jack Warner. The prologue gives the background and history of the falcon so that the audience can better understand the story's premise:

"In 1539, the Knight Templars of Malta, paid tribute to Charles V of Spain, by sending him a golden falcon encrusted from beak to claw with the rarest jewels—but pirates seized the galley carrying this precious token and the fate of the Maltese falcon remains a mystery to this day."

As the plot develops, Sam Spade pressures Brigid O'Shaughnessy into confessing that her story about her sister running away with Floyd Thursby was a hoax. When Joel Cairo and Kasper Gutman get to hear that Brigid has been in touch with Spade, "they flock to Sam like bees to honey."[33] Spade learns that Brigid was previously in cahoots with Cairo and Gutman to track down the falcon. But Brigid and Thursby had recently located it during an expedition to Istanbul. They subsequently made a pact in Hong Kong, whereby they would make their way back to the States separately, while Captain Jacobi, skipper of the *La Paloma*, smuggled the falcon to San Francisco aboard his ship.

After Miles Archer and Floyd Thursby are both liquidated, Capt. Jacobi shows up mortally wounded in Spade's office and gives him the package containing the falcon before he expires. (Capt. Jacobi is played by Walter Huston, the director's father, in an uncredited cameo.) So Spade now has three murders to investigate: Miles Archer, Floyd Thursby, and Capt. Jacobi. The San Francisco fog is gathering around the case faster than Spade can lift it.

Spade in due course arranges a showdown in his apartment with all the principals present. Gutman admits that he had Wilmer kill Thursby, Brigid's ally, because Thursby and Brigid planned to keep the black bird for themselves. Gutman assumed that he could reason with Brigid once Thursby was out of the way. Gutman, Cairo, and Wilmer later went to Brigid's apartment for a confrontation with her, and found Capt. Jacobi there. Jacobi, another ally of Brigid's, suddenly snatched the falcon, which he had brought to Brigid from Hong Kong, and fled down the fire escape. Wilmer shot Jacobi as he made a run for it, but Jacobi managed to make it to Spade's office with the black bird before dying.

Spade convinces Gutman to let Wilmer take the fall for murdering Thursby and Jacobi. Wilmer is distraught that the man who is both his boss and his lover is willing to sacrifice him. Gutman apologizes to Wilmer by saying, "I couldn't be fonder of you if you were my own son; but, if you lose a son, it's possible to get another. There is only one Maltese falcon!" Wilmer, who refuses to be the fall guy, makes his getaway from Spade's apartment.

Spade arranges to have Effie, his secretary (Lee Patrick), deliver the falcon (which Spade has kept hidden) to his apartment. Gutman unwraps the package feverishly and begins scraping the black enamel off the statue with a knife to reveal the bejeweled figuring underneath. Everyone is devastated to discover that the statue is a fake, made of lead. Gutman composes himself, however, and invites Cairo to accompany him to Istanbul, to obtain the genuine falcon from the duplicitous fence who sold

Brigid the false falcon; Gutman and Cairo leave together. Spade phones the police and tells them to pick up Wilmer, Gutman, and Cairo before they blow town: Wilmer, who was working for Gutman, shot Thursby and Jacobi, and Cairo was in with them.

Then Spade turns his attention to Brigid, whom he accuses of slaying Miles Archer. She killed Miles with the gun she had earlier obtained from Thursby. That way, she figured, Thursby would be convicted of Miles's murder, and she could acquire the falcon for herself. (She had not counted on Wilmer shooting Thursby.) Miles was too experienced a private eye, Spade points out, to have gone up a blind alley after a man he was following. "But he'd have gone up there with you, angel. He was just dumb enough for that." Brigid is the only person involved in the case who could have lured Miles to his death in a dark alley.

Sam's determination to find Miles's killer reflects his loyalty to his partner. As he puts it, "When a man's partner is killed, he's supposed to do something about it. It doesn't make any difference what you thought of him. He was your partner, and you're supposed to do something about it."

Spade may be portrayed as an ambiguous figure, involved in a dubious business, comments Steven Gale, "but ultimately he is found to be admirable because he adheres to" his professional code: "partners are supposed to look out for each other."[34] And so Sam informs Brigid that he is turning her over to the police. Although Sam finds Brigid attractive, he will not violate his code for her.

Moreover, Sam is painfully aware that Brigid has sought to manipulate him all along. As a matter of fact, if he had accompanied Brigid that first night, instead of Miles, she would not have hesitated to murder him, just as she did not hesitate to shoot Miles. To Brigid, the femme fatale, Sam was just part of her overall scheme "to acquire the Maltese falcon for herself."[35] When the cops take Brigid away, Huston photographs the iron grille on the hotel elevator closing across her face in close-up. This foreshadows the prison bars that Brigid must look forward to.

One of the police detectives, Tom Polhous, looks at the scarred, counterfeit falcon and asks Spade, "What's that?" Sam replies, "The stuff that dreams are made of." This line of dialogue does not appear in the novel, and has been attributed to Huston. But Huston maintained that the phrase was "Bogie's idea." Before they shot the scene, Bogart said to Huston, "John, don't you think it would be a good idea, this line? Be a good ending?"[36] The line may have been Bogart's idea, but the primary source is Shakespeare's *The Tempest* (1611), where Prospero, the magician, intones, "We are such stuff / As dreams are made of" (IV.i.156–57).

The focus in the movie's ending is on the phony falcon, and the capacity of human beings for self-delusion. The falcon thus takes on a symbolic significance; it represents what Tennessee Williams once called "the long delayed, but always expected something that we live for."[37] All of us know the experience of building our expectations of something we look forward to so much that we are inevitably doomed to disappointment if and when it comes to pass. The gang of fortune hunters in *The Maltese Falcon* waste their lives pursuing a fabled treasure they will never find.

As for the genuine, priceless falcon, it still is stashed away somewhere between Istanbul and Hong Kong; and, as the movie's printed prologue declares, its fate "remains a mystery to this day."

Not surprisingly, Hammett considered Huston's film to be superior to the previous two adaptations of his novel. "Have you seen *The Maltese Falcon* yet?" he wrote to his estranged wife Josephine Dolan Hammett, on October 20, 1941. "They made a pretty good picture of it this time, for a change."[38] For the record, Warner Bros. released a DVD set in 2006 comprising all three versions of *The Maltese Falcon*, so the reader can compare the three.

The reviewers of Huston's movie agreed that it was an outstanding crime film. Most of them marveled that Huston's initial foray as a film director produced such an accomplished work. As Berg observes, Huston "establishes the cramped, claustrophobic cosmos from which none of the characters escapes unscathed. For a first-time director, Huston's ability to keep the tone unrelentingly arch and nasty is remarkable."[39] In the last analysis, Huston's seminal movie opened the door for film noir.

When *The Maltese Falcon* opened in Paris in the summer of 1946, Nino Frank, who shortly thereafter wrote a groundbreaking article about film noir in *The French Screen* (August 28, 1946), enthusiastically reviewed Huston's picture three weeks earlier in the same journal (August 7, 1946). "I will not insult my reader by telling him who Dashiell Hammett is: a private detective turned writer," whose influence "remains profound." In place of the British school of detective fiction, which is "a pleasant substitute for crossword puzzles," Hammett presents the hard-boiled private detective "who lives on the fringe of the law." Like Hammett's novel,

Frank concluded, Huston's picture is an unsparing, pitiless depiction of the criminal milieu. "I defy anyone to resist the grip of the story."[40]

The Maltese Falcon has become not only a classic film noir, but a cult favorite. Indeed, the city of San Francisco has paid tribute to both the novel and the film. On the southwest corner of the intersection of Bush and Stockton Streets, across from Dashiell Hammett Street, a plaque states: "On approximately this spot Miles Archer, partner of Sam Spade, was done in by Brigid O'Shaughnessy."[41]

Joe Gores published a prequel to Hammett's novel entitled *Spade and Archer* (2009), in which he fills in the backstories of the major characters in *The Maltese Falcon*. But Gores's spin-off does not really add to our appreciation of Hammett's original novel, since, as David Gates notes, in *The Maltese Falcon* "we already know these people perfectly well."[42]

The Library of Congress bestowed a singular honor on *The Maltese Falcon*, and some other noirs treated in this study, when it selected them to be preserved in the permanent collection of the National Film Registry of the Library of Congress as culturally, historically, and aesthetically important.

In *America's Film Legacy: Landmark Movies in the National Film Registry*, Daniel Eagan writes that Huston always claimed that when he filmed *The Maltese Falcon* he simply "made the book." Eagan replies, "But Huston's work went beyond simply staging scenes from the novel. He recognized the queasy underside of Hammett's plot, the allure of thieves, of getting away with sleeping with your partner's wife," and putting one over on the cops. In sum, *The Maltese Falcon* "marks one of the most auspicious directorial debuts in movies."[43]

Hammett followed *The Maltese Falcon* with *The Glass Key* (1931). Paramount brought the novel to the screen in 1935 with moderate success. When the studio's executives noticed the widespread popularity of the Warner Bros. remake of *The Maltese Falcon* in 1941, they decided that they would follow suit in 1942 with a remake of *The Glass Key*—the novel Hammett thought was his best.

Notes

1. Hammett, "Introduction," in Dashiell Hammett, *The Maltese Falcon*, vii.
2. Undated summary of historical data; *The Maltese Falcon* file in the Warner Bros. Collection in the Archive of the Library of the University of Southern

California; see also Edmund Wright, ed., *The Oxford Encyclopedia of World History* (New York: Oxford University Press, 2006), 352–53.

3. Dashiell Hammett, "The Whosis Kid," in Dashiell Hammett, *The Continental Op*, ed. Steven Marcus (New York: Vintage Books, 1992), 217.

4. Dashiell Hammett, "The Gutting of Couffignal," in Dashiell Hammett, *The Big Knockover*, 34.

5. Dashiell Hammett, *The Maltese Falcon* (New York: Vintage Books, 1992), 274.

6. Hammett, "Introduction," in Hammett, *The Maltese Falcon*, vii.

7. Symons, *Dashiell Hammett*, 66.

8. Metress, "Introduction," in *Critical Response to Dashiell Hammett*, xix.

9. *The Maltese Falcon* (1931) file, in the National Film Archive of the Library of the British Film Institute.

10. Thomas Doherty, *Hollywood's Censor: Joseph I. Breen* (New York: Columbia University Press, 2007), 70.

11. *Satan Met a Lady* file, in the Warner Bros. Collection in the Archive of the Library of the University of Southern California.

12. Hammett, *The Maltese Falcon*, 3.

13. John Huston, interview by the author; London, July 31, 1972. All quotations from Huston that are not attributed to another source are from this interview.

14. Joseph McBride, *Hawks on Hawks* (Los Angeles: University of California Press, 1982), 60.

15. Jeffrey Meyers, *Bogart: A Life in Hollywood* (New York: Houghton Mifflin, 1997), 124; see also John Huston, *An Open Book* (New York: Knopf, 1980), 78.

16. Lawrence Grobel, "John Huston Interview," in *John Huston: Interviews*, ed. Robert Emmet Long (Jackson: University Press of Mississippi, 2001), 163.

17. James Naremore, *More Than Night: Film Noir in Its Contexts*, rev. ed. (Los Angeles: University of California Press, 2008), 60.

18. Kristen Thompson and David Bordwell, *Film History: An Introduction*, rev. ed. (New York: McGraw-Hill, 2010), 215.

19. Raymond Borde and Etienne Chaumeton, *A Panorama of American Film Noir*, trans. Paul Hammond (San Francisco: City Light Books, 2000), 34.

20. Philip Kiszely, *Hollywood through Private Eyes: The Hard-Boiled Novel in the Studio Era* (New York: Peter Lang, 2006), 83.

21. George Perry, *Bogie: The Life and Films of Humphrey Bogart* (New York: St. Martin's Press, 2006), 126.

22. David Thomson, *New Biographical Dictionary of Film*, rev. ed. (New York: Knopf, 2010), 545.

23. Richard Barrios, *Screening Out: Playing Homosexual in Hollywood* (New York: Routledge, 2003), 137.

24. Meyers, *Bogart*, 129.

25. Compare Hammett, *The Maltese Falcon*, 33.

26. Stephen Cooper, "*The Maltese Falcon*: John Huston's Adaptation," in *Perspectives on John Huston*, ed. Stephen Cooper (New York: G. K. Hall, 1994), 122.

27. Roger Ebert, *The Great Movies I* (New York: Broadway Books, 2003), 280.

28. Charles Berg, "*The Maltese Falcon*," in *The Encyclopedia of Novels into Film*, ed. John Tibbetts and James Welsh, rev. ed. (New York: Facts on File, 2005), 278.

29. "Dialogue on Film: John Huston," in *Conversations with the Great Moviemakers*, ed. George Stevens, Jr. (New York: Knopf, 2006), 347.

30. M. S. Fonseca, "Arthur Edeson," in *International Dictionary of Films and Filmmakers*, ed. Nicolet Elert, Andrew Sarris, and Grace Jeromski, rev. ed. (New York: St. James, 2000), vol. 4, 236.

31. Mary Astor, *A Life on Film* (New York: Delacorte Press, 1967), 160.

32. Geoff Mayer, "Introduction: Readings in Film Noir," in *Encyclopedia of Film Noir*, 8.

33. Burkhard Rowekamp, "*The Maltese Falcon*," in *Movies of the Forties*, ed. Jurgen Muller (Los Angeles: Taschen/BFI, 2005), 30.

34. Steven Gale, "*The Maltese Falcon*: Melodrama or Film Noir?" *Literature/Film Quarterly* 24, no. 2 (Spring 1996): 146.

35. Deborah Knight, "On Reason and Passion in *The Maltese Falcon*," in *The Philosophy of Film Noir*, 230.

36. Meyers, *Bogart*, 130.

37. Gene D. Phillips, *The Films of Tennessee Williams* (Cranbury, N.J.: Associated University Presses, 1980), 46.

38. Richard Layman and Julie Rivett, eds., *Selected Letters of Dashiell Hammett* (Washington, D.C.: Counterpoint, 2001), 173.

39. Berg, "*The Maltese Falcon*," 279.

40. Nino Frank, "*The Maltese Falcon*," in John Huston, *The Maltese Falcon: A Screenplay*, ed. William Luhr (New Brunswick, N.J.: Rutgers University Press, 1998), 130.

41. Meyers, *Bogart*, 337.

42. David Gates, "Becoming Sam Spade," *New York Times Book Review*, February 8, 2008, 12.

43. Daniel Eagan, *America's Film Legacy: Landmark Movies in the National Film Registry* (New York: Continuum, 2010), 339.

CHAPTER FOUR

STUART HEISLER: *THE GLASS KEY*
EDWARD BUZZELL: *SONG OF THE THIN MAN*

Dashiell Hammett set *The Glass Key* in an unnamed city on the Eastern Seaboard—most likely Baltimore, where he grew up and was first employed as a Pinkerton operative. Hammett's first novel, *Red Harvest*, looked forward to *The Glass Key* in that it was about violence and corruption in the city. Specifically, *Red Harvest* is set in Personville, nicknamed Poisonville. When the last honest citizen in town is murdered, the Continental Op, Hammett's familiar private eye, is determined to punish the guilty.

The hero of *The Glass Key* is Ned Beaumont, personal assistant and sidekick of political boss Paul Madvig. Although Ned is not a private detective in the usual sense of the term, like the Op, Beaumont is a special investigator for the district attorney's office. As such, Ned attempts to solve a murder case in which Paul is accused of the crime. He is not only Paul's henchman, but his loyal friend.

Ned Beaumont in some ways resembles Dashiell Hammett: Beaumont "wears a neatly trimmed mustache (like Hammett) and drinks a lot (as Hammett was already doing)."[1] He is also, like Hammett, a natty dresser, who chides Paul about wearing "silk socks with tweeds."[2] Paul's poor taste in clothes underscores how he would like to raise his social status but is not adept in doing so.

Admittedly, Ned is in the employ of Paul Madvig, a powerful, dishonest ward boss, who operates in the corrupt world of city politics. Still, Ned is doggedly determined to clear his boss of the murder charge, even if it means taking on the city's mobsters. "In the matter of integrity," comments Dooley, "Ned Beaumont is cut from the same cloth as the rest of Hammett's heroes."[3] Ned is well aware that, even after he has captured the culprit who committed the murder, the corrupt urban environment will outlast his efforts to see justice done. In short, the city, in Hammett's bleak vision, remains essentially lawless.

Unlike Sam Spade, Ned Beaumont does wind up at novel's end in a love relationship. The novel concludes with Ned and Janet Henry telling Paul that they are leaving town together. Nevertheless, the symbolism of the book's title undercuts the "happy ending." Specifically, the title refers to Janet's dream, which she relates to Ned at one point. In her dream Janet and Ned get lost in a forest and happen upon an apparently abandoned house. They find the key under the doormat and unlock the front door, only to discover inside hundreds of snakes, which slither through the door and go off into the forest.

Janet later confesses to Ned, after she and Ned have fallen in love, that her dream was really a nightmare. The key was made of glass and shattered in Ned's hand after he got the door open. "We couldn't lock the snakes in and they came out all over us; I woke up screaming."[4] Of course, commentators on the novel have had a field day with Janet's nightmare. The simplest explanation, however, is perhaps the best. Julian Symons writes that "the common sense view of the fragile key is this: The glass key is meant to symbolize only that the relationship between Ned Beaumont and Janet Henry" is likewise fragile; "it may not last."[5]

With the publication of *The Glass Key* in 1931, several critics agreed that this novel along with *The Maltese Falcon* were the best detective stories to come along in a long time. Hammett biographer Diane Johnson believes *The Glass Key* to be "as elegant and controlled in style as anything Hammett ever wrote."[6] Furthermore, it was a best seller, and so Hollywood came calling.

Hammett's novels had proved easily adaptable for the screen. "Writers on the order of Dashiell Hammett," brandishing incredibly laconic prose and razor-sharp dialogue, "wrote books that had almost the skeletal structure and style of a script," Lawrence O'Toole points out. Hammett was adept at conveying a great deal of exposition through dialogue. O'Toole adds that film noirs such as *The Glass Key* "capitalized on the filmic qualities of hard-boiled fiction: crisp, clever plotting; locales where light and shadow could disport themselves; and characters short on talk and big on action."[7]

The Glass Key (1935)

Paramount purchased the screen rights of the novel for $25,000—considerably more than the $8,500 Warner Bros. had paid for *The Maltese Falcon*. The studio inquired of the industry censor's office, known as "the Hays Office" after its director, Will Hays, if the Hammett novel was suitable for filming. The Hays office replied that the novel was objectionable because it painted an exaggerated picture of a large American city as a politically corrupt and crime-ridden slum. The censor's negative response made Paramount decide to shelve the project for the time being, with a view to overhauling the plot for filming later on.

Moreover, when Joseph Breen became administrator of the Censorship Code in 1934, he upheld the Hays office's verdict on *The Glass Key*. Breen, who had also discouraged the studios from optioning other hard-boiled novels for filming, such as James M. Cain's *Double Indemnity*, "held hard-boiled crime fiction to be everything" he was protecting the American public from, as Tom Hiney puts it.[8]

A steady stream of news stories at the time documented the rise of organized crime across the nation, which went hand in hand with political corruption in big cities.[9] So Breen's judgment of Hammett's novel as unfair to American politicians as a group was manifestly unjustified. Nevertheless, Paramount capitulated to the censor by submitting a screenplay to Breen in which "the politics of the novel were toned down," and Breen approved the script.[10]

Frank Tuttle directed the first screen adaptation of *The Glass Key*, released in 1935. Tuttle was a dependable filmmaker who directed movies in a variety of genres, including the Eddie Cantor musical *Roman Scandals* (1933). Tuttle turned Hammett's novel into a glossy thriller as a vehicle for the limited talents of George Raft as Ed Beaumont (Ned Beaumont in the novel).

Raft is only adequate in the role of the henchman of the good-natured political big shot Paul Madvig (Edward Arnold), who is saved from being framed for murder by the intrepid Ed Beaumont. When compared to Bogart as Sam Spade, Raft is a less convincing screen tough guy. Furthermore, Clare Dodd as Janet Henry, the movie's love interest, does not register any too well. Only Edward Arnold in the supporting role of Paul Madvig, "the political mover and shaker," gives a worthy performance.[11]

Ed Beaumont (Alan Ladd) and Janet Henry (Veronica Lake) in Stuart Heisler's film of Dashiell Hammett's *The Glass Key*.

At seventy-seven minutes, *The Glass Key* was standard length for a low-budget programmer. "As murder mystery material, the story provides interesting plot situations," *Variety* opined, "but *The Glass Key* will have to struggle to strike above moderate grosses."[12] That estimate of the movie fits David Thomson's overall assessment of Frank Tuttle: "There is no reason to build him up as an important director; none of his films have survived as more than a typical studio product."[13]

Tuttle's main claim to fame was directing Alan Ladd in his break-out film as the contract killer in *This Gun for Hire* (1942), opposite Veronica Lake. Indeed, the success of that film prompted Paramount to costar Ladd and Lake in the remake of *The Glass Key* the same year.

Alan Ladd, at five feet, five inches, proved that a short man could achieve star status in Hollywood. Veronica Lake, his costar in *This Gun for Hire* and *The Glass Key*, was, at five feet, two inches, a perfect match for Ladd. Alan Ladd was an effective actor who had played in *This Gun for Hire* a lonely man alienated from society. His impact on the public was so great that Paramount had rushed him into production in a new version of *The Glass Key*, "continuing his guise as a quiet little tough guy."[14] Furthermore, there was a sexual chemistry between Ladd and Lake that would undoubtedly work well in *The Glass Key*, which, as things turned out, was released just six months after *This Gun for Hire*.

The Glass Key was chosen as a vehicle for Ladd because Paramount figured that if Warner Bros. could make a killing with a remake of Hammett's *Maltese Falcon*, they could do the same with a remake of Hammett's *Glass Key*. Accordingly, the remake would have a bigger budget and a stronger cast than the 1935 version.

The Glass Key (1942)

Paramount's second adaptation of Hammett's novel was in the capable hands of Stuart Heisler. Heisler had been relegated to directing "B" pictures from 1936 until he was elevated to making "A" features with *The Remarkable Andrew* (1942). This movie was a whimsical fantasy with Brian Donlevy as the ghost of Andrew Jackson besting some crooked politicians in the present day. But Heisler demonstrated in his next picture, *The Glass Key*, that he was at his best with the thriller genre.

Hammett had worked as a screenwriter in Hollywood throughout the 1930s without much success. By 1940 he had just about given it up, so Paramount's head of production, B. G. "Buddy" De Sylva, turned to another hard-boiled crime novelist, Jonathan Latimer, to compose the script for the remake of *The Glass Key*. Latimer was a wise choice. Although he was not an innovator like Hammett, he was associated with Hammett, Chandler, and Cain in "the Golden Age of Hard-Boiled Fiction" in the 1930s. Between 1934 and 1939, Latimer turned out five crime novels featuring the exploits of Bill Crane, a hard-drinking, wisecracking, tough private eye modeled on Sam Spade. In fact, Bill Crane reads *Black Mask* (!).

Latimer flippantly described these five mystery novels as dealing with "booze, babes, and bullets."[15] In retrospect, the Crane novels "helped further define and popularise the private eye genre."[16] In 1940 Latimer published his first non-Crane novel, *Dark Memory*, which was something of a homage to Hammett. Indeed, *Dark Memory* took on a more somber, hard-edged tone, much like Hammett's *Glass Key*.

Around this time, Latimer, a native Chicagoan, moved to Southern California and began writing screenplays. He became a good friend and drinking companion of Raymond Chandler, but he recalled meeting Hammett only once. It was in the lobby of the Beverly Wilshire Hotel around 3 a.m.; Hammett was drunk, so he probably did not remember the meeting. Afterward Latimer reflected, "Hell of a writer, though, drunk or sober."[17]

Latimer coscripted *Topper Returns* (1941) for Roy Del Ruth, who had directed the 1931 *Maltese Falcon*. This spooky mystery was a big hit, so De Sylva assigned Latimer to do the new screenplay for *The Glass Key*. Latimer had an ear for colloquial language and was particularly adept at creating lively, tough-sounding dialogue. For example, Madvig says at one point in Latimer's script for *The Glass Key*, "I just met the swellest dame— she smacked me right in the kisser!" Latimer subsequently specialized in writing screenplays for film noirs, such as *The Big Clock* (1948). Latimer's screenplays "skillfully assimilated many of the central attributes of film noir, such as the morally flawed male," exemplified by Ed Beaumont (Ned in the novel) in *The Glass Key*.

De Sylva sent the completed screenplay to Breen's office before principal photography commenced. The production chief would simply not go into production with a script for *The Glass Key* that the censor had not read in advance. Breen felt that the present screenplay had overcome in large measure his original objections to the novel back in 1935. After all, Breen observed, political chicanery was no longer quite so objectionable as it once was.[18]

Breen at this juncture objected only to some lurid phrases cropping up in the script that were prohibited by the Censorship Code. The censor took exception, for example, to a line of a thug named Jeff, who has beaten up Ed Beaumont. Jeff later calls Ed "a goddamned massacrist." Since the code explicitly forbade profanity, the offending adjective disappeared from the movie's dialogue.[19]

The ritual beating of Ed, which Jeff refers to, takes place when Ed invades gangster territory, with a view of absolving Paul Madvig from a threatened murder indictment. Ed is captured and cruelly tortured by the hoodlum Jeff on the orders of Nick Varna, a rival crime boss to Madvig. It seems incredible that the sequence in which Ed is beaten to a pulp got by the censor in 1942.

Actually this brutally violent scene also figured in the 1935 version of *The Glass Key*, and the critics did not complain about the scene at the time. Thus Andre Sennewald, in the *New York Times* (July 17, 1935), merely mentioned the sequence in passing, observing that Ed is subjected to a savage beating "by a sadistic gunman who is at heart just a good-natured booby."[20] Since the critics had not taken issue with the torture scene in 1935, Breen let it pass in the remake.

The impressive supporting cast in the remake was headed by Brian Donlevy and William Bendix. As Paul Madvig, Donlevy reprises his role as the governor involved in civic corruption in Preston Sturges's *Great McGinty* (1940). In *The Glass Key* Donlevy once again plays an amiable roughneck with appealing vitality. William Bendix was new to movies when he took the role of Jeff in the present movie. He is a striking presence in the film, as a "gravel-voiced Brooklyn-accented mug type." His bravura performance in *The Glass Key* presaged that his best performances would always be in "noir enterprises."[21]

Heisler engaged Theodor Sparkuhl as director of photography for this picture, since Sparkuhl had been his cinematographer on *Among the Living* (1941), a low-budget horror movie. Sparkuhl, another German émigré, had worked with Ernst Lubitsch in Berlin on silent films like *Carmen* (1918) and had become familiar with German expressionism before departing Germany when Hitler came to power. En route to Hollywood Sparkuhl made a stopover in Paris, where he photographed *La Chienne* for Jean Renoir in 1933.

Because of his adroit use of low-key lighting effects in *The Glass Key* and other pictures, Sparkuhl became associated with film noir in Hollywood. What's more, Heisler's *Glass Key*, in retrospect, was seen as a crucial movie in the trend of film noir. Yet this version of Hammett's novel "has been almost totally ignored by most studies of film noir."[22]

Sparkuhl displays his expertise with the camera in the long tracking shot that opens *The Glass Key*. Gang boss Paul Madvig enters the campaign headquarters of Senator Ralph Henry (Moroni Olsen), who is running on the reform ticket for governor. Madvig is head of the Voters League, yet he is flanked by members of his gang in the recognizable "gangster attire of pinstriped suits and snap-brimmed fedoras."[23] As the camera tracks beside Madvig while he moves through the foyer, it picks up snatches of various comments about him. One onlooker refers to Madvig as "the biggest crook in the state," and another acknowledges that he runs the Voters League, a respectable organization.

This opening scene establishes that Madvig is a mob boss who is striving for respectability in the city. In fact, he hopes to marry Senator Henry's blue-blooded daughter Janet (Veronica Lake), which would "sanction the entry of the gangsters into legitimate society."[24] When reporters suggest to Madvig that he has no business being linked to the senator's reform party, he replies by referring to the gambling debts of Senator Henry's wayward son Taylor. He adds that the senator should start by reforming his son, "who gets into more jams than the Dead End Kids!"

Ed Beaumont, Paul Madvig's personal assistant, advises him that he is making a mistake in aligning himself with the reform candidate. For Madvig is thereby alienating racketeer Nick Varna (Shad O'Rory in the novel), with whom Madvig had previously enjoyed a peaceful coexistence. Madvig disagrees, and reacts by pressuring the police chief (who is in his pocket) into shuttering a gambling casino operated by Varna (Joseph Calleia), in order to impress Senator Henry, not to mention Janet Henry, whom Madvig is courting. Nonetheless, the notorious Varna will inevitably seek to take revenge on Madvig for turning against him.

Paul Madvig learns that Taylor Henry, a playboy-gambler, is romancing his younger sister Opal (Madvig's daughter in the novel). He angrily warns Taylor to stay away from his sister. Consequently, when Ed later finds the corpse of Taylor Henry in the gutter, suspicion falls on Paul Madvig as the killer. Ed realizes that in order to free Paul from being incriminated in Taylor's death, he will have to find the real murderer.

Ed urges Paul to disassociate himself from Senator Henry's reform party and to give up wooing Janet Henry, and make peace with Varna—but Paul refuses. In exchange for Senator Henry's using Paul's political pull to get elected governor, Paul boasts, "Ralph Henry has practically given me the key to his house." Ed responds, "Yeah, a glass key; be sure it doesn't break up in your hand."

Ed is suggesting to Paul that Senator Henry and his daughter are ingratiating themselves with him so that he will help to get the senator elected. After the election, when they have no further use for him, Paul will discover that the key to their home was merely glass after all; and it will shatter in his hand—their door will be closed to him for good. Since Hammett's symbolism in the novel's title, mentioned above, was deemed too elaborate and sophisticated for the film, Latimer came up with a simpler explanation for the title.

Despite their differences, Ed remains loyal to Paul, both as his assistant and his friend. Ed decides to utilize his position as a special investigator in the office of District Attorney Farr to track down Taylor Henry's killer. After all, Farr deputized Ed in the first place because of Paul's pulling strings on Ed's behalf.

When Ed confronts Varna about his efforts to pin Taylor Henry's murder on Paul Madvig, his sworn enemy, Varna sics Jeff, his vicious henchman, on Ed. The notorious Varna threatens Ed that Jeff will go to work on him until he is willing to betray Paul by saying that Paul murdered Taylor. Shortly thereafter Ed finds himself in a sleazy den, where Jeff beats him senseless with maniacal glee, all the while calling him "sweetheart" and "cuddles."

Heisler hints at the sexual ambiguity "strikingly implicit in the homo-erotic undertow of the sadomasochistic beating of Ed by Varna's heavy, Jeff."[25] Indeed, the masochistic link between Ed and Jeff is suggested by the manner in which Ed submits to being repeatedly slugged by Jeff. "I never seen a guy who liked being hit so much," Jeff exclaims. Manny Farber calls their relationship "a strange mixture of sadism and affection."[26] While shooting this sequence, the rugged William Bendix accidentally landed a punch on Ladd's jaw that knocked him cold. Heisler, "never one to allow a convincing shot to go unrecorded," ordered that shot to be used in the film.[27]

In the end, Ed decides he has had enough and sets fire to the mattress in the room where he is imprisoned. While Jeff is preoccupied with putting out the flames, Ed escapes by jumping through a window. Janet Henry comes to visit Ed while he is recuperating in the hospital. Asked why he took such a pummeling for Paul, Ed answers, "Because he is my friend, and he's square. He would have taken a beating for me." Janet admires Ed's stubborn loyalty to his friend and realizes that she is falling for Ed.

While he is hospitalized, Ed learns that Varna has cajoled Clyde Matthews, publisher of the *Observer*, a local newspaper, into agreeing to publicly accuse Madvig in print of slaying Taylor Henry. The "exposé" is to appear in the paper the following morning. So Ed decides to check himself out of the hospital and pay a visit to Matthews's country estate, where Matthews is holed up with Varna and his goons.

Ed forces Clyde Matthews to admit that his newspaper is bankrupt and that he is heavily in debt to Varna; that is why he is willing to do Varna's bidding. Eloise Matthews, Clyde's philandering wife, displays contempt for her husband when she hears that he is broke; after all, she only married him for his money. She accordingly begins flirting crassly with Ed on the couch.

When Clyde witnesses his wife openly kissing Ed, the distraught husband goes upstairs to his bedroom and blows his brains out.

Geoff Mayer claims that Ed, in order to prevent the publication of Varna's accusation against Madvig, "provokes the suicide" of the publisher by "seducing his wife."[28] On the contrary, there is no indication that Ed actually "seduces" Eloise by having sex with her on the living room couch, either in the novel or in the film, at this point. Ed does accept Eloise's advances, but their smooching is interrupted by the gunshot from upstairs. Ed simply could not have foreseen that his having indulged in heavy petting with Eloise would have driven her husband to take the extreme measure of committing suicide. In any case, with Clyde Matthews out of the picture, Ed moves quickly to kill the story about Madvig's murdering Taylor Henry so that it will not be front page news in the *Observer*.

Ed, still desperate to smoke out Taylor Henry's killer and exonerate Paul, seeks out the inebriated Jeff in a dingy basement bar. While Ed is attempting to pump Jeff for information about the killing, Varna shows up. He ominously warns Jeff that he talks too much when he is drunk and smacks him harshly. Jeff goes berserk and strangles Varna to death in retaliation. Ed watches impassively, but does not intervene. After throttling Varna, Jeff blurts out, "I'm just a good-natured slob everybody thinks they can push around." Ed calls the police, who take Jeff into custody. Ed accordingly wreaks vengeance on his enemies without lifting a finger: the ruthless Varna is dead, and the savage Jeff will be executed for his murder. As Nash and Ross observe, "This is a tough, raw crime yarn that pulls no punches, with taut direction from film noir specialist Heisler."[29]

At the movie's climax, Ed goads the real murderer of Taylor Henry into confessing to the district attorney. Ralph Henry admits that he killed his son during an argument on a deserted street at night. "I told him he would ruin my political career" with his dissolute lifestyle, the senator explains. "Taylor hit me; we scuffled." The senator hit his son with his walking stick. "Somehow he fell down, and his head hit the curb. He was dead—it was an accident." Ralph Henry adds that Paul was present, but, for Janet's sake, Paul helped him cover up the killing.

The movie concludes in a sentimental fashion. Ed and Janet tell Paul they are going to go away together and make a fresh start in life elsewhere. Paul responds that they are "two kids who have got it bad for each other." He magnanimously gives them his blessing: "Get going, before I change my mind." Bruce Crowther wryly terms the picture's happy ending "a Hollywood confection." In the novel "Ed is clearly less sure that he had done the right thing in pairing off with Janet and retains a lingering attachment to Paul."[30]

Despite the sentimental ending, *The Glass Key* has an underlying layer of perversity, thanks to Jonathan Latimer's vigorous, nifty screenplay, which is fundamentally as faithful to Hammett as was Huston's script for *The Maltese Falcon*. Like that movie, *The Glass Key* is blessed with a superior cast, ably directed by Stuart Heisler. Although the Alan Ladd–Veronica Lake team struck cinematic sparks, the picture belongs to Ladd. He is able to convey the stoic, self-possessed Ed Beaumont, aided by his deeply timbered voice. Ladd makes Beaumont a genuinely noir antihero.

Donlevy is superb as the good-natured political boss who fought his way up from the wrong side of the tracks. The rest of the supporting cast is likewise top-notch, with Joseph Calleia as the heartless racketeer Nick Varna and William Bendix, who steals nearly every scene he appears in, as the frightening, cretinous Jeff. The critics, besides praising the film's script and direction, acknowledged the masterful score supplied by Victor Young, all quavering strings and chattering clarinets. Young would go on to compose the music for many noirs, including Lang's *Ministry of Fear*.

One other picture derived from a Hammett novel was also a critical and popular success. Hammett published *The Thin Man* in 1934, and it was filmed and rushed into release the same year. What's more, the first *Thin Man* movie spawned no less than five sequels.

In the early winter of 1930, Hammett began a novel entitled *The Thin Man*. By the time he reached page 65 of the typescript, he decided to interrupt his work on the novel, after he had written ten chapters, and accept an invitation to go to Hollywood. He spent a year writing screenplays with indifferent success. In a handwritten note appended to the typescript of the novel, dated January 14, 1942, Hammett recalled, "I didn't return to work on the story until a couple more years had passed; and then I found it more satisfactory to keep only the basic idea of the plot and otherwise to start over."[31]

The 18,000-word typescript of *The Thin Man* is much more akin to the hard-boiled fiction Hammett had done in his previous books than to the published novel. In fact, Nick and Nora Charles do not appear in the first version, which is known as "The First Thin Man."[32] Nevertheless, the preliminary draft of *The Thin Man* does bear some marked similarities to the completed novel. In both versions an eccentric, not to say mad, inventor named Wynant has vanished without a trace. As the story line develops in the finished novel, Wynant is really dead, in spite of the fact that his crooked lawyer, Herbert Macaulay, insists that he is still alive.

The main character in "The First Thin Man" is John Guild, a private detective. Hammett apparently abandoned the first draft of the book because Guild was turning out to be a pedestrian gumshoe, much less distinctive than the colorful Sam Spade. In rewriting this material Hammett transformed the central figure into the charming, dapper ex–private eye, Nick Charles. Nick has retired from his profession to manage the business affairs of his wife, Nora, a lumber heiress.

The thin man of the title in Hammett's novel is Clyde Wynant, who is so called because his corpse fits conveniently into a very narrow hiding place in the cellar of his laboratory, where it is concealed by the murderer. But most readers assumed that the thin man was Nick Charles, "because thin is cool and suave," and because Nick prefers drinking to eating.[33] Certainly the term refers to Nick in the film version and in the five sequels.

In his completed novel Hammett leavened the darker aspects of the mystery story with comedy, which sets it apart from the first draft, as well as from all of Hammett's previous novels. Nick and Nora are a sophisticated couple, whose clever repartee and breezy badinage endeared them to the reading public. Lillian Hellman observed that the Charleses have one of the few marriages in modern literature where "the man and woman actually like each other."[34] It is Nora who coaxes Nick out of retirement to unravel the murder mystery. Nick eventually figures that Macaulay killed Wynant when the inventor discovered that Macaulay was guilty of embezzling funds from Wynant's fortune.

The Thin Man received good reviews and was a best seller when it was published in 1934. MGM bought the screen rights for $21,000 at the behest of director W. S. "Woody" Van Dyke.

The Thin Man (1934)

Louis B. Mayer, Metro's chief executive, saw *The Thin Man* as a routine detective movie, and allotted Van Dyke a short three-week shooting schedule and a budget of $230,000 to make the picture. Van Dyke selected William Powell and Myrna Loy, whom he had just directed in

Manhattan Melodrama (1934) to play Nick and Nora Charles. He assigned Frances Goodrich and Albert Hackett, a husband-and-wife writing team, to compose the screenplay.

Van Dyke was a no-nonsense director, who was known as "One-Take Woody" because of the speed and economy with which he directed a picture. *The Thin Man* was no exception; he shot the film in a brisk sixteen days. It was evident that Powell and Loy shared a real chemistry on screen. "Bill was so naturally witty and outrageous," Loy explained, "that I stayed somewhat detached, always a little incredulous." Between them, she added, was a sense of complete understanding, "an instinct for how one could bring out the best in the other."[35] Powell and Loy made Nick and Nora a legendary screen couple, "for whom matrimony did not signal the end of sex, romance, and adventure."[36]

At the movie's climax Nick brings together all of the suspects for a dinner, complete with plainclothesmen dressed as waiters. He then explains how he solved the mystery—and collars the culprit, Herbert Macaulay, Clyde Wynant's devious attorney. This ritual of collecting the suspects at the finale, so that Nick could nail the guilty party, would be repeated in each of the sequels to *The Thin Man*.

The Thin Man was not a grim whodunit but a drawing room comedy with a murder or two thrown in for good measure. It is punctuated with witty dialogue, as when Nick is asked by a reporter about the murder case. He responds, "It's putting me behind in my drinking!" In the words of Van Dyke, *The Thin Man* "proved that murder mysteries on screen did not necessarily have to be morbid nightmares. . . . A murder mystery can be turned into a pleasing, laughable entertainment and still retain every element of a first-class baffling mystery."[37]

Because *The Thin Man* was a smash hit for MGM, it served as the basis for a lucrative series of five sequels. Dashiell Hammett, who had been a consultant on the set for *The Thin Man*, wrote a prose treatment (detailed outline) for the first two sequels, *After the Thin Man* (1936) and *Another Thin Man* (1939), both scripted by Goodrich and Hackett. Hammett borrowed some incidents from the first version of the novel in his scenario for *After the Thin Man*, such as having one of the suspects surreptitiously renting an apartment in the city under an assumed name.

After *Another Thin Man* Hammett declared that he was "bored" with the franchise and sold to MGM the screen rights of the *Thin Man* title and the characters of Nick and Nora for $40,000. He commented that no one had "ever invented a more insufferably smug pair of characters. They can't take that away from me, not even for $40,000."[38] Hammett ultimately earned $1 million in royalties from the novel and its spin-offs, including a radio show (1941–1950), a TV series (1957–1959), and, of course, the original movie and its five sequels.[39] *Song of the Thin Man* is the last and the best of the sequels—and qualifies as film noir.

The Song of the Thin Man (1947)

The final entry in the series was scripted by Steve Fisher, aided by the film's producer, Nat Perrin, from a scenario by Stanley Roberts. In *Song of the Thin Man* the urbane Nick and the sweet, sassy Nora still are a fun couple, whose marriage never stands in the way of their going off on detective capers. As befits a film noir, however, *Song of the Thin Man* is a grimmer movie than the previous sequels, with Nick and Nora searching for clues in dark and mysterious New York jazz hangouts. In addition, there is an insane musician who suffers from neurotic guilt and threatens Nora's life—deeply disturbed characters are a commonplace in film noirs.

To confirm the picture's credentials as film noir, *Song of the Thin Man* features Gloria Grahame, who appeared in other film noirs like Fritz Lang's *Human Desire*. Grahame was easily the most blatantly sexual female on the screen. Any film noir, writes Michael Buckley, was "enlivened by her saucy delivery."[40] This film is, in essence, closer to the dark tone of Hammett's first draft of *The Thin Man* than to the somewhat lighter tone of the published novel. *Song of the Thin Man* portrays a grim world marred by conspiracy and betrayal, in which no one can be trusted.

Edward Buzzell was assigned to direct *Song of the Thin Man*; he was a sure-handed and versatile director, who had turned out the madcap Marx Brothers' *Go West* (1940), for example. He would make *Song of the Thin Man* a good closing entry for the series, with the help of director of photography Charles Rosher. It was Rosher, who had founded the American Society of Cinematographers with Arthur Edeson (the cinematographer on Huston's *Maltese Falcon*), who made *Song of the Thin Man* a nifty noir.

Rosher had won an Academy Award as co-cinematographer on F. W. Murnau's *Sunrise* (1927). Émigré directors like Murnau had brought German expressionism to Hollywood, and Rosher utilized it in

Song of the Thin Man. There is an uncanny interplay of light and shadow in the present film, which creates a brooding atmosphere of tension and uncertainty that smacks of German expressionism.

Just as Paramount selected a writer of hard-boiled fiction, Jonathan Latimer, to write the screenplay of *The Glass Key*, so Metro wisely chose mystery writer Steve Fisher (*I Wake Up Screaming*) to be principal screenwriter for *Song of the Thin Man*, aided by the movie's producer, Nat Perrin. Fisher was a *Black Mask* alumnus like Hammett and had recently taken up screenwriting; he had adapted Raymond Chandler's *Lady in the Lake* for MGM, released in February 1947. Fisher fashioned a tough, gritty script for *Song of the Thin Man*, which avoided superficial melodrama.

Song of the Thin Man exemplifies the kind of film that Manny Farber called "termite art"—a small, unpretentious movie that "evades affectation." It has no ambition to be a pompous, inflated "elephantine" drama that smacks the viewer with "artiness." It rather "nibbles away" at "a few spots of tingling, jarring excitement."[41]

William Powell and Myrna Loy did their last star turn as Nick and Nora Charles in *Song of the Thin Man*. The supporting cast was headed by Gloria Grahame. Grahame had "opened her noir career" by playing a weary dance hall hostess in Edward Dmytryk's film noir *Crossfire* (1947), just before appearing in *Song of the Thin Man* as Fran Page, a sultry nightclub thrush.[42] Judith Williamson has said of Grahame, "Neither we nor the other characters know whether to believe what she says; elusive as a cat," she is all but unknowable herself.[43]

Silver and Ursini single out the scene in the present film as typical noir in which Grahame as Fran Page sings a torch song in a smoky café. "She seems to lean on the piano for support, and her face is sullen and suspicious."[44] Rosher's adroit lighting of the scene makes Fran stand out from the darkness and gloom that surround her. At this point Fran has all the earmarks of a femme fatale.

Kevin Brownlow has told me that the noir look of *Song of the Thin Man* is largely due to Rosher, and not to Buzzell: "I would not have credited Buzzell with any photographic expertise, whereas Rosher was a photographic genius."[45] Indeed, Rosher had earned a second Oscar for photographing *The Yearling* (1946) just prior to beginning work on *Song of the Thin Man*.

The film opens with Nick and Nora Charles attending a charity ball aboard the S.S. *Fortune*, a floating gambling casino operated by Phil

Brant. Tommy Drake's dance band, with featured clarinetist Buddy Hollis (Don Taylor), is on hand. In the course of the evening Mitchell Talbin (Leon Ames), Drake's business manager, warns Drake about his wayward personal life. In fact, Drake, with his gambling and womanizing, is cut from the same cloth as the dissolute playboy Taylor Henry in *The Glass Key*. Like Taylor Henry, Tommy Drake will meet a violent end.

Drake attempts to steal cash from the safe in Brant's office in order to cover a gambling debt. But he is shot to death in the middle of the robbery. Brant is the prime suspect in the killing of Drake because he had quarreled with Drake earlier in the evening about Drake's compulsive gambling.

Brant entreats Nick Charles to help him clear his name, but Nick—as always—maintains that he has retired from sleuthing. Whereupon Nora—as always—coaxes him into taking the case. Another important suspect is Buddy Hollis. The mentally unstable Buddy, who is a hopeless alcoholic, disappears shortly after the murder, thereby casting suspicion on himself.

Another clarinetist in Drake's band, Clarence "Clinker" Krause (Keenan Wynn) steers Nick and Nora around to several New York jazz clubs frequented by musicians like Buddy for after-hours jam sessions. (The sequence recalls *The Phantom Lady*, Robert Siodmak's 1944 noir, in which the heroine visits several jazz clubs looking for the fabled lady of the title.) In one nightery, Fran Page sings with a combo. While Fran is warbling a romantic ballad, Clinker tells Nick that she had been Buddy's heartthrob—until she jilted him for Drake. Buddy was inconsolable at the loss of Fran, and he has continued to carry the torch for her.

Nick encounters Clinker Krause again when he sneaks aboard the S.S. *Fortune*, which has been moored offshore near the wharf since Drake's murder. As Nick prowls the dark corridors of the gambling ship, the beam of his flashlight pierces the darkness, signifying how Nick is endeavoring to shed light on the dark mystery. When Nick meets up with Clinker, who has come aboard to retrieve his clarinet, he enlightens Nick by informing him that Fran regrets ditching Buddy for Drake, who turned out to be nothing but "a road company Casanova" (an example of Fisher's smart dialogue).

Hoping that Fran can help him in his investigation, Nick goes to her apartment—only to find that Buddy's old flame has been stabbed to death. Nick's practiced eye spies a matchbook from the Hotel Vesta in Poughkeepsie. He rightly deduces that Fran had been visiting Buddy at the Valley Rest Home near the hotel. It seems that Buddy, whose mind has been shattered by alcohol, has developed a deeply rooted guilt complex and believes that he shot Drake while he was in a drunken stupor.

When Nick and Nora get nowhere questioning Buddy at the rest home, Nora goes back to see Buddy on her own. Nora assures Buddy that she is a friend of Fran's. Buddy erupts in a paranoid tantrum, raving, "They sent you to spy on me because I killed Drake; and now I'll kill you!!" As Buddy hallucinates, Nora's face is multiplied on the screen and melts into a blur. Just then Nick breaks into the room and saves her from Buddy. The hapless Buddy's hallucinatory image of Nora, depicted on the screen in a bizarre fashion, is a salient example of Rosher's skillful use of German expressionism in the film.

Nick collects all of the suspects in the case in the ballroom aboard Brant's gambling ship, ostensibly for the reopening of the S.S. *Fortune*, but really to unmask the murderer. This obligatory ritual of gathering the suspects together takes place at the climax of all six of the *Thin Man* movies. Once again Nick has plainclothesmen disguised as waiters on hand for the showdown, just as he did in the original *Thin Man* movie.

The ballroom is dimly lit, with everyone bathed in shadows—a typical noir setting. Buddy is leading Drake's band, and Nick pretends that Buddy has recovered from his psychosis and supplied Nick with the facts he needs to solve the case. By this ploy Nick aims to unnerve the culprit and make him show his hand.

Nick ultimately zeroes in on Mitchell Talbin, who finally cracks and blurts out that he killed Drake because he had seduced Mitchell's wife Phyllis. Nick adds that Mitchell then convinced Buddy that he had killed Drake by planting the murder weapon on Buddy. What's more, Mitchell murdered Fran because she had figured out during her visits to Buddy at the sanatorium that Mitchell had shot Drake.

After Mitchell confesses to the killings, his wife Phyllis empties her gun into him. "I swore I'd kill the man who shot Tommy Drake," she declares to Mitchell as he draws his last breath. Phyllis thus reveals herself to be the movie's femme fatale, and not Fran Page. Fran seemed to be a femme fatale at the outset, when she dumped Buddy for Drake, but she wound up sacrificing her life for Buddy in the end. Having broken the case, Nick announces that perhaps he should not give up being a private eye after all.

Song of the Thin Man was underrated by some reviewers when it premiered in August 1947, simply because they assumed that it was merely a routine follow-up to the four previous sequels to *The Thin Man* that had gone before. Yet some other critics genuinely appreciated it. The *New York Times* stated that fans of the franchise could rest assured that William Powell and Myrna Loy "exhibit the same old zest and bantering affection" they did in the original *Thin Man* thirteen years earlier. "They are as good company now as they ever were."[46]

In describing *Song of the Thin Man* as "this new Dashiell Hammett detective thriller," *Variety* reminded fans of the series about the roots of the *Thin Man* movies in Hammett's novel. The picture "puts the Metro series right back in full stride. *Song of the Thin Man* is one of the better pictures in the *Thin Man* grouping. Edward Buzzell keeps interest at a high pitch."[47]

The reputation of *Song of the Thin Man* has improved over the years. This is not surprising, given the contributions of noir specialist Steve Fisher and of the superior director of photography Charles Rosher. Silver and Ursini cite the movie as a significant film noir in their book *The Noir Style*, as mentioned. Nash and Ross observe, "The last entries in a series are, as a rule, bad. This one breaks the mold," and can hold its own with other mystery movies of the period.[48]

More recently Ben Brantley has written that Dashiell Hammett was the creator of Nick and Nora Charles, "the chic, martini-loving husband-and-wife sleuths. Incarnated on screen by William Powell and Myrna Loy, the Charleses became the template for marriage as a sophisticated test of cleverness; and they have been copied ad infinitum." But copies are never as good as the originals.[49]

The screen credits for *Song of the Thin Man* state that the screenplay is "based on characters created by Dashiell Hammett." That is the last official screen credit Hammett ever received on a motion picture. His influential series of detective novels had come to an end with *The Thin Man* in 1934. One of the reasons "behind Hammett's silence for more than a quarter-century before his death in 1961," according to Symons, was that "he felt he had come to the end of what he could do with the crime story."[50]

In January 1936, Hammett attended a *Black Mask* writers dinner; it was the only time that Raymond Chandler ever met Hammett. "Often wonder why he quit writing after *The Thin Man*," Chandler wrote to a friend. "Met him only once, very nice-looking, tall, quiet, gray-haired." Chandler concluded, "Seemed quite unspoiled to me."[51]

William Powell and Myrna Loy as Nick and Nora Charles in the fifth and final sequel to *The Thin Man*, entitled *Song of the Thin Man*.

Ironically, Hammett did not admire his own work. Lillian Hellman believed that he was ashamed of having written "mere detective stories," on which he squandered his obvious gifts.[52] Hammett wanted to write "socially significant novels, but he never indicated exactly what he had in mind," writes Hammett biographer William Nolan in his overview of Hammett's career. His only significant piece of fiction in later years was "Tulip" (1952), an aborted novel that he abandoned at 17,000 words. "Tulip," published posthumously, is the story of an author with writer's block.[53]

Kiszely notes that there is no question that alcoholism "blighted Hammett's productivity." Incidents of his self-destructive behavior under the influence of alcohol "are numerous and well-documented." As the years slipped by, Hammett continued to drink, gamble, and womanize.[54] Furthermore, because Hammett suffered from tuberculosis, which got worse as he got older, Nolan suggests that Hammett found the strain of writing too much to bear.[55]

Dashiell Hammett never seemed to grasp that he had raised the crime novel to the level of literature. Indeed, *The Maltese Falcon* and *The Glass Key*, his best novels, can survive comparison with Hemingway. They give a raw, unvarnished portrait of violence and corruption in modern life.

James Thurber once complained that even the work of the most popular writers does not always stay in print continuously "in a country of fickle and restless tastes that goes in for the Book of the Month and the Song of the Week."[56] Be that as it may, Hammett's fiction has never disappeared into a literary limbo as he always feared it might. In the realm of the detective story, Hammett remains a master, both on page and screen.

There remains one screen adaptation of a Hammett novel yet to be treated. In 1978 his 1929 novel *The Dain Curse* was made into a neo-noir film for television. This movie will be considered in chapter 12, which looks at neo-noir.

Notes

1. Dennis Dooley, *Dashiell Hammett* (New York: Unger, 1984), 109.
2. Dashiell Hammett, *The Glass Key* (New York: Knopf, 1989), 62.
3. Dooley, *Dashiell Hammett*, 112.
4. Hammett, *The Glass Key*, 211.
5. Symons, *Dashiell Hammett*, 84.
6. Johnson, *Dashiell Hammett*, 85.

7. Lawrence O'Toole, "Now Read the Movie," *Film Comment* 18, no. 6 (November–December, 1982): 37.

8. Tom Hiney, *Raymond Chandler: A Biography* (New York: Atlantic Monthly Press, 1997), 138.

9. Lee Server, "Bad Company," *Sight and Sound* 19 (n.s.), no. 8 (August, 2009): 30.

10. Woody Haut, *Heartbreak and Vine: Hard-Boiled Writers in Hollywood* (London: Serpent's Tail, 2002), 14.

11. Nash and Ross, eds., *Motion Picture Guide*, vol. 3, 1034.

12. *"The Glass Key,"* in *Variety Film Reviews*, vol. 6, n.p.

13. Thomson, *The New Biographical Dictionary of Film*, p. 910.

14. Thomas, *The Films of the Forties*, 64.

15. Geoff Mayer, "Introduction," in *Encyclopedia of Film Noir*, 35.

16. Haut, *Heartbreak and Vine*, 186.

17. Haut, *Heartbreak and Vine*, 187.

18. Letter of Joseph Breen to B. G. De Sylva, December 15, 1941, in Production Code Administration Archive, at the Margaret Herrick Library of the Motion Picture Academy.

19. Production Code of the Motion Picture Association of America (June 13, 1934), "V. Profanity," 4. Production Code Administration Archives, at the Margaret Herrick Library.

20. Andrew Sennewald, *"The Glass Key,"* in *New York Times Film Reviews* (New York: New York Times, 1997), vol. 2, n.p. This collection of reviews is unpaginated.

21. Sarris, *You Ain't Heard Nothin' Yet*, 117.

22. Mayer, "Introduction," in *Encyclopedia of Film Noir*, 12.

23. Fran Mason, *American Gangster Cinema* (New York: Macmillan, 2002), 61.

24. Mason, *American Gangster Cinema*, 61.

25. Jim Hillier, *"The Glass Key,"* in Alastair Phillips, *100 Film Noirs* (London: British Film Institute, 2009), 106–7.

26. Manny Farber, "Mystery Movie," *Farber on Film: The Complete Film Writings of Manny Farber*, ed. Robert Polito (New York: Library of America, 2009), 46.

27. Nash and Ross, eds., *Motion Picture Guide*, vol. 3, 1034.

28. Mayer, "Introduction," in *Encyclopedia of Film Noir*, 12.

29. Nash and Ross, eds., *Motion Picture Guide*, vol. 3, 1034.

30. Bruce Crowther, *Film Noir: Reflections in a Dark Mirror* (New York: Unger, 1989), 28.

31. Steven Marcus, *"The Thin Man*: An Early Typescript," in Dashiell Hammett, *Crime Stories and Other Writings*, ed. Steven Marcus (New York: Library of America, 2001), 929–30.

32. See Dashiell Hammett, "The First Thin Man," in *Nightmare Town*, 347–96. This presents the complete typescript of the first draft of the novel.

33. Thomson, *Have You Seen . . . ?*, 880.

34. Dooley, *Dashiell Hammett*, 124.

35. Thomson, *Have You Seen . . . ?*, 880.

36. Sarris, *You Ain't Heard Nothin' Yet*, 419.

37. W. S. Van Dyke, "R for a Thin Man," in *Hollywood Directors, 1914–40*, ed. Richard Koszarski (New York: Oxford University Press, 1976), 311–12.

38. Dooley, *Dashiell Hammett*, 118.

39. Robert Gale, *A Dashiell Hammett Companion* (Westport, Conn.: Greenwood Press, 2000), 248.

40. Michael Buckley, "Gloria Grahame," *Films in Review* 40, no. 12 (December 1989): 580.

41. Farber, "White Elephant Art vs. Termite Art," in *Farber on Film*, 540, 534.

42. Brian McDonnell, "Gloria Grahame," in *Encyclopedia of Film Noir*, 199.

43. David Thomson, *The New Biographical Dictionary of Film*, 359.

44. Alain Silver and James Ursini, *The Noir Style* (Woodstock, N.Y.: Overlook Press, 2003), 108.

45. Kevin Brownlow to the author, May 16, 2009.

46. "*Song of the Thin Man*," in *New York Times Film Reviews*, vol. 3, n.p.

47. "*Song of the Thin Man*," in *Variety Film Reviews*, vol. 7, n.p.

48. Nash and Ross, eds., *Motion Picture Guide*, vol. 7, 3036.

49. Ben Brantley, "In a Gilded World, Theirs Is but to Quip and Sigh," *New York Times*, February 23, 2010, sec. C:1.

50. Symons, *Dashiell Hammett*, 4.

51. Raymond Chandler to Alex Barris, April 16, 1949, in *Selected Letters of Raymond Chandler*, ed. Frank MacShane (New York: Columbia University Press, 1981), 165.

52. Dooley, *Dashiell Hammett*, 133.

53. Nolan, "Introduction," in Dashiell Hammett, *Nightmare Town*, xi. Hellman included "Tulip" in *The Big Knockover*, 301–48.

54. Kiszely, *Hollywood through Private Eyes*, 61.

55. Nolan, "Introduction," in Dashiell Hammett, *Nightmare Town*, xi.

56. James Thurber, *Credos and Curios* (New York: Harper & Row, 1967), 162–63.

Part Three

DARKNESS AT NOON: REPRESENTATIVE NOIR FILMS

FRITZ LANG:
MINISTRY OF FEAR AND *SCARLET STREET*

F ive major directors of film noir emigrated from Europe to Hollywood after Hitler came to power: Fritz Lang, Billy Wilder, Robert
Siodmak, Otto Preminger, and Fred Zinnemann. These émigré
directors played a large part in establishing classic film noir. Brian Mc-
Donnell states, "Among them, Fritz Lang was a central figure, contribut-
ing in a substantial way to the cycle," with a string of film noirs.[1]

Although *Ministry of Fear* is an overlooked Lang noir, preeminent
Lang scholar Lotte Eisner terms *Ministry of Fear* "a definite part of the
film noir tradition."[2] In fact, Graham Greene's 1943 novel, *The Ministry
of Fear*, with its "dark streets and sinister neighborhoods, the shabby
offices and shabbier hotel rooms," seems to be perfectly attuned to the
atmosphere of film noir.[3]

It is an axiom of commentators on spy fiction that nearly all of the
genre's greatest authors worked in intelligence before writing spy novels:
Somerset Maugham, Ian Fleming, as well as Graham Greene. They all
were familiar with the world of espionage from personal experience.

In 1941 Graham Greene was chief of the British Secret Intelligence
Service in Freetown, Sierra Leone. Greene composed *The Ministry of Fear*
while he was in Freetown—the only novel he wrote during the war years.
Despite the straightened circumstances in which he penned the novel, "his
prose is spare and elegant, his pacing masterly."[4]

The novel moves with what has rightly been called scenario swiftness
and deals with Arthur Rowe (Stephen Neale in the film), an unhappy man
who has been detained in an asylum ever since he was convicted for killing

his invalid wife. Almost immediately after his release from the asylum, he finds himself stalked and pursued by an assortment of menacing individuals. At first he wonders if it is his imagination, but soon discovers that a cake he won at a charity bazaar on the first day of his release from the institution actually contained a roll of microfilm intended for a Nazi spy who was to smuggle this secret information out of the country.

It is easy to understand why Lang was attracted to the novel. One often finds in Lang's work what can be called his "paranoid theme": the hero is surrounded by an unseen enemy whose forces are everywhere. Stephen gradually finds that no one can be trusted, for even people who on the surface seem good more often than not turn out to be in league with the enemy.

In *The Ministry of Fear*, then, we have a ready-made Lang situation. Lang recalled, "I have always admired Graham Greene, and when I came back to Hollywood from New York, where I had signed the contract, and read the script, I did everything I could to get out of making that picture; but Paramount wouldn't cancel the contract. That was one of the times that my agent had failed to get a clause in my contract that allowed me to work on the script."[5]

One reason that he would have liked to have revised the screenplay was that the searching examination of the hero's psychological problems, so evident in Greene's novel, was mostly missing from the script. Greene portrays Stephen, the hero, as a deeply neurotic man in the novel, but in the screenplay Stephen's emotional problems seem to be largely behind him. In the movie, as a matter of fact, Stephen is not responsible for his wife's death because she commits suicide. Hence he is not guilty of euthanasia, as he is in the book.

This whole probing of Rowe's psyche is missing from the film, but Greene still had a soft spot for the movie in his heart: "*The Ministry of Fear* was made by dear old Fritz Lang," he said, "and I was delighted that a veteran director of his reputation was involved in the film. But unfortunately the script that he was given to work with cut out the whole middle third of the book in which Rowe goes into a nursing home with amnesia and tries to sort out his life. Without this section the whole point of the novel is missing, and the story doesn't exist."[6]

The screenplay for *Ministry of Fear* was by Seton Miller, who was an experienced screenwriter in Hollywood, having won an Academy Award for coscripting *Here Comes Mr. Jordan* (1941). Miller had a reputation for "taut dialogue, well-drawn characters, and solid construction."[7] So Miller was not the neophyte Lang often called him.

In 1943 Miller became a producer as well as a writer; his first picture as a writer-producer was *Ministry of Fear*. Given Miller's dual role as both producer and author of the screenplay, he was in a position to veto Lang's suggestions to amend the script. Withal, *Ministry of Fear* is generally considered one of Miller's best films as a writer-producer.

Ray Milland, a stalwart leading man at Paramount, was slated to play Stephen Neale. But the member of the cast most associated with film noir is Dan Duryea, who has the role of a Nazi gent known as Cost. "With his slicked-down hair, sharp features, and wolfish grin, Duryea was one of the most distinctive figures in film noir," and would be seen in Lang's *Scarlet Street* the following year.[8]

Because of wartime conditions, the film could not be shot on location in London and had to be made almost entirely in a Hollywood studio. As in Lang's German film *M*, the studio-built city is "a created environment of uncannily deserted streets and menacing storefronts," which evoke the protagonist's paranoia and isolation. As such, the sets are in the tradition of German expressionism. Thus "the shadowy wartime noir streets and claustrophobic confines become a place of anxiety, . . . a dark world where nothing is certain."[9]

As his pursuers track Stephen down, "the city streets become increasingly shadowed and solitary," thanks to the superb low-key lighting by cinematographer Henry Sharp, who had photographed the 1935 film of *The Glass Key*.[10]

Lang's version of *Ministry* turned out to be one of his most accomplished spy melodramas. He was, after all, a master at creating noir thrillers. Writing of Lang's thrillers, more recently, Iain Sinclair observes that Lang brought with him to Hollywood "the notion of the city as an incubator of violence," which is mirrored in his German movies like *M*.[11] Lang's ability to turn out a suspenseful thriller is clearly on view in a chase melodrama like *Ministry of Fear*.

The film begins in a darkened room; a door opens, admitting a shaft of light that reveals Stephen (Ray Milland) sitting in the shadows and facing the door. He is staring silently at the swinging pendulum of the clock on the opposite wall. A doctor enters; he informs Stephen that he is now free to leave the asylum, where he has been confined these last two years, following his nervous breakdown after the death of his invalid wife. When Stephen walks out of the dark room and into the brightly lit corridor, his action conveys that he is now endeavoring to turn his back on his murky past and to walk into the light of the present. Ironically, he soon enters an even more uncertain world than the one he has just left.

On his way to the train depot to catch a train for London, Stephen visits a charity bazaar sponsored by the Mothers of the Free Nations. Stephen is drawn to the clairvoyant's dark tent, where Mrs. Bellane (Mrs. Bellairs in the novel) reads his palm with a flashlight. Stephen says, "Forget the past; just tell me the future." He does not wish to recall his dead wife's ordeal. Without realizing it, Stephen has given the secret password to Mrs. Bellane, who then divulges to Stephen the weight of the prize cake. Stephen wins the cake by guessing its correct weight. But just as he is about to leave the fairgrounds, the sponsors of the fete insist that he has been awarded the prize through an oversight and that the cake really belongs to someone else, a Mr. Cost (Dan Duryea). Stephen nevertheless stubbornly insists on keeping the cake and heads for the railway station.

While he is waiting to board the train, Stephen sees a blind man coming down the platform toward him. The appearance of a blind man fits in perfectly with the atmosphere of uneasy anticipation Lang is striving to establish at this point. In describing the blind man, Paul Jensen writes: "Preceded by the sound of his tapping cane, he appears through a cloud of steam that gives him almost supernatural overtones."[12] As the blind man chats with Stephen in the course of the journey, there is a close-up of his face, which shows his eyes furtively darting around the train compartment. This indicates to the viewer, if not yet to Stephen, that the man is pretending to be blind for some malevolent purpose of his own. While the train is halted during a Nazi air raid on the area, the man suddenly snatches the cake and runs off into the night, only to be killed by a falling bomb. When it came to staging a gripping scene of this sort, Lang was without a peer in film noir.

Once in London, Stephen visits the headquarters of the Mothers of the Free Nations, which sponsored the charity fair, in order to see if he can ascertain the significance of the stolen cake. There he meets a brother and sister, Willi Hilfe (Carl Esmond) and Carla Hilfe (Marjorie Reynolds). They are Austrian refugees who run the organization, but they prove to be of little help in solving the mystery.

As the film unreels, Scotland Yard investigators discover that the crucial cake contained a roll of microfilm intended for a Nazi spy who was to smuggle this secret information about British defense plans out of the country. Further investigation reveals that the Mothers of the Free Nations, which sponsored the charity bazaar, is actually a front for a bureau of Nazi agents known as the Ministry of Fear. This term refers to the "Nazi method of blackmailing foreign nationals into betraying their countries."[13] As Carla puts it, "The Nazis work all around you; they know where to find you." They infiltrate organizations like the Mothers of the Free Nations for their own nefarious purposes.

Initially Willi Hilfe seems friendly to Stephen and accompanies him to a séance at the home of Mrs. Bellane, the medium. This Mrs. Bellane turns out to be an elegant lady (Hilary Brooke), nothing like the frumpy Mrs. Bellane Stephen encountered at the carnival. It seems that the Mrs. Bellane at the bazaar was a volunteer pinch-hitting for the real Mrs. Bellane at the clairvoyant's booth at the fair. The real Mrs. Bellane, like Willi

Stephen Neale (Ray Milland) and Carla Hilfe (Marjorie Reynolds) view the corpse of Nazi spy Willi Hilfe (Carl Esmond)—her brother—in Fritz Lang's film of Graham Greene's *The Ministry of Fear.*

and Carla, claims to know nothing about the mysterious significance of the prize cake. Mr. Cost, the man Stephen saw at the fair, shows up just as the séance begins; and the room is plunged into darkness.

Mrs. Bellane, whose face is visible in the dark, is lit from below, giving her an eerie quality. She calls forth an invisible spirit who accuses Stephen of being responsible for his wife's death. Gunfire suddenly pierces the darkness, and the lights are turned on. Mr. Cost lies dead on the floor, and Stephen is accused of murdering him. Stephen flees the scene of the crime and phones Carla, the only person he dares trust. They agree to meet at a subway station, which turns into an air raid shelter when an air raid siren sounds.

As Stephen and Carla wait out the air raid on the underground subway platform, he tells her about his wife's demise. His wife was incurably ill and begged Stephen to obtain poison for her, so she could end her suffering. Stephen purchased the poison, which he could not bring himself to give to her. But she found the poison hidden in a drawer, where Stephen had concealed it, and took it herself. He spent the whole night holding her hand, watching the slowly swinging pendulum on the clock in her bedroom, until her torment ended. This explains why Stephen was staring at a clock pendulum in the opening scene of the movie. Stephen was convicted of euthanasia anyway and sentenced to a term in the asylum. In the novel Stephen is actually guilty of mercy killing; but "the film seeks to make the hero more acceptable" by having his wife administer the poison to herself, as Quentin Falk comments.[14] Because the film renders Stephen in no way responsible for his wife's death, the crucial section in the novel in which Rowe goes to a sanatorium to come to grips with his past became irrelevant to the film and was deleted—much to Greene's disappointment.

When Stephen is interrogated by Inspector Prentice, a Scotland Yard detective, about the death of the blind man and other matters, Stephen cajoles the detective into returning with him to the site of the bomb crater where the blind man was killed, in search of evidence to corroborate his story about Nazi agents stalking him—for the so-called blind man, in retrospect, was surely a Nazi agent. They discover a chunk of cake in a bird's nest, and inside the morsel of cake is a canister of microfilm containing vital military secrets. So Stephen is vindicated.

Stephen and Inspector Prentice eventually trace the enemy spy ring to a haberdashery store, where Stephen realizes that Travers, one of the tailors, is none other than Cost—the man he was accused of murdering at the séance. Recognizing Stephen, Cost realizes that the jig is up; he dials a phone number with a huge tailor's scissors and informs a fellow spy cryptically that he will not be able to keep his promise: "Personally, I have no hope at all." Then Cost dashes into the fitting room, locks the door, and stabs himself in the stomach with the scissors.

Stephen soon learns that Cost had phoned Willi Hilfe, who is really a Nazi spy, and that he has used his sister as an innocent pawn for his subversive activities. When Stephen at last confronts Willi in front of Carla, Willi pulls a gun on him in an effort to make his getaway, but Carla manages to snatch the weapon away from him. Willi then switches off the lights and runs out of the room, saying to Carla, "You couldn't kill your own brother." She can—and in fact, she does. As Willi slams the door behind him, a shot is fired in the dark, and we see a pinpoint of light in the door where the bullet pierced it. When the door is opened, the light falls across the body of Carla's brother. Thus, with the last member of the spy ring disposed of, Stephen's troubles are over and at the final fadeout he rides off with Carla in his sports car into the sunset.

Some film critics have questioned the plausibility of Carla's shooting her brother without hesitation. On the contrary, her action is clearly credible: Carla and Stephen, after all, have developed a love relationship by this point in the film; she is more committed to Stephen than to her nefarious brother. Moreover, Carla's behavior is entirely consistent with that of the typical Lang heroine. In many of Lang's films the heroine represents the values of innocence and integrity so sorely lacking in the shadowy nightmare world that Lang often depicts. As Andrew Sarris states, Lang makes exceptions to his bleak vision of life "in the pure, trustworthy love of beautiful girls. Romantic love, with its intimations of Christian self-sacrifice," flows through Lang's films.[15]

John Russell Taylor points out the implicit continuity between Lang's German films and his American movies by drawing attention to the references to Lang's German pictures that occasionally surface in his Hollywood output. For example, *Ministry of Fear* is "haunted with the shadows of the nightmare world" Lang had portrayed in *M*.[16]

Paramount did not have much faith in Lang's film from the outset. *Ministry of Fear* was premiered in October 1944 but not given a full-sale release until the following February. Lotte Eisner complained that *Ministry of Fear* has always been reckoned as a minor Lang film, when it is really an important film noir.[17]

Pauline Kael called *Ministry of Fear* "an unmemorable Paramount picture."[18] David Thomson replied that he simply could not accept that the film was forgettable. Furthermore, Thomson believes that Miller's screenplay is underrated. It is, after all, loaded with incidents that convey a pervasive atmosphere of fear, dread, and a malign fate. Thomson went so far as to state that *Ministry of Fear* "may yet be appreciated as Lang's greatest film in America, more delicately poised over the razor's edge of war and madness" than any of his other movies.[19]

While Thomson's reassessment of *Ministry of Fear* is a welcome corrective to the negative judgments of Kael and others, the movie cannot be called Lang's greatest American film noir. That accolade belongs to *Scarlet Street*.

Scarlet Street (1945)

Lang's *Scarlet Street*, like Renoir's *La Chienne* (which is discussed in chapter 2), is based on the novel of the same name by Georges de la Fouchardiere, in which an upright citizen is entrapped by a treacherous femme fatale.

Lang said that he had seen Renoir's film during its original release, but he did not use it as a model for his version of the same story, since he wanted to make a new film, not a mere copy of Renoir's French original. If it is true that Lang did not look at *La Chienne* (*The Bitch*) again, Tom Gunning wryly observes, "it is not from lack of trying." Lang's correspondence from the period indicates that he did in fact endeavor to locate a print of *La Chienne* for screening, but failed to do so, since French films were generally not available in the United States during World War II.[20]

Paramount had purchased the screen rights to the novel at Ernst Lubitsch's request in the early 1930s, but Lubitsch could never come up with a screenplay that would get past the censors. Producer Walter Wanger, who was married to Joan Bennett, had recently formed an independent production unit at Universal Studios with Lang and his wife. Wanger, an enterprising producer of films like *Stagecoach* (1939), was able to buy the screen rights to the novel from Paramount fairly cheaply. Lang and his screenwriter Dudley Nichols decided to transplant the story from bohemian Montmartre in Paris to bohemian Greenwich Village in New York City. Nichols, who had scripted Lang's movie *Man Hunt* (1941), spent three months constructing the screenplay for *Scarlet Street*, in consultation with Lang.

In general Nichols followed the novel almost scene by scene in composing the screenplay. He created "a brooding urban underworld of lights and shadows."[21] As in the book the central character Chris Cross (Maurice Legrand in the novel) is devastated to learn that Kitty March (Lucienne Pelletier in the novel) loves her pimp Johnny Prince (Dédé in the novel), not him. So he murders Kitty and contrives to frame Johnny for the crime.

It was a cinch that Lang's film could not use the title of Renoir's film, *The Bitch*, for his movie. After much discussion Lang settled on *Scarlet Street* for the title. Lang had in mind "the passage in the Apocalypse of St. John, where the whore of Babylon" is described as a scarlet woman.[22] In addition, illicit sex is associated with the color red, as in the term *red light district*.

Lang was blessed with a superior cast in *Scarlet Street*. Joan Bennett excelled at playing a deceitful and seductive femme fatale, and her role as Kitty March is "her most accomplished role in the classical noir cycle."[23] Edward G. Robinson took a range of parts in film noirs; from playing Chris Cross, the fallen hero of *Scarlet Street*, he went on to portray the dogged government agent in Welles's *The Stranger* the following year. Rounding out the principal cast members was Dan Duryea as Kitty's nattily dressed, oily boyfriend Johnny Prince. All three actors had appeared in Lang's *Woman in the Window* (1944).

Since Chris Cross is an amateur painter, Lang commissioned his friend, the artist John Decker, to paint Chris's pictures. Because Chris is an untrained amateur, Lang had Decker give his paintings "a kind of Primitive style."[24] The sets were designed by Alexander Golitzen, Universal's reigning production designer, who had won an Academy Award for his work on *The Phantom of the Opera* (1943).

As in the case of *Ministry of Fear*, the exteriors for *Scarlet Street* were shot on indoor sets in the studio, with no scenes shot on location. "What the studio-bound noirs sacrifice in authenticity, they make up in a heightened claustrophobia," writes Terrence Rafferty. The characters exist in a confined, closed-in world. Moreover, cinematographer Milton Krasner underscored that claustrophobic feeling "by means of dim, expressionistic lighting, hemming the nervous characters in with walls of shadows."[25]

The film's background music was composed by Hans Salter, an immigrant born in Austria, like Lang. Salter specialized in dark, melodramatic scores for films like *The Black Cat* (1941). In *Scarlet Street* he employs "Melancholy Baby," the old standard popular song, throughout the score. The tune is first heard on the jukebox of the bar where Chris and Kitty go for a drink on the night they first meet. Moreover, Kitty frequently plays the same song on her record player. "Melancholy Baby" suggests that Chris is a lonely man, who lives in a state of gloom.

Lang approved of Salter's score, except for his closing theme. "The idea of my film is that crime doesn't pay," Lang advised Salter. At film's end Chris is crushed by guilt, Lang continued. "Your end title is too hopeful; I want it more downbeat."[26] Salter complied with a tragic theme that was more appropriate for a ruined, self-destructive man.

During the editing period Lang deleted the scene in which Chris goes to Sing Sing on the night of Johnny's execution. He climbs a telephone pole, so he can see the lights in the death house dim at the moment when Johnny is electrocuted. Lang feared that watching Chris rejoice at Johnny's death might appear grotesque, "and have an unintentional comic effect on the audience"; so he eliminated the scene.[27]

Lang remembered that the studio was worried that Joseph Breen, the film industry censor, might object to the fact that Johnny was executed for a crime that he did not commit, rather than Chris, who actually committed the murder. Lang said that he mollified the censor by pointing out that "Chris is punished more by living with his guilt than he would have been by going to prison. At the end of the movie he is a man driven by the Furies, at his wits' end." Lang added that since he was raised a Catholic, he firmly believed that a sinner pays for his sins by mental suffering, as Chris does. In addition, not a single critic complained that Johnny was unjustly executed. The critics presumably felt that Johnny got what was coming to him since he was an unregenerate scoundrel who had cruelly connived with Kitty to bilk Chris out of his last cent and ruin his life.

Lang then had to cope with the Legion of Decency, a Roman Catholic organization that rated the moral suitability of movies for its Catholic constituency. In the absence of an industry rating system, which would not come to pass until 1968, the legion's ratings were followed by many non-Catholics. The studio bosses tended to do the legion's bidding, to avoid receiving an objectionable rating from the legion for a movie, which could damage the film's chances at the box office. The legion placed *Scarlet Street* in its disapproving "objectionable" category, for "films that can be a moral danger to spectators," because of the movie's "undue emphasis on illicit love."[28]

The New York State Board of Censors, headed by Irwin Conroe, was one of several local censorship boards across the country in those days. The New York censor originally banned the film in New York State, objecting to the number of bedroom scenes, particularly the one in which Chris stabs Kitty repeatedly. David Kalat remarks that initially Chris plunged an ice pick into Kitty seven times. Conroe found the number of stabbings excessive, given the sexual connotations of the multiple phallic thrusts involved. Producer Walter Wanger, who negotiated with the New York censor, agreed to reduce the stabbings to four thrusts. "The film was so altered in all prints (not just in New York state)."[29] Conroe accepted this concession and a couple of other minor alterations in the film, and approved the movie for exhibition in New York State.

Lang commented laconically, "*Scarlet Street* was originally banned in New York State. . . . The ban was removed only after prolonged representation."[30] He subsequently quipped to me, "It is apparently immoral to stab a woman seven times, but moral to stab her only four times."

Scarlet Street begins with Chris Cross receiving an award from his boss, J. J. Hogarth, at a testimonial dinner, for twenty-five years of service as a cashier for Hogarth's clothing firm. Chris afterward wanders home through the winding streets of Greenwich Village, where the streetlights barely penetrate the darkness. "By one of those unlucky chances that were a staple of noir films," Chris happens upon a young woman being cuffed by a man who runs off when Chris shouts for a policeman.[31]

The girl identifies herself as an actress and says she was attacked by a purse snatcher. Actually Kitty March is no damsel in distress, but a prostitute who was being roughed up by her pimp, Johnny Prince. (Kitty's relationship with Johnny smacks of sadomasochism.) Chris, in turn, misleads Kitty into thinking that he is a wealthy painter. Chris and Kitty have a drink in a nearby bar. Chris, who is trapped in an unhappy marriage, becomes infatuated with Kitty. She is able to coax him into renting an apartment where she can live—and he can spend time painting, away from the unpleasant company of his shrewish wife, Adele.

Chris is eventually reduced to embezzling funds from his company in order to meet Kitty's continued demands for money, demands that are made at the behest of Johnny, her pimp. More than once Lang shows Chris in his cashier's cage in the office where he is employed. Tom Conley suggests that these shots of Chris imply that this cubicle seems to "incarcerate the cashier," that is, Chris lives in "an infinitely constraining world," where he is imprisoned by his obsession with Kitty, from which he is powerless to liberate himself.[32]

Johnny takes some of Chris's paintings to a Greenwich Village art fair, to see if they will sell. The pictures are noticed by Damon Janeway, a prominent art critic, who is impressed with their "primitive power." Janeway traces them to Kitty's apartment and offers to have them exhibited in Dellarowe's fashionable art gallery. Aware that Chris never signs his canvasses, Johnny coerces Kitty into telling Janeway that she painted them. Kitty accordingly signs Chris's paintings, and Johnny sells them to Dellarowe.

When Chris discovers what Kitty has done, he is so infatuated with her that he sees her appropriating his work as her own as the symbol of a bond between them. "It's as if we were married," he says, "only I take your name." Chris even titles his painting of Kitty *Self-Portrait*.

Chris fails to realize that, in allowing Kitty to take credit for his paintings, he is, in essence, forfeiting his own self-identity. He allows Kitty to control him, to the point where he hardly exists any longer as an individual with a will of his own. Chris's subservient relationship with Kitty is "a role-reversal reply of her relationship with Johnny," who dominates Kitty in the same manner as she dominates Chris, as Bould notes.[33]

Chris is likewise dominated by his wife Adele (Rosalind Ivan). He wears an apron at home to do domestic chores; this implies that his wife Adele wears the pants in the family. At one point Chris is wielding a butcher knife while he cuts a slab of meat for dinner. Adele mentions a newspaper account of a wife in Queens being murdered by her husband. When Chris turns toward Adele with the knife in his hand, she backs away, exclaiming, "Get away with that knife—do you want to cut my throat?" Chris is "obviously seething with murderous rage." The scene thus prefigures his stabbing of Kitty at the movie's climax: "he clearly has the capacity for committing murder."[34]

Adele's long-lost first husband, Homer Higgins, suddenly turns up. He had been thought to have died a hero's death while endeavoring to rescue a drowning woman. In fact Homer is a corrupt ex-cop who had

Chris Cross (Edward G. Robinson) and Kitty March (Joan Bennett) in *Scarlet Street*, Fritz Lang's remake of Jean Renoir's dark film *La Chienne*.

faked his own death in order to escape being arrested for taking bribes—and to be rid of his nagging wife.

Chris realizes that he is now free to marry Kitty. He goes to Kitty's apartment to tell her the good news. Chris is so besotted with love for Kitty that he is confident she will accept his marriage proposal; instead, Kitty laughs him to scorn. Suddenly, it becomes painfully clear to Chris that she has loved her boyfriend Johnny all along, and has never loved him. Chris is so enraged by Kitty's cruel rejection that he seizes an ice pick from an ice bucket and brutally stabs her to death. Chris murders Kitty "by stabbing at her ice-cold heart with the most appropriate of weapons, an ice pick," comments Julie Kirgo in *Film Noir: The Encyclopedia*. "He finally penetrates her long-withheld body."[35] Then he makes a hasty retreat from her apartment without being seen.

A little later Johnny shows up, roaring drunk, and finds Kitty dead; he is subsequently accused of murdering Kitty while he was in a drunken stupor, since he is the only person known to have visited her on that fateful night. Chris keeps silent while Johnny is convicted of the homicide on circumstantial evidence and is executed in the electric chair. Chris's involvement in the deaths of both Kitty and Johnny brings in to relief the symbolic significance of his name, Chris Cross. To begin with, when an individual double-crosses the same persons who have double-crossed him, it is known in common parlance as a "criss-cross." Thus, by killing Kitty and allowing her lover to be electrocuted for the crime, Chris has double-crossed the two people who had double-crossed him. Chris's revenge amounts to a criss-cross and hence accounts for his name.

Later on, Chris is discharged by his employer for embezzling company funds; he eventually becomes a pathetic hobo. As he wanders the streets aimlessly, he is haunted by Kitty's voice saying, "He brought us together, Johnny, forever." Lang employs expressionistic technique by having Kitty's voice echoing inside Chris's head. That Chris is haunted by Kitty's words suggests that he will remain obsessed to the end of his days by the realization that by killing Kitty and allowing Johnny to be executed for her death, he has unwittingly united them forever in the hereafter.

Chris is reduced to living in a fleabag motel with a neon sign incessantly flickering outside his curtainless window. He is driven to make an unsuccessful suicide attempt by trying to hang himself in an effort, in effect, to execute himself for his crimes. He is then evicted from the tawdry transient motel and winds up a homeless vagrant, wandering the city streets and sleeping on park benches. Chris expiates his guilt, says Donald Phelps, "by having to endure the nightly spooning of the loving couple Kitty and Johnny. Pursued by this demonic duo, Chris . . . is seen shuffling down the Bowery, a bewhiskered derelict."[36]

On Christmas Eve Chris walks past the Dellarowe Gallery, where his painting of Kitty (entitled *Self-Portrait*) has just been purchased by a rich matron. "Here is the man who made it, and nobody knows it," Lang commented. "He goes away down the street, with Kitty's voice ringing in his ears."[37]

As he diminishes into the distance, the pedestrians passing him on the pavement simply evaporate into thin air. Lang employs this expressionistic visual metaphor to indicate symbolically that Chris has so withdrawn himself from human contact that he does not see the people on the sidewalk. In other words, Chris's isolation from others implies that he has sentenced himself to live virtually in solitary confinement, as the self-imposed penalty for his crimes.

Among the many fine elements in the film, one that must not be overlooked, is Lang's adroit use of the standard romantic ballad "Melancholy Baby" throughout the movie, as already noted. Richard Younger writes, "From the opening credits, where the cheery strains of the song give no hint of the road to hell Chris will take, to the thunderous Wagnerian finale, the song is heard in numerous versions, each one more emotional than the last. . . . The mere title of the song evokes a potentially dark mood."[38]

The pessimistic ending of Lang's *Scarlet Street* is quite different from the more upbeat conclusion of Renoir's *La Chienne*. Suffice it to say that unlike Chris, Maurice, the central figure of Renoir's film, is not particularly troubled by avenging himself on the pair who had so ruthlessly exploited him. Furthermore, he apparently enjoys his life as a bum more than he ever liked being a cashier. For my money, Lang's ending is more thought provoking and powerful than Renoir's, and ranks as one of the most painfully tragic endings of a motion picture in all of American cinema. *Scarlet Street* was Lang's favorite among his American films. The film, he explained, "seemed to have all the right touches, and to turn out the way that I had hoped it would."

Scarlet Street premiered in December 1945, but its general release was delayed until the following February. Universal was afraid that the New York censor's original denunciation of the film would earn the picture an unjustified reputation with the public at large as a salacious movie, and waited until the New York censor had lifted the ban on the film to release it nationwide. *Scarlet Street* opened at the Loew's Criterion in Manhattan on February 20, 1946.

The film was heralded by enthusiastic reviews, and the mass audience flocked to the much-discussed movie. *Scarlet Street* has since been recognized as a major film noir. As Giannetti and Eyman observe, "Some of the best works of the American cinema" deal with "the ensnarement of a hapless male by a conniving seductress," among them *The Maltese Falcon* and *Scarlet Street*.[39]

Notes

1. Brian McDonnell, "Fritz Lang," in *Encyclopedia of Film Noir*, 259.

2. Lotte Eisner, *Fritz Lang*, trans. Gertrud Monder (New York: Da Capo, 1986), 239.

3. Alan Furst, "Introduction," in Graham Greene, *The Ministry of Fear* (New York: Penguin Books, 2005), xii. Although Greene's novel is entitled *The Ministry of Fear*, Lang's film is called *Ministry of Fear*, omitting the initial article.

4. Joseph Finder, "Five Best Novels on Political Conspiracy," *Wall Street Journal*, August 30, 2009, 147.

5. Fritz Lang, interview by the author, Beverly Hills, June 9, 1974. All quotations from Lang that are not attributed to another source are from this interview.

6. Graham Greene, interview by the author, Antibes, France, July 23, 1977.

7. John Gallagher, "Seton I. Miller," in *International Dictionary of Films and Filmmakers*, vol. 4, 579–80.

8. Brian McDonnell, "Dan Duryea," in *Encyclopedia of Film Noir*, 176.

9. Sheri Biesen, *Blackout: World War II and the Origins of Film Noir* (Baltimore: Johns Hopkins University Press, 2005), 92, 93.

10. Hirsch, *The Dark Side of the Screen*, 116, 57.

11. Iain Sinclair, "*M*: Murder in the City," *Sight and Sound* 20 (ns), no. 4 (April 2010): 44.

12. Paul Jensen, *The Cinema of Fritz Lang* (New York: Barnes, 1969), 148.

13. James Welsh, "Graham Greene's *Ministry of Fear*: Part I," *Literature/Film Quarterly* 2 (Fall 1974): 312.

14. Quentin Falk, *Travels in Greeneland: The Cinema of Graham Greene*, rev. ed. (New York: Quartet Books, 1984), 38.

15. Andrew Sarris, "Fritz Lang," in *The American Cinema: Directors and Directions, 1929–68*, rev. ed. (New York: Da Capo, 1996), 65.

16. John Russell Taylor, *Strangers in Paradise: The Hollywood Emigrés* (New York: Holt, Rinehart, and Winston, 1983), 192.

17. Eisner, *Fritz Lang*, 239, 246.

18. Pauline Kael, *5001 Nights at the Movies* (New York: Holt, 1991), 482.

19. Thomson, *Have You Seen . . . ?*, 556; see also Falk, *Travels in Greeneland*, 40.

20. Tom Gunning, *The Films of Fritz Lang* (London, British Film Institute, 2000), 308.

21. Rodney Farnesworth, "Dudley Nichols," in *International Dictionary of Films and Filmmakers*, vol. 4, 609.

22. Eisner, *Fritz Lang*, 257.

23. Brian McDonnell, "Joan Bennett," *Encyclopedia of Film Noir*, 98.

24. Charles Higham and Joel Greenberg, "Interview with Fritz Lang," in *Fritz Lang: Interviews*, ed. Barry Grant (Lexington: University of Mississippi, 2003), 114.

25. Terrence Rafferty, "Noir and the City," *New York Times*, July 22, 2007, sec. 2:11.

26. Patrick McGilligan, *Fritz Lang: The Nature of the Beast* (New York: St. Martin's Press, 1997), 323.

27. Eisner, *Fritz Lang*, 265.

28. *Scarlet Street* file, Legion of Decency files, in the Archives of the National Catholic Office for Motion Pictures.

29. David Kalat's remarks are taken from the audio commentary track included on the DVD of *Scarlet Street* (released by Kino Video in 2005).

30. Fritz Lang, "The Freedom of the Screen," in *Hollywood Directors: 1941– 76*, ed. Richard Koszarski (New York: Oxford University Press, 1977), 141.

31. John Irwin, *Unless the Threat of Death Is behind Them: Hard-Boiled Fiction and Film Noir* (Baltimore: Johns Hopkins University Press, 2006), 253.

32. Tom Conley, *Film Hieroglyphics: Ruptures in Classical Cinema* (Minneapolis: University of Minnesota Press, 1998), 34.

33. Mark Bould, *Film Noir: From Berlin to Sin City* (New York: Columbia University Press, 2005), 33.

34. Hirsch, *The Dark Side of the Screen*, 7.

35. Julie Kirgo, "*Scarlet Street*," in *Film Noir: The Encyclopedia*, ed. Alain Silver, James Ursini, Robert Porfirio, and Elizabeth Ward (New York: Overlook Duckworth, 2010), 256.

36. Donald Phelps, "*La Chienne* and *Scarlet Street*," *Film Comment* 32, no. 1 (January–February 1996): 71. This is the best essay in English on the comparison of the two films.

37. Peter Bogdanovich, *Who the Devil Made It: Conversations with Film Directors* (New York: Ballantine, 1998), 205.

38. Richard Younger, "Song in Contemporary Film Noir," *Films in Review* 44, nos. 7–8 (July–August, 1996): 99.

39. Louis Giannetti and Scott Eyman, *Flashback: A Brief History of Film* (Boston: Allyn and Bacon, 2010), 89.

CHAPTER SIX

ALFRED HITCHCOCK:
SPELLBOUND AND *STRANGERS ON A TRAIN*

Alfred Hitchcock is not often labeled as a director of film noirs; he is certainly not associated with noir to the same degree as Fritz Lang. And yet some of his thrillers, like *Spellbound* and *Strangers on a Train*, are richly designed noirs. As Hirsch maintains, Hitchcock, like all noir directors, "is attracted to stories of confinement." He depicts in *Spellbound*, for example, how "the pressure of events forces the characters into hiding," as their world becomes "a place of lurking threats and potential pitfalls" in true noir fashion.[1]

Spellbound (1945)

Spellbound was the first Hollywood movie to employ psychiatry as its fundamental premise. As a result, a number of critics have found the film long and slow, and have ranked it with undistinguished Hitchcock efforts of the period like *The Paradine Case* (1948) and *Under Capricorn* (1949). Indeed, James Agee termed *Spellbound* in the *Nation* "Hitchcock's surprisingly disappointing thriller about psychoanalysis."[2] Consequently, *Spellbound* deserves reassessment as a first-class film noir, since it focuses on the dark recesses of the human mind in a way that places it securely within the parameters of film noir.

Hitchcock made *Spellbound* at a time when Sigmund Freud's titilating grab bag of theories about sex and dreams, and the dramatic case histories he utilized to exemplify them, gradually captured the public's imagination. After all, dream sequences provide a shorthand method by which the filmmaker can project the subjective view of reality that the characters nurture for themselves. In fact, at that time the press was recommending the advantages of psychoanalysis to veterans of World War II who were "struggling with the aftereffects of shell shock."[3]

Hitchcock made *Spellbound* under the banner of producer David O. Selznick, who had produced Hitchcock's *Rebecca* (1940). Hitchcock had little trouble selling the concept of the film, which employed Freudian psychology to "explain" the characters' actions, to Selznick, who had himself been in psychoanalysis.

To write the screenplay, Hitchcock engaged playwright-screenwriter Ben Hecht, who had served as an uncredited "script doctor" for Hitchcock on *Foreign Correspondent* (1940). As it happened, Hecht had, like Selznick, been in analysis.[4] As his credits on films like *Wuthering Heights* attest, Hecht managed "to achieve commercial success while maintaining a level of artistry and originality that was the envy of his profession."[5]

Hitchcock chose, as the basis of Hecht's screenplay, a 1927 novel by Francis Beeding (joint pen name for John Palmer and Hilary Saunders), *The House of Dr. Edwardes*. The book dealt with an imposter who passes himself off as the director of a mental institution. Hitchcock and Hecht visited asylums in the New York area before they set to work hammering out a script in a New York hotel room, far away from Selznick's kibitzing.

The screenplay of *Spellbound* became the heavily Freudian tale of John Ballantyne, who is obsessed with the notion that he murdered his psychiatrist, Dr. Edwardes, while they were skiing together. An amnesiac, Ballantyne unconsciously assumes the identity of Edwardes at Green Manors, the private sanatorium in Vermont of which Edwardes was to have been the new superintendent, had his untimely death not intervened. When Ballantyne's true identity is inevitably discovered, one of the staff psychiatrists, Dr. Constance Petersen, who by then has fallen in love with John, flees from the asylum with him in the hope of finding out what really happened during Edwardes's last skiing expedition.

Hitchcock cast Ingrid Bergman, who had just won an Academy Award for George Cukor's *Gaslight*, as Dr. Constance Petersen, the psychiatrist who uncovers Ballantyne's deception. John Ballantyne was played by Gregory Peck, a rising young star (*The Keys to the Kingdom*). Hitchcock accomplished a casting coup by engaging Michael Chekhov to play Constance Petersen's mentor, Dr. Brulov. Michael Chekhov, the nephew of the Russian playwright Anton Chekhov, was a renowned acting coach, who seldom appeared in films.

The movie's director of photography, George Barnes, had already received an Oscar for photographing *Rebecca*. A consummate cinematographer, Barnes's interplay of light and shadow gave the film a foreboding, brooding quality, particularly to the asylum scenes in *Spellbound*.

To supply the haunting background music for *Spellbound*, Hitchcock commissioned Miklos Rozsa, who was becoming a prominent contributor to film noirs. In 1945 Rozsa composed two important symphonic scores for film noirs: Hitchcock's *Spellbound*, as well as Billy Wilder's *Lost Weekend*, which dealt with an alcoholic writer.

In his score for *Spellbound* Rozsa for the first time made extensive use of the theremin, an electronic musical instrument that produces a high-pitched, quavering sound that was perfectly attuned to a movie dealing with mental illness. The eerie sound of the theremin augmented the weird atmosphere of the picture's scarier scenes. Rozsa skillfully featured the theremin in his symphonic score for *Spellbound*, and it likewise proved a highlight for *The Lost Weekend*.

Postproduction was completed in February 1945, but Selznick tinkered endlessly with the final cut, as was his custom. He held a series of previews, and made minor adjustments in the finished film accordingly. As a result, Selznick delayed the release of *Spellbound* until late October 1945.

After the premiere, Selznick was exasperated to hear that Rozsa had already utilized the theremin again in *The Lost Weekend*, which was opening in November. Selznick phoned Rozsa and asked him if this was true. Rozsa responded curtly, "Yes, I have used not only the theremin, but also the piccolo, the trumpet, the triangle, and the violin!"[6] Selznick, Rozsa suggested, did not have a monopoly on the use of the theremin.

Rozsa later declared that his pioneering use of the theremin in *Spellbound* had made the instrument "the official Hollywood mouthpiece for mental disorders."[7] On a more serious note, Richard Ness writes that Rozsa's Academy Award–winning score for *Spellbound* "demonstrated that film music could be serious and contemporary, while still remaining within the symphonic tradition."[8]

Selznick insisted that the picture begin with a printed preface, written by Ben Hecht, which stated: "Our story deals with psychoanalysis, the method by which modern science treats the emotional problems of the sane. The analyst seeks only to induce the patient to talk about his hidden problems to open the locked doors of his mind. Once the complexes that have been disturbing the patient are uncovered and interpreted, the illness and confusion disappear."

Selznick intended the preface "to authenticate the film's psychiatric content."[9] For good measure, he employed his own psychiatrist, May Romm, as a consultant on the film, and gave her a screen credit as "Psychiatric Advisor." Be that as it may, the movie's portrayal of psycho-analysis is fairly elementary in the script so that the average moviegoer can comprehend it. After all, Hitchcock said, he was not making a docu-mentary about Freudian psychology. He saw the film as a "manhunt story, wrapped up in pseudo-psychoanalysis."[10]

Hitchcock visualizes on the screen the concept of opening "the locked doors of the mind" mentioned in the preface when John and Constance kiss for the first time. Superimposed on their passionate embrace is a shot of a series of doors, which recede down a seemingly endless corridor, opening one by one. This signifies that the constant Dr. Petersen will give John the courage to open the secret doors beyond which lie the traumatic experiences by which he has been spellbound.

Constance takes John to visit Dr. Alex Brulov, her teacher and friend, at his home in Rochester, New York, for a few days. One night during their stay, John falls into a trance and prowls around the house in a daze—all the while carrying the straight razor he shaves with. He encounters Dr. Brulov, who gives him a glass of drugged milk. Hitchcock photographs Dr. Brulov through the bottom of the glass, which is tilted toward the camera, as John drains the glass. The screen goes white, as milk fills the frame, indicating that the bromide in the milk has rendered John unconscious.

With the help of her mentor Dr. Brulov, Constance is able to uncover the hidden meaning of several psychological clues with which John has provided them. The prongs of a fork indenting a white tablecloth, the stripes on a white bathrobe, the ridges on a white bedspread, the foamy swirl of hairs on a soapy shaving brush: this network of images symbol-izes ski racks on a snowy slope such as the one on which Edwardes met his death at the Gabriel Valley winter resort. Edwardes's demise in turn is subconsciously linked with the death of John's brother in a childhood accident for which John still feels responsible.

In flashback we see John as a youngster sliding down the banister of a stone porch toward his brother who is sitting at its foot. John unintentionally collides with the lad, causing him to pitch forward and become impaled on a spiked fence.

As Constance puts it, in her simplified explanation, "People often feel guilty for something they never did, and it usually goes back to something in their childhood." If a child believes he has caused something terrible to happen to someone else, "he grows up with a guilt complex over a sin that was only a child's bad dream."

Because of his abiding sense of guilt for making his younger brother die in such a manner, John has convinced himself that he somehow must have precipitated Edwardes's fatal fall into Gabriel Valley's ravine. In short, because John believes that he caused his brother's death, he likewise feels he caused Dr. Edwardes's death—a misconception boiled up in the kitchen of his unconscious.

To ascertain the true facts about the skiing accident, Constance must interpret John's recurring dream about this episode. Hitchcock brought

Dr. Brulow (Michael Chekhov) and Dr. Constance Petersen (Ingrid Bergman) interrogate John Ballantyne (Gregory Peck) in Hitchcock's *Spellbound*.

in the Spanish avant-garde painter Salvador Dali to design this sequence, because he wanted to have the dream photographed in the vivid way Dali painted. Traditionally, he explained, dream scenes in films had always been enveloped in swirling smoke and filmed slightly out of focus to make them look misty and blurred. "But dreams are not like that; they are very, very vivid."[11] So Hitchcock chose Dali to conceive this fantasy sequence in his own personal style, which had a clear-cut, solid architectural sharpness to it. The fantasy sequence was then filmed with the (uncredited) help of William Cameron Menzies, the production designer of Hitchcock's *Foreign Correspondent* (1940). Menzies, who was familiar with German expressionism, supervised the final version of the bizarre dream sequence.[12]

Hitchcock himself was familiar with German expressionism; he made his first movie in 1926 in Munich at the Emelka Studios, with which his home studio in London had a coproduction deal. While there he observed German directors at work.

The asylum scene in John Ballantyne's dream recalls the expressionist asylum scenes in *The Cabinet of Dr. Caligari*. Ingrid Bergman subsequently recalled that the dream sequence was originally "a wonderful twenty-minute sequence that really belongs in a museum."[13] James Bigwood, in his exhaustive essay on this film, emphasizes that Bergman's memory has played her false. "The dream sequence lasts three minutes in the film," he explains. "The sequence was indeed originally intended to be longer. Never twenty minutes long—Ingrid Bergman exaggerates a bit"—but certainly a minute longer than it finally wound up.[14] The deleted footage pictured Bergman as a statue draped in a Grecian gown with an arrow inexplicably piercing her neck. That image, Hitchcock conceded, was too grotesque for a commercial Hollywood movie, and so this vignette was excised.

The hallucinatory sequence starts with John and Edwardes playing cards in a bizarre gambling house. Its walls are hung with black velvet draperies on which are painted enormous staring eyes, and a man goes around cutting the eyeballs on the curtains with a gigantic scissors. As a matter of fact, Dali borrowed the image from *The Andalusian Dog*, an experimental short film on which he collaborated with Luis Buñuel in 1928, as film cultists will have recognized. (The short film begins with a shot of Buñuel himself apparently slitting open the eyeball of a young girl.)

The grotesque behavior of the man with the shears in *Spellbound* implies that he is a patient in an insane asylum, presumably Green Manors, and that he is apparently expressing his resentment of the watchful eyes of the institution's staff and guards. A further covert reference to Green Manors is made when the faceless proprietor of the casino insists with Edwardes most emphatically that he is the sole owner and operator of the establishment. This is an implicit allusion to Dr. Murchison (Leo G. Carroll), the outgoing director of the sanatorium who was known to have been deeply disturbed by the prospect of being supplanted by Edwardes.

The next time the anonymous proprietor materializes in John's nightmare, he is holding a wheel in his hand (which suggests a revolver) and hiding behind a chimney on a slanted roof, as he watches Edwardes slide off the roof to his death. Constance finally cracks the code of this last episode of the dream by reasoning that this is a disguised representation of how the crazed Murchison, in a last desperate attempt to retain his position at Green Manors, shot Edwardes from behind a tree while the latter was skiing down a hillside with John, and left John to take the blame.

The death of Dr. Edwardes was a traumatic experience so horrible that it caused John to lose his memory so that he would not have to remember that dreadful incident. Constance says that John has put the horrible memory behind a closed door, and she must help him open it (another reference to the film's printed prologue). Constance is eventually able to get John to recall what actually happened to Dr. Edwardes on the Gabriel Valley ski slopes.

When Constance confronts Murchison with this explanation, the demented psychiatrist pulls out a pistol and threatens to kill her on the spot. The camera is behind Murchison as it photographs the gun in his hand slowly turning away from Constance toward himself and then firing straight at the lens. To keep Constance and the pistol both in focus while this shot was being photographed, Hitchcock placed a giant artificial hand holding a revolver, which was itself four times the normal size, in the foreground while she stood in the background facing the gun. The use of the huge prop gun was effective here in making the revolver loom threateningly large on the screen.

In the original release prints of *Spellbound*, Murchison's gun went off in a burst of Technicolor scarlet in an otherwise black-and-white movie. The red coloring has been restored in the DVD version of the movie released in 2008. Even without the unexpected flash of color, however, the explosion of the pistol in the filmgoer's face is a startling surprise, as is the discovery that the dapper, staid Dr. Murchison has turned out to be the proverbial lunatic who has taken over an asylum.

Spellbound was a commercial triumph when it was finally released. The public seemed to have willingly swallowed the mixture of murder and psychoanalysis whole, but the critical reaction to the picture was less enthusiastic. Manny Farber grumbled in the *New Republic* that the movie unreeled in "slow motion," and he parsed the plot as complicated and unbelievable.[15] Other reviewers said that the Freudian psychology in the film was on the level of an article in a newspaper's Sunday supplement, forgetting that the mass audience was not familiar with the intricacies of psychoanalysis.

On the one hand, *Spellbound* has not worn well with the critical establishment over the years. Thus Pauline Kael wrote it off as "a confection whipped up by jaded cooks."[16] On the other hand, Donald Spoto has at least endorsed *Spellbound* in his book on Hitchcock, *Spellbound by Beauty*. He reminds us that "once released, *Spellbound* never lost its popularity." Spoto writes that "the enduring appeal of *Spellbound* derives from "the understated performance of Ingrid Bergman and the vulnerable characterization by Gregory Peck."[17]

Furthermore, *Spellbound* has at last been acknowledged, in retrospect, as a trendsetter. After *Spellbound*, mental illness became a subject for a series of popular film noirs.[18] In fact, Hitchcock's *Strangers on a Train* presents a textbook case in Freudian psychology in its deeply disturbed villain, Bruno Antony.[19] Moreover, *Strangers on a Train* is based on a novel by Patricia Highsmith; her biographer, Joan Schenkar, calls her "our most Freudian novelist"—another link with *Spellbound*.[20]

Hitchcock first approached Dashiell Hammett to write the screenplay for *Strangers on a Train*, but Hammett replied that his last screenplay was for the film version of Lillian Hellman's *Watch on the Rhine* (1943), and that was his final effort at writing for the screen.[21] Hitchcock then commissioned Raymond Chandler, another major writer of crime fiction, to compose the script for *Strangers on a Train*, based on the prose treatment of the scenario Hitchcock and Whitfield Cook (*Stage Fright*) had prepared.

Strangers on a Train (1951)

Hitchcock chose Chandler because he was interested in working with this eminent crime novelist and screenwriter. Chandler, in turn, accepted

Hitchcock's invitation "because I thought I might like Hitch," whom he judged to be one of the few intelligent filmmakers in Hollywood.[22]

Chandler was also interested in Highsmith's book because the novel clearly indicates that Highsmith believed that "there was evil in everyone," that it was a part of human nature, as Nora Sayre has noted.[23] "I'm very concerned," Highsmith herself stated, with the way that good and evil exist in everyone "to a greater or lesser degree."[24]

Hitchcock, like Highsmith, was very much preoccupied with bringing light into the dark corners of the human psyche. Indeed, many filmgoers have come away from his movies, *Newsweek* once noted, with some sobering thoughts about human nature as Hitchcock viewed it: that people are not always what they seem, neither as good nor as bad as they might perhaps at first appear; "that good and evil can bundle together, like sly lovers, in the same personality."[25] Furthermore, Highsmith's first novel has the kind of hook that is a hallmark of film noir: a man is roped into coping with circumstances beyond his control.

Preferring to work alone, Chandler resented the preliminary script conferences that Hitchcock imposed on him before he was allowed to get to work on his own and was not mollified even when Hitchcock agreed to come to his home in La Jolla, California, for the sessions. Like Hammett, Chandler was a heavy drinker, and sometimes he was somewhat tipsy by the time Hitchcock arrived. Thus one day, while watching Hitchcock get out of the studio limousine in front of his house, the disgruntled writer mumbled testily to his secretary, "Look at that fat bastard trying to get out of his car," adding that he cared not if the director overheard him. Hitchcock probably did, since that was the director's last trip to La Jolla.[26]

Chandler later grumbled that he detested these "god-awful jabber sessions, which seem to be an inevitable although painful part of the picture business."[27] For his part, Hitchcock was none too happy with Chandler's interaction with him during their story conferences. Hitchcock recalled that he would say to Chandler, "Why not do it this way?" and Chandler would snap back, "Well, if you can puzzle it out, what do you need me for?"[28]

Chandler followed his literary source very closely in the early scenes of the screenplay. *Strangers on a Train* begins with a railway journey, in the course of which Bruno Antony (Robert Walker), a wealthy homosexual, ingratiates himself with Guy Haines (Farley Granger), a handsome tennis champion. The slightly effeminate, effete Bruno exemplifies Freud's fundamental concept of the homosexual; he combines a deep-seated, implacable hatred of his tyrannical father with a curious attachment to his eccentric mother. As the two lunch together on the train, it is evident that Guy, who is unhappily married to a conniving, promiscuous spouse, is fascinated by this fey, coyly ingratiating creature. So much so that from the start there is an unacknowledged homosexual undertone to their relationship. "The meeting on the train," Roger Ebert points out, plays like the classic pickup of one man by another.[29]

At the time homosexuality was a taboo topic for American films, according to the Censorship Code. Hence "the homoeroticism that Highsmith hinted at in Bruno's idolization of Guy," writes McGilligan, had to be portrayed in a very subtle manner in the movie.[30] The mass audience was simply not prepared for references to homosexuality in commercial Hollywood movies. Only the cognoscenti were alert enough to pick up the homosexual implications of the plot.

Before they part company at journey's end, Bruno attempts to manipulate Guy into agreeing to exchange a murder with him, with Guy killing Bruno's father and Bruno doing away with Guy's wife, Miriam. Since neither has an ostensible motive for committing the other's crime, they would both, according to Bruno, successfully elude detection. The script's dialogue at this point is very close to that of the novel, in which Bruno says, "We meet on a train, see, and nobody knows we know each other." He continues, "We murder for each other, see? I kill your wife and you kill my father."[31]

In fact, Bruno's proposal appeals to Guy more than he is prepared to admit even to himself. Consequently, Jane Sloan observes, Guy does not decisively reject it. Instead, "Guy humors him" by saying that Bruno's theory is "O.K."[32] Taking Guy's hedging for tacit approval, the deranged Bruno soon dispatches Miriam and demands forthwith that Guy keep his part of the bargain; Guy agrees to do so, just to put Bruno off. The manner in which Bruno plays on the baser instincts of the fundamentally good-natured Guy signifies the duality that lies at the heart of human nature—a recurring theme in Highsmith's fiction.

Screenwriter Arthur Laurents (*Rope*) said, "Farley Granger told me once that it was Robert Walker's idea to play Bruno Antony as a homosexual."[33] On the contrary, it should be obvious from the foregoing remarks about Bruno's background and behavior that his approach to Guy, as a rather blatant homosexual courting a heterosexual, is embedded in the supple screenplay and not something Walker, as brilliant as he is in the part, superimposed on the characterization on his own. After all, Bruno is marked as a homosexual "by his importunate pursuit of Guy, his readily assumed hatred of Miriam, his silk dressing gown," as well as by his very Freudian "resentment of his father and his closeness to his mother."[34]

Alfred Hitchcock and Robert Walker take a breather while shooting the climactic merry-go-round sequence in *Strangers on a Train*. Walker plays Bruno Antony, the role for which he is most remembered.

Years later, after he had retired from the screen, Farley Granger came out of the closet and acknowledged that he was homosexual. So *Strangers on a Train* presents "a straight actor (Robert Walker) playing Bruno, a homosexual," while a homosexual actor (Farley Granger) plays Guy, a heterosexual.[35] (In fact, Laurents remembered having a fling with Granger while Granger was filming *Rope*.) Joan Schenkar reflects that Highsmith, who was herself a lesbian, could not have been aware that Granger was homosexual, "nor could Granger have known what Pat Highsmith's sexual tastes were. And that was the underworld of homosexuality in mid-century America."[36]

Patricia Highsmith subsequently said that adapting *Strangers on a Train* for film "gave Chandler fits."[37] Actually, it was Hitchcock, not Highsmith, who gave Chandler fits. To his chagrin, Chandler discovered that Hitchcock seemed less preoccupied with the fundamental plausibility of the story than with creating a series of striking visual scenes. On August 17, 1950, he wrote to Ray Stark, his Hollywood agent, "Hitchcock seems to be a very considerate and polite man, but he is full of little suggestions and ideas, which have a cramping effect on a writer's initiative. . . . He is always ready to sacrifice dramatic logic (in so far as it exists) for the sake of a camera effect." This is very hard on the screenwriter "because the writer not only has to make sense out of the foolish plot if he can; but he has to do it in such a way that any sort of camera shot that comes into Hitchcock's mind can be incorporated into it."[38] It was as if Hitchcock simply directed the picture in his head, with little concern for the sorts of questions about narrative logic and character development that troubled Chandler.

Chandler was particularly worried about the scene in which Guy tentatively promises to take the life of Bruno's father. Guy must convince a reasonable percentage of the audience, Chandler recorded in his notes, that "a nice young man might in certain circumstances murder a total stranger just to appease a lunatic." Otherwise the viewers would not be sufficiently involved in the subsequent development of the plot. "The premise is that if you shake hands with a maniac, you may have sold your soul to the devil." He concluded with some exasperation, "Or am I still crazy?"[39]

In the book Guy does in fact carry through his promise to murder Bruno's father, but Chandler contended that, given Guy's status as the likable hero of the movie, the film audience would not be prepared to believe that he is capable of committing a homicide. So, in consultation with Hitchcock, Chandler made a substantial change in the scenario at this point. Guy merely pretends that he plans to kill Bruno's father. Explaining that he simply wants to get the whole affair over with once and for all, Guy informs Bruno that he has decided to do what Bruno wants that very night. Guy actually intends to warn Mr. Antony about his son's desire to have him slain. With noir inevitability, Guy's plan goes hideously wrong. Bruno rightly suspects Guy's actual reason for showing up at the Antony mansion and heads him off before he can see Mr. Antony. Bruno also serves notice to Guy in a threatening tone that he does not take kindly to being double-crossed.

Chandler continued to criticize Hitchcock for being more interested in riveting his audience's attention with a number of visually exciting scenes than he was in knitting together the overall continuity of the story. Since *Strangers on a Train* is set in and around Washington, D.C., Hitchcock decreed that certain scenes take place at various landmarks in the nation's capital—picturesque sites that in themselves have precious little to do with the story. Robert Corber comments, "In shot after shot, the dome of the Capitol building appears in the background brilliantly lit up, and the Jefferson Memorial provides the setting for a suspenseful encounter between the all-American hero, Guy Haines, and the murderous villain, Bruno Antony."[40]

In Hitchcock's defense, Paul Jensen has written that Chandler's approach to script writing was in open conflict with Hitchcock's concept of how a screenplay should be devised; it was inevitable that they would clash. In essence, Hitchcock tended "to sidestep the demands of logic," which were uppermost in Chandler's mind, in favor of creating what Chandler termed visually striking scenes.[41] As Hitchcock remarked in conversation, "I am not so much interested in the stories that I tell, as in the means I use to tell them."[42]

Specifically, Hitchcock believed that the fast-paced plot of a thriller like *Strangers on a Train* was not meant to be analyzed too closely. The moviegoer should be so caught up in a suspense melodrama that he buys the story completely, warts and all, while he is seeing it. Pauline Kael has written that part of the fun of seeing a Hitchcock suspenser was that it "distracted you from the loopholes, so that, afterwards, you could enjoy thinking over how you'd been tricked and teased."[43]

An example of one of Hitchcock's clever little set pieces is the opening sequence of *Strangers on a Train*: A taxi drives up to a railway station and discharges a passenger. We see only the feet of a man wearing flashy two-toned shoes getting out. Then a second taxi pulls up and unloads another traveler: we see a pair of plain brown Oxfords emerging from the cab. The ostentatious saddle shoes that belong to Bruno indicate that he is a fancy dresser and perhaps a frivolous type. By contrast, the modest, dark wing-tip shoes Guy is wearing suggest that he is a conservative dresser and probably a more sensible individual.

Both men approach the train from opposite directions, and once the train leaves the depot, there is a shot of intersecting railroad tracks, as the train proceeds along its route. The crisscrossing rails foreshadow how the lives of these two individuals will likewise converge. Soon after, the shoes of Guy and Bruno accidentally touch as they cross their legs in the parlor car. They take the occasion to strike up a casual conversation, which will in fact lead Guy into a dangerous relationship with Bruno that Guy could not have foreseen. This is precisely the sort of apparently harmless chance meeting in film noir that can lead to unexplained consequences.

One of the tense scenes to which Chandler refers is that in which Bruno follows Miriam, Guy's estranged wife, and her two escorts to the Leeland Lake Carnival. They all take a ride on the carousel and sing along with the calliope as it plays "The Band Played On." Then Bruno lures Miriam away from her boyfriends to a secluded corner of the amusement park and strangles her.

The murder is ironically accompanied by the distant music of the merry-go-round's calliope as it grinds out its cheery rendering of "The Band Played On." Horrified, we watch the murder as it is reflected in Miriam's glasses, which have fallen to the grass during her struggle with Bruno. Photographed in this grotesquely distorted fashion, the strangling looks as if it were being viewed in a fun-house mirror, another reminder of the grimly incongruous carnival setting of the crime.

Given the fact that Guy subconsciously wanted to kill Miriam himself, he has in effect done so through the mediation of Bruno as his proxy; to that extent Bruno embodies the underside of Guy's own personality, which underlines Highsmith's statement that the good and evil forces warring within Guy reflect the duality of human nature itself. In *Strangers on a Train* we have a perfect example of a basically decent person who is morally stained by capitulating in some degree to a wicked influence on his life.

That Guy has become, however inadvertently, allied with the perverse force for evil that Bruno represents is concretized in the scene in which the two men stand on opposite sides of a wrought iron fence as Bruno informs Guy that he has taken Miriam's life. When a squad car appears across the street, Guy instinctively joins Bruno on the same side of the barrier and thus implicitly acknowledges his share of the guilt for Miriam's demise. In his essay on German expressionism in *Strangers on a Train*, Peter Dellolio comments that the expressionistic imagery of the iron gate implies that Guy, like Bruno, belongs behind bars.[44] Moreover, the image of Guy's troubled face barred by the sinister shadows of the gate grille signals his imprisonment by Bruno in an unholy alliance from which he is for now unable to extricate himself.

This dark tale of obsession and murder clearly belongs to the realm of film noir. The milieu of noir is essentially one of shadows and is exemplified in the scene just described. For the shadows that fall across Guy's figure imply the morbid, murky world in which he is imprisoned with Bruno.

In Highsmith's novel, as mentioned, Guy actually murders Bruno's father in order to stop Bruno from ceaselessly tormenting him to do it. Guy is then wracked by guilt and eventually surrenders to the private detective who has been investigating Miriam's death. Bruno, meanwhile, gets drunk during a party on a yacht, accidentally falls overboard, and drowns. Guy reflects afterward that "he knew now that Bruno had borne half his guilt."[45]

It is clear, therefore, that Chandler kept Highsmith's plot intact up to and including Miriam's murder. But when Chandler had Guy draw the line at slaying Mr. Antony, Chandler parted company with the book in a substantial way and took the story in another direction, after the halfway mark. Chandler, who regularly submitted pages of the script to the studio while he was writing the screenplay, mailed the final pages on September 26, 1950. His draft concludes with Bruno, wearing a straightjacket, confined in a padded cell in a lunatic asylum.[46] Chandler felt that some of the scenes in his draft were admittedly "far too wordy," but by and large he thought he had done an acceptable job.[47]

Chandler was chagrined to learn that Hitchcock had borrowed Ben Hecht's assistant, Czenzi Ormonde, to revise his screenplay, with an assist from Hitchcock himself and Barbara McKeon, the movie's associate producer. After all, it was common in those days for scriptwriters to work in teams, like piano movers, a practice Chandler deplored.

In any case, Ormonde sharpened the dialogue—which Chandler himself had admitted was "too wordy"—and tightened the narrative structure of the script. In consultation with McKeon, Ormonde sometimes would condense Chandler's draft by eliminating whole sequences from his screenplay; at other times she would simply combine two of his scenes into one scene. On the other hand, Ormonde often incorporated Chandler's crackling dialogue into the final draft, which was dated October 18, 1950.[48]

Hitchcock confirmed that in the final screenplay Guy is painfully aware that Miriam's death has freed him of the two-timing wife he despised. Consequently, Guy strives to bring Bruno to justice in the film in order to expiate his own subconscious guilt for Miriam's slaying, since "Guy felt like murdering her himself."

Guy is given the chance to redeem himself by pursuing Bruno back to the scene of Miriam's murder and forcing Bruno to confess the truth about her death. As they wrestle with each other aboard the carousel, the mechanism suddenly goes berserk, changing what is normally a harmless source of innocent pleasure into a whirling instrument of terror. The carousel thus serves as still another reflection of Hitchcock's dark vision of our chaotic, topsy-turvy planet. As the runaway merry-go-round continues to swirl at top speed, its rendition of "The Band Played On" is also accelerated to a dizzying tempo, and mingles macabrely with the screams of the hysterical riders trapped on board. A mechanic at last manages to bring it to a halt, but it stops so suddenly that the riders go sailing off in all directions as the machinery collapses into a heap of smoldering wreckage, bringing this sequence to a spectacular climax. Bruno dies in the debris, unrepentant to the last.

The climactic amusement park scene has no parallel in Chandler's original draft nor in Highsmith's novel. Hitchcock had recalled a runaway carousel in a 1946 British novel entitled *The Moving Toyshop* by Edmund Crispin (pen name of Robert Bruce Montgomery). So Hitchcock decided to stage the climax of the film in the same amusement park where Miriam had been murdered. He accordingly opted to use the suspenseful fairground scene from Crispin's book in the film.

The carousel scene in *Strangers on a Train* as filmed, with Bruno Antony (Robert Walker) and Guy Haines (Farley Granger, dark blazer) locked in a death struggle.

In *The Moving Toyshop* the detective, Gervase Fen, slugs it out with Sharman, the villain, aboard a merry-go-round that is out of control. When the carousel finally comes to a halt, Fen is uninjured and Sharman is hurt, but still alive. The question still remains as to why Hitchcock never gave Crispin credit for the use of the fairground scene from his novel in the movie. As Graham Petrie emphasizes, "There can be no doubt that Edmund Crispin's novel provided the (unacknowledged) source for the ending of Hitchcock's film."[49]

The film ends with the happy prospect of Guy marrying Anne. "Guy's pleasant future of marriage to Anne," MaryKay Mahoney wryly notes, "has been provided for him courtesy of Bruno, who removed Miriam, the only obstacle to Guy's happiness."[50] That final irony is surely one that is savored by the savvy filmgoer. For Guy not only benefited from the crime but also subconsciously wanted Miriam dead.

Raymond Chandler and Czenzi Ormonde received a shared screen credit as coauthors of the screenplay of *Strangers on a Train*. John Russell Taylor, Hitchcock's authorized biographer, with whom I compared notes on the film, believes that the studio's decision to acknowledge Chandler's contribution to the picture was entirely appropriate. Taylor confirms that "there are very Chandlerish elements in the film as made."[51] For example, once Chandler had opted to have Guy decide against killing Bruno's father, the film's plotline develops along lines similar to that of Chandler's original screenplay for *The Blue Dahlia* (1946), in which the hero is also suspected of slaying his estranged wife.

Moreover, some scenes in Ormonde's revised version of the screenplay were transplanted from Chandler's draft directly into the final shooting script. For example, the movie's opening sequence, with the two pairs of feet approaching the train and finally touching in the parlor car, was incorporated into the final shooting script just as Chandler wrote it.[52]

Chandler's final word on the subject of *Strangers on a Train* was recorded in a letter to his literary agent Carl Brandt on December 11, 1950. "The fallacy of this operation was my being involved in it at all, because it is obvious to me now . . . that a Hitchcock picture must be all Hitchcock," he said.[53] Screenwriter Ernest Lehman told me that although he spent several months working on the script for Hitchcock's *North by Northwest*, "somehow the picture turned out the way *he* wanted it to. He always got his own way, and I have never figured out how he did it." Neither could Raymond Chandler, who grudgingly admitted that in the last analysis *Strangers on a Train* was clearly a Hitchcock picture, not a Chandler picture.[54]

In 1991 an alternate version of *Strangers on a Train* was unearthed in the vaults at Warner Bros. It was "erroneously believed to have been the British theatrical version when it was first discovered." It turned out to be the preview version Hitchcock had prepared for test screenings in Los Angeles in March 1951, prior to the final version released to theaters.[55] This prerelease version contains two scenes that were revised in minor ways; but another crucial scene differs noticeably from the theatrical version.

The preview version contains some dialogue in this scene Hitchcock excised from the release prints. These lines occur in the scene in which Guy and Bruno first meet aboard the train and point up Bruno's homosexuality in a rather overt fashion. For example, some of the additional lines of dialogue bring into relief Bruno's stereotypical hatred of women, epitomized by his utter contempt for Miriam, who has been unfaithful to Guy. "Let's not talk about it anymore," Guy responds stoically. But Bruno is not to be dissuaded: "Women like that can sure make a lot of trouble for a man." Bruno then brings up the subject of revenge by expressing his theory that "everybody is a potential murderer. Now, didn't you ever feel that you wanted to kill somebody? Say, one of those useless fellows that Miriam was playing around with?" Guy brushes aside Bruno's question, but Bruno persists in following this line of thought by unveiling his plan that he could liquidate Miriam, and Guy could reciprocate by disposing of Bruno's father.

Bill Desowitz declares that the complete Bruno-Guy dialogue contained in the earlier cut of the movie amplifies Bruno's homosexual attitudes by foregrounding his hatred for the opposite sex and his corresponding preference for the members of his own sex. The result, says Desowitz, is that "the complete Bruno-Guy sequence is richer and more outlandish" than the subsequent compressed version; "it enlivens the exchange between Bruno and Guy" and makes Bruno appear "more evil, more seductive."[56]

In short, it appears that Hitchcock deleted this passage of dialogue, amounting to two minutes of screen time, from the release prints because of the strong homosexual content, which he assumed the industry film censor would disapprove of. Hitchcock was aware that at the time that he made *Strangers on a Train*, Joseph Breen, the censor, maintained that homosexuality was too strong a subject for American motion pictures. He was backed up by the Censorship Code, which stated flatly that any reference to "sex perversion" was forbidden. As Thomas Doherty comments, Breen was committed to keeping homosexuals in "the celluloid closet."[57]

Withal, the film was a phenomenal critical and popular success when it premiered in July 1951, with reviewers toasting the film as a top-notch thriller. One critic even mentioned how subtly the film appeals to the outlaw lurking in all of us. There were some dissenters. More than one critic called the plot implausible, while Manny Farber went much further when he called *Strangers on a Train* "fun to watch, if you check your intelligence at the box office." Farber contended that Hitchcock cleverly masked the movie's implausibilities "with a honey-smooth patina of sophistication . . . and general glitter"—a remark that is in complete harmony with Chandler's criticism of the film.[58]

Be that as it may, Malcolm Jones, a contemporary critic, writes that the secret of the film's success is fairly simple: "At the heart of nearly all of Hitchcock's movies, and certainly his greatest ones, are ordinary people caught up in circumstances they can neither explain nor control."[59] That, in a nutshell, is what *Strangers on a Train* is all about.

Some cinephiles claim to have discovered that, twelve minutes into *Strangers on a Train*, a previously unnoticed figure standing behind Miriam in the early scene in the music store where she is employed is Patricia Highsmith herself, looking into a notebook. But Highsmith was twenty-nine when the film was shot, and the lady standing behind Miriam is clearly middle aged. Besides, Highsmith declined Hitchcock's invitation to visit the set during shooting.[60] So there is no Highsmith cameo in *Strangers on a Train*.

Patricia Highsmith stated in *Plotting and Writing Suspense Fiction* that she considered *Strangers on a Train* "one of the best of the films" made from her novels.[61] In fact, when she was asked before her death in 1995 which of the movies from her work she preferred, she had not changed her mind, largely because of Robert Walker's peerless performance as the silky psychopath.[62] His Bruno is on a par with the legendary villains of film noir.

In addition, *Strangers on a Train* can be favorably compared to Anthony Minghella's *The Talented Mr. Ripley* (1999), in which Matt Damon plays a sly homosexual psychopath reminiscent of Bruno Antony. In fact, the *New Yorker* affirms that "the prototype of Ripley was Bruno in *Strangers on a Train*, immortalized by Robert Walker in Hitchcock's film."[63] Minghella's film will be considered in chapter 13 as a neo-noir.

Notes

1. Hirsch, *The Dark Side of the Screen*, 142.
2. James Agee, *Film Writings and Selected Journalism*, ed. Michael Sragow (New York: Library of America, 2005), 209.

3. Jonathan Freedman, "Alfred Hitchcock: Therapeutic Culture in America," in *Hitchcock's America*, Jonathan Freedman and Richard Millington (New York: Oxford University Press, 1999), 81.

4. *Spellbound* file, Ben Hecht papers, Newberry Library, Chicago.

5. Kiszely, *Hollywood through Private Eyes*, 60.

6. Miklos Rozsa, *Double Life: The Autobiography of Miklos Rozsa* (New York: Wynwood Press, 1989), 128.

7. Rozsa, *Double Life*, 129.

8. Richard Ness, "Miklos Rozsa," in *International Dictionary of Films and Filmmakers*, vol. 4, 724.

9. Patrick McGilligan, *Alfred Hitchcock: A Life in Darkness and Light* (New York: HarperCollins, 2004), 356.

10. Francois Truffaut, *Hitchcock*, with the collaboration of Helen Scott, rev. ed. (New York: Simon and Schuster, 1985), 18.

11. Charles Higham and Joel Greenberg, *The Celluloid Muse* (New York: New American Library, 1972), 103.

12. Floyd Martin, "William Cameron Menzies," in *International Dictionary of Films and Filmmakers*, vol. 4, 562.

13. McGilligan, *Alfred Hitchcock*, 353.

14. James Bigwood, "Solving a *Spellbound* Puzzle," *American Cinematographer* 72, no. 6 (June 1991): 39.

15. Manny Farber, *Farber on Film: The Complete Film Writings of Manny Farber*, ed. Robert Polito (New York: Library of America, 2009), 265.

16. Kael, *5001 Nights at the Movies*, 701.

17. Donald Spoto, *Spellbound by Beauty: Alfred Hitchcock and His Leading Ladies* (New York: Harmony Books, 2008), 142.

18. Thomson, *Have You Seen . . . ?*, 176.

19. On Freud and film, see "Sigmund Freud," in Gene Phillips and Rodney Hill, *The Encyclopedia of Stanley Kubrick* (New York: Facts on File, 2002), 120–21; on Freud and film noir see Irwin, *Unless the Threat of Death Is behind Them*, 148–52.

20. Patricia Cohen, "The Haunts of Miss Highsmith," *New York Times*, December 11, 2009, sec. C:1.

21. Thomas Leitch, *The Encyclopedia of Alfred Hitchcock* (New York: Facts on File, 2002), 32.

22. Frank MacShane, *The Life of Raymond Chandler* (New York: Dutton, 1976), 170.

23. Nora Sayre, "In the Shoes of a Scary Stalker," *New York Times*, April 12, 1998, sec. 2:12.

24. Gordon Gow, "The Fifties," in *Hollywood: 1920–70*, ed. Peter Cowie (New York: Barnes, 1977), 184.

25. "Hitchcock: Three Nightmares," *Newsweek*, January 24, 1966, 89.

26. John Russell Taylor, *Hitch: The Life and Times of Alfred Hitchcock* (New York: Da Capo, 1996), 214.

27. MacShane, *Life of Raymond Chandler*, 171.

28. Francois Truffaut, *Hitchcock*, rev. ed. (New York: Simon and Schuster, 1985), 193.

29. Roger Ebert, *The Great Movies II* (New York: Broadway Books, 2005), 429.

30. McGilligan, *Alfred Hitchcock*, 442.

31. Patricia Highsmith, *Strangers on a Train* (New York: Norton, 1993), 34.

32. Jane Sloan, *Alfred Hitchcock: A Guide to References and Resources*, rev. ed. (Los Angeles: University of California Press, 1995), 239.

33. Vito Russo, *The Celluloid Closet: Homosexuality in the Movies*, rev. ed. (New York: Harper and Row, 1987), 94.

34. Leitch, *The Encyclopedia of Alfred Hitchcock*, 322.

35. McGilligan, *Alfred Hitchcock*, 451.

36. Joan Schenkar, *The Talented Miss Highsmith: The Secret Life and Serious Art of Patricia Highsmith* (New York: St. Martin's Press, 2009), 276.

37. Patricia Highsmith, "Introduction," in *The World of Raymond Chandler*, ed. Marian Gross (New York: A and W, 1978), 5.

38. Taylor, *Hitch*, 215.

39. Raymond Chandler, "Notes about the Screenplay of *Strangers on a Train*," in Chandler, *Raymond Chandler Speaking*, ed. Dorothy Gardiner and Kathrine Walker (Los Angeles: University of California Press, 1997), 133–35.

40. Robert Corber, "Hitchcock's Washington and 'the Homosexual Menace,'" in *Hitchcock's America*, ed. Freedman and Millington, 99.

41. Paul Jensen, "Film Noir and the Writer: Raymond Chandler," *Film Comment* 10, no. 6 (November–December 1974): 25.

42. Alfred Hitchcock, interviewed by the author, New York, May 4, 1974. Unless specifically noted otherwise, any quotations from Alfred Hitchcock in this chapter are from the author's conversation with him.

43. Pauline Kael, *I Lost It at the Movies* (New York: Boyars, 1994), 9.

44. Peter Dellolio, "Expressionist Themes in *Strangers on a Train*," *Literature/Film Quarterly* 31, no. 4 (Fall 2003): 262.

45. Highsmith, *Strangers on a Train*, 264.

46. Raymond Chandler, *Strangers on a Train: A Screenplay* (Los Angeles: Warner Brothers, 1950), 101. Extensive revisions to the screenplay by Czenzi Ormonde are not included in this version of the script.

47. Chandler, *Raymond Chandler Speaking*, 125.

48. Charlotte Chandler, *It's Only a Movie: Alfred Hitchcock* (New York: Simon and Schuster, 2005), 192; see also Al Clark, *Raymond Chandler in Hollywood* (Los Angeles: Silman-James, 1996), 141.

49. Graham Petrie, "Transfer of Guilt: *Strangers on a Train*," *Sight and Sound* 19 (ns), no. 7 (July 2009): 49.

50. MaryKay Mahoney, "A Train Running on Two Sets of Tracks: High-smith and Hitchcock's *Strangers on a Train*," in *It's a Print: Detective Fiction from Page to Screen*, ed. William Reynolds and Elizabeth Tremley (Bowling Green, Ohio: Bowling Green University Press, 1994), 107.

51. Taylor, *Hitch*, 216.

52. Chandler, *Strangers on a Train: A Screenplay*, 1–2.

53. Raymond Chandler, *Selected Letters of Raymond Chandler*, ed. Frank Mac-Shane (New York: Columbia University Press, 1981), 247–48; see also Andrew Wilson, *Beautiful Shadow: A Life of Patricia Highsmith* (New York: Bloomsbury, 2003), 169.

54. Ernest Lehman, interview by the author, Cannes, May 10, 1976.

55. Andrea Toal, "DVD of the Month: *Strangers on a Train*," *Sight and Sound* 14 (ns), no. 12 (December 2004): 74.

56. Bill Desowitz, "Strangers on Which Train?" *Film Comment* 28, no. 3 (May–June 1996): 5. Desowitz is wrong in calling the preview version of the film "the British cut," but he is right in his analysis of the two versions of the film.

57. Thomas Doherty, *Pre-Code Hollywood: Sex and Immorality in American Cinema* (New York: Columbia University Press, 1999), 363, 125.

58. Farber, *Farber on Film*, 359.

59. Malcolm Jones, "*Psycho:* The Mother of All Horror Films," *Newsweek*, January 18, 2010, 61.

60. Schenkar, *The Talented Miss Highsmith*, 275.

61. Patricia Highsmith, *Plotting and Writing Suspense Fiction* (New York: St. Martin's Press, 1985), 106.

62. "Patricia Highsmith," *Premiere* 18, no. 1 (September 2004): 116.

63. Anthony Lane, "Killing Time: *Mr. Ripley*," *New Yorker*, January 3, 2000, 130.

GEORGE CUKOR: *A DOUBLE LIFE*
BILLY WILDER: *SUNSET BOULEVARD*

George Cukor is chiefly known for his stylish, sophisticated romantic comedies like *Holiday* (1938) and *The Philadelphia Story* (1940), both with Katharine Hepburn and Cary Grant. He dipped into film noir most notably on two occasions, with *Gaslight* (1944), a gothic thriller with Ingrid Bergman, and *A Double Life* (1947), a psychological drama with Ronald Colman. Of the two, *Gaslight* is still considered an important noir, while *A Double Life* is unfortunately not held in similar esteem.

A Double Life (1947)

Cukor made *A Double Life* from an original screenplay by the husband-wife writing team of Garson Kanin and Ruth Gordon, who between them would be responsible for six more film scripts for Cukor. The film deals explicitly with Cukor's ongoing theme about the need for one to distinguish between illusion and reality in life. This theme applies in a special way to show-business types who, like the hero of *A Double Life*, are apt to become lost in the world of illusion that they create for others.

In *A Double Life* Ronald Colman portrays Anthony John, an actor who becomes so identified with his stage roles that he develops a murderous streak of jealousy while playing Othello, the Moor of Venice, during a long Broadway run. With increasing difficulty he tries to divorce himself from the role when he is offstage, until he ultimately goes insane and strangles a prostitute. As the publicity layouts for the film declared, Tony is an actor "consumed by the fires of his own greatness." Putting it another way, Stanislavsky baldly stated, "When an actor begins to believe the part he's playing, fire him!"[1]

The dark, brooding atmosphere of the film, coupled with the equally cynical, somber vision of life reflected in this tale of obsession, despair, and death, marks the movie as an example of film noir. Like *Spellbound* and other film noirs of the period, *A Double Life* dramatizes mental illness as a motive for murder.

Noir was flourishing when Cukor filmed *A Double Life*. The grim realism of noir is reflected in the location sequences shot around New York City, so many of which ominously take place under cover of darkness. Cukor insisted with the front office at Universal-International that he would have to do some location work in New York to "get away from the studio back lot," and to give the picture documentary-like realism.[2] He used the old Empire theater, which was demolished in 1953, to shoot all of the scenes in the film that take place on the stage.

Cukor cast Ronald Colman against type as Anthony John. The urbane Colman usually played "the mature, amused romantic," as when he enacted the judge in George Stevens's *Talk of the Town* (1942).[3] Cukor prodded Colman "out of his shell of British reserve to get a more expansive and demonic performance than he had ever given."[4]

Colman was somewhat insecure about playing the scenes from Shakespeare's play that occur in the film, since he had not performed on the stage for many years. So Cukor, Garson Kanin recalled, "brought in the classical stage actor Walter Hampden from New York" to coach Colman in the Shakespeare scenes.[5]

"While I don't think he was as great an Othello as Lawrence Olivier was on the stage," Cukor commented, "I thought it was a respectable try. . . . I thought Colman spoke some of the lines very movingly."[6]

Cukor hired Shelley Winters to play the blowsy, buxom, and voluptuous waitress in *A Double Life*. Winters had mostly played small parts in some forgettable movies up to this point, but her role as Pat Kroll in the present film proved to be a breakout performance for her. Dave Kehr says that the femme fatale in a noir film is "usually a bottle blonde, stuffed into a tight sweater that outlines her oddly conical breasts. Her mouth is wide, painted, and clamped on a cigarette, her eyes burn too brightly." She is, finally, a "carnal, blatantly sexual, and self-interested creature."[7] That describes Pat Kroll to a T.

Edmond O'Brien took on the role of Bill Friend, the play's enterprising publicity agent (and Tony's nemesis). "O'Brien played the lead in a number of the most interesting and significant films of the classical noir cycle," including Siodmak's *The Killers* (1946).[8]

Director of photography Milton Krasner earned his spurs as a noir cinematographer by photographing an influential group of film noirs, particularly Lang's *Woman in the Window* and *Scarlet Street*. In *A Double Life*, Krasner's skillful camerawork features some of the most fundamental imagery in the film noir canon, such as the rain-soaked pavements of the gloomy, deserted streets where brownstones recede into the distance, and where Tony wanders, brooding, late at night.

While filming portions of a performance of *Othello* on the Empire's stage, Cukor had cinematographer Milton Krasner shoot directly into the banks of spotlights and footlights on the stage, thereby giving the filmgoer some sense of what a theatrical performance is like from the point of view of the actors.

Photographing the actors on stage at close range serves to involve the viewer in the action much more deeply than if the scene had been photographed from the more distant point of view of the audience in the theater. Bruce Crowther adds that Tony's inner turmoil is "powerfully reflected by the photography, which contrasts the dark recesses of his tortured mind with the brilliant yet dislocating footlights which illuminate his stage performance."[9]

Cukor spent extra time tutoring Shelley Winters, who was still relatively new to pictures. He told her that Pat Kroll is doomed: "I want the audience to know she is doomed from the first time they see her." He suggested that she go and observe the harlots in the back streets of Los Angeles. "Try to get some sense of the girls who trade on sex in their misspent lives."[10]

Cukor was patient with Winters, even though she proved sassy and temperamental at times. She said to him one day, "I don't like this line; I think I should say something else." Cukor stormed at her, "Ruth and Garson have written this wonderful part, and you want to rewrite the dialogue!"[11]

Signe Hasso as Brita and Ronald Colman as Anthony John, a deeply disturbed actor, in *A Double Life*.

The film's producer, Michael Kanin (brother of Garson Kanin), remembered that at that point Cukor finally lost patience with her and slapped her on the face.[12] Asked about the story that Winters's behavior so exasperated the director at one point that he gave her a whack to shut her up, Cukor responded with a twinkle, "If I did I am sure she deserved it. She was inexperienced, pushy, and brash, and I had to tell her to pipe down and listen to direction many times."

During postproduction Cukor was fortunate enough to have Miklos Rozsa contribute the background score to *A Double Life*. Having copped an Academy Award for scoring *Spellbound*, Rozsa was much in demand to provide background music for psychological dramas. Yet the studio brass at Universal-International turned thumbs down on Rozsa's music for *A Double Life*. So he was called on the carpet by the director of the music department and told to make the music more pleasant by eliminating the dissonant passages.

Rozsa recalled, "I went immediately to George Cukor, who flew into a rage, and told me that he would personally kill me if I changed one single note." Rozsa, who had stood up to Selznick over his score for *Spellbound*, forthwith dispatched a memo to the head of the studio, saying "that he should jump in the lake and that Lake Toluca was the nearest."[13]

Suffice it to say that Rozsa contributed another Oscar-winning score to *A Double Life* and was becoming the "spokesman" for the anguished, obsessed characters of film noir. Page Cook calls Rozsa's coruscating music for *A Double Life* "one of the finest noir scores ever." Rozsa's score, Cook writes, "brings an eloquence to the film with a sinewy, driving force that intimates undercurrents of nervous tension."[14]

Among the performances singled out for praise by preview audiences was that of Signe Hasso (*The House on 92nd Street*), who plays Brita, Tony's ex-wife. Although Brita still costars with Tony on the stage playing Desdemona in *Othello*, she is all too aware that his winning charm evaporates when the cruel underside of his nature asserts itself, and that his personality is deeply influenced by the parts he plays. As she explains it, "We were engaged doing Oscar Wilde, married doing Kaufman and Hart, and divorced doing Chekhov."

Cukor adroitly employs expressionism to dramatize how the role of Othello has entered into Tony's consciousness. During the opening night party, Tony hears snatches of dialogue from the play echoing in his consciousness; he claps his hands over his ears to shut out the voices of the players. Later on a fiendish face of Othello is conjured up in a nightmare as he sleeps; Othello's image is superimposed on a shot of Tony rolling and tossing in bed. Both scenes have a decidedly expressionistic flavor.

In the movie's strongest scene Anthony John is spending the evening with his mistress Pat Kroll, a full-time waitress at a café appropriately called the Venezia and a part-time prostitute. The scene is bathed in noir-ish darkness. When Tony becomes obsessed with the idea that she is still seeing other men, Othello's obsessional jealousy begins to seep into the actor's consciousness and to possess him completely. As Pat asks him to switch off the light, she unwittingly brings to his mind a bit of dialogue from the murder scene of *Othello*, which was shown in performance earlier in the film. Tony, now transported into this scene of the play, hears the voice of Desdemona request him to extinguish the lamp in her bedroom before she drifts off to sleep. In his role as Othello, Tony quenches instead the life within Pat Kroll, thinking all the while that it is Desdemona that he is sending off to sleep forever.

While Tony throttles the life out of this wretched creature, an elevated train thunders by the window of Pat's squalid flat; its nerve-jangling clamor is a fit accompaniment for the ugly violence taking place inside. Indeed, this unsettling noise is more effective than any background music could have been at this point.

The creative use of sound in this sequence is matched by equally creative camerawork. As Pat falls backward on the bed in death, the camera catches in close-up her hand pulling across the foot of the bed the curtain that separates her bedroom from the rest of her scruffy little flat. Her action recalls the way in which Desdemona in a similar fashion reaches up from her bed and closes the drapery of her sumptuous four-poster as she breathes her last. These complementary images accentuate still more the close parallel between Pat's murder in real life and that of Desdemona in the play.

Tony, increasingly identifying with Othello, becomes insanely jealous of press agent Bill Friend, whom he suspects of having an affair with Brita. He finally attacks Bill and nearly strangles him—while muttering some of Othello's lines. Bill calls him a maniac; and thereafter Bill becomes increasingly convinced that Tony is insane. Indeed, Bill picks up on Tony's attempt to strangle him while quoting Othello's dialogue and recalls that the tabloid press has linked Pat Kroll's murder with Othello's strangling Desdemona in the current production of the play. With that, Bill steadily builds up a convincing case, based on circumstantial evidence, that points to Tony as Pat Kroll's killer. He takes his case to the police, who arrange to arrest Tony following a performance of *Othello*.

The movie ends with a striking bit of visual imagery. After the police have discovered, with the help of Bill, that the actor is the killer they are after, they go to the theater and wait for him backstage while he finishes what is to be his last performance. Once more merging illusion with reality, Tony plays Othello's suicide scene with a real dagger, and ends his own life as he ends the play. Tony expires with Brita's name on his lips. Like Othello, he is "a man that loved not wisely but too well."[15] The film's final, unforgettable image is that of the curtains parting to allow the star to take his bows—while the spotlight reveals only an empty stage. The slow dimming of the spotlight beam into darkness thus signals the fading away of a once-great star in the theatrical firmament.

"When I discussed the suicide scene with Ronnie Colman," Cukor remembered, "I said that a light should come into Tony's eyes just before he dies," as if his entire life is illuminated in his eyes at the moment of death. "When I looked at the rushes the next day there it was! He really knew how to act for the camera."

Tony's suicide in *A Double Life* recalls a similar scene in Fritz Lang's silent movie *Spione* (*Spies*, 1928). At the conclusion of *Spies*, Haghi, an enemy agent, is performing on stage as Nemo the clown. He notices the police in the wings, waiting to arrest him after his performance. Rather than submit to capture, Haghi substitutes real bullets for the blanks he usually employs in his act, and kills himself on stage while laughing maniacally. The audience assumes that this is all part of his performance and erupts into wild applause as the curtain falls and the movie ends.

The obvious parallels between the suicide of Tony and that of Haghi were nevertheless a coincidence, since Garson Kanin indicated that he and Ruth Gordon were not familiar with Lang's film, which had not been widely seen in this country at the time they wrote their script.

The Motion Picture Academy conferred an Oscar on Colman for his performance in *A Double Life*. "The statuette," Colman biographer Sam Frank notes, "was as much a lifetime achievement award as it was sincere applause for a fine job of acting."[16]

The film was a huge hit and garnered enthusiastic reviews. *Variety* stated, "George Cukor's direction has found all of the merit in the characters written by Ruth Gordon and Garson Kanin." *Variety*'s comments refer not only to Colman, but to Shelley Winters, Edmond O'Brien, and Signe Hasso, all of whom did "impressive work" in the movie.[17]

The enthusiasm for *A Double Life*, displayed at the time of its original release, cooled over the years; and the film has not continued to be appreciated by film historians as the grand film noir that it is. But *A Double Life* is a film still worth watching, and it has attracted on DVD some of the wider audience it deserves. As Tony Thomas, one of the movie's few champions, states in *The Film of the Forties*, "Even for those with little interest in the theater, it is an arresting and disturbing film."[18]

117

If George Cukor's *A Double Life* centers on an aging actor who goes insane and murders his lover, Billy Wilder's *Sunset Boulevard* focuses on a has-been actress who goes crazy and slays her inamorata. Yet the two movies are rarely if ever mentioned as companion pieces, even though they were made only three years apart. Both films depict a noir character who is haunted "by deep psychological scars which lead to . . . psychotic behavior."[19]

Although *Sunset Boulevard* is revered as one of Wilder's most respected films, it is seldom mentioned in studies of film noir. William Relling asserts that *Sunset Boulevard* "is more of a gothic horror story than a noir story, since my personal definition of noir demands that as a key component of the plot there has to be a crime committed."[20] Brian McDonnell responds that, admittedly, "almost all noir scenarios contain a crime. Technically, *Sunset Boulevard* fits this prescription because it certainly begins with a man's body being recovered by police from a swimming pool." The movie goes on to depict the shadowy world of self-deceit and exploitation that "embodies the thematic preoccupations of film noir."[21]

The picture also resonates with the theme that pervades Wilder's films. As Wilder himself formulated that theme: "People will do anything for money—except some people, who will do *almost* anything for money."[22] Joe Gillis, the antihero of *Sunset Boulevard*, it becomes apparent, "will do almost anything for money."

Sunset Boulevard (1950)

Like *A Double Life*, *Sunset Boulevard* is based on an original screenplay. Wilder coscripted the screenplay with Charles Brackett, with whom he had collaborated on several scripts; a third writer, D. M. Marshman, Jr., also contributed to the screenplay.

They decided to call the aging movie queen Norma Desmond. Her first name was a reference to Mabel Normand, the silent film comedienne. Her surname referred to William Desmond Taylor, a director of silent films who was murdered on the night of February 2, 1922. Taylor had had love affairs with several actresses, among them Normand, who was implicated in Taylor's unsolved murder. The scandal ended her career.[23] So Norma Desmond's name was tinged with tragedy.

At the suggestion of George Cukor, who had already directed *A Double Life*, Wilder hired Gloria Swanson to play Norma Desmond. George

Cukor told me that he assured Wilder that Swanson could play a movie goddess hoping for a comeback convincingly, since at that point she was a Hollywood has-been. But Swanson did not withdraw into seclusion after her Hollywood days. By the time Wilder wanted her for his movie, she had moved to New York and become the hostess of a local TV talk show.

Another actor on Wilder's wish list was Erich von Stroheim, whom he wanted to play Norma's butler, Max von Mayerling. Like Stroheim, Max had been a director of silent films; in fact, Max had directed Norma Desmond in a silent picture, just as Stroheim had directed Gloria Swanson in a silent movie. But, like Stroheim, Max's directorial career did not survive the coming of sound. Max winds up as Norma's dignified butler and last admirer.

At first, Stroheim wanted no part of the role, because Max was a relic of Hollywood's past—like Stroheim himself. Stroheim finally accepted the part, though he thought it demeaned him. Nevertheless, forever after he referred to the role of Max as "that goddamned butler."[24]

In addition, Wilder got Cecil B. DeMille to play himself in *Sunset Boulevard*. In the film's scenario DeMille had directed Norma as a young actress, when in reality DeMille had directed Gloria Swanson in films like *Male and Female* (1919) "in the old days." DeMille appeared in the sequence in *Sunset Boulevard* in which Norma visits him on the set of *Samson and Delilah* (1949). Actually DeMille had just finished shooting his picture. "We used his sets when Norma visits him," which were still standing, Wilder remembered.[25]

In the screenplay Wilder and Brackett mention that Norma has Max screen "one of Norma's old silent pictures" for Joe.[26] Wilder told me, "I used a clip from *Queen Kelly* in the course of *Sunset Boulevard*," in the scene in which Norma shows Joe one of her vintage films. "It was an interesting tie-in, that the clip of Gloria Swanson as a younger film star was actually from the one picture in which she was directed by Stroheim, who was playing Norma's former director in *Sunset Boulevard*. This added a more genuine flavor to the film."

When I asked Wilder why he substituted his own intertitle for the one in the scene he was using from *Queen Kelly*, he replied, "I couldn't use the intertitle for the one in the scene he was using from *Queen Kelly* because *Queen Kelly* was a movie starring Gloria Swanson, while the clip being projected in *Sunset Boulevard* was supposedly from a film starring Norma Desmond."

It is while looking at a close-up of herself in this silent film that Norma utters the celebrated remark, "No dialogue—we didn't need dialogue. We had *faces* then."

Principal photography lasted from mid-April to mid-June, 1949. Wilder commandeered the camera crew to shoot various locations around Hollywood and Beverly Hills, prior to the start of principal photography. His purpose was to establish the authentic atmosphere of the film colony for the movie, just as Cukor had shot location footage in the Broadway theater district and its environs for *A Double Life*.

"Stroheim was enormously helpful with the script," Wilder told me; "it was he who suggested that Norma be receiving fan letters that are ultimately disclosed as having been written by Max. Stroheim had a fine celluloid mind; he knew what worked." As Stroheim told Wilder, Max writes the letters "because Max still loves her and pities her."

Composer Franz Waxman, who scored *Sunset Boulevard*, was, like Wilder, an émigré from Berlin who came to Hollywood during the Nazi period. By the time Waxman composed the background music for *Sunset Boulevard*, he had written scores for some outstanding Hollywood films, including Hitchcock's *Rebecca* (1940).

"The main theme is one of a tango character," Waxman explained; "it stems from a scene in which Gloria Swanson makes reference to the early days of Hollywood and dancing the tango with Rudolph Valentino. This is the atmosphere in which she still lives in 1950." Norma, as Joe reflected, is still living in the past.

John Caps, who named Waxman's score for *Sunset Boulevard* among the best ever composed for a film, states, "The dark, pulsing introductory passages place the audience in the sonic world" of a thriller—all tense strings and strident brass. "Waxman spins his material into an essay on dead dreams and self-delusion." By the end, Waxman himself adds, the music has "become twisted and tortured," to accompany Norma's ghastly descent into madness.[27]

Wilder commented that "two Europeans," Rozsa, who scored *A Double Life*, and Waxman, who scored *Sunset Boulevard*, provided some of the best film music of the classic film noir period.

The original draft of the screenplay at the Herrick Library of the Motion Picture Academy, dated December 21, 1948, begins with a prologue that did not make it into the finished film. This sequence takes place in the Los Angeles County Morgue. Avram Fleishman, in his book *Narrative Films*, wonders whether the morgue sequence was ever filmed.[28] Indeed it was. As a matter of fact, Paramount archivists discovered some of the footage of this sequence and included it as a special feature in the 2008 release of *Sunset Boulevard* on DVD.

The morgue prologue originally appeared after the opening credits. The sequence shows the dead body of a young man named Joe Gillis being wheeled into the morgue. He then starts to recount to his fellow corpses the tale of how he came to die. But preview audiences found the sequence ludicrous rather than sad, and so Wilder scrapped it.

Many film historians assume that Wilder devised a whole new opening sequence, on which he expended additional time and money filming. But that is not the case. Cinematographer John Seitz testifies that the footage of Joe's corpse floating in Norma's pool, while the police fish him out, had already been shot for use toward the end of the film. "We already had both," that is, the morgue sequence, plus the scene at the pool.[29] Wilder himself stated, "No new footage was shot." He simply added a voice-over narration by Joe Gillis, telling posthumously of the events leading up to his demise; and his story makes up the bulk of the film.[30]

Paramount hosted a full-dress preview screening at the studio in April 1950, to which three hundred members of the Hollywood industry were invited. Wilder was particularly concerned about how the film community would accept the picture.

After the opening credits, in which the film's title is seen stenciled in wedge-shaped letters on a curb, the police are shown swarming around a swimming pool. The pool is on the grounds of an immense baroque estate on Sunset Boulevard; it is just after dawn. A corpse is floating facedown in the pool. The dead man is Joe Gillis, who begins to tell the filmgoer his story, voice-over on the sound track. Joe is thus narrating the film "from beyond the grave," writes Avram Fleishman, "from the detached perspective of the dead."[31] This is one of the few instances in film history wherein a movie's narration is supplied by a dead person.

The film's dark, morbid atmosphere implies that *Sunset Boulevard*, like *A Double Life*, is in the film noir style. Joe narrates the film "in the tough, florid style of a film noir hero," says Terrence Rafferty, "that is, in the defensive voice of a born loser."[32]

As Joe's story unfolds in flashback, we see him as a debt-ridden, failed screenwriter—as was Wilder in his early years in Hollywood. One day Joe's car has a blowout on Sunset Boulevard, and he turns into the curving private driveway of a garish, shuttered villa, which belongs to Norma Desmond, a faded star of the silent screen. When Norma learns that Joe is a screenwriter, she promptly engages him to revise her elephantine screenplay for *Salome*, a proposed biblical epic, in which she desperately hopes to make her comeback. "Poor devil," Joe muses, "still waving to a parade that has passed her by." Joe eventually stays on with Norma, says Barry Norman, "to become her lover, her dependent, and finally her victim."[33]

As noted above, *Sunset Boulevard* is a film noir with some elements of the horror genre mixed in. For example, the demented dowager prowling around a spectral mansion that is haunted by memories of a dead past is a reference to the archetypical "old dark house," which is a staple of horror films.

Norma plays bridge once a week with some old friends that Joe wryly christens "the Waxworks, dim figures from the silent days." Wilder strove to give the film documentary-like realism by having three stars of silent pictures join Norma's bridge game: H. B. Warner, Anna Q. Nilsson, and Buster Keaton. Warner had played Christ in DeMille's 1927 biblical spectacle *The King of Kings*; Nilsson was imported to Hollywood from Sweden in 1911—a dozen years before Garbo—to appear in silent pictures like Raoul Walsh's *Regeneration* (1915); and Keaton was the silent clown who made the comic masterpiece *The General* (1927).

"The cameo appearances of these silent film stars added a more genuine flavor to the film," as an evocation of the old Hollywood, Wilder told me. (Gossip columnist Hedda Hopper also plays herself in this film.)

Wilder also got Cecil B. DeMille to play himself in *Sunset Boulevard*, as mentioned. DeMille gently tries to dissuade Norma from attempting to do a film based on her truly atrocious *Salome* script. DeMille took direction like a pro; he made no suggestions to Wilder about how to stage the scene he was in. DeMille was "total perfection," Wilder told me. "He was very disciplined and gave a subtler performance, I thought, than any actor ever gave in a film that he directed."

In the sequence in which Norma visits DeMille while he is shooting *Samson and Delilah*, DeMille puts her in the director's chair so she can watch a rehearsal. "While she is sitting there," David Freeman observes, "a boom microphone passes behind her, disturbing her hat and casting a shadow over her face. . . . Norma scowls at the microphone, the very thing that ended her era."[34]

Norma mentions to DeMille that the studio has been calling her urgently, but it is not, as she thinks, about making her *Salome* movie; it is merely to arrange to borrow her car, a venerable Isotta-Fraschini with leopard-skin upholstery, for a Crosby picture. "DeMille manages to suppress this fact, to forestall her humiliation."[35]

On New Year's Eve Joe has a quarrel with Norma, who is drunk; he walks out on her. But Max soon phones him, to inform him that Norma has attempted suicide; so Joe returns to the house and finds Norma lying in her gondola-shaped bed, and they are reconciled. At the stroke of midnight, as the strains of "Auld Lang Syne" waft into the room, "she reaches up and pulls him toward her with nails that look like talons," comments Morris Dickstein.[36] Joe has indeed fallen into the hands of a typical femme fatale of film noir.

Cecil B. DeMille plays himself in Billy Wilder's *Sunset Boulevard*, with Gloria Swanson as Norma Desmond, the role that crowned her career.

The film's title refers to the passing of the old Hollywood: it recalls the tragic lives of has-been film stars like Norma Desmond, whose careers in silent pictures were eclipsed by the advent of sound. In effect, the sun set on their careers when they failed to make a successful transition to sound films. The decaying swimming pool on Norma's estate, in which John Gilbert swam ten thousand midnights ago, is a relic of the grandeur of Norma's long-lost heyday as a superstar in Hollywood. It is cracked and empty at the film's start, but Norma subsequently restores the pool and fills it when Joe enters her life. Norma's restoration of the pool symbolizes how she hopes to revive her lost youth and to relive her past through Joe by arresting the decay of her own life. "I picked up the image of the pool from a Raymond Chandler story: Nothing is emptier than an empty swimming pool," said Wilder.

"Still, I didn't conceive the pool so much as a metaphor for Norma's personal decay, but as an authentic depiction of the way a woman like Norma, living in the past, would allow her property to slide in to ruin," Wilder explained. "Even today there are old Hollywood estates with empty swimming pools, with rats running around in them, and cracked tennis courts with sagging nets. That is part of our community; people are up, and then they are down."

Norma's romance with Joe is doomed to be short lived; as time goes on, Joe finds it intolerable to allow himself to be supported by a wealthy, aging woman. He realizes that he is an opportunist who has sold himself to the highest bidder. He thus reflects Wilder's favorite theme: Joe can no longer bring himself to do *anything* for money.

Joe strikes up a relationship with Betty Schaefer (Nancy Olson), another aspiring screenwriter. She sees one sequence in a scenario of Joe's, entitled *Dark Windows*, to be "moving and true." She is confident that it could be made in to a screenplay about "teachers and their threadbare lives." Unlike Norma's script for her creaky melodrama, Joe and Betty are writing a screenplay that is vital and compelling. After Joe catches her enthusiasm he works on it surreptitiously with Betty several nights a week. But Norma inevitably discovers that Joe is seeing Betty and becomes insanely jealous.

One fateful night Joe finally summons the courage to tell Norma that he is terminating their sordid liaison once and for all. "Norma, you're a woman of fifty," Joe tells her. "There is nothing tragic about being fifty, unless you try to be twenty-five!" When she threatens to kill herself if he leaves, he replies, "You'd be killing yourself to an empty house. The audience left twenty years ago."

Norma, who has been emotionally disturbed for some time, finally crosses the brink into insanity. As Joe leaves her mansion and walks across the patio, the deranged woman empties a revolver into his retreating figure; he pitches forward into the swimming pool. She shoots Joe dead, comments Steffen Haubner, "to prevent him from abandoning her, as everyone else did long ago."[37] We are now back at the point where the film began, with Joe being fished out of the floodlit pool by the police; hence Joe comments laconically on the sound track to the filmgoer, "Well, this is where you came in."

Shortly afterward, a crew of newsreel cameramen enter the house to photograph the fallen star as she is taken away by the police. But Norma mistakes the newsreel cameramen for the camera crew on a movie set, and accordingly believes that she is at long last making her comeback film. Max, who has supported her fantasies about a new career all along, makes believe, for her sake, that he is Cecil B. DeMille directing her in *Salome*. A look of anguish crosses Max's face when he directs the cameras toward Norma as she sweeps down the grand staircase of her exotic mansion for her final close-up. "So they were turning after all, those cameras," Joe says over the sound track. "Life, which can be strangely merciful, had taken pity on Norma Desmond. The dream she had clung to so desperately had finally enfolded her." The stunning finale of *Sunset Boulevard* makes for one of the greatest moments in classic film noir. And so Norma Desmond finally becomes swallowed up in the role of Salome, just as Anthony John was enveloped in the role of Othello.

American films at the time that *Sunset Boulevard* was made tended to have more positive endings than this film does because the studios feared that the public would reject downbeat endings. "*Sunset Boulevard* did not have a happy ending," said Wilder, "because it was inevitable that Norma would go mad. No other ending would have worked for the film, and the studio at no point questioned this." So happy endings were not always the rule in Hollywood films when *Sunset Boulevard* was made; the same holds true of *A Double Life*, which likewise ends in tragedy.

Most of the audience at Paramount's advance screening of *Sunset Boulevard* for the Hollywood community on that April night in 1950 stood up and cheered at the film's conclusion. Wilder said that Swanson later looked around for Mary Pickford, another star of silent pictures;

Erich von Stroheim and Gloria Swanson in *Sunset Boulevard*, Wilder's dark fable about Hollywood.

but an old-time producer told her, "She can't show herself, Gloria. She's overcome; we all are."

But Louis B. Mayer, the pompous chief executive of MGM, threw a tantrum in the lobby, Wilder remembers. Then, spying Wilder, he shook his pudgy fist at him, denouncing him as a disgrace to the industry. "You have dirtied the nest. You should be kicked out of this country, tarred and feathered, you goddamned foreigner son-of-a-bitch." In the heat of the moment Mayer apparently lost sight of the fact that he too was an immigrant, having been born in Minsk, Russia. By Wilder's own testimony, he responded to Mayer in kind. "Yes, I directed this picture," Wilder said; "Mr. Mayer, why don't you go fuck yourself?!"[38]

Discussing Mayer's tirade later, Wilder insisted that *Sunset Boulevard* "was not anti-Hollywood," as Mayer contended. Joe Gillis was a hack and Betty Schaefer tried "to put Joe back on the right track," Wilder explained. "I don't say anything derogatory about pictures" in this film.

Very few critics panned *Sunset Boulevard* when it premiered at the Radio City Music Hall on August 10, 1950; admittedly one reviewer dismissed it as "a pretentious slice of Roquefort," but he was the exception that proved the rule.[39] In general audiences and critics wholeheartedly embraced the film.

James Agee, who was committed to writing capsule film reviews for the *Nation*, contributed a five-page essay on the picture to the November 1950 issue of *Sight and Sound*. "It is one of those rare movies," he rhapsodized, "that can be talked about, almost shot for shot and line for line, for hours on end. . . . I am willing to bet that it will be looked at and respected long after most of the movies too easily called great have been forgotten."[40]

After all, *Sunset Boulevard* is blessed with a superb screenplay and inspired direction, topped off by Gloria Swanson's superlative performance as Norma and Erich von Stroheim's indelible portrayal of Max. Moreover, the movie is sterling for Wilder's consummate craftsmanship in producing well-defined, plausible characters. Swanson, as the obsolete screen star, has the threat of madness throughout—the cockeyed glint in her eyes implies the unruly and unmanageable passions that lie beneath her surface glamour. This keeps us watching as she leads us down the treacherous path to tragedy.

Manny Farber believed that the acting honors should be shared with William Holden. As the ruined screenwriter, "Holden is one of the most quietly charming hard-luck guys a moviegoer ever watched."[41] When the Academy Awards rolled around, Holden received a well-deserved nomination for best actor. All told, *Sunset Boulevard* nabbed no less than eleven nominations. But the only winners were Wilder, Brackett, and Marshman for best original screenplay; Waxman for best score; and John Meehan and Hans Dreier for production design. Presumably, Wilder's altercation with Mayer cost him some votes for the picture among Hollywood's old guard, just as he suspected it would.

Over the years *Sunset Boulevard* has continued to be singled out as a masterpiece. Indeed, the release of the picture on DVD in 2008 was the occasion for renewed acclaim for the film.

When the American Film Institute honored the best one hundred films made during the first century of American cinema with a TV special on CBS-TV July 3, 2003, *Sunset Boulevard* was at the top of the list. In observing that *Sunset Boulevard* had been chosen to be preserved by the National Film Registry of the Library of Congress, Daniel Eagan termed the movie "a withering tale of disillusionment" told with "psychological honesty."[42]

Taken together, *A Double Life* and *Sunset Boulevard* are two film noirs that offer the darkest accounts of Broadway theater and the Hollywood film industry on record.

Notes

1. Page Cook, "The Sound Track: *A Double Life*," 33, no. 1 (January 1982): 53.

2. George Cukor, interview by the author, Los Angeles, August 18, 1980. All quotations from Cukor that are not attributed to another source are from this interview.

3. Thomson, *The New Biographical Dictionary of Film*, 176.

4. Sam Frank, *Ronald Colman: A Bio-Bibliography* (Westport, Conn.: Greenwood Press, 1997), 20.

5. Garson Kanin, interview by the author, Beverly Hills, March 4, 1981.

6. Charles Higham and Joel Greenberg, "George Cukor," in *George Cukor: Interviews*, ed. Robert Emmet Long (Jackson: University Press of Mississippi, 2001), 58.

7. Dave Kehr, "Dangerous to Know," *New York Times*, February 7, 2010, sec. 2:14.

8. Brian McDonnell, "Edmond O'Brien," in *Encyclopedia of Film Noir*, 343.

9. Crowther, *Film Noir*, 65.

10. Patrick McGilligan, *George Cukor: A Double Life* (New York: St. Martin's Press, 1991), 196.

11. Emmanuel Levy, *George Cukor: Master of Elegance* (New York: William Morrow, 1999), 166.

12. Michael Kanin, interview by the author, Beverly Hills, July 10, 1987.

13. Cook, "The Sound Track," 54.

14. Cook, "The Sound Track," 53.

15. William Shakespeare, *Othello*, V.ii.351.

16. Frank, *Ronald Colman*, 20.

17. "*A Double Life*," in *Variety Film Reviews*, vol. 7, n.p.

18. Thomas, *The Films of the Forties*, 222.

19. Silver and Ursini, *The Noir Style*, 27.

20. William Relling, "A Walk on the Wilder Side," in *The Big Book of Noir*, 39.

21. Brian McDonnell, "*Sunset Boulevard*," in *Encyclopedia of Film Noir*, 398.

22. Billy Wilder, interview by the author, Hollywood, September 30, 1975. Any quotations from Wilder that are not attributed to another source are from this interview.

23. Thomson, *New Biographical Dictionary of Film*, 656.

24. Arthur Lennig, *Stroheim* (Lexington: University Press of Kentucky, 2000), 445.

25. David Freeman, "*Sunset Boulevard* Revisited," *New Yorker*, June 21, 1993, 77.

26. Billy Wilder, Charles Brackett, and D. M. Marshman, Jr., *Sunset Boulevard: A Screenplay*, ed. Jeffrey Meyers (Los Angeles: University of California Press, 1999), 43.

27. John Caps, "Movie Music," *Film Comment* 39, no. 6 (November–December 2003): 37; see also Tony Thomas, *Film Score: The View from the Podium* (London: Yoseloff, 1977), 57.

28. Avram Fleishman, *Narrated Films: Storytelling Situations in Cinema History* (Baltimore: Johns Hopkins University Press, 1992), 94–95.

29. James Ursini, "John F. Seitz Interviewed," in *Film Noir Reader 3*, ed. Alain Silver, James Ursini, and Robert Porfirio (New York: Limelight, 2002), 301.

30. Cameron Crowe, *Conversations with Wilder* (New York: Knopf, 2001), 255.

31. Fleishman, *Narrated Films*, 96.

32. Terrence Rafferty, "He's Nobody Important, Really, Just a Movie Writer," *New York Times*, July 27, 2003, sec. 2:18.

33. Barry Norman, *100 Best Films* (New York: Carol, 1993), 219.

34. Freeman, "*Sunset Boulevard* Revisited," 77.

35. Jeffrey Meyers, "Introduction," in Wilder, Brackett, and Marshman, *Sunset Boulevard: A Screenplay*, ix.

36. Morris Dickstein, "*Sunset Boulevard*," in *The A List: 100 Essential Films*, ed. Jay Carr (New York: Da Capo, 2002), 282.

37. Steffen Haubner, "*Sunset Boulevard*," in *Movies of the Forties*, 543.

38. Gerd Germunden, *A Foreign Affair: Billy Wilder's American Films* (New York: Berghahn, 2008), 95. Germunden has a detailed account of the infamous encounter between Mayer and Wilder, pointing out that, ironically enough, Mayer would be dethroned as head of MGM only a year later because he had not kept up with the climate of change in the industry; see pp. 95–99.

39. Sam Staggs, *Close-Up on Sunset Boulevard* (New York: St. Martin's Press, 2003), 158.

40. Agee, *Film Writing and Selected Journalism*, 468–69.

41. Farber, *Farber on Film*, 339.

42. Eagan, *America's Film Legacy*, 439.

ROBERT SIODMAK: *THE KILLERS* (1946)
DON SIEGEL: *THE KILLERS* (1964)

R obert Siodmak is a puzzling paradox among film noir directors. He was "a talented director with an unquestionable flair for film noir," according to Jean Pierre Coursodon. Yet "little has been written about him," despite the fact that films like *The Killers*, derived from the Hemingway short story, are quintessential noir, featuring a doom-ridden hero.[1]

In Ernest Hemingway's short story cycle about Nick Adams, young Nick comes under the temporary influence of some older men, most notably Ole Andreson in "The Killers." Under the spell of such men Nick gradually grows in maturity from adolescence to young manhood; for it is by observing their behavior under stress that he learns how to face the harsher and more perplexing aspects of adult life.

"The Killers" has been filmed twice in Hollywood. The role of Nick Adams is slighted in the first film and is nonexistent in the second. The reason that Nick appears to be fairly expendable in the two film adaptations of "The Killers" is that in this particular short story he is not so much an actor as an observer.

As Hemingway conceived the story, the title documents the young man's first direct encounter with the forces of evil, as represented by the two paid assassins from Chicago who invade a small town to murder an ex-prizefighter called Ole Andreson, whose nickname is "Swede." Nick is shattered by the way in which the killers have methodically gone about the business of tracking down their victim, and then announce with total impunity their intent to murder Swede in the diner where Nick is having supper.

More positively, Nick is deeply impressed by the stoic courage with which Swede accepts his unavoidable fate. After Nick warns him that the two gunmen are after him, Swede continues to await their inevitable appearance in his boardinghouse room because, as he tells Nick, he is tired of running.

Hemingway scholar Joseph Flora comments that "The Killers" thus represents another sobering step in Nick Adams's education in learning to cope with a cruel and disordered world.[2] But this aspect of the story's meaning is completely passed over in both film versions of "The Killers."

Instead, each of the two motion pictures utilizes the plot of Hemingway's short story as a prologue to the film proper and then proceeds in a series of flashbacks to develop in detail the tangled web of events that lead to Swede's murder, the motive for which Hemingway never explicitly explained in the story. In effect, the two movies opt for focusing on Ole Andreson, rather than on Nick Adams, in order to explain more fully why Swede was so willing to accept his death.

Hemingway's short story has been called "one of the most influential works in American literature."[3] This is because in it Hemingway pioneered the hard-boiled mode of fiction. Hammett, as we know, acknowledged the influence of Hemingway's lean, spare prose on his fiction, especially on the dialogue of his stories. "The dialogue, particularly that between the killers," writes Philip Booth, "relies on notably short, clipped sentences, offering the sensation of words being spit out and exchanged rapidly, like machine-gun fire. The technique was common to the era's hard-boiled fiction."[4]

"The Killers" was first published in *Scribner's Magazine* in 1927, the year that the movies learned to talk. Gangster pictures did not get rolling until after the advent of sound; and then Hemingway's story "affected the way gangsters spoke on the screen."[5] For example, gangster films like *Little Caesar* (1930) and *Scarface* (1932) imitated Hemingway's tough, rhythmic pattern for the gangsters' dialogue.

The screenplay of Robert Siodmak's 1946 film adaptation of "The Killers" was written by John Huston, with the assistance of Anthony Veiller, in the same way that Alan Rivkin had helped out Huston with the screenplay for *The Maltese Falcon*. "Scripts of the caliber of *The Killers* do not come along every day," Siodmak said. "This one happened to be written by my friend John Huston." Huston, a distinguished writer-director in his own right of such crime melodramas as *The Maltese Falcon*, received no screen credit for collaborating on the screenplay of *The Killers* because technically he was under contract at the time to Warner Bros. and could not officially be credited with a screenplay for Universal.

Veiller made some contributions to the script of *The Killers* around the same time he wrote the screenplay for Orson Welles's *The Stranger*, which is treated later in this book. "Incidentally," Siodmak continued, "Hemingway's original was only eleven pages, which was used for the opening. The rest was invented."[6]

The opening sequence of the 1946 film transfers Hemingway's short story to the screen virtually intact in the opening moments of the film. The balance of the screenplay veers into the realm of film noir. Indeed, the movie presents a typical film noir milieu, represented by tawdry cabarets, stale cigarette smoke, naked lightbulbs, and dark alleys. Colin McArthur writes in *Underworld USA* that Siodmak often invites his audience into the dark and sinister film noir world of his crime melodramas by a forward tracking shot seen from the filmgoer's point of view, and *The Killers* is no exception to this rule: "In the opening of *The Killers*, the point of view is from the back seat of the killers' car as it hurtles through the darkness towards the little town of Brentwood, New Jersey, where Swede waits to be killed."[7]

The darkness that surrounds them until they enter the brightly lit diner seems to presage that during their brief stay in town the powers of darkness will hold sway. The two gunmen (William Conrad and Charles McGraw) casually announce that they plan to kill Pete Lunn (the alias Ole Andreson has been using) when he comes in for supper. They then proceed to hold Nick, George the counterman, and Sam the cook at bay. When Swede does not appear, they disappear once more into the darkness from which they had materialized a few minutes before.

Nick rushes to the boardinghouse where Ole Andreson (Burt Lancaster) lives to warn him, but it is already too late. The powers of darkness are already enveloping Swede, who lies on his bed in the murky shadows of his shabby room. He is aware that his death has only been temporarily postponed by his failure to appear in the diner for supper. After Nick departs, Swede continues to stare at the door of his room, until it suddenly bursts open and the two gunmen, minions of darkness seen only in silhouette, blast away at the camera, which then cuts to Swede's hand slowly sliding down a brass bedpost in death.

Aside from a few minor discrepancies, the film has up to this point been fairly faithful to its literary source. But the script omits the final scene of the short story, which takes place back at the diner, where Nick's brief conversation with George and Sam makes it clear what a traumatic experience this brush with evil has been for Nick; for his helplessness to save Swede fills him with horror and grief. It is this scene that substantiates the fact that Hemingway's short story really centers on Nick's reaction to what has happened and is not principally about Ole Andreson at all.[8]

Asked by boxer Gene Tunney about the real-life counterpart of Ole Andreson, Hemingway replied that it was Andre Andreson, who had agreed to throw a fight, but then went on to win it. "All afternoon he had rehearsed taking a dive," Hemingway explained, "but during the fight he had instinctively thrown a punch he didn't mean to." The fighter whom Andre Andreson decked in a 1916 bout was Jack Dempsey. Andreson was shot to death in a Chicago tavern in 1926, the year Hemingway wrote "The Killers."[9] In the film Swede is murdered, not for failing to throw a fight, but because he allegedly double-crossed some gangsters.

The short story serves as a prologue to the rest of the screenplay. Huston constructed a cleverly conceived backstory that centers on Jim Reardon, an insurance investigator who is making an official inquiry into Swede's death because Swede carried a policy with Atlantic Casualty, Reardon's agency. Hemingway's "hard-boiled dialogue and laconic style" pervades much of the additional material appended to Hemingway's story by Huston.[10]

According to Siodmak biographer Deborah Alpi, "Huston was solely responsible for the final draft of the script."[11] Since Huston composed the screenplay for *The Maltese Falcon*, it appears that he modeled Reardon in *The Killers* on Sam Spade in *The Maltese Falcon*. As played by Edmond O'Brien, Reardon's cocky assertiveness marks him as an intrepid Sam Spade figure, "cast in the mold of the hard-boiled detective."[12] Reardon is as grimly determined to solve the mystery of Swede's murder as Spade was to unravel the mystery surrounding the slaying of Miles Archer.

At times Reardon talks like Spade. Thus Reardon, almost in spite of himself, is fascinated by the manner in which Kitty Collins had slyly manipulated Swede into participating in a payroll robbery some time back; he comments, "I would like to have known the old Kitty Collins"—a wry remark worthy of Sam Spade. "And it's no knock on O'Brien's performance," comments Jonathan Lethem, "to savor his meticulous imitation of Bogart," particularly during the shoot-out at the Green Cat Lounge, where Reardon encounters Al and Max, the pair that liquidated Swede.[13]

Huston turned his finished screenplay over to Mark Hellinger, the enterprising producer of the movie; it was Hellinger who originally had the inspiration to build Hemingway's short story into a feature film. Hellinger had been a New York journalist, a colleague of columnist Damon Runyon; he graduated to becoming a movie producer in 1940. *The Killers* was Hellinger's first production at Universal. He chose Robert Siodmak, whose noir thriller *The Spiral Staircase* (1945) had been a huge success, to helm *The Killers*.

Siodmak, as mentioned previously, had directed *Menschen am Sonntag* in Berlin in 1929, in collaboration with Billy Wilder and Fred Zinnemann. After the commercial and critical success of that film, Siodmak was hired to direct movies at Ufa, until Hitler came to power in 1933. Wilder and Zinnemann in due course headed for Hollywood.

Siodmak, when he learned one day that storm troopers were hunting for him in Berlin, also fled Germany. He migrated to Paris, where he directed French films until the war broke out in Europe in 1939, at which point Siodmak decided to relocate in America, as Wilder and Zinnemann had done before him. *Pièges* (*Personal Column*, 1939) was the last and best movie Siodmak made in France, a psychological thriller that presaged his film noirs in Hollywood. It concerns a serial killer who lures hapless women through want ads in the newspaper.

Siodmak did not make much of an impact in Hollywood with the early pictures he directed there, routine efforts like *Son of a Dracula* (1943). He complained that no one even knew how to pronounce his surname properly and took to wearing a jacket that had the phonetic transcription of his name displayed on the back: "SEE-odd-mack."[14] But he made a name for himself when he directed the first of a series of important film noirs, *Phantom Lady* (1944).

Siodmak brought with him to Hollywood his experience in working in both the German and French film industries. His film noirs like *The Killers* were spiced with Teutonic sauce, which created an expressionistic atmosphere that was morbid and haunting. By the same token, French naturalism is reflected in his inclination to shoot on location whenever possible. For example, Swede's last boxing match was filmed at Hollywood Legion Stadium.

Hellinger, who had a knack for recognizing talent, selected two virtual unknowns to star in *The Killers*. The movie was Burt Lancaster's debut film. "In *The Killers* I was a big, dumb Swede," Lancaster remembered; "there was no need to be highly ostentatious. For a new actor this is much easier than something histrionic."[15]

Lancaster went on to play in several more film noirs, because he so perfectly embodied the vulnerability of the classic noir antihero who is victimized by a femme fatale. Similarly, Ava Gardner, who had previously played only minor parts in movies, became the iconic figure of the femme fatale in other noir films after her portrayal of the devious, remorseless Kitty Collins in *The Killers*.

In contrast to Lancaster and Gardner, Edmond O'Brien was an established star when he took the part of the dogged claims investigator, Jim Reardon, who dominates the movie after the prologue. O'Brien would continue to play significant roles in several more noirs, including *A Double*

Lily (Virginia Christine), Ole Andreson (Burt Lancaster), and Kitty Collins (Ava Gardner) in Robert Siodmak's film of Ernest Hemingway's *The Killers*.

Life. So too Albert Dekker was a pro at this point in his career, and often played strong, menacing types like crime boss Big Jim Colfax in *The Killers*. And Sam Levene was typically cast as a soft-tough cop, as he was in *After the Thin Man*, before taking a similar part in the present film, that of Lieutenant Sam Lubinsky.

Behind the camera there was director of photography Elwood "Woody" Bredell, who had worked with Siodmak on *Phantom Lady*. In *The Killers* Bredell presents a virtual inventory of noir cinematography. Because Bredell employed low-key lighting throughout the film, he cut back drastically on lighting the sets, reducing the number of arc lamps, especially for night scenes.

Accordingly a sinister atmosphere was created in certain interiors by infusing them with menacing shadows looming on the walls, which gave a Gothic quality to the faces. All in all, Bredell's chiaroscuro cinematography, with its night-shrouded streets and alleys, ominous corridors, and dark archways, gave the picture a rich texture. After being coached by Siodmak, Bredell later observed, "he could light a football field with a match."[16]

The Killers reflects "a moody intensity that is reminiscent of the German Expressionism of Fritz Lang, whose work heavily influenced Siodmak," according to Borde and Chaumeton.[17] But Siodmak also favored location shooting. Thus the present movie combined dark, brooding studio sets with actual locations. For example, the daring payroll robbery at a Hackensack factory was filmed on location in a documentary style, and photographed in a single, continuous take that was as smoothly executed as the crime itself.

The shot begins from the point where the gang, disguised as workmen, enter the main gate of the Prentiss Hat Company. The camera then peers through the window of the payroll office as the mobsters take the money. It then rises to a high angle, as they exchange gunfire with guards on the factory grounds; the camera then proceeds to film their escape out the main gate. The narrator of this flashback is Kenyon, Reardon's boss; he comments that one of the guards "fell to the ground with a bullet in the groin." This underscores the notion that the movie portrays a chaotic world prone to eruptions of grisly violence.

In keeping with the conventions of film noir, the movie is characterized throughout by an air of grim, unvarnished realism, typified by the payroll robbery sequence. Siodmak photographed the scene with a harsh, newsreel-like quality.

The robbery sequence is accompanied by a throbbing theme smacking of urgency; it was provided by Miklos Rozsa, whose scores for film noirs like *Spellbound* would earn him the title of "the voice of the noir." For *The Killers* Rozsa "dreamed up a leitmotif that rumbles whenever the two hitmen appear on screen: four solid beats played by low brass, accompanied by insistent snare drums. Rozsa entitled this passage in his score "Danger Ahead."[18] It was later employed for the theme of the TV series *Dragnet*. In general Rozsa's hard-hitting music for *The Killers* is "powerful and brutal," comments Larry Timm, "perfect for the actions of the cold-hearted characters on screen."[19] (A concert suite from Rozsa's score was released in 1996 on a CD, entitled "Miklos Rozsa: *Double Indemnity* and Other Scores.")

After the prologue, which portrays Swede's death, the movie introduces Jim Reardon, the claims investigator charged with conducting an inquiry into Swede's murder because Swede had been insured by Reardon's company. In the course of the film Reardon's investigation takes the form of a quest to uncover the reason for Swede's stoically submitting to his own death. "That enigma drives the narrative," as Reardon painstakingly cobbles together the story of Swede's past.[20] It is his inquiry into Swede's death, a gangland killing, that takes Reardon into the world of film noir.

Siodmak considered *The Killers* a gangster picture, since the term *film noir* was not yet in use in those days. As Siodmak put it, the ideal hero for a gangster picture is someone "who has failed in life and has therefore committed a crime. . . . If you give such a person a good enough motive for the crime," the audience will be on his side. This, of course, is the recipe followed by the scriptwriter of *The Killers* and neatly sums up the way in which Huston shrewdly extended Hemingway's plot to fill out a full-length screenplay.[21]

The Killers has an intricate narrative structure, involving no less than eleven flashbacks, comprising testimony given to Reardon by the individuals he interviews. As Hirsch points out, "In Siodmak the past is often a maze that has to be penetrated, its mysteries uncovered only gradually by means of a complex web of intersecting viewpoints."[22]

In the course of the flashbacks Reardon discovers that it was Swede's failed boxing career that led him into a life of crime, once he became an ex-pug. This particular flashback is narrated by Lt. Sam Lubinsky, who had known Swede since boyhood. During the bout Swede smashes his hand beyond repair. The fight thus brings into relief how Swede is a born loser.

Siodmak portrays Swede's last prizefight as one of the most savage boxing matches ever seen on the screen. He had Bredell photograph much of the fight through the ropes, to make the viewer feel that the bout is being seen from ringside. At crucial moments Bredell moves the camera inside the ring, first showing Swede's opponent, Tiger Lewis, lunging at Swede's jaw, and then showing Swede slumping to the floor in a daze.

A spectator tells Lubinsky that Swede is "getting murdered" and that his opponent is "killing him." After Swede is KO'd, his manager departs with, "No use hanging around here; I never did like wakes." Shadoian remarks, in what is perhaps the best essay on the film, that these observations about Swede's last bout show how Swede's death haunts the flashbacks. (What's more, in another flashback "we are present at his funeral.")[23] Manny Farber, in his review of *The Killers* in the *New Republic*, sums up the fight sequence by saying that an action scene like this one has been "filled with a vitality all too rare in current movies."[24]

The failure of Swede's boxing career is employed to establish Swede's desperate need for money, a need that leads him to participate in a payroll robbery with a gang that later arranges his murder for apparently double-crossing them. In fact, we learn in the series of flashbacks that Swede is the scapegoat for Colfax, the leader of the gang, and his mistress Kitty, who use the unsuspecting Swede to cover up their own double cross of the gang. Because of his long-standing devotion to Kitty, Swede is an easy foil for their scheme. It is Kitty and Colfax who have kept the entire proceeds of the robbery for themselves while making it look like it was Swede who absconded with the funds; they leave him to take the rap and finally to be murdered once his whereabouts are discovered.

The film suggests, as does the Hemingway story, that by electing to take his medicine for consorting with criminals in the first place and by facing death with dignity and courage, Ole Andreson, the once honest boxer, redeems his recent past. Swede is, therefore, as sympathetic a figure in the film as he is in the short story.

Siodmak supplies a touch of expressionism to the flashbacks by a scarf decorated with golden harps that functions as a visual symbol of Swede's dedicated love of Kitty, from whom he got the scarf as a keepsake. It first appears early in the movie in the hands of Reardon, the insurance investigator, who has discovered it among Swede's effects after the boxer's murder. Later in the film when we see Swede fondling it during the planning session for the robbery it is an emblem of his willingness to go along with the caper in order to ingratiate himself still further with Kitty by making some easy money. Swede even wears the scarf as a mask during the actual robbery as a good luck charm, but the only kind of luck that Kitty brings Swede is bad. And it is painfully ironic, therefore, that at the time of his death this scarf embroidered with angelic harps is his sole memento of the devilish female who coauthored his murder.

In a rare moment of frankness, Kitty expresses to Swede at one point her view of herself. "I'm poison, Swede, to myself and everybody around me." A legendary femme fatale, "Kitty is beautiful, duplicitous, and willing to use her erotic appeal to manipulate and destroy men, in order to get what she wants."[25] The fact that she is unattainable, however, does not prevent men like Swede from desiring her.

Reardon tracks Kitty to Pittsburgh, where she now lives with her husband, Big Jim Colfax. Reardon arranges to meet her at the Green Cat Lounge to interrogate her about her involvement in Swede's murder. The two killers, Al and Max, had followed Reardon and Kitty to the club, where Reardon is now their target. Their arrival is announced by the theme that Rozsa employed for them in the movie's prologue, called appropriately "Danger Ahead." Colfax has ordered them to slay Reardon so that he cannot incriminate him in Swede's killing. Lubinsky, in turn, has also shadowed Reardon and Kitty to the cabaret, and is likewise present.

"The shootout that ensues is dynamically choreographed."[26] The killers open fire on Reardon, who overturns a table to provide cover for himself, while Lubinsky shoots the killers dead. When the smoke clears, Reardon discovers that the wily Kitty has taken a powder—she has escaped through the window in the powder room.

Reardon and Lubinsky, plus a squad of policemen, follow Kitty to the suburban mansion she shares with Colfax. This is where Siodmak stages the movie's final showdown. Reardon and the police arrive just as Colfax and a mobster named "Dum-Dum" Clarke—the last surviving member of Colfax's gang—are engaged in a gun battle. Reardon had tipped off Dum-Dum that it was Colfax, and not Swede, who had double-crossed the gang. Dum-Dum endeavors to settle his accounts with Colfax, but both men are fatally wounded.

Kitty implores her dying husband to exonerate her of any complicity in the plot to kill Swede. But Colfax's dying words to his wife are merely,

"I guess our luck's run out, Kitty." Reardon watches Colfax die and taunts Kitty, saying, "Your would-be fall guy is dead." Colfax simply would not lie to the cops with his dying breath by declaring Kitty's innocence. "In classic film noir," Wager comments, "the femme fatale's actions almost always prove fatal to her as well as to her male victims."[27]

James Agee opined in his notice of The Killers in the Nation that the dialogue Huston concocted for the screenplay, "though generally skillful and talented, isn't within miles of Hemingway's in quality."[28] On the contrary, Hemingway wrote in a 1959 essay on the films of his fiction that he much admired Huston's work. "It's a good picture, and the only good picture ever made of a story I wrote. One reason for that is that John Huston wrote the script."[29]

Mary Hemingway told me that Hemingway himself was pleased with the movie. "The only film made from his work of which Ernest entirely approved was The Killers."[30] The studio presented him with a print of the film, and he frequently ran it for guests at his home in Cuba, although he invariably fell asleep after the first reel—the only portion of the picture based directly on his story.

Hemingway scholar Melissa Harmon writes that Siodmak's Killers is a "truly moving and terrifying adaptation of one of Hemingway's best stories."[31] Moreover, Siodmak's film has been incorporated into the group of films preserved by the National Film Registry at the Library of Congress. Daniel Eagan states in his book on the registry movies that Siodmak films like The Killers offer "a compelling and seductive equivalent" to hard-boiled fiction.[32]

In 1952 Siodmak reteamed with Burt Lancaster for his last Hollywood movie, a swashbuckler entitled The Crimson Pirate. He then returned to Europe and eventually settled in his native Germany in 1954, where he continued to direct brisk thrillers. In 1959 Siodmak made a film in Britain, The Rough and the Smooth (U.S. title: Portrait of a Sinner). It was actually a film noir featuring Nadja Tiller as a calculating femme fatale who betrays three men—including William Bendix (The Glass Key), whom she drives to suicide. But this movie is no match for Siodmak's American noirs.

Siodmak made some outstanding noirs in Hollywood, as did Wilder and Zinnemann. (Wilder's Sunset Boulevard and Zinnemann's Act of Violence are represented in this book.) Yet Hirsch rightly laments that Wilder and Zinnemann "have received the kind of acknowledgment that Robert Siodmak, whose career parallels theirs, has not."[33] Perhaps Siodmak is best remembered in his native Germany, where, a quarter century after his death, the Berlin International Film Festival held a comprehensive retrospective of his movies.

Hemingway did not live to see the 1964 remake of *The Killers*. To cash in on the Hemingway name, the movie was called on its initial release *Ernest Hemingway's The Killers*. Siodmak's film likewise had Hemingway's name in its official title, but reviewers invariably referred to each movie as simply *The Killers*; and film historians have followed suit.

Including Hemingway's name in the title of the remake was misleading, since the remake of *The Killers*, directed by Don Siegel, was considerably less faithful to its literary source than the first version.

The Killers (1964)

As it happened, Don Siegel was Mark Hellinger's first choice to direct *The Killers* in 1946, because Hellinger had been impressed by Siegel's very first film, *The Verdict*, a film noir set in Victorian London with Peter Lorre and Sydney Greenstreet (*The Maltese Falcon*). But Siegel was under contract to Warner Bros. (as was John Huston), and Jack Warner would not lend Siegel to Universal. So Hellinger got Siodmak instead.

Siegel went on to direct some first-class film noirs like *The Lineup* (1958). Andrew Sarris termed the climactic shoot-out in *The Lineup* "among the most stunning displays of action montage in the history of the American cinema."[34] Seventeen years after Siodmak's *Killers* appeared, Siegel wrote in his autobiography, "Lou Wasserman, head of Universal, asked me to do a new version—the first two-hour movie made for TV."[35]

Siegel welcomed the opportunity to make his version of *The Killers*, since his remake of Howard Hawks's film of Hemingway's *To Have and Have Not*, entitled *The Gun Runners* (1958), was a resounding failure. Siegel's version had Audie Murphy, a mediocre actor at best, in the role created by Humphrey Bogart in Hawks's 1944 movie; and Murphy was no Bogart.

Siegel was determined not to make his version of *The Killers* a carbon copy of the Siodmak movie. Indeed, he wished to call his film *Johnny North*, the name of the fall guy played by Burt Lancaster in Siodmak's film, but he was overruled by the front office. "The only idea from the original picture I wished to use was the catalyst of a man knowing he's going to be killed and making no attempt to escape sure death," he explained.[36]

Though the remake of *The Killers* has little connection with Hemingway, it is an excellent thriller in itself. Siegel collaborated (uncredited) with screenwriter Gene Coon, who had written some episodes of *Dragnet*, on the script. They sought to avoid making a mere rehash of the Siodmak film by introducing some neat plot twists of their own, such as having the killers themselves, rather than an insurance investigator, probe the motives for the hero's steadfast refusal to avoid his own murder.

Even the look of Siegel's film is different from that of Siodmak's movie. Since Siodmak shot his film in black and white and Siegel's movie was to be in color, the latter decided to replace the ominously dark atmosphere of Siodmak's film noir with several scenes of mayhem shot in bright sunshine to imply that in the savage world of the film, evil is just as likely to strike in broad daylight as under the cover of darkness. Siegel's movie is "pervaded with noir-like sadism and double dealing, but is photographed in band-box colors," writes James Naremore.[37] The killers are willing to do their dirty work in the afternoon sunshine.

The movie's prologue takes place in Miami, Florida. The opening sequence only remotely resembles the short story, whereas the parallel sequence in Siodmak's movie encapsulated most of the key elements of Hemingway's short story.

The opening sequence in the remake is set in a home for the blind. The peaceful atmosphere of a warm, sunny afternoon is shattered by the chilly intrusion of two killers, Charlie (Lee Marvin) and Lee (Clu Gulager), who have come to murder Johnny North (John Cassavetes), a failed auto racer who teaches a course in auto repair to the blind residents of the home.

Charlie inquires of the blind receptionist, Miss Watson, the whereabouts of Jerry Nichols, the assumed name that Johnny has been going by. (Miss Watson is played by Virginia Christine, who was Lt. Lubinsky's wife in the Siodmak film.) When she replies that Jerry cannot meet with them until after his class, Charlie says with feigned nonchalance, "Lady, we just haven't got the time." With that, Charlie knocks Miss Watson unconscious, and he and Lee proceed to Johnny's classroom.

A blind old man (instead of young Nick Adams) warns Johnny that two sinister strangers are looking for him, but Johnny does not flee. Instead, he resolutely stands his ground as the two assailants burst into his classroom and fill him with lead. The passing years have not blunted the shocking violence of this scene, made all the more authentic by Siegel's employing real blind people as Johnny's students.

Charlie and Lee are impressed by the tranquility with which Johnny North has met his fate, and they resolve to find out why, particularly because Charlie remembers that four years before, North was implicated in a million-dollar mail truck heist from which the stolen money was never recovered.

Siegel films often deal with "the antisocial outcast," writes Andrew Sarris; "his gallery of loners" includes Dancer (Eli Wallach), the psychopathic professional killer in *The Lineup* and Charlie Strom, the cold-blooded veteran hit man in *The Killers*.[38] Just as Huston apparently modeled Reardon in his script for the 1946 *Killers* on Sam Spade in *The Maltese Falcon*, so too Siegel seems to have modeled Charlie Strom in the 1964 *Killers* on Dancer, a sociopath with a wicked glint in his eye. Charlie, like Dancer, has survived as a hired gun by relying on meticulous planning. Dancer in *The Lineup* must track down a cache of heroin seized by some criminals who have double-crossed a drug czar; and he does so with a relentlessness that is likewise evident in Charlie in *The Killers*.

"The progress from Dancer in *The Lineup* to Charlie in *The Killers* is a short one," according to Silver and Ursini. "Charlie wears the same dark business suit as Dancer and carries the same caliber handgun with a slightly longer silencer."[39] Dancer is gunned down on an unfinished highway; Charlie dies, after a bloody shoot-out, on a suburban lawn. Too late they both learn that eventually everyone loses.

Siegel insisted that the cast of *The Killers* was a major factor in the movie's success as an important gangster movie. Siegel elicited from Marvin the best performance of his career as a psychotic killer who dresses impeccably, sports dark shades, and carries his revolver in a businesslike attaché case emblematic of his cool professionalism.

Geoffrey O'Brien writes, "If Angie Dickinson," as the femme fatale Sheila Farr, "lacks the aura of Ava Gardner, she does at least perfectly communicate the chic rapacity" that her role requires.[40] As for John Cassavetes, although he acted in films to gather funding for the independent films he directed, his role as the earnest, obsessed Johnny North in *The Killers* is one of his best performances. Lastly, there is Siegel's great casting coup: Siegel cast Ronald Reagan against type as the villain of the piece in what turned out to be, interestingly enough, the actor's last film before

Charlie (Lee Marvin) as one of the killers in Don Siegel's remake of Siodmak's *The Killers.*

launching a career in politics. "There *is* something ironic," said Siegel wryly, "about the man who was to become the governor of California two years later, executing the robbery of a mail truck in the movie disguised as a California state trooper."[41] Quite apart from this curious sidelight on Reagan's farewell performance in the film, he gave a fine, sharp-edged performance as Browning: at one point Reagan, as Jack Browning, petulantly slaps Sheila Farr around, just to remind her who is boss.

Although Siegel's film was designed to be the first made-for-TV movie ever done, Siegel told me that he did not shoot the picture any differently because of that: "I shot it the way I shoot every film I make, in a very taut, lean style with great economy, and at a very fast pace. This is the way I work best." Siegel shot much of the movie on location, in order to give the picture the documentary flavor that was standard for his other movies, like *The Lineup.*

Yet shooting had gotten off to a bad start when Lee Marvin took to showing up on the set in no condition to work, and Siegel became increasingly worried that Marvin's drinking was hurting the picture. The crucial final scene of the film had been shot on the first day of production on location in a posh suburban home the studio had rented for the day. But it had to be reshot later because Marvin had arrived drunk; and redoing the scene, of course, meant an expensive return to the location site.

When similar incidents occurred, Siegel finally decided to take the actor aside during a break in shooting and tell Marvin of his concern: "Look, you just can't work when you're like this," Siegel said. "So let's go through it one more time for show, call it a day, and do it right tomorrow." Later in the day Marvin remarked to Siegel: "I liked the fact that you talked to me alone." From then on, adds Siegel, Marvin did not show up drunk for the duration of shooting.

Clu Gulager, who played Lee, Charlie's deranged cohort in the film, said that Marvin's drinking problem was rooted in the fact that "he was the most insecure actor I've ever known." Nevertheless, Marvin's understated performance in this film "is the apex of his career."[42]

Although Siegel shot a film with economy and speed, he took his time in the editing room, where he and editor Richard Belding spent twenty-five days working round the clock to turn the 180,000 feet of the rough cut of *The Killers* into a final print of 9,000 feet, so that the film would fit into a two-hour TV time slot.[43]

Composer John Williams (*Star Wars*) was still known as Johnny Williams when he scored *The Killers* in 1964. He had drifted into scoring TV dramas for series like *Playhouse 90* in the mid-1950s, and also had scored some low-budget features. Williams's music for *The Killers* showcases prominent brass motifs and pounding percussion rhythms, mingling dissonant themes with sweeping lyrical melodies. Still Ronald Schwartz is correct in saying that Williams's music for the remake of *The Killers* is no match for "Miklos Rozsa's masterpiece, which punctuated the action of the 1946 original."[44]

After the prologue, in which the killers slay Johnny, the remake proceeds in flashback fashion, the same format used in the previous movie, to fill in the background behind the hero's death. Charlie and Lee are at the center of the film, as they seek out the individuals who knew Johnny North. This time the femme fatale who suckers the hero into getting involved in a robbery is Sheila Farr. Like Kitty, her predecessor in the first movie, she then manages to con the rest of the gang into believing that Johnny has double-crossed them and made off with all of the plunder, when in fact it is Sheila and her lover, Jack Browning, who have done the double-crossing.

When Johnny discovers that Sheila's loyalty all along has been to Jack Browning, and that she and Jack are now husband and wife, he is crushed by Sheila's betrayal. Indeed, Charlie declares to Sheila at one point, "Now I understand why Johnny just stood there when we shot him. The only man who isn't afraid to die is the man who is dead already. *You* killed Johnny; you didn't need us." That line of dialogue is worthy of Huston.

After strong-arming several people who knew Johnny for information about his past, Charlie and Lee decide to blackmail Browning by threatening to tell the mob that it is he and Sheila who should have been murdered. Browning, using a high-powered rifle, ambushes the two blackmailers from his office window, killing Lee instantly and mortally wounding Charlie. But Charlie lives long enough to follow Browning to his fashionable home, where Sheila is anxiously waiting for him. Browning stuffs his briefcase with the stolen money, hoping to leave town with Sheila before Charlie catches up with them. But it is already too late.

As Charlie draws a bead on them, Sheila begs him to listen to her spurious excuses for her part in the whole affair. Before firing, Charlie shakes his head wearily and murmurs for the last time in the film his oft-repeated remark, "Lady, I just haven't got the time." The middle-aged Charlie has known all along that, given the many years he has already survived the perils of his profession as a paid assassin, he is living on borrowed time; he is now aware that his time has at last run out.

After he shoots Browning and Sheila, Charlie staggers out of the house into the bright sunlight with the briefcase full of money. He collapses, dumping the money all over the lawn. Hearing a police siren in the distance, he raises his arm, points his index finger as if it were his revolver, and dies. Charlie knows his arsenal is exhausted, just as he knows his life is spent, but he nevertheless makes this one final futile gesture of defiance against the forces of law and order as he expires and the movie ends.

As things turned out the movie was first released as a theatrical feature and not premiered on television after all. The network censors thought the film too violent for the home screen, and NBC executives concurred, especially since the recent assassination of President Kennedy had sparked protests from the public about TV violence promoting violence in real life. Moreover, the scene in which Browning ambushes Charlie and Lee from a vantage point high above the street was thought to resemble the circumstances of the president's death too closely, although the similarity was purely coincidental. The picture achieved a successful theatrical release that confirmed Siegel's position as a preeminent director of fast-paced thrillers, although it does not quite come up to Siodmak's classic film noir version of the Hemingway story. For one thing, whatever the movie's other merits, the Siegel film has precious little to do with the original Hemingway short story. Moreover, Siegel's movie is not cast in the mold of a traditional noir, as Siodmak's picture was—although Naremore calls Siegel's film "noirlike." After all, Siegel's movie does have a doomed hero, a femme fatale, and villains plotting dark deeds.

With Siegel's *Killers* a new type of gangster emerged from film noir. The gangster movie, from William Wellman's *Public Enemy* (1930) through Samuel Fuller's *Underworld U.S.A.* (1961), had stressed the criminal's displays of neurotic aggression and ferocious savagery. By contrast, Charlie Strom in *The Killers* is a "cold, restrained psychotic" individual, a laconic, implacable, menacing figure.[45] Lee Marvin enacted this iconic character in other movies as well, most notably John Boorman's *Point Blank* (1967), in which Marvin again plays a ruthless, hard-boiled criminal.

Siegel's version of *The Killers* can be appreciated as a fine film, when considered apart from the original 1946 movie. As Siegel told me, "I endeavored to come up with a movie that was not a pale imitation of Siodmak's picture, but a movie that would stand on its own as quality entertainment." In this he succeeded. "For a made-for-television movie," according to David Thomson, Siegel's *Killers* "is way above average," especially because of Lee Marvin's immaculate performance—a sterling addition to Siegel's gallery of "tough, solitary outsiders."[46]

Perhaps Andrew Tudor said it all when he toasted Siegel as a director who "combined entertainment with perception; skilled filmmaking economy with nicely delineated characters; and overall detachment with sympathy for his hard-pressed protagonists" like Johnny North. Tudor's remarks certainly apply to *The Killers*, a movie that demonstrated that Siegel's "skill and subtlety have deserved rather more in the way of critical attention" than they have received.[47]

In short, Siodmak's *Killers* may be the more accomplished film, but Siegel's movie of the same name deserves to be seen. So it was a stroke of genius for Criterion to package both movies as a double feature for a two-disc DVD set, affording the viewer an interesting study in cinematic contrasts.

Notes

1. Jean Pierre Coursodon, "Robert Siodmak in Black and White," in *The Big Book of Noir*, 41.

2. Joseph Flora, *"Men without Women,"* in *Hemingway: Eight Decades of Criticism*, ed. Linda Wagner-Martin (East Lansing: Michigan State University Press, 2009), 289.

3. *"The Killers," Time*, September 4, 2006, 74.

4. Philip Booth, "Hemingway's 'The Killers' and Heroic Fiction," *Literature/Film Quarterly* 35, no. 1 (Winter 2007): 405.

5. Carlos Clarens, *Crime Movies: A History of the Gangster Genre*, rev. ed. (New York: Da Capo, 1997), 196.

6. Robert Siodmak, "Hoodlums: The Myth," in *Hollywood Directors: 1941–76*, ed. Richard Koszarski (New York: Oxford University Press, 1977), 286.

7. Colin McArthur, *Underworld USA* (New York: Viking, 1972), 105.

8. Ernest Hemingway, "The Killers," in *The Short Stories of Ernest Hemingway* (New York: Scribner, 2003), 288–89.

9. Philip Young, "Big World Out There: The Nick Adams Stories," in *The Short Stories of Ernest Hemingway: Critical Essays*, ed. Jackson Benson (Durham, N.C.: Duke University Press, 1975), 35.

10. McDonnell, *"The Killers,"* in *Encyclopedia of Film Noir*, 242–43.

11. Deborah Alpi, *Robert Siodmak: A Biography with Critical Analyses of His Film Noirs* (Jefferson, N.C.: McFarland, 1998), 154.

12. Mason, *American Gangster Cinema*, 78.

13. Jonathan Lethem's remarks are taken from his essay *"The Killers* (1946)," included with the DVD of the film (released by Criterion in 2003), 2.

14. *Cinema's Exiles: From Hitler to Hollywood* (Karen Thomas, 2007, television documentary). This documentary contains rare footage of Siodmak giving a brief interview about working in Hollywood.

15. Karen Hannsberry, *Bad Boys: The Actors of Film Noir* (Jefferson, N.C.: McFarland, 2003), 372.

16. Hillier and Phillips, *100 Film Noirs*, 205.

17. Borde and Chaumeton, *A Panorama of American Film Noir*, 79.

18. Robert Horton, "Music Man: Miklos Rozsa," *Film Comment* 31, no. 6 (November–December, 1995): 2–3.

19. Larry Timm, *The Soul of Cinema: Film Music* (Upper Saddle River, N.J.: Prentice-Hall, 2003), 144.

20. Booth, "Hemingway's 'The Killers' and Heroic Fatalism," 408.

21. Siodmak, "Hoodlums: The Myth," 286.

22. Hirsch, *The Dark Side of the Screen*, 118.

23. Jack Shadoian, *Dreams and Dead Ends: The American Gangster Film* (New York: Oxford University Press, 2003), 81.

24. Manny Farber, *Farber on Film: The Complete Film Writings of Manny Farber*, ed. Robert Polito (New York: Library of America, 2009), 290.

25. Jans Wager, *Dames in the Driver's Seat* (Austin: University of Texas Press, 2005), 92.

26. Michael Walker, "Robert Siodmak," in *The Book of Film Noir*, ed. Ian Cameron (New York: Continuum, 1992), 113.

27. Wager, *Dames in the Driver's Seat*, 42.

28. Agee, *Film Writing and Selected Journalism*, 252.

29. Joseph Flora, *Ernest Hemingway: A Study of the Short Stories* (Boston: Twayne, 1989), 139.

30. Mary Hemingway, letter to Gene Phillips, August 20, 1978.

31. Melissa Harmon, "Ernest Hemingway: The Man and His Demons," *Biography* 2, no. 5 (May 1998): 93.

32. Eagan, *America's Film Legacy*, 396.

33. Hirsch, *The Dark Side of the Screen*, 117.

34. Andrew Sarris, *The American Cinema: Directors and Directions, 1929–68*, rev. ed. (New York: Da Capo, 1996), 137.

35. Don Siegel, *A Siegel Film* (London: Faber, 2003), 235.

36. Siegel, *A Siegel Film*, 235.

37. James Naremore, *More Than Night: Film Noir in Its Contexts*, rev. ed. (Los Angeles: University of California Press, 2008), 190.

38. Sarris, *The American Cinema*, 137.

39. Silver and Ursini, *The Noir Style*, 249.

40. Geoffrey O'Brien's essay, "*The Killers* (1964)," is included with the DVD of the film (released by Criterion in 2003), 2; it is in the same set with Siodmak's film.

41. Don Siegel, interview with the author, Chicago, November 13, 1979. Any quotation from Siegel that is not attributed to another source is from this interview.

42. Clu Gulager, interview included in the DVD of *The Killers* (1964).

43. Stuart Kaminsky, *Don Siegel, Director* (New York: Curtis Books, 1974), 176.

44. Ronald Schwartz, *Noir, Now and Then* (Westport, Conn.: Greenwood Press, 2001), 34.

45. Shadoian, *Dreams and Dead Ends*, 237.

46. Thomson, *New Biographical Dictionary of Film*, 829.

47. Andrew Tudor, "Don Siegel," in *International Dictionary of Films and Filmmakers*, vol. 2, 466.

CHAPTER NINE

OTTO PREMINGER:
LAURA AND *ANATOMY OF A MURDER*

Charles Derry has observed that the public persona of European-born filmmaker Otto Preminger was that of a Teutonic tyrant, "terrorizing his actors and bullying his subordinates"—an image augmented by his acting appearances as a heel-clicking Nazi in films like Billy Wilder's *Stalag 17* (1953). Derry adds, "It may have been this public persona, more than anything else," that impeded an appreciation of the director's achievements as a worthy film director.[1]

During the 1930s American film executives made periodic trips to Europe in search of fresh talent. Joseph Schenck, the head of Twentieth Century-Fox, interviewed Preminger during a visit to Vienna in the spring of 1935. He was impressed with Preminger's experience in the theater and invited him to come to Hollywood. Preminger accepted Schenck's offer.

Preminger, who hailed from Vienna, as did Fritz Lang and Billy Wilder, followed them to Hollywood a few years after they migrated there. Preminger and the other European exiles remained in Hollywood and contributed to American movies their technical and artistic talent for filmmaking. Film historian Robert Sklar writes, "It's hard to imagine the shape of American cinema without the contribution of" these exiles.[2] In point of fact, foreign directors, precisely because they are not native-born Americans, are sometimes able to view American life with a vigilant, perceptive eye for the kinds of telling details that homegrown directors might easily overlook or simply take for granted. In fact, European directors, like Preminger, were able to catch the authentic atmosphere of the United States as surely as any native-born filmmakers.

When he arrived at Fox in the winter of 1936, Preminger was chosen by Darryl Zanuck, the production chief, to direct two featherweight comedies. Preminger duly became part of the Austrian-German colony in Hollywood. In 1937 he was assigned to direct *Kidnapped*, derived from Robert Louis Stevenson's classic novel. But Preminger had an angry falling-out with Zanuck over the screenplay and was taken off the picture. Zanuck then banished him from the ranks of directors. Preminger saw the handwriting on the wall and left Hollywood; he went on to direct a variety of plays on the New York stage.

Because of his success on Broadway, Preminger was invited back to Fox in the early 1940s with the endorsement of Fox executive William Goetz. Zanuck, who still would not reinstate Preminger as a director, made him a producer instead; and in due course he appointed him to produce *Laura*, a murder mystery, with Rouben Mamoulian (*The Mark of Zorro*) set to direct. *Laura* was relegated by Zanuck to the B-picture unit at Fox, to be made into a low-budget program picture.

Laura (1944)

Preminger was not satisfied with the screenplay of *Laura*, adapted from the 1942 novel by Vera Caspary. So he revised it extensively, in tandem with the screenwriters. He was particularly pleased with the revisions done by Samuel Hoffenstein, who had coscripted the fine film of *The Phantom of the Opera* (1943) with Claude Rains. "Hoffenstein practically created the character of Waldo Lydecker," the waspish, Machiavellian gossip columnist, in the script, Preminger recalls in his autobiography. "From the book we retained only the gimmick of Laura first appearing to be the victim of a murder, and afterward, when she reappears, becoming the chief suspect."[3] Truth to tell, Mark McPherson, the detective in charge of the murder investigation, arrests Laura as a ploy to lure the real killer out in the open.

Vera Caspary took one look at the script and voiced her disappointment with it to Preminger. "Why are you making a B-picture out of my novel?" she inquired. Preminger answered that that was Zanuck's decision, not his.[4] (Film noirs, as we know, were often low-budget films.) Caspary later complained that Preminger "wanted to make it a conventional detective story."[5] She pointed out that Mark McPherson in her novel was a fairly sophisticated police detective, while the script had retooled him into a tight-lipped, uncouth cop, who was born in a low-slung fedora and cheap trench coat.

Caspary was convinced that Preminger had done violence to her book in the screenplay. He responded in his autobiography, where he explains, "When I prepare a story for filming, it is being filtered through my brain. . . . I have no obligation, nor do I try, to be 'faithful' to the book."[6]

Preminger submitted the revised script to Bryan Foy, the executive in charge of the B-picture unit at Fox. Foy rejected the rewrite. "Otto complained that I didn't read the script of *Laura* when I turned it down," Foy told me. "I asked Dave Stevens, my assistant, to read it and to compare notes with me. I subsequently informed Otto that Dave read it and said it was lousy. Otto insisted that I should send the screenplay to Zanuck for his opinion, and so I did."[7]

After Preminger appealed to Zanuck, the latter not only approved the revised screenplay that Preminger had supervised, but personally took over the supervision of the picture from Foy. That meant that *Laura* was automatically placed in the schedule of the A-picture unit.

Zanuck likewise sided with Preminger about the choice of Clifton Webb to play the villain in *Laura*. The casting director had vetoed Webb because he thought Webb effeminate. Preminger countered that the audience would never suspect that the witty and urbane Webb was the murderer, and that would make for a nifty surprise ending.[8] He was right in holding out for Webb, since Webb's polished performance in his screen test impressed Zanuck considerably.

Preminger selected Gene Tierney to play the sultry Laura and Dana Andrews to play the determined police lieutenant Mark McPherson. Tierney and Andrews would both appear in other Preminger film noirs. Indeed, Preminger reteamed them in *Where the Sidewalk Ends* (1950), an underrated noir about a rogue cop (Andrews) who accidentally slays a suspect, and Tierney played the dead man's widow.

Rounding out the cast of *Laura* were Vincent Price as the opportunistic playboy Shelby Carpenter, to whom Laura becomes briefly engaged; and Judith Anderson as Ann Treadwell, Laura's aunt, a socialite who has her sights set on Shelby. Price and Anderson both won plaudits for their performances.

Principal photography commenced on April 27, 1944, with Rouben Mamoulian directing. When Preminger viewed the rushes of each day's shooting, he was simply appalled. Preminger felt that "Mamoulian just didn't understand the picture."[9] Mamoulian was making an old-fashioned, florid melodrama, while Preminger saw the movie as a sleek psychological thriller. He wanted to impart an atmosphere of sleazy chic to this story about the decadent upper crust.

After Zanuck saw the footage that Mamoulian had shot over a period of two weeks, he lifted the ban on Preminger's directing at Fox. Specifically, Zanuck allowed Preminger to replace Mamoulian as director and to produce the picture as well. Preminger commented laconically, "And that is how I became a director again."[10]

Preminger took the reins as director on May 15; he brought along cinematographer Joseph LaShelle, who had shot Clifton Webb's screen test. After Preminger was at the helm, Vincent Price noticed that "Otto gave our characters a feeling of evil underneath their sophistication, a façade these high society people had. When you saw the picture, you realized their characters were essentially very, very evil—beneath their high society veneer." Preminger, Price concluded, understood this in a way that Mamoulian did not.[11]

Thus the film hints that Shelby Carpenter may well be a homosexual who caters to affluent females who can provide him with the finer things in life to which he would like to become accustomed. Shelby goes to the highest bidder, and that turns out to be the wealthy grande dame Ann Treadwell. She states candidly her kinship with Shelby. "He is right for me," she says, "because I can afford him. He's no good, but he's what I want. I'm not a good person; neither is he. So we belong together; we are both weak and can't seem to help it."

Since homosexuality, as we know, was forbidden by the Censorship Code, Joseph Breen, the industry censor, reminded Preminger as producer of the film (as Breen had reminded John Huston about Joel Cairo) that a homosexual character like Waldo Lydecker must be portrayed as a "debonair man about town," and not as a pansy.[12] Preminger did not follow Breen's directive exactly when he took over as director. In the opening sequence Waldo is shown getting dressed up in a dandyish tweed suit, complete with a silk handkerchief for the jacket pocket and a carnation in his lapel, thereby signifying to the alert viewer that he is homosexual. By the same token, Shelby has something of a mincing quality in his demeanor, which is likewise tinged with lavender.

Waldo Lydecker (Clifton Webb) and Laura (Gene Tierney) in Otto Preminger's *Laura.*

Naremore refers to the fact that both Clifton Webb and Vincent Price were homosexual and observes that any film that placed Clifton Webb and Vincent Price "in the same drawing room is inviting a mood of fey theatricality."[13] Foster Hirsch adds in his biography of Preminger that the movie's oblique handling of Waldo's and Shelby's sexuality gives *Laura* intriguing noir shadings."[14]

As a matter of fact, *Laura* is typical of film noir, in the manner in which it examines the dark side of the human condition. It places Preminger in the company of other émigré directors like Lang, Wilder, and Siodmak, who all made significant noirs.

Foster Hirsch opines that "the best *noir* directors were German or Austrian expatriates who shared a world view that was shaped by their bitter personal experiences of . . . escaping from a nation that had lost its mind." In point of fact, "the group of expatriate directors who were to become the masters of the *noir* style," Hirsch continues, brought to their American films a predilection for "stories about man's uncertain fate, and about psychological obsession and derangement."[15]

155

Laura is very much in keeping with the conventions of film noir. The dark world of film noir, notes Barton Palmer in his book on the subject, is one where a woman with a past can encounter a man with no future.[16] That *Laura* was in the vanguard of film noir movies is evident from a seminal essay on film noir written in 1946 by French critic Nino Frank; he terms *Laura* an example of "a new type of crime film" coming out of Hollywood, which he designates as film noir.[17]

Preminger directed a series of excellent film noirs throughout the 1940s and 1950s, but his detractors acknowledge only *Laura* as a worthy noir. They overlook, for example, *Fallen Angel*, with Dana Andrews as a con man in cahoots with a femme fatale (Linda Darnell), as well as *Where the Sidewalk Ends* and *Anatomy of a Murder*. Nevertheless, a limited group of film historians, which includes Andrew Sarris, take Preminger seriously as an artist and recognize his later noirs as "moody, fluid studies in perverse psychology," in the tradition of *Laura*.[18]

When David Raksin was commissioned to compose the background music for *Laura*, Preminger informed him that, for the principal theme of the score, he wanted him to use Duke Ellington's "Sophisticated Lady." Raksin objected that the tune was already too familiar to moviegoers. "So Otto gave me the weekend to come up with a song to replace 'Sophisticated Lady.' Coincidentally, that Saturday I received a letter of farewell from a lady I was in love with. I put the letter on my piano on Sunday evening, . . . and it was in my mind as I began to compose. The tune came to me: The melody of our theme song needed to evoke melancholy, and I had just been given a heavy dose."[19]

Raksin poured all of his feelings of unrequited love into the melody, and the music gave a nostalgic, regretful dimension to the movie's score. Later on Johnny Mercer wrote a lyric for the theme, which is not in the film. The title tune struck a chord with the movie-going public; it subsequently became a standard popular song. Cole Porter even said that, out of all the romantic ballads ever written, he would have liked to have composed the theme from *Laura*.[20]

After Zanuck watched the rough cut of *Laura*, he muttered, "Well, we missed the bus on this one." He especially had misgivings about the last fifteen minutes of the movie, which seemed a little flat. Then Zanuck remembered that Laura herself had narrated a section of the novel.[21] Hence he decided that the last quarter hour of the film should be reshot from Laura's point of view. When Preminger received the revised ending of the script, he thought Laura's monologue in the scene was pointless and confusing. In it Laura contradicts Waldo's account of their first meeting—which is shown in flashback earlier in the film.

In Waldo's version of their first encounter, which he narrates on the sound track, Laura buttonholes him in a restaurant and entreats him to endorse a fountain pen she is promoting in an ad campaign for the advertising agency she works for. Laura tells Mark in the new scene, "That never happened; that is a story Waldo wrote for his column. He likes to make things up; and, once he writes something, he believes it."[22] She says that Waldo first met her in night court, where he was gathering material for his column. She had been arrested for nonpayment of rent, and Waldo bailed her out. She concludes that she will never forget what he did for her.

Preminger told me that he pointed out to Zanuck that the critics would scold the filmmakers for "cheating" the audience by labeling Waldo's flashback as spurious later in the film, since the filmgoer initially accepted it as genuine, when Waldo narrated it earlier in the movie. Moviegoers, after all, usually assume that the camera does not lie. But Zanuck was adamant and insisted that Preminger film the new ending, with Laura's monologue intact.

Zanuck scheduled a private screening of the revised rough cut and invited his friend Walter Winchell, the influential newspaper columnist and radio commentator. After the picture was over, Winchell congratulated Zanuck, saying, "Big time! Great!" Then he said, "But the ending; I didn't get it. You've got to change it." Zanuck turned to Preminger and inquired, "Do you want your old ending back?" Preminger replied, "Of course."[23]

So Preminger excised the scene in which Laura negated Waldo's flashback about how he met her, and the flashback now stood as true and authentic. Preminger was grateful to Winchell for intervening and later repaid him by giving him a cameo appearance in the Joan Crawford vehicle he directed, *Daisy Kenyon* (1947).

Laura begins with Waldo Lydecker, a cynical, sardonic newspaper columnist intoning in a voice-over: "I shall never forget the weekend Laura died. With Laura's horrible death, I was alone—with only my poignant memories of her." Laura is thought to have been murdered when a young woman's corpse is found in her apartment.

157

Mark McPherson, the police detective investigating the case, subconsciously falls in love with the ravishing portrait of Laura that hangs over the mantelpiece in her living room. McPherson is a more complex character than he at first appears.

When Mark prowls around Laura's bedroom, apparently searching for clues about her murder, he sniffs the perfume and fondles the lingerie of the dead enchantress. Barry Norman wonders if there is "a touch of necrophilia in McPherson's obsession with Laura," or a hint of fetishism in his investigation of the girl's apartment. Since these questions are never explicitly answered in the thought-provoking movie, Norman concludes, "Well, yes—or anyway, maybe."[24]

After all, Mark, who is a down-at-the-heels policeman, is bewitched by the portrait of a woman he presumes to be dead. Waldo asks Mark, "Have you sublet her apartment? You are there often enough to pay rent." Then Waldo warns him, "You'll end up in a psychiatric ward. I don't think they've ever had a patient who fell in love with a corpse." Stuart Minnis cites Spencer Selby's astute observation that, at this point in the movie, "Laura's most alluring quality is her unattainability."[25]

Then, in a totally unexpected reversal of events, Laura turns up alive. It develops that the murderer, who had intended to shoot Laura, killed by mistake a girl who was staying in Laura's apartment while Laura herself was out of town. Shelby Carpenter, who ostensibly is courting Laura at the time, had brought her there—unbeknownst to Laura. Because the girl's face was obliterated by the shotgun blast, she was assumed to be Laura.

The milieu of film noir is essentially one of shadows and fog, and is exemplified in *Laura* in the shadowy scene in which McPherson falls asleep in a chair beneath Laura's portrait; he awakens to find Laura, who is very much alive, standing before him for the very first time. For a moment she seems to McPherson to be an apparition rather than a living person. When he realizes that she is the real Laura in the flesh, "she pales somehow beside her ethereal portrait, which remains a more dominant image than the woman herself."[26]

Since the heroine does not make her first appearance in the film until the movie is well under way, Catherine Henry indicates how Preminger nevertheless makes her presence felt by the audience, both visually and aurally, from the outset. For one thing, Laura's portrait hanging over the fireplace dominates several scenes; for another, "a piece of music which she liked—the 'Laura theme'—is played repeatedly." The "haunting quality of both the portrait and the musical theme," Henry concludes, "not only helps to explain the detective's increasing obsession with Laura, . . . but also keeps her foregrounded for the audience as well."[27]

Although Laura is "perfectly groomed and pretty," she is "merely human"; hence Mark is subconsciously disappointed that she is so ordinary, when compared to the "goddess" in the painting.[28] Nevertheless, it gradually becomes clear that Laura and Mark have fallen in love.

The killer is ultimately revealed to be Waldo Lydecker, Laura's former mentor. "The madly jealous Lydecker had been so attached to Laura," Tony Thomas writes, "that he vowed that she should never belong to anyone else"; and so he sought her death, not once, but twice.[29] Laura is for Waldo his prized possession. Consequently, he found her involvement with a callow stud playboy like Shelby Carpenter intolerable.

Waldo likewise recoils when he thinks of her in the arms of Mark McPherson. "The best part of myself; that's what you are," Waldo declares to Laura when he appears in her apartment, prepared to shoot her a second time. "Do you think I am going to leave you to the vulgar pawings of a second-rate detective, who thinks you are a dame?" Mark shows up just in time with another cop, who guns down Waldo before he can blast Laura with his double-barreled shotgun.

Although Laura and Mark clearly plan to marry at film's end, Eugene Archer long ago threw cold water on the movie's happy ending. "One can visualize their future—the tormented detective brooding into his liquor before the omnipresent portrait, while poor, unwitting Laura, the merest shell of his erotic fantasy, ponders her unhappy life."[30] In other words, David Thomson adds, "the Laura who might have had hopes once of being a Madison Avenue socialite, ends up in a trailer park" (like Laura Manion, Laura Hunt's namesake, in *Anatomy of a Murder*), or sitting next to Mark in the bleachers at the ball game.[31]

Laura was judged a top-notch thriller when it opened in October 1944. "The whole film is of a piece," Roger Ebert has since written; it achieves "a kind of perfection in its balance between low motives and high style. The materials of a B-grade crime potboiler are redeemed" by a great cast.[32]

There were a few dissenting voices in the original reviews of the movie. The idiosyncratic critic, Manny Farber, criticized Gene Tierney's performance as possessing "no other qualities than those there are in a fashion mannequin on parade." Yet her Laura is the object of "the kind of gaga-eyed reverence that you find in perfume ads." He also dismissed Dana Andrews's "wooden" performance as Mark McPherson.[33] Liahna Babener (who calls Farber "Manny Farrell") laments his lack of appreciation for Tierney and Andrews, whose performances in this and other Preminger film noirs are still insufficiently appreciated.[34]

But Farber was definitely in the minority among reviewers of the film. Furthermore, Joseph LaShelle won an Academy Award for his cinematography (Preminger and Webb were also nominated).

Perhaps of all the praise that this polished, suspenseful thriller has received, British director Ken Russell said it best. He recalled reflecting, after viewing *Laura* as a teenager, that had he died right after seeing the film, "it would have been with the certain knowledge that *Laura* was better than any British picture I'd ever seen."[35]

Nonetheless, none of the critics of the film when it premiered could have predicted that *Laura* would be considered a landmark in the emerging trend of film noir. Daniel Eagan, in his book on the films incorporated into the National Film Registry, writes that, after *Laura*, Preminger's "greatest successes for the next decade were in film noir," so that Preminger played a significant role in the shaping of film noir.[36]

Film historians usually name *Angel Face* (1952) as marking the last of Preminger's classic noirs and totally overlook *Anatomy of a Murder* (1959). Admittedly, *Angel Face* is an interesting noir, in which Jean Simmons portrays a femme fatale, a psychopath who is doomed to compulsively destroy her loved ones. But *Anatomy of a Murder*, not *Angel Face*, is really the last of Preminger's striking series of noirs, and may possibly be his best. . . .

After a decade at Twentieth Century-Fox, Preminger decided that he would not renew his contract with Fox when it expired, but would set up shop as an independent. By 1953 he was free to become an independent filmmaker. As such, Preminger from now on was at liberty to choose his own subjects for filming and secure financial backing from a major studio, which would then market the finished film through its distribution facilities.

Preminger proved his mettle as an independent producer-director, not only by crusading for the freedom of the screen, but also by performing all the functions required to make and market his films. What's more, he championed the independent filmmakers movement by choosing projects that the major studios were hesitant to tackle. Furthermore, in refusing to make any concessions to the industry censor, Preminger believed that he was defending the fundamental human right of freedom of expression.

We recall that he allowed a homosexual undercurrent to be present in *Laura*, by way of the character of Waldo Lydecker in particular. "I always resisted film censorship," he maintained, "because I believe that the right of free expression is something that we will lose if we do not defend it." He added (no doubt with the Nazi takeover of his native Austria in mind): "Freedom of expression is so important because no totalitarian government has ever been able to exist without strict censorship."

He went on to make films that demonstrated once again that he, more than any other European-born director, sought to gain for the serious filmmaker the right to treat mature subject matter on the screen. If *The Man with the Golden Arm* was Hollywood's first substantial treatment of drug addiction, *Anatomy of a Murder* was Hollywood's first attempt to deal with the subject of rape in frank terms.

But the real significance of the film lies in the fact that it is a superlative courtroom drama. This is due in no small measure to the fact that before coming to America Preminger had earned a law degree at the University of Vienna, which enabled him to depict legal procedures throughout the film in an accurate and precise manner. Perhaps that is why fellow director Barbet Schroeder (*Reversal of Fortune*) said of the film, "I really thought I was seeing a documentary and a drama at the same time."[37]

Anatomy of a Murder (1959)

Preminger's film is an adaptation of the best-selling novel by Robert Traver, aka John Voelker, a retired justice of the Michigan Supreme Court. In 1952, when Voelker was a practicing attorney, he defended Coleman Peterson, a U.S. Army lieutenant who was accused of murdering Mike Chenoweth, a bartender at the Lumberjack Tavern in Big Bay, Michigan, for allegedly raping Peterson's wife. The jury's verdict was that Peterson was "not guilty by reason of insanity."[38]

In 1958 Voelker published a fictionalized account of the trial as *Anatomy of a Murder*. In the novel Voelker became defense lawyer Paul Biegler; Peterson was renamed Lt. Frederick Manion; his wife is Laura; and Chenoweth is Barney Quill.

The author writes in the novel that the murder and subsequent trial took place in the distant Upper Peninsula of Michigan, "a wild, harsh, and broken land," with a forlorn look in the late winter.[39] When Preminger went to Michigan to scout locations for the film, Voelker said later, "he decided to film the entire picture here," interiors as well as exteriors.[40] Preminger's thirst for realism was reflected in his predilection for shooting on location, and for having the cinematographer utilize a newsreel-like style in filming the action.

Preminger was convinced that the special atmosphere of the area could not be re-created on a Hollywood sound stage, "It's not the *look* of the place I want to get on the screen," Preminger explained; "I want the actors to *feel* it, to absorb a sense of what it's like to live here." Transplanting his cast and crew to the Upper Peninsula, he concluded, "will help to make the film more 'real' than any single thing I can do." What's more, "by using only real locales," Richard Griffith writes in his book about the making of the movie, "Preminger made one of the first American movies" ever to be shot entirely on location.[41]

Filming on location had become linked with film noir, with George Cukor shooting scenes on the streets of New York for *A Double Life* and Billy Wilder filming scenes around Los Angeles for *Sunset Boulevard*, in order to strive for a greater sense of realism.

Preminger chose locations in Marquette and Ishpeming, Michigan, including the Lumberjack Tavern itself, to represent the fictitious town of Iron City in the novel. Voelker's own law office, which was in his home, would serve as the law office and home of Paul Biegler in the movie. It is precisely the grim, rugged landscape of the Upper Peninsula, with its bleak skies and weather-beaten houses, that gives the movie the stark look of film noir. In fact, the film's authentic locations reflect the world of film noir, with its succession of sleazy roadhouses, downbeat transient motels, and dingy jails.

When I asked Preminger if he thought of *Anatomy of a Murder* as film noir, he replied, "You are a film historian; I am not. Call it film noir if you like." As a matter of fact, Preminger is best known for the series of dark psychological thrillers that he directed in the 1940s and 1950s, beginning with *Laura*. He was making film noirs, of course, before that term became common outside of France.

Anatomy of a Murder relates to Preminger's postwar noir period, not only because Laura Hunt and Laura Manion share the same first name, but because the prototype of Frederick Manion in *Anatomy* is found in Waldo Lydecker in *Laura*. Both Waldo and Manion jealously obsess over an alluring female. Moreover, Preminger's use of low-key lighting depicts the relationship of Laura Manion and her husband as existing in the shadows. Manion seems to dominate his wife with his possessiveness and sadistic tendency to physical violence. "Is theirs a love story or a sordid relationship?" asks Jeanine Basinger.[42]

A witness testifies in court that Manion had said, referring to his wife, that, when the trial is over, he is going to "kick that bitch from here to kingdom come." Laura frankly admits to Biegler that she is afraid of her husband, but she cannot bring herself to leave him. Their ambiguous relationship remains immersed in darkness throughout the movie. Paul Mayersberg mentions that love relationships in Preminger's cinema sometimes fail because the two parties are "imprisoned in their own states of mind, unable to make contact."[43] This observation certainly is borne out in the relationship of Laura and her husband.

Preminger commissioned Wendell Mayes to write the screenplay for *Anatomy of a Murder*, on the recommendation of Billy Wilder, for whom Mayes had scripted *The Spirit of St. Louis* (1957). Following the book, Wendell Mayes's skillful screenplay is filled with the kind of behind-the-scenes legal maneuverings that keep the story from becoming a battle of words instead of a battle of wits. The plot, simply put: Lieutenant Frederick Manion is accused of murdering Barney Quill, a bartender he claims brutally raped his wife, Laura. Manion's attorney is Paul Biegler, a small-town lawyer who seems to have taken on a case bigger than he can handle.

Throughout the period in which Preminger was directing *Porgy and Bess* in the daytime, Mayes met with him every night to confer about the screenplay. Mayes wrote during the day; and he and Preminger would discuss the script pages he had turned out that day. They did not call it quits until they had worked out the narrative construction "to please us both," Mayes remembered.[44] Furthermore, the script is peopled with a host of cleverly written supporting characters. As it happened, Mayes finished the script on Preminger's birthday, December 5, 1958.

Preminger dispatched the completed screenplay immediately to Geoffrey Shurlock, who had succeeded Joseph Breen as industry censor. When they met on December 8, Shurlock was especially concerned about the candid language used in the trial scenes. Terms such as "sperm" and "penetration" surfaced in the course of the testimony at the trial—words that had never been uttered in a Hollywood film before. In addition, the word "rape" was articulated in the screenplay "more frequently than in any previous American film."[45] Jack Vizzard, Shurlock's chief assistant, remembered that Preminger "drew up a written response that read like a legal document"; he even cited *Black's Law Dictionary*.[46] Preminger contended that the graphic clinical language employed in the dialogue was common in trials involving sexual offenses; the dialogue in question was handled with dignity and taste in the film.

Preminger absolutely refused to eliminate words like "contraception" and "seduce." But he *did* accede to Shurlock's demand that he reduce the number of references to "rape," and he substituted "violation" for "penetration" in the courtroom discussion of rape.[47] Shurlock and his advisor, Jack Vizzard, finally approved the screenplay—"they were tired of fighting with Otto Preminger."[48]

Early on Preminger quarreled with Lana Turner when he was casting the picture. He selected a pair of slacks for her, and she declined to wear them, Preminger recalled. "She wanted to have her costumes done by Jean Louis; I felt that the wife of a second lieutenant couldn't afford Jean Louis."

Preminger reminded Lana Turner that she was no longer at MGM, where she had made *The Postman Always Rings Twice* (1946). In that film noir Turner insisted on wearing glamorous outfits, even though she was playing a waitress in a roadside diner. Preminger pointed out rather harshly that he was an independent producer-director, and she would wear whatever he chose for her. She thought he was bluffing, he concluded, "but I never am."[49] With that, Preminger cancelled her contract. Twelve hours later Lee Remick was signed to play Laura Manion, since she had the ability to look both trashy and wholesome. Laura Manion is a promiscuous wife, and Lee Remick was at her best displaying a come-hither look.

Otherwise, the casting process went smoothly. James Stewart accepted the role of Paul Biegler, a provincial Michigan lawyer, "an All-American guy" who reflects the grassroots virtues of honor and simplicity. And yet he is canny and shrewd, and not to be taken for granted. Stewart biographer Marc Eliot writes that "the always wholesome actor gave the film the necessary moral heft it needed to balance out its increasingly sordid plot."[50]

To offset the familiar faces of actors like James Stewart in the cast, Preminger selected some New York stage actors, on the theory that the general public would not associate them with other roles they had played. Preminger signed Ben Gazzara to play the defendant, Lt. Manion, because he possessed a menacing quality that implied that Manion was prone to violence. George C. Scott was given the role of the slick, big-time special prosecutor from Lansing, Claude Dancer.

Preminger pulled a casting coup in convincing a well-known lawyer, Joseph N. Welch, to play Judge Weaver in the film. Michael Sragow dismissed Preminger's casting of a real lawyer in the film as a "gimmick."[51] But Preminger offered a different explanation: "The reason that I approached Welch," he said, "was that no first-rate actor that I wanted to play the part, such as Spencer Tracy, would accept it, because they thought it was too small. My assistant suggested that I ask a real-life lawyer, and I thought of Welch, who was famous for his role in the televised hearings that led to Senator Joseph McCarthy's censure by the Senate."[52] Welch's rebuke to McCarthy—"At long last, have you no decency, sir?"—spelled the beginning of the end of McCarthy's career. "I called him in Boston and sent him the script, and he agreed to play the part." Welch brought to the role, Preminger concluded, an authenticity that "no professional actor could have matched."

Preminger's director of photography, Sam Leavitt, who had already photographed three previous Preminger pictures, had just won an Oscar for *The Defiant Ones* (1958). Leavitt managed to pack an enormous amount of visual detail into the compositions of his shots, even though the movie was not in widescreen, as some reviews said.

In order to avoid the inclement weather when principal photography began on March 23, 1959, Preminger arranged to shoot the trial scenes first. He used the local courthouse in Marquette, Michigan, which added to the naturalistic flavor of the film. The courtroom scenes were shot in chronological order, thereby enabling the actors to build their parts throughout the trial sequences.

Hollywood columnists reported that Preminger had foregone his "Gestapo" tactics in directing actors during the shoot. But Ben Gazzara remembered Preminger as maintaining a "German formality" on the set. Nevertheless, "the occasional eruptions," said George C. Scott, "were with the technical people, not with the actors."[53] Principal photography wrapped on May 15, 1959.

Film editor Louis Loeffler, like Sam Leavitt, was a Preminger veteran; he has in fact cut most of the movies Preminger had directed since

Laura. Because Preminger wanted to release *Anatomy of a Murder* while the novel was still a best seller, he had Loeffler edit the film during the shooting period, instead of waiting until the completion of filming to cut the picture during postproduction.

Preminger selected Duke Ellington to score the movie. Contrary to the customary Hollywood practice, Preminger had Ellington come to Michigan during the shooting period for ongoing conferences about the score. "By watching the progress of the shooting," Preminger explained, the composer "becomes part of the film."[54] So Ellington finished his score, which he had written throughout filming, shortly after the production wrapped. Peter Bogdanovich writes that Ellington's score "remains extraordinarily fresh and modern nearly half a century later."[55]

Geoffrey Shurlock passed *Anatomy of a Murder* without any trouble, because Preminger had discussed the picture with him in detail at the script stage. Moreover, the Legion of Decency approved the movie as suitable for mature audiences. A legion spokesman, Father Patrick Sullivan, under whose influence the legion was becoming more enlightened in its approach to serious, artistic motion pictures, remembered that the adroit defense attorney, Paul Biegler, "was the moral compass of the picture." He further noted that, while *Anatomy of a Murder* was "definitely not family entertainment," any subject can be proper material for the screen "if treated with the kind of discretion and artistry that this movie exhibits."[56]

Nonetheless, Preminger was not yet out of the woods. Some local censorship boards still existed across the country. We recall that Fritz Lang ran afoul of the New York board of censors with *Scarlet Street*. Preminger learned that the Chicago censor board was considering banning *Anatomy* if he did not delete certain words from the film. Having made some excisions in the script for the industry censor, Preminger was not prepared to make additional concessions at the behest of the Chicago censor board.

Preminger flew to Chicago and had a conference with police chief Timothy O'Connor, who was also the head of the Chicago board. "My board suggests five cuts," he declared, "but I will settle for just one." Chief O'Connor demanded that the word "contraception" be eliminated, because "I would not want my eighteen-year-old daughter to go to a movie and hear that word."[57] Preminger refused, and the Chicago censor accordingly banned *Anatomy of a Murder* in Chicago.

But Preminger, ever the attorney-at-law, brought suit against the City of Chicago in the Federal District Court of Illinois. Judge Julius Miner viewed the movie with his two preteen sons and reversed the Chicago censor's decision, declaring that the Chicago censor "had exceeded constitutional bounds" in banning the film, which did not undermine public morality.[58] Preminger commented, "The days of arbitrary censorship were coming to an end."

As David Thomson makes clear in discussing the film, Manion is a calculating, insolent individual who barely troubles to conceal his own violent nature, and his wife "makes no effort to disguise her provocative sensuality."[59] After sizing up Lieutenant Manion's wife, the filmgoer cannot help wondering if the flirtatious Laura Manion might not have invited Barney Quill's advances. In that case, Manion would have been more wronged by his wife than by Barney Quill, the man he killed.

The first time Biegler meets Laura, she is wearing dark glasses to hide her black eye. Laura claims that Barney Quill gave her the shiner when he took her against her will. It is also feasible, legal experts Paul Bergman and Michael Asimow state, that her husband gave Laura the black eye when he made her admit that she had willingly made love with Barney Quill, and that he deliberately killed Quill in a jealous rage. "Together they concocted the rape story to cover their tracks."[60]

Preminger once said that his films are often about people who are neither black nor white, but "infinite shades of gray"; *Anatomy of a Murder* is patently no exception to this rule. Like Jean Renoir, Preminger firmly believed that everyone has their reasons for what they do, though their motives are not always easy to discern.[61]

Anatomy of a Murder, according to V. F. Perkins, is a salient example of how Preminger attempts in his films to portray "characters, actions, and issues clearly and without prejudice." More precisely, in the present film "Preminger presents the evidence, but he leaves the spectator free to draw his own conclusions."[62] In other words, the audience is asked to become the jury and to decide to what extent each of the key characters who figures in the trial is telling the truth. That is no easy task.

Preminger opted against portraying Laura's rape in flashback; instead, Biegler asks her to show him the site of the assault one evening. The director employs German expressionism in this scene. Leavitt's noirish low-key lighting creates a dark, sinister atmosphere in this wooded area; Biegler and Laura are enveloped in almost total darkness. The expressionistic lighting emphasizes symbolically how Quill sought to hide his evil deed under a cloak of darkness.

Jeanine Basinger endorses Preminger's decision not to depict in flash-back the fateful night on which Laura contends that she was raped. If the filmgoer were permitted to see the episode as Laura describes it in her testimony, they would have no doubts about what happened. "Not having seen the event through flashback," Basinger continues, leaves the viewer no choice "but to listen carefully to Laura's description of it and try to determine if she is telling the truth."[63]

It is precisely in this fashion that Preminger puts the audience in the position of the jury, forcing them to make up their own minds about *all* of the testimony presented at the trial. In brief, the unique merit of the film is that none of the issues is permitted to be clear cut for the sake of a lazy audience. Preminger depicts the characters as complex and inscrutable human beings whose motives are open to question.

Laura testifies that Quill "tore my panties off and did what he wanted." At the first mention of the word "panties" the crowd in the courtroom bursts into raucous laughter. So Judge Weaver delivers instructions from the bench to those present. Since Joseph Welch addresses himself directly to the camera, it is evident that the instructions are for the filmgoers as well:

"For the benefit of the jury, and especially the spectators," the record will show that "the undergarment referred to in the testimony was her panties. When this pair of panties is mentioned again in the course of this trial, there will not be one snicker, or even one smirk in my courtroom. There isn't anything comic about a pair of panties which figures in the violent death of one man and the possible incarceration of another."

Once the question of the panties has been raised in court, Biegler calls Mary Pilant (Kathryn Grant), the manager of the Thunder Bay Inn where the slain bartender was employed, as a witness for the defense. She testifies that she found a pair of torn panties, which Quill had apparently hurled down the motel's laundry chute. Mary then produces the tattered panties in open court. Claude Dancer, the special prosecutor, in cross-examining Mary, attempts to discredit her testimony by accusing her of being Quill's spurned mistress. Mary is reduced to tears and reveals that Barney Quill was her father; she was his illegitimate daughter. Mary was painfully aware that he was quite capable of violent behavior; he must have ripped off the panties during a brutal sexual act.

Defense Attorney Paul Biegler (James Stewart) confronts witness Mary Pilant (Kathryn Grant) in Preminger's *Anatomy of a Murder*.

As Bergman and Asimow point out, "A cross-examiner is never supposed to ask a question to which he doesn't know the answer. Here Dancer does not know of the actual relationship between Quill and Mary Pilant," and should not have cavalierly assumed that he did.[64] With that, a verdict favorable to Lt. Manion seems almost assured.

In photographing this courtroom drama, Preminger often employs long takes, in order to allow the camera to move around and thus keep the film from looking static and stagey. During these long takes Preminger cleverly works the camera around the actors as it unobtrusively glides about the courtroom, so that the pace of action never slackens.

An extended take, uninterrupted by cuts to other angles, enables an actor to give a sustained reading of a long speech, and thus build it steadily to a dramatic climax. There is, for example, the scene in which Paul Biegler and his assistants are waiting for the verdict. His principal assistant is Parnell McCarthy (Arthur O'Connell), a has-been lawyer whose once-keen legal mind has been dulled by alcohol. McCarthy ruminates about juries while he and the defense team await the verdict.

"Twelve people from twelve different walks of life go off into a room. . . . These twelve people are asked to judge another human being, as different from them as they are from each other. And in their judgment, they must become as one mind: unanimous. It's one of the miracles of man's disorganized soul that they can do it—and in most instances do it right well. God bless juries." These observations constitute a tribute by Preminger, the trained lawyer, to due process of law. And the fact that Preminger encompasses McCarthy's lengthy speech in a single unbroken take makes O'Connell's delivery of it all the more effective.

The jury's verdict, when it finally comes, declares the defendant not guilty. From the beginning of the trial, Biegler has been aware that if he is to get his client acquitted, he has to come up with a justifiable reason for this act of homicide. The reasonable cause that Biegler ultimately hits upon is, in fact, suggested by Manion himself. Manion claims that he is not guilty by reason of temporary insanity. To be more specific, throughout the trial Biegler pleads that Manion has been driven by an "irresistible impulse" to kill Barney Quill. In the end, the jury sides with Biegler and agrees with him that the accused is innocent.

Claude Dancer, the big-city lawyer, had been confident that he could demolish the less sophisticated Biegler's defense of Manion. But, as Basinger shrewdly observes, Biegler wins at least partly because, "unlike Dancer, he lives in the town where the trial is taking place and knows the kinds of people who are on the jury."[65] Perkins reminds us that "our primary involvement is with the lawyer, not his client." We are gratified that Biegler has won his case, not necessarily that he got Manion off.[66] In fact the film celebrates the rural-American virtues of honesty and folk wisdom of the unpretentious Biegler.

Nevertheless, Preminger ends the movie with a sly twist that implicitly casts doubt upon the verdict. When Biegler goes to the trailer camp where the Manions have been living, he finds that they have skipped town without paying his fee. The only souvenir they have left behind is a note from the husband, informing Biegler that he was seized by "an irresistible impulse" to get out of town. Biegler is left at film's end in a quandary: if an irresistible impulse is a convenient excuse for Manion to cheat Biegler out of his fee, perhaps, in the last analysis, it was likewise a convenient excuse for Manion to murder Quill. After all, it was Manion himself who suggested the plea of temporary insanity to Biegler in the first place. At the fade-out, Biegler is no longer certain that Manion was innocent.

The ambiguous ending of *Anatomy of a Murder* is typical of the somber, cynical vision of life reflected in film noir. Indeed, film noirs present a pessimistic outlook that emphasizes the grim, dark side of life. Thus *Anatomy* is a tale of a murder trial that ends with the thought that a killer may have gone scot-free.

In most of Preminger's films, writes Murray Smith, there is no doubt by film's end what motives have driven the characters; for example, in *Laura* it becomes evident that Waldo was motivated by jealousy to try to murder Laura. But in *Anatomy of a Murder*, "the ambiguities are sustained and left ambiguities at the end of the film."[67]

In 1962 Preminger screened *Anatomy of a Murder* in Moscow, at the invitation of the Russian Film Academy. Preminger stated after the screening that he personally concurred with the jury's verdict at the trial. In fact, when a Russian filmmaker insisted with Preminger that Manion should have been convicted, he replied, "The evidence was not conclusive; and in our country a man is presumed to be innocent until he is proved guilty beyond a shadow of a doubt."[68]

Anatomy of a Murder was, like *Laura*, an enormous success. After its premiere on July 7, 1959, the film earned over $5 million in domestic rentals, plus another $1 million in foreign markets. The picture also received seven Academy Award nominations: acting nominations for James Stewart, Arthur O'Connell, and George C. Scott, as well as nominations for cinematographer Sam Leavitt, editor Louis Loeffler, and screenwriter Wendell Mayes. The nomination that went to Preminger as producer of the film was that for best picture. But, because the academy membership was "made up of older, more conservative members," who shied away from voting for such a controversial picture, *Anatomy* won no Oscars at all.[69]

Stewart's performance, however, did receive a Golden Lion when the film was shown at the 1959 Venice Film Festival. And rightly so; with his portrayal of an easygoing but cagey rural attorney, Stewart etched a depiction of a trial lawyer that would be hard to surpass.

It is hard to fathom why *Anatomy* has been denied the status of one of Preminger's major film noirs. Paul Mayersberg, in his penetrating essay on Preminger's noirs, for example, excludes *Anatomy*.[70] Curiously, the movie has often been classified as a murder mystery—even though there is simply no mystery whatever about who committed the sole murder in the picture! Nash and Ross offer one of the few assessments of the film that correctly pegs it as a "slick, terse noir."[71]

Be that as it may, the majority of commentators on the movie consider it as one of Preminger's finest achievements. Little wonder that Basinger terms *Anatomy* "a perfect lesson in law and a piece of first-class movie entertainment."[72] As such, the picture richly deserves to be called, in this writer's view, one of the greatest courtroom dramas ever made, and Preminger's masterpiece as well. In fact, film noirs like *Laura* and *Anatomy of a Murder* move one to reconsider problematic noirs like *Angel Face*.

And so, despite Preminger's public image as a harsh, arrogant "storm trooper" (an image Lana Turner certainly endorsed), film historians in recent years have been willing to grant him an honored place in the pantheon of American directors. He is also a major contributor to the classic period of film noir.

Notes

1. Charles Derry, "Otto Preminger," in *International Dictionary of Films and Filmmakers*, vol. 6, 398; see also Dave Kehr, "A Tyrant with a Focus on Love's Uncertainty," *New York Times*, December 30, 2007, sec. 2:23.

2. Robert Sklar, "The Ufa Story," *New York Times Book Review*, October 13, 1996, 20; see also John Russell Taylor, *Strangers in Paradise: The Hollywood Emigrés* (New York: Holt, Rinehart, and Winston, 1983), 16.

3. Otto Preminger, *Preminger: An Autobiography* (Garden City, N.Y.: Doubleday, 1977), 72.

4. *Preminger: An Autobiography*, 72.

5. Vera Caspary, "My *Laura* and Otto's," *Saturday Review*, June 26, 1971, 36.

6. *Preminger: An Autobiography*, 111.

7. Bryan Foy, interview by the author, Los Angeles, September 4, 1975.

8. Otto Preminger, interview by the author, New York, April 22, 1979. Any quotations from Preminger that are not attributed to another source are from this interview.

9. Chris Fujiwara, *The World and Its Double: The Life and Work of Otto Preminger* (New York: Faber and Faber, 2008), 40.

10. Gerald Pratley, *The Cinema of Otto Preminger* (New York: Barnes, 1971), 61.

11. Gregory Catsos, "Priceless: A Farewell Interview with Vincent Price," *Filmfax* 42, no. 6 (December 1993–January 1994), 46.

12. Memo dated November 2, 1943, Production Code Administration Archive, at the Margaret Herrick Library of the Motion Picture Academy.

13. Naremore, *More Than Night*, 98.

14. Foster Hirsch, *Otto Preminger: The Man Who Would Be King* (New York: Knopf, 2007), 113.

15. Hirsch, *The Dark Side of the Screen*, 115.

16. Barton Palmer, *Hollywood's Dark Cinema: The American Film Noir* (New York: Twayne, 1994), 52.

17. Frank, "The Crime Adventure Story," 21.

18. Sarris, *The American Cinema*, 105.

19. Hirsch, *Otto Preminger*, 106–7.

20. Timm, *The Soul of Cinema*, 118.

21. See Vera Caspary, *Laura*, in *Laura, Bedelia, Evvie: 3 Novels* (New York: Houghton Mifflin, 1992); the narrators of *Laura* are Waldo Lydecker, Mark McPherson, and Laura Hunt.

22. Fujiwara, *The World and Its Double*, 45.

23. Bogdanovich, *Who the Devil Made It*, 620.

24. Barry Norman, *The One Hundred Best Films* (New York: Carol, 1997), 163.

25. Stuart Minnis, *"Laura,"* in *The Encyclopedia of Novels into Film*, 240.

26. Nicholas Christopher, *Somewhere in the Night: Film Noir and the American City* (New York: Free Press, 1997), 247.

27. Catherine Henry, *"Laura,"* in *International Dictionary of Films and Filmmakers*, vol. 1, 564.

28. Jim Hillier, *"Laura,"* in Hillier and Phillips, *100 Film Noirs*, 161.

29. Thomas, *The Films of the Forties*, 129.

30. Eugene Archer, *"Laura," Movie* 1, no. 2 (September 1962), 13. This essay is one of the eleven articles in the special Preminger issue of *Movie*.

31. David Thomson, "Impulse: Otto Preminger," *Sight and Sound* 15 (ns), no. 5 (May 2005): 33; see also Julie Kirgo, *"Laura,"* in *Film Noir: The Encyclopedia*, 177.

32. Ebert, *The Great Movies II*, 241.

33. Farber, *Farber on Film*, 197–98.

34. Liahna Babener, *"Laura*: Novel to Film," in *It's a Print: Detective Fiction from Page to Screen* (Bowling Green, Ohio: Bowling Green State University Press, 1994), 89.

35. Ken Russell, *The Lion Roars: Ken Russell on Film* (Boston: Faber and Faber, 1994), 16.

36. Eagan, *America's Film Legacy*, 377.

37. Holly Sorensen, "The Ten Best Courtroom Dramas," *Premiere* 7, no. 6 (June 1994): 119. *Anatomy of a Murder* is numbered among the top ten courtroom dramas ever made; the list was drawn up by a jury of both lawyers and filmmakers, headed by attorney F. Lee Bailey.

38. Shirley Bergman, "The Reel Trial," *Michigan History* (November–December, 2001): 90–91.

39. Robert Traver, *Anatomy of a Murder* (New York: St. Martin's Press, 1958), 1.

40. Robert Traver, "Preface," in Richard Griffith, *Anatomy of a Motion Picture* (New York: St. Martin's Press, 1959), 1.

41. Griffith, *Anatomy of a Motion Picture*, 25–26, 28.

42. Jeanine Basinger, "*Anatomy of a Murder*: Life and Art in the Courtroom," in *Columbia Pictures: Portrait of a Studio*, ed. Bernard Dick (Lexington: University Press of Kentucky, 1992), 180.

43. Paul Mayersberg, "From *Laura* to *Angel Face*," in *Movie Reader*, ed. Ian Cameron (New York: Praeger, 1972); this book reprints six of the eleven articles from the special Preminger issue of *Movie* (September 1962).

44. Rui Nogueria, "Wendell Mayes," in *Backstory 3: Interviews with Screenwriters of the 1960s*, ed. Patrick McGilligan (Los Angeles: University of California Press, 1997), 263.

45. Hirsch, *Otto Preminger*, 311.

46. Jack Vizzard, interview by the author, Berlin, May 19, 1977.

47. Walsh, *Sin and Censorship*, 292.

48. Louis Giannetti and Scott Eyman, *Flashback: A Brief History of Film*, rev. ed. (Boston: Allyn and Bacon, 2010), 183.

49. Bogdanovich, *Who the Devil Made It*, 631.

50. Marc Eliot, *Jimmy Stewart: A Biography* (New York: Random House, 2006), 330.

51. Michael Sragow, "*Anatomy of a Murder*," *New Yorker*, May 16, 1994, 36.

52. For further background on Senator Joseph McCarthy's witch hunt for communists and his subsequent censure by the Senate, see Giannetti and Eyman, *Flashback*, 182–85.

53. Hirsch, *Otto Preminger*, 308–9.

54. *Preminger: An Autobiography*, 156.

55. Peter Bogdanovich, *Who the Hell's in It: Hollywood's Legendary Actors* (New York: Ballantine Books, 2006), 425.

56. Father Patrick Sullivan, interview by the author, New York, January 28, 1977.

57. *Preminger: An Autobiography*, 157.

58. Dawn Sova, *Forbidden Films: Censorship* (New York: Facts on File, 2001), 18.

59. Thomson, *New Biographical Dictionary of Film*, 779.

60. Paul Bergman and Michael Asimow, *Reel Justice: The Courtroom Goes to the Movies* (Kansas City, Mo.: Andrews and McMeel, 1996), 234.

61. Basinger, "*Anatomy of a Murder*," 170; see also Thomson, *New Biographical Dictionary of Film*, 715.

62. V. F. Perkins, "Why Preminger?" in *Movie Reader*, 43.

63. Basinger, "*Anatomy of a Murder*," 176.

64. Bergman and Asimow, *Reel Justice*, 236.

65. Basinger, "*Anatomy of a Murder*," 180.

66. V. F. Perkins, *Film as Film* (New York: Penguin, 1978), 148.

67. Murray Smith, *Engaging Characters: Fiction, Emotion, and the Cinema* (New York: Oxford University Press, 1995), 184.

68. Willi Frischauer, *Behind the Scenes of Otto Preminger* (New York: Morrow, 1974), 181.

69. Eliot, *Jimmy Stewart*, 332.

70. Paul Mayersberg, "From *Laura* to *Angel Face*," 44–46.

71. Nash and Ross, eds., "*Anatomy of a Murder*," in *Motion Picture Guide*, vol. 1, 63.

72. Basinger, "*Anatomy of a Murder*," 181.

CHAPTER TEN

FRED ZINNEMANN: *ACT OF VIOLENCE*
STANLEY KUBRICK: *THE KILLING*

red Zinnemann broke into motion pictures in 1929 by collaborating on *Menschen am Sonntag*, a semidocumentary made in Berlin, as the assistant cameraman. This was the same film that gave Billy Wilder and Robert Siodmak their start in the movie business as well. Like Wilder, Zinnemann was an Austrian, working in the Berlin film industry, who immigrated to Hollywood after Hitler took over the German film industry.

Menschen am Sonntag, in retrospect, can be seen as a forerunner of the trend in American film toward greater realism that followed World War II, a trend that Zinnemann was very much a part of. Zinnemann sought to establish himself in Hollywood primarily by making documentary shorts at MGM from 1937 to 1941. Jack Ellis writes that Zinnemann consequently "remained close to the documentary impulse of *Menschen am Sonntag* when he graduated from making short documentaries to directing features."[1] He started with a low-budget whodunit called *Kid Glove Killer* (1942), starring Van Heflin as a police scientist who solves a murder.

Zinnemann moved on to making more important pictures like *The Search* (1948), a solid realistic drama about displaced European children after World War II. It was the first film that he had shot in Berlin since *Menschen am Sonntag*. The strong realism of *The Search* coincided with the movement toward naturalism in American cinema in postwar Hollywood. Zinnemann's "documentary impulse" inspired him to take a documentary-like approach to making fiction films. Silver and Ursini sum up the situation in Hollywood at the time that Zinnemann made his first film noir, *Act of Violence*. Film noirs were often low-budget pictures, "which dictated

177

the recycling of existing sets, . . . and generally minimizing shooting times." European "refugees" like Zinnemann "helped to refine film noir's distinctive visual style," not just with low-key photography, but with German expressionism.[2]

Zinnemann made a series of three movies about the postwar disillusionment associated with the readjustment of American veterans to civilian life. He recalled, "There were some American veterans with psychological scars that they developed during the war," as depicted in *Act of Violence*.[3]

Act of Violence (1948)

Zinnemann made a trio of semidocumentaries about the rehabilitation of American GIs after World War II. The trilogy begins with *Act of Violence*, in which Frank Enley, an ex-GI, is stalked by another ex-soldier, Joe Parkson, who bears him a grudge that goes back to their days in a Nazi prisoner-of-war camp. At that time Frank had betrayed Joe's escape plans for himself and some fellow prisoners to the camp commandant. Since the war Frank has been trying to bury the past by becoming a responsible member of his small-town community, but the arrival of Joe precludes this.

The trilogy continued with *The Men* (1950), with Marlon Brando in his film debut as a paraplegic vet; and *Teresa* (1951), about an Italian war bride married to a GI. All three movies are film noirs, working within the documentary format (called docu-noirs).

The problems of returning veterans, after all, were a staple of postwar noirs. "The veteran, suffering from wounds, both external and internal," Hirsch says, "is one of noir's most vulnerable figures."[4] *Act of Violence* is the best film noir in Zinnemann's trio of films about maladjusted war veterans. Yet, as Paul Arthur attests, the film was "critically neglected and rarely screened" for years. It has only become regarded as a superior noir relatively recently.[5]

The "docu-noir" tradition, which these films exemplify, represent a combination of documentary realism and film noir, intended to give a documentary realism to a film noir. (Preminger's *Anatomy of a Murder*, filmed in the Upper Peninsula of Michigan, is a late docu-noir.) Docu-noirs tend to portray a frank, unglamorous version of the human condition that is often reflected in the shabby settings of the movies. Furthermore, the directors of these films peopled the noir landscape with troubled and desperate characters. "A seedy back room, a bottle of cheap booze, a glaring overhead light, unshaven men dressed in rumpled suits"—these details tell us we are "in the world of film noir."[6]

In 1947 James Agee applauded the tendency in Hollywood movies to be shot, "not in painted studio sets, but in actual places."[7] Zinnemann shot several sequences of *Act of Violence* in actual Los Angeles surroundings, imparting a sober realism to the movie. For example, he used Santa Monica, California, for the scenes set in Santa Lisa, the suburb where Frank lives; Big Bear Lake stands in for Red Wood Lake, where Frank goes fishing; and the scenes in which Frank wanders in the squalid Los Angeles slums were filmed in the old Bunker Hill district of the city. This was a popular location for film noirs because of its aging buildings, which had a faded, deteriorated look, and its dilapidated flophouses. Film noirs "took to the streets of real cities," adds Foster Hirsch. "The location thrillers gave the action the look of an on-the-spot journalistic report."[8]

In the course of *Act of Violence* Frank Enley hides from the light of day in the depths of the shadowy urban underworld. The film offers a sharp contrast between the grim downtown area and the suburban haven where Frank lives with his wife, Edith, and their child. The darkness that gradually envelops Frank's idyllic home "is an image of the persisting shadow cast" by Frank's past on him and his family.[9]

Paul Arthur astutely notices that *Act of Violence* came from MGM, an unlikely studio. Compared to Universal or Fox, "MGM was a cautious latecomer to the volatile field of late-1940s crime melodrama. . . . Under the newly installed head of production Dore Schary," MGM did make a few film noirs.[10] But, *Act of Violence* at the outset did not seem a very promising project. After all, the screenplay was by a marginal screenwriter, Robert Richards, and it was derived from an unpublished story by Collier Young, a former assistant to Columbia mogul Harry Cohn.

Still, the movie had an up-and-coming director who had made *The Search*, and an experienced director of photography, Robert Surtees (*Thirty Seconds over Tokyo*). Moreover, Richards managed to come up with a taut, highly compressed screenplay. Once Joe arrives in California, the plot unfolds in just two days and nights.

The movie "begins in daylight, in unthreatening surroundings," and ends a couple of nights later in a seamier environment, as Frank wanders the empty inner-city streets, "desperately seeking a hiding place."[11] David

Thomson is one of the few film historians who recognizes how Richards's "tough, tight script, done economically and effectively," pitilessly depicts a story "crowded with weak people and desperate compromises." This is one of the few Zinnemann pictures devoid of hope, in which the protagonist "cannot avoid being destroyed by consequences."[12] As such, *Act of Violence* is typical of film noir, presenting as it does a man whose life is disrupted by his own weakness and misfortune.

The film's opening scenes, as portrayed in the script, are riveting. The hardened war veteran, Joe Parkson, wears a trench coat and a snap-brim fedora that immediately suggest film noir. The disabled veteran has a limp; his physical affliction is symbolic of his twisted personality; that is, his mind is crippled. Joe lives in a seedy, cold water flat in a New York slum, which is portrayed with the gritty realism of the docu-noirs of the period.

Joe soon catches a Greyhound bus for California, where he plans to kill an old army buddy, Frank Enley, who is now an admired citizen living in the sunny Los Angeles suburb of Santa Lisa. As Joe leaves the bus station in Santa Lisa and crosses the street to his hotel, he has to make way for the Memorial Day parade, while some elderly veterans march by, proudly displaying the American flag.

Zinnemann commented, "I liked the idea of this man, who was the veteran of an inhuman experience in the war, having to step back because a few old guys were walking past him, carrying the American flag, as though they owned it."[13] Joe first traces Frank to Red Wood Lake, where Frank is fishing. As soon as Frank spots Joe, rowing in broad daylight on the placid lake, he realizes that Joe has pursued him to California with vengeance on his mind; Frank panics and hurries back to town.

Frank arrives home at nightfall, and Robert Surtees's cinematography gives the encroaching darkness an atmosphere of foreboding. "The script offered a great range of possibilities for visual treatment," Zinnemann writes in his autobiography; "they were thoroughly explored by Bob Surtees, our cameraman."[14] Zinnemann first met Surtees in Berlin in the mid-1920s, when Surtees came over from Hollywood to serve his apprenticeship as a camera assistant at a Berlin studio. By the time Surtees photographed *Act of Violence*, he was recognized as one of Hollywood's most reliable cinematographers.

Although *Act of Violence*, like many film noirs, had a limited budget, Zinnemann could still afford to fill the key role with seasoned actors. He chose Van Heflin, who had appeared in Zinnemann's first feature, *Kid*

Glove Killer, to play Frank Enley. Heflin had already won a best supporting actor Oscar for his own film noir, *Johnny Eager* (1941). The director cast Robert Ryan as Joe Parkson. "Ryan's angular, sharp facial features, his ability to convincingly suggest violence and seething hatred" had made him one of film noir's most prominent villains.[15] Yet these roles were at complete variance with his real nature, which was very benign. "I like stories about guys who get knocked around," Ryan explained, "because most people do get knocked around"—Joe Parkson was crippled in the Nazi POW camp.[16]

Mary Astor, the legendary temptress of *The Maltese Falcon*, gives a peerless performance in the present film in the role of Pat, a tired streetwalker who gives Frank shelter as he flees from Joe's vengeance. She recalled that she actually found the dress she wore in the movie "on the rack at the cheapest department store. We made the hem uneven, put a few cigarette burns and some stains on the front." Astor also wore an unbecoming wig and "used too much lipstick and too much mascara." Surtees obligingly employed unflattering lighting to help her look like a hooker past her prime.[17] Pat is drawn to try and help Frank because he is, like herself, an unlucky traveler in the urban netherworld.

The musical score was provided by another émigré from Hitler's Germany, the Polish composer Bronislau Kaper. He had scored some romantic films in Hollywood, but he preferred darkly serious movies like Orson Welles's *The Stranger* (1946) and *Act of Violence*. The jagged theme Kaper provided for the scene in which Frank first meets up with Pat, the shady barfly, in a dive is particularly noteworthy. Zinnemann noted that "the score was conducted by a promising young musician—none other than André Previn," who would become a film composer in his own right.[18]

At the beginning of the movie Frank Enley is known as a prominent local citizen of Santa Lisa, where he has been instrumental in the building of prefabricated houses to accommodate returning veterans and their families. Frank has done so in order to expiate his act of cowardice during the war. "It is no coincidence that Frank is a builder," writes Wheeler Dixon; "he has built a new life for himself in Santa Lisa," where he lives with his wife and son.[19]

But Joe knows Frank only as "a stool pigeon for the Nazis." When Frank explains to his wife Edith (Janet Leigh) why Joe is stalking him, he says that while he was a prisoner of war during World War II he informed on Joe and some other prisoners who planned to escape from the

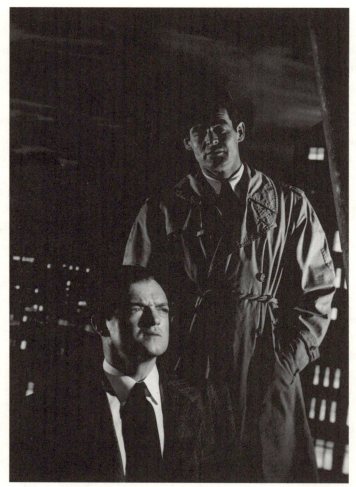

Frank Enley (Van Heflin) is menaced by Joe Parkson (Robert Ryan) in Fred Zinnemann's *Act of Violence* (1949).

internment camp. Frank made a deal with the SS commandant of the camp to spare the lives of the prisoners involved in the escape. But the Nazis ruthlessly killed the ten men attempting to escape—except for Joe, who survived as a cripple. Frank ultimately confesses to his wife that he suspected all along that the camp commandant would not keep his word and let the escapees live. "I was an informer!" he shouts.

In order to avoid a deadly confrontation with Joe, Frank takes off for a builders' convention at the Blake Hotel in Los Angeles. Meanwhile,

Ann Sturges (Phyllis Thaxter), Joe's fiancée, follows him to his hotel in Santa Lisa and pleads with him to give up his plan to liquidate Frank. To no avail; Joe in turn follows Frank to the Blake Hotel. When Frank encounters Joe at the convention, he again panics and runs out of the hotel into the pitch-black night. Frank in effect is descending into the dark underworld of Los Angeles.

Frank's entry into Los Angeles's netherworld symbolizes his downhill spiral into moral degeneracy; it is "punctuated by an endless series of descents down one staircase after another." Frank's passage through the lower depths of Los Angeles "is among the most mordantly gripping, gorgeously composed episodes in all of film noir," according to Paul Arthur.[20] Frank finally lands in "one of the seediest bars ever seen in an MGM film" where he comes across Pat, a slatternly prostitute; Johnny, a tough gangster (Berry Kroeger); and Mr. Gavery (Taylor Holmes), a shyster lawyer.[21]

Pat introduces Frank to Gavery, the unscrupulous attorney, and they retire to the bar's dingy back room for a conference. Gavery advises Frank to employ Johnny to "dispose of his problem" with Joe. Gavery all the while plies Frank with liquor, as he proposes to Frank that Johnny should confront Joe and be forced to shoot him "in self-defense." When Frank balks at the idea of murdering Joe, the heartless Gavery replies, "You sent ten men off to die; what's one more?"

With that, Frank abruptly leaves the bar and walks through the dark alleys and narrow passageways of the neighborhood; he finally wanders into a railway tunnel. Once again Zinnemann adroitly employs expressionism, as Frank hears the inner voices of Joe and the duplicitous Nazi commandant echoing in his mind. Lost in deep despair, Frank eventually steps onto the railroad tracks, right in the path of an oncoming train. But he jumps out of the way just in time, and we know that he at least has conquered his impulse to commit suicide.

Pat, who has been shadowing him, takes Frank to her shabby apartment. Zinnemann makes good use of this atmospheric set, bathing it in a bleak, sickly half-light. It is here that Frank finally strikes a deal with Johnny to liquidate Joe for him. Joe is to meet Frank at the Santa Lisa train depot the following night for a showdown, but it is Johnny—and not Frank—who will be waiting at the station to confront Joe. When Frank sobers up the next day, he realizes what he has done and heads for the Santa Lisa depot to thwart Johnny's murder of Joe.

As Frank arrives at the depot, he sees Johnny hiding in his black sedan, prepared to shoot Joe. Frank and Joe slowly advance toward each other, in the tradition of a gunfight in a western movie. Frank finally shouts to Joe, "I came to warn you!" Then Frank is shot by Johnny as he dashes into the path of the bullet Johnny intended for Joe. Frank, mortally wounded, jumps on the running board of Johnny's car as Johnny attempts to flee the scene. As Frank struggles to grab control of the steering wheel from Johnny, the sedan crashes into a lamppost. Both Frank and Johnny are killed instantly in the wreck.

Ann Sturges appears on the scene as Joe kneels over Frank's body, realizing that Frank saved his life. Frank sacrificed his life for Joe's, as an act of atonement. Joe assures Ann that he did not murder Frank. "I didn't do it, Ann!" He vows to tell Edith how and why Frank died.

Act of Violence reflects Zinnemann's favorite theme: "Man's fate, and the need to face up to it," writes Robert Horton. "Almost always in Zinnemann's films," he reminds "the hero of a date with destiny."[22] This German fatalism was congenial to Zinnemann's thematic vision, for he was convinced that we cannot escape the consequences of our actions. Robert Ryan commented, "It was a downbeat story, not common when the film was released."[23] It is true that Frank pays for his sins with his life, but other film noirs also had downbeat endings too, like *Sunset Boulevard* and *Scarlet Street*.

Zinnemann went on to make grander films than *Act of Violence*. But few of them are as challenging or as absorbing as this ruggedly realistic, tautly constructed film noir. Like Fred Zinnemann, Stanley Kubrick made a significant film noir early in his career that helped to establish him as an important filmmaker.

Writing in the mid-1950s, film critic Manny Farber praised certain Hollywood directors like Billy Wilder who would "tunnel" beneath the surface of the stories they were filming and seek to illuminate in a shrewd and unsentimental fashion deeper truths, usually about the unglamorous side of this human condition. These directors did not get bogged down in "significant" dialogue but told their stories in a straightforward fashion that nonetheless implied subtle thematic implications beneath the surface of their basically plot-oriented scripts. In short, these filmmakers took "private runways to the truth."[24] Stanley Kubrick's *The Killing* is a fine example of what Farber was writing about.

The Killing (1956)

Stanley Kubrick's *Killer's Kiss* (1935) has often been cited by film historians as a film noir, rather than *The Killing*. For example, James Naremore, in his study of film noir, *More Than Night*, discusses *Killer's Kiss*, but not *The Killing*. The preference for *Killer's Kiss* over *The Killing* by some film scholars puzzled Kubrick, since he considered *Killer's Kiss* part of his juvenilia, an amateur movie made on a shoestring when he was still learning his craft. He told me that he "much preferred to be represented in the noir canon by *The Killing*."[25]

Kubrick's first important film, *The Killing*, was a tough and tightly knit crime thriller about a racetrack robbery carried out by a group of down-at-the-heels small-time crooks who hope to pull off one last big job to solve all of their individual financial crises. As Foster Hirsch points out, "The failed heist, which demonstrated the truism about the lack of honor among thieves, was a classic noir staple."[26]

In *The Killing*, "a combination of bad luck and personality flaws brings about the destruction of the gang and foils what would have been the perfect crime," adds Arthur Lyons. "Life is unforgiving in noir films. You can make one mistake, and you're finished."[27] Putting it another way, Martin Scorsese notes in his commentary for his documentary *A Personal Journey through American Movies* (1995), "There are no dispensations in film noir; you pay for your sins."

As a matter of fact, *The Killing* came toward the end of the cycle of classic film noir, which ran roughly from 1941 to 1958.

"After ten years of steadily shedding romantic conventions," Paul Schrader writes in his renowned article on the cycle, "the later noir films finally got down to the root causes" of the disillusionment of the period: the loss of heroic conventions, personal integrity, and finally psychic stability. The last films of the trend seemed to be painfully aware that "they stood at the end of a long tradition based on despair and disintegration and did not shy away from the fact."[28]

Furthermore, *The Killing* also reflects another element of film noir that Schrader points out as endemic to that type of movie: it utilizes "a complex chronological order to reinforce a sense of hopelessness and lost time" in a disoriented world.[29] Based on Lionel White's novel *Clean Break*, Kubrick's tightly constructed script follows the preparations of the makeshift gang bent on making a big pile of money by holding up a racetrack. They have planned the robbery to coincide with the actual running of the seventh race, and Kubrick photographs the heist in great detail with all of its split-second timing. He builds suspense with great intensity by quickly cutting from one member of the gang to another in a series of flashbacks that show how each has simultaneously carried out his part of the plan. All of these parallel lines of action lead inexorably to the climactic moment when the ringleader gets away with the loot.

Edward Buscombe remarks, "This early Kubrick picture shows all of the characteristic precision and care in the construction of the narrative, pieced together through flashback and voice-over narrations."[30]

Kubrick was a fan of Jim Thompson, the author of several hard-boiled crime novels dealing with violent and self-destructive behavior like *The Killer inside Me* (1952). Kubrick had been particularly impressed by Thompson's ear for dialogue, so he asked this leading author of pulp fiction to work on the dialogue for *The Killing*. Thompson's dialogue "was lively and acerbic," as terse and understated as Kubrick's direction of the film.[31]

Kubrick wanted to introduce a homosexual subtext into the film (which is not present in the novel) in terms of the older conspirator having a crush on the young leader of the gang. This precipitated a censorship problem. At the time that Kubrick began making films, in the 1950s, Geoffrey Shurlock, the industry censor, maintained that homosexuality was too strong a subject for American motion pictures.

Shurlock insisted that the restrictions of the industry's censorship code be upheld; the code prohibited Kubrick from depicting homosexuality in any explicit way. But Kubrick managed to suggest a hint of homosexuality in *The Killing*. He implies that Marvin Unger, one of the accomplices of Johnny Clay in planning the robbery, has a covert homosexual attachment to the much younger Johnny. Marvin sees Johnny as a surrogate son, and this "blurs into a homoerotic attraction on the part of Marvin," as Fran Mason explains.[32] "There's nothing I wouldn't do for Johnny," he says. In fact, Marvin's participation in the caper seems to be motivated by his need to be near Johnny, rather than by greed for money.

Marvin even suggests in Thompson's laconic dialogue that he and Johnny go off together after the heist, "and let the old world take a couple of turns," while they live alone together without any women along, so they can "have a chance to take stock of things" on their own. But his invitation is tactfully ignored by Johnny. A clever director like Kubrick could get around the restriction on portraying homosexuality by hints and suggestions. Indeed, this is an example of the sort of subtle implication that Farber had in mind, as noted above, that lurk beneath the surface of the plot.

Pauline Kael, who agrees with Kubrick that *The Killing* marks the real beginning of his career, says in *Going Steady* that robbery pictures tend to be terribly derivative of earlier robbery movies, but that it is still possible for a director to bring a fresh approach to the project: "to present the occupational details of crime accurately (or convincingly), to assemble the gang so that we get a sense of the kinds of people engaged in crime and what their professional and non-professional lives are like. A good crime movie generally has a sordid, semi-documentary authenticity about criminal activities," she concludes, "plus the nervous excitement of what it might be like to rob and tangle with the law."[33]

All of these elements are evident in *The Killing*. In giving us a glimpse into the seedy lives of each member of the gang involved in the robbery, Kubrick has given the film a touch of sleazy authenticity that raises it well above the level of the ordinary crime movie. The director elicited a high order of ensemble acting from a group of capable Hollywood supporting players who rarely got a chance to give performances of such substance. Sterling Hayden plays Johnny Clay, the tough organizer of the caper. Jay C. Flippen is Marvin Unger, the cynical older member of the group; Elisha Cook, Jr., is George Peatty, the timid track cashier who hopes to impress his voluptuous wife, Sherry (Marie Windsor), with stolen money, since he cannot otherwise give her satisfaction; and Ted De Corsia is Randy Kennan, a crooked cop.

Some of the actors had been cast in noir films before. Sterling Hayden played a character similar to Johnny in John Huston's *Asphalt Jungle* (1950), another noir heist film. Elisha Cook, Jr., had become the iconic loser in noir films, having made a lasting impression as the hapless hoodlum Wilmer in *The Maltese Falcon*. Marie Windsor had played a gangster's wife in *Song of the Thin Man* (1947) and a marked woman in *Narrow Margin* (1952). "Many people have asked me how it was working in film noir. As far as I know, no one had put a name to it at that time," Windsor said later. "I think after a great collection of film noir pictures, the term became generally known."[34]

George Peatty (Elisha Cook, Jr.), Johnny Clay (Sterling Hayden), Marvin Unger (Jay C. Flippen) plan a heist in Kubrick's *The Killing*.

Although *Clean Break* is set in New York City, Kubrick shot *The Killing* on location in Los Angeles—and in San Francisco, the setting of Dashiell Hammett's stories.[35] Veteran cinematographer Lucien Ballard was engaged to shoot the film. Occasionally friction developed between director and cameraman when they disagreed on how a shot should be lit. Eventually, however, a mutual respect developed between the two men. Kubrick, after all, was one of the few movie directors who belonged to the cinematographers' union.

The Killing was scored by Gerard Fried, who composed the music for all of Kubrick's films of the 1950s. The pulsating theme for the opening credits, comments David Wishart, "both elicits the hustle and bustle of the racetrack" and grimly foreshadows the violent outcome of the caper "with urgently etched staccato tones." Moreover, "the bellowing, brassy horns in the main title music" give the music "a forward thrust," Fried says. "The movie has gotten started and, like a runaway train, it just never lets up."[36]

Kubrick was confident that his method of telling the story by means of fragmented flashbacks would work as well on the screen as it did in the novel. "It was the handling of time that may have made this more than just a good crime film," he said. Another thing that attracted him to White's book, Alexander Walker points out very perceptively in *Stanley Kubrick, Director*, is that the novel touches on a theme that is a frequent preoccupation of Kubrick's films: the presumably perfect plan of action that goes wrong through human fallibility and/or chance. "It is characteristic of Kubrick that, while one part of him pays intellectual tribute to the rationally constructed master plan, another part reserves the skeptic's right to anticipate human imperfections or the laws of chance that militate against its success."[37] Kubrick's theme was in harmony with the tenets of film noir, which created "a dark, menacing, paranoid universe," notes Michael Cristofer, "into which many a film hero was drawn and then destroyed by forces he could not understand or control."[38]

It is clear from the outset in *The Killing* that the tawdry individuals whom Johnny Clay has brought together to execute the racetrack robbery compose a series of weak links in a chain of command that could snap at any point. Add to this the possibility of unexpected mishaps that could dog even the best of plans, and the viewer senses that the entire project is doomed from the start. Nevertheless, one is still fascinated to see how things will go wrong, and when.

Because of the intricate structure of the film's convoluted story line, it is appropriate to comment on the plot in some detail.

During the credits of *The Killing* there are several shots of the preparations before a race: the starting gate is brought into place, the horses line up in their positions, and so on. It is a tribute to Kubrick's naturalistic direction that when the film cuts from these documentary shots of the track to the betting area, few filmgoers suspect that the action has shifted to a studio set. The voice of the narrator further contributes to the documentary air of the picture. He introduces each of the characters, describing why each is implicated in the plot. The narrator is Art Gilmore (uncredited), who often spoke the voice-over narration for newsreels.

First there is Marvin Unger. "At exactly three forty-five on a Saturday afternoon in September," the narrator begins, "Marvin Unger walked toward the cashiers' windows at the racetrack. Despite his lifelong antipathy for gambling, he had bet on all of the horses in the same race. He that this method would cause him to lose in the long run, but he was shooting for higher stakes." Marvin is helping to set up a well-planned robbery so that he can obtain enough money to retire with financial security. He stands at the window of cashier George Peatty. When the winner of the race is confirmed, Marvin writes an address and meeting time on the back of his winning ticket and pushes it through the window to Peatty. He gives a similar note to track bartender Mike O'Reilly (Joe Sawyer).

At 7 p.m. that same evening Johnny Clay is opening a bottle of beer in the dingy kitchen of a flat while he describes his accomplices to his girlfriend Fay (Coleen Gray). "None of these guys are criminals in the ordinary sense of the word," he explains. "They all have little problems they have to take care of. Take Marvin Unger, who is nice enough to let me stay here in his apartment. He is no criminal." To quell Fay's misgivings about Johnny's getting involved in a major crime after recently getting out of prison, her lover says, "Anytime you take a chance you had better be sure that the stakes are worth it because they can put you away just as fast for taking ten dollars as for taking a million." Johnny arranges to meet Fay at the airport after the robbery so that they can go away together, and sends her away.

Some of the strongest dramatic scenes in the film are those between mousy George Peatty and his sluttish wife Sherry. George is hopelessly in love with Sherry and is constantly afraid that she will two-time him with another man—something she has done repeatedly. George is trapped in a sadomasochistic relationship with his high-maintenance wife, a treacherous femme fatale. The two performers breathe a great deal of credibility into their handling of these scenes, particularly Cook, whom Penelope Houston describes as "the prototype of all sad little men."[39]

Thompson had "an interest in sadomasochistic relationships," James Naremore points out in his book on Kubrick. The dialogue in the scenes involving the bickering couple "has the true Thompson ring."[40] Maddened by her constant condescension, George blurts out that he is involved in a big operation that will make them rich. Sherry shrewdly tries to pry more of the details from him, but George, aware that he has already said too much, becomes evasive. "My own husband doesn't trust me," she pouts. Sherry later tells her lover Val (Vince Edwards) what she has been able to wheedle out of her husband. Ironically, she is as submissive to this cheap crook as George is to her.

At the meeting Johnny has called with his fellow conspirators, he goes over the intricate plans he has laid. A single overhead lamp illumines their worn, defeated faces as they talk, leaving them surrounded by a darkness that is almost tangible. It is this darkness that seems to hover around Kubrick's characters in many of his films and which they desperately seek to keep from engulfing them—usually without success.

Sherry unexpectedly interrupts these deliberations when she is heard snooping around in the corridor outside Marvin's apartment. George weakly whimpers that she must have found the address while going through his pockets, since she is a very jealous wife. This incident shakes the whole group's sense of security about the venture, but Johnny is able to reconfirm their confidence that the plan has not been damaged by Sherry's interference.

"Three days later," the narrator says, "Johnny Clay began the final preparations." He hires a wrestler named Maurice to start a fight with the track bartender to distract the police from the robbery.

Clay next visits sharpshooter Nikki Arcane (Timothy Carey) at his farm. Johnny hires Arcane to shoot down Red Lightning, the favored horse, during the course of the seventh race. This will delay the official decision on the winner of the race and enable Johnny to make a bigger haul before the bettors arrive at the cashiers' windows for their payoffs. Nikki fondles a puppy all the time that he and Johnny discuss the proposition, which explains his hesitation to shoot an animal. "You're not being asked to commit first degree murder," Johnny chides; "it isn't even murder. The worst they could get you for is shooting horses out of season." The last item on Johnny's agenda is to rent a motel room where he can temporarily store his rifle and hide the loot immediately after the robbery.

Tension begins to mount as the day of the holdup dawns. "Four days later, at 7 a.m., Sherry Peatty was wide awake," says the narrator. Badgering her nervous spouse at the breakfast table, she gets him to admit that today is the day.

From this point onward Kubrick begins to follow each separate strand of the robbery plot through to its completion, doubling back each time to show how each of the elements of the elaborate plan is implemented simultaneously with all of the others. Kubrick repeats the shots from the credit sequence of the horses getting into starting position for the seventh race each time he turns back the clock to develop a different step in the complex

191

robbery plan, thereby situating the viewer temporarily. (Kubrick did location work at a track on the outskirts of San Francisco for these scenes.)

The narrator takes us to 11:43 a.m., when Nikki Arcane left his farm in his sports car. He arrives at the track parking lot at 12:30, and bribes the black parking attendant to let him have the position he requires in order to draw a bead on Red Lightning. The attendant mistakes Nikki's patronizing manner as genuine kindness and comes over from time to time to chat with Arcane. At one point the attendant offers Nikki a lucky horseshoe.

Nikki tensely watches the race through his gunsight. At precisely 4:23 p.m. he pulls the trigger and brings Red Lightning down. Thirty seconds later Arcane is dead. His sports car blows a tire as he tries to drive out of the parking lot, leaving him within the range of a track guard's pistol shot. Lying next to Nikki on the cement is the lucky horseshoe that he had been given a few minutes before. A shot like this, comments Naremore, makes *The Killing* seem "more slyly cruel" than an ordinary thriller.[41]

Kubrick has built his film from the beginning toward the peak where all of Johnny's meticulous planning suddenly converges on the moment when he enters the cashiers' office and scoops up $2 million. Johnny puts on a rubber mask and gloves; with typical Kubrick irony, the face on the mask is frozen with a perpetual grin.

Thus disguised, Johnny bursts into the cashiers' room and orders them to fill his large laundry sack with all the money it will hold. As they do so the track announcer can be heard in the background: "We don't have any exact information on Red Lightning's spill, but we do know that the jockey was not seriously injured." Then Johnny makes his getaway, heaving the bulky bag, which now contains his mask, gloves, and gun as well as the cash, out of an open window. Later we learn that Officer Kennan was stationed below the window to catch the loot as it hit the ground and transfer it to the motel room where Johnny would pick it up later.

Kubrick begins to draw the last threads of the plot together as Johnny's companions in crime assemble in Marvin's shabby living room to await Clay's appearance with the money. The men sit around drinking nervously and listening to radio reports of the "daring holdup" at the track. George's hand, anxiously nursing a glass, is in the foreground, suggesting the tension that permeates the room.

"Where is Johnny?" George whines. "Why does his timetable have to break down *now*?" There is a knock at the door, but instead of Johnny and the cash it is Val, Sherry's boyfriend, and one of his mobsters. They force their way into the room, expecting to grab the swag for themselves. A shoot-out ensues that leaves everyone in the room dead—except for George, who is mortally wounded. For a moment Kubrick trains his camera on the pile of corpses spread around the living room. The room is silent, except for the sound of bouncy Latin music pouring from the radio, providing an ironic contrast to the carnage of the scene. It has been quite a killing.

George Peatty has enough life left in him to struggle into his car and drive home. George is moving with the determination of a man who knows he must accomplish something before he takes his last breath. Once home he finds Sherry packing to go away with Val, as he suspected she would. She tries to mollify him with a prefabricated alibi, but for once in his life George is not to be forestalled by his scheming wife. "Why did you do it?" he asks plaintively, already knowing the answer. "I loved you, Sherry." He then blasts away with his pistol, the impotent husband finally penetrating his wife with bullets. As George himself falls forward toward the camera he knocks over the birdcage, symbol of his pitifully narrow existence, which is now at an end. Sherry too has expired; she learned too late that the worm had finally turned.

Although she appeared in only a few scenes of *The Killing*, the role of Sherry Peatty proved the most significant role of Marie Windsor's career. In this regard Windsor exemplifies the fact that the size of a part does not matter if one is under the direction of an expert director like Kubrick. Her riveting portrayal of Sherry won her a place in film history as a quintessential femme fatale of film noir.

Because of heavy traffic around the track, Johnny shows up late at the gang's meeting place, only to find a squad car arriving on the scene with its siren wailing. Aware that something terrible has happened, Johnny proceeds straight to the airport to meet Fay as planned. En route he buys the largest suitcase he can find and stashes the loot in it. He finds Fay and they proceed to the check-in counter, passing two men who are quite clearly sizing up everyone who enters the air terminal. With nervous nonchalance Johnny demands that the airline allow him to lug his huge suitcase on board with him rather than stow it in the luggage compartment. Throughout his bickering with the airline personnel, which Kubrick records in a single take, the bulky bag stands inertly in the center of the frame, as Johnny tries to minimize its size. Realizing that he is causing a scene, Clay capitulates and watches apprehensively as the bag is tossed onto a conveyor belt and disappears from sight.

Johnny and Fay arrive at the departure gate just in time to see the baggage truck drive out onto the windy airfield. They watch in mute horror as the ramshackle case falls off the top of the mountain of luggage and springs open, flooding the airstrip with stolen bills that blow right at the camera. The fate of the money in *The Killing* recalls how the gold dust in John Huston's *Treasure of Sierra Madre* (1948) blows across the desert sands. In that film the men who have slaved to acquire the gold can only laugh hysterically when they contemplate how it drifted away from them.

But Fay and Johnny are in a daze. She supports his arm as they walk to the street and hopelessly try to hail a taxi before the two FBI agents who have been watching them all along can reach them. Fay tells Johnny to make a run for it, but he can only murmur, almost inaudibly, "What's the difference?" Resigned to their fate, Johnny and Fay turn resolutely around to face the two men advancing toward them through the glass doors of the flight lounge.

Johnny and Fay had hoped to escape the corrosive atmosphere of the big city by flight to a cleaner climate. Earlier Marvin had encouraged Johnny to go away "and take stock of things." But for Johnny, brutalized by a life of crime, it was already too late.

When *The Killing* was released, Pauline Kael saw it as "an expert suspense film, with fast, incisive cutting," and "furtive little touches of characterization."[42] *Time* applauded Kubrick for having shown "more imagination with dialogue and camera than Hollywood has seen since the obstreperous Orson Welles went riding out of town. . . . The camera watches the whole show with the keen eye of a terrier stalking a pack of rats."[43]

Other critics besides *Time* recognized Kubrick as a new genius on the cinema's horizon. Yet United Artists, the film's distributor, released the film on the bottom half of a double bill with *Bandido*, a now-forgotten action picture. UA obviously did not appreciate the classic film that Kubrick had delivered.

Working out of the grand noir tradition, Kubrick managed in *The Killing* to give a new twist to the story of a man trapped by events he cannot control. The defeat of Johnny and his cohorts, comments Andrew Dickos, "leaves these outsiders with the inevitable negation of their dreams—dreams that they could not buy."[44] As for Johnny himself, his character owes something to that of Ole Andreson in *The Killers* (1946). Like Ole, Johnny is "wearily fatalistic and stoical, and consistently sympathetic—despite his criminality."[45]

Notes

1. Jack Ellis, *A History of Film*, rev. ed. (Boston: Allyn and Bacon, 1996), 272.
2. Silver and Ursini, "Introduction: The Classic Period," in *Film Noir: The Encyclopedia*, 18.
3. Fred Zinnemann, interview by the author, London, May 15, 1994. Any quotations from Zinnemann that are not attributed to another source are from this interview.
4. Hirsch, *The Dark Side of the Screen*, 217.
5. Paul Arthur, "Noir Happens: *Act of Violence*," *Film Comment* 35, no. 4 (July–August 1999): 58.
6. Giannetti and Eyman, *Flashback*, 140.
7. Agee, *Film Writings and Selected Journalism*, 430.
8. Hirsch, *The Dark Side of the Screen*, 17.
9. Brian McDonnell, "*Act of Violence*," in *Encyclopedia of Film Noir*, 85.
10. Arthur, "Noir Happens: *Act of Violence*," 58.
11. Alain Silver and Blake Lucas, "*Act of Violence*," in *Film Noir: The Encyclopedia*, 26.
12. Thomson, *Have You Seen . . .?*, 5.
13. Arthur Nolletti, Jr., "Conversation with Fred Zinnemann," in *Fred Zinnemann: Interviews*, ed. Gabriel Miller (Jackson: University Press of Mississippi, 2005), 116.
14. Fred Zinneman, *A Life in the Movies: An Autobiography* (New York: Scribner's, 1992), 74.
15. Geoff Mayer, "Robert Ryan," in *Encyclopedia of Film Noir*, 359.
16. Hannsberry, *Bad Boys*, 572.
17. Wheeler Dixon, "*Act of Violence* and the Early Films of Fred Zinnemann," in *The Films of Fred Zinnemann: Critical Perspectives*, ed. Arthur Nolletti, Jr. (Albany: State University of New York Press, 1999), 43–44.
18. Zinnemann, *A Life in the Movies*, 74.
19. Dixon, "*Act of Violence*," 52.
20. Arthur, "Noir Happens: *Act of Violence*," 57.
21. Dixon, "*Act of Violence*," 99. Nicholas Joy was originally elated to play Gavery, but was replaced by Taylor Holmes; yet some sources, including Dixon, list Joy as Gavery; see Dixon, 49.

22. Robert Horton, "Day of the Craftsman: Fred Zinnemann," *Film Comment* 33, no. 5 (September–October, 1997): 62.

23. Hannsberry, *Bad Boys*, 572.

24. *Farber on Film*, 490.

25. Stanley Kubrick, interview by the author, London, July 18, 1973; see Naremore, *More Than Night*, 156–58.

26. Hirsch, *Detours and Lost Highways*, 254.

27. Arthur Lyons, *Death on the Cheap: Film Noir and the Low-Budget Film* (New York: Da Capo, 2001), 284.

28. Schrader, "Notes on Film Noir," 463.

29. Schrader, "Notes on Film Noir," 463.

30. Edward Buscombe, "*The Killing*," in *The BFI Companion to Crime*, ed. Phil Hardy (Los Angeles: University of California Press, 1997), 192.

31. Joseph Bevan, "The Nothing Man: Jim Thompson," *Sight and Sound* 20 (ns), no. 6 (June 2010): 43.

32. Mason, *American Gangster Cinema*, 102.

33. Pauline Kael, *Going Steady* (New York: Boyars, 1994), 183.

34. Vincent LoBrutto, *Stanley Kubrick: A Biography* (New York: Da Capo, 1999), 92.

35. Christiane Kubrick, *Stanley Kubrick: A Life in Pictures* (London: Little, Brown, 2002), 57.

36. David Wishart, CD liner notes for *Music from the Films of Stanley Kubrick* (New York: Silva Screen Records, 1999), 6, 10.

37. Alexander Walker, *Stanley Kubrick, Director*, rev. ed. (New York: Norton, 1999), 52.

38. Michael Cristofer, "Lost Hollywood: Film Noir," *Premiere* 14, no. 7 (March 2001): 58.

39. Penelope Houston, *Contemporary Cinema* (Baltimore: Penguin Books, 1969), 66.

40. James Naremore, *On Kubrick* (London: British Film Institute, 2007), 68.

41. Naremore, *On Kubrick*, 75.

42. Kael, *5001 Nights at the Movies*, 394.

43. "*The Killing*," *Time*, June 4, 1956, 99.

44. Dickos, *Street with No Name*, 202.

45. Hillier, "*The Killing*," in *100 Film Noirs*, 146.

ORSON WELLES:
THE STRANGER AND *TOUCH OF EVIL*

Orson Welles's *Touch of Evil* is considered by many to be the last great film noir of the classic period. Meanwhile, *The Stranger* is largely ignored in most of the standard books on film noir. The critical apathy about *The Stranger* is partially Welles's own fault, since he consistently dismissed the movie in interviews as "the one of my films of which I am least the author." He thought it was a failure.[1] Simply put, the picture is a good deal better than Welles was prepared to admit.

After the commercial failure of Welles's first two Hollywood films, *Citizen Kane* (1941) and *The Magnificent Ambersons* (1942), Welles was persona non grata as far as the major studios were concerned. He desperately wanted to direct another film. Hence when independent producer Sam Spiegel asked him to play the lead in *The Stranger*, Welles offered to direct the movie as well. Spiegel, a newcomer to Hollywood, took him up on his offer.

Like Fred Zinnemann, Sam Spiegel was an Austrian Jew who got his start in the film industry in Berlin. Spiegel was employed by the Berlin branch of Universal Pictures, preparing its films for European distribution. He fled Hitler's Germany in 1933 and went to London, where he had a brief career as a con man and a check forger. After serving a short jail sentence for fraud, Spiegel immigrated to Hollywood, where he was known officially as S. P. Eagle, in order to bury his checkered past.[2] Some of the production team on *The Stranger* accordingly called the film the *S. T. Ranger*, as a droll reference to Spiegel's alias.

Spiegel bought the screen rights to a story by Victor Travis and Decla Dunning entitled "Date with Destiny." As producer of the film, he asked William Goetz, who had an independent production company, International Pictures, that distributed its films through RKO, to join forces with him. Spiegel arranged for Goetz to finance the film and to act as its executive producer. Spiegel then engaged Welles to play the lead, and Welles accepted the part—so long as he could direct the film as well. In fact, Welles, who was eager to direct again, would not appear in the movie unless he could direct it. Goetz, who had supported Preminger's bid to return to directing at Fox after Preminger's notorious falling-out with Zanuck, likewise favored Welles's wish to direct *The Stranger*.

Spiegel and Goetz allowed Welles to direct—but with certain stringent conditions. Although Welles was free to collaborate on the screenplay before principal photography commenced, he could not deviate from the shooting script once filming was under way. (Spiegel had heard tales about Welles rewriting scenes just before the cameras turned.) Moreover, Spiegel retained final cut so that he had the final say about the editing of the film during postproduction.

"The contract that he signed in order to make the movie tied his hands tighter than a Victorian corset," quips Welles biographer Clinton Heylin.[3] But Welles signed the contract because he was anxious "to prove to the industry that I could direct a standard Hollywood picture, on time and on budget, just like anyone else."[4]

The Stranger (1946)

In *The Stranger* Welles plays Franz Kindler, a key Nazi who escaped from Europe at the end of World War II. He is now Charles Rankin, a teacher at a New England prep school. Rankin/Kindler hopes to hide there indefinitely from Inspector Wilson, the government agent who hopes to bring him to justice.

In *The Stranger* Welles is working in the tradition of international intrigue, which is part of many film noirs, like Fritz Lang's *Ministry of Fear*. What's more, Welles's film is clearly linked to some postwar noirs. Such films, as Sheri Biesen emphasizes, examined social ills like the emotional problems of returning veterans, as did Fred Zinnemann's *Act of Violence*;

and, in the case of *The Stranger*, "the danger of war criminals" still at large exemplifies another type of postwar noir.[5]

John Huston, who had a hand in the writing of the screenplay of *The Killers* with Anthony Veiller for Robert Siodmak, also collaborated with Veiller on the first draft of the script for *The Stranger*. As in the case of *The Killers*, Huston received no screen credit for his work on the screenplay for *The Stranger* for contractual reasons: he could not officially work for International Pictures while under contract to Warner Bros.

Veiller, in collaboration with Huston, composed the first draft of the screenplay, adapted from the Travis-Dunning story.[6] When Welles came on board, he reworked some scenes with Veiller. He also added a long prologue to the script, in which Konrad Meinike, Franz Kindler's executive officer, searches for Kindler in Latin America, where Kindler is believed to be in hiding, along with several other unrepentant war criminals.

Meinike, in turn, is shadowed by Inspector Wilson, a Nazi hunter who hopes Meinike will lead him to Kindler. Wilson wears a wide-brimmed felt hat and a somewhat rumpled top coat, which make him resemble the typical film noir detective. Meinike ultimately discovers that Kindler is now teaching history in a New England prep school, and proceeds to look for him there, pursued, of course, by Wilson.

Welles thought "the big chase in South America was much the best thing in the picture, . . . probably because I wrote it."[7] Welles shot this material, which initially accounted for the first two reels of the picture; but Spiegel excised most of it during postproduction because it was not relevant to the main plot, which was set in a New England village.

Nevertheless, snippets of Welles's prologue remain in the film: Meinike reaching a South American port and lying to the authorities about his reason for being there; Meinike finally coaxing a photographer who is forging him a new passport to divulge the current whereabouts of Kindler. David Thomson rightly believes that Spiegel's cuts in the prologue were appropriate: "Truly we do not need that part of Meinike's story."[8]

Welles himself deleted from the shooting script a bizarre dream of Rankin's new wife, Mary, who initially has no knowledge of her husband's sordid past. He had designed this hallucinatory dream to depict how Mary was beginning to suspect that Wilson's allegations that Charles Rankin is actually Franz Kindler may really be true. According to Heylin, "throughout this delirious vision the camera was supposed to slowly close in on

Rankin until one of his eyes fills the screen," as Rankin is transformed into the monstrous Franz Kindler.[9]

After Hitchcock released *Spellbound* in the fall of 1945, Welles decided to cut Mary's nightmare from the script of *The Stranger*, in order not to risk the comparison of Mary's dream sequence with the dream sequence designed by Dali for Hitchcock's film. After the deletion of Mary's dream, however, Wilson's remark to her at film's end, "Pleasant dreams, Mary," loses some of its significance.

Welles managed to get a covert reference into *The Stranger* to *Hearts of Age* (1934), a silent short he made at age nineteen on the campus of his alma mater, the Todd School for Boys in Woodstock, Illinois. For one thing, Welles filmed *Hearts of Age* on the campus of a prep school, and much of *The Stranger* takes place at a prep school.

For another, if one combines the images of the bell tower in *Hearts of Age* with the shots of the young Welles's death fall from a fire escape in the short, one gets a premonition of Welles's death fall from the clock tower at the finale of *The Stranger*. At any rate, Welles's contention that *The Stranger* is an impersonal film, and that there is nothing of him in it, seems more of an exaggeration than ever.[10]

While revising the screenplay, Welles wrote most of the dialogue in the scenes set in the local drugstore, where Wilson shrewdly gleans information from the wily checker-playing pharmacist, Mr. Potter, about Charles Rankin. Welles also wrote the subtle scene at the dinner party, wherein Wilson, who is posing as an antique dealer, broaches the topic of a Nazi resurgence. This is a subject Welles had addressed in some of his think pieces for the *New York Post* in the winter of 1945. "Rankin, waxing arrogant, launches a disquisition on the German character," whereby he inadvertently betrays his deeply rooted Nazi philosophy.[11]

"The German sees himself as conspired against, set upon by inferior nations," Rankin pontificates. Mary's younger brother Noah intervenes, "All Germans aren't like that; what about Karl Marx?" Rankin responds without thinking, "But Marx wasn't a German; Marx was a Jew." Wilson is struck by the remark, which makes him begin to consider that Rankin might just be Kindler. As he later reflects ruefully, "Who but a Nazi would deny that Karl Marx was a German because he was a Jew?"

Screen credit for the script was eventually assigned solely to Anthony Veiller by the Screen Writers Guild. Veiller, after all, was primarily responsible for establishing the characters and for the basic plot of the screenplay. Welles had only been involved in revising the screenplay.

The enterprising Spiegel brought together a sterling cast for *The Stranger*. Besides Welles, there was Edward G. Robinson as Wilson, a member of the Allied War Crimes Commission. As it happened, Welles's preferred choice to play Wilson was Agnes Moorhead, who had been with Welles since his early days in radio. "I thought it would be much more interesting to have a sinister lady on the heels of the Nazi," he explained.[12] But Spiegel would not hear of such unconventional casting. Loretta Young, who had been a movie star since the 1930s, did a serviceable job as Mary, Charles Rankin's wife.

Welles managed to hire two of his former associates for his production team. Russell Metty, an experienced director of photography, had given Welles a hand on *The Magnificent Ambersons* by shooting some additional scenes without screen credit. He subsequently photographed Welles's late, great film noir, *Touch of Evil*. Production designer Perry Ferguson had been responsible for the sets of *Citizen Kane* (with Van Nest Polglase). Ferguson erected a 124-foot clock tower that was important to the plot (Rankin/Kindler has a passion for repairing antique clocks). Ferguson discovered a huge discarded clock in the basement of the Los Angeles County Museum and had it placed in the tower.

In the film the clock becomes a sixteenth-century German Gothic clock in the town's church tower. (One wonders how an antique Strasbourg clock turned up in a Connecticut village.)

Early in the film Metty photographs the town square of the village where Rankin is hiding out, from a high angle. This overhead shot gives the viewer a sense of the quiet atmosphere of the sleepy little New England town where Rankin lives. The peaceful atmosphere of the village belies the fact that a monstrous war criminal is lurking there.

During shooting Metty found that the scenes in the clock tower gave him the greatest technical challenge. Metty recalled that "the tower was boxed in on all four sides, and the walls could not be removed to allow for the camera."[13] Moreover, it was difficult to keep the lights that were illuminating the scene out of camera range within the narrow confines of the tower. Withal, Welles staged tense confrontations between Rankin and his wife and with Wilson, within the tower set, all adroitly photographed by Metty.

Franz Kindler (Orson Welles), a Nazi fugitive, on the clock tower, next to a gargoyle, at the climax of *The Stranger*.

Bronislau Kaper, who also wrote the score for *Act of Violence*, provided the background music for *The Stranger*. Kaper churned out a fine, suspenseful score, capturing the tense feeling of the drama, right from the beginning with his riveting music for the opening credits, which is in fact a mini–piano concerto.

Spiegel engaged Ernest Nims to edit the picture. Welles remembered that Nims, like Spiegel, "believed that nothing should be in a movie that did not advance the story."[14] Accordingly Nims, with the approval of both Sam Spiegel and William Goetz, trimmed away most of the movie's first two reels, which portrayed Meinike's quest for Kindler in South America. Nims also made some other minor cuts in the finished film; as a result, Welles's preliminary edit was 115 minutes, while Nims's official final cut, much to Welles's displeasure, was 95 minutes.[15] Welles would have to cope with Nims again on *Touch of Evil*, for which Nims was supervising editor.

The Stranger starts out with Welles's abbreviated prologue, in which Konrad Meinike (Konstantin Shayne) pursues Franz Kindler throughout Latin America, while Inspector Wilson is hot on Meinike's trail. The film proper begins when Meinike arrives by bus (accompanied by Wilson) in Harper, Connecticut, where Kindler, in the guise of Charles Rankin, teaches European history at the Harper School for Boys. (There is a poster on the grounds advertising a sports contest between Harper and Woodstock, Welles's alma mater.) That very evening Rankin is to wed Mary Longstreet, the daughter of a Supreme Court justice.

The movie's title obviously refers to Franz Kindler, who is a notorious war criminal masquerading as a respectable citizen of the community. But the title also refers to Wilson, another outsider, who pretends to be an antiques dealer looking for product, but is actually investigating Rankin and anyone associated with him.

Meinike has a clandestine meeting with Rankin in the woods on the edge of town. Rankin realizes that the War Crimes Commission freed Meinike so that he would lead the authorities to him. So Rankin embraces Meinike as an old comrade—and forthwith strangles Meinike amid the intricate noirish shadows of the woods at nightfall. He hastily buries Meinike's corpse on the spot in a shallow grave. Wilson eventually suspects Rankin to be Kindler still more when Mr. Potter, the local druggist, corroborates the fact that Rankin—like Kindler—is an authority on antique clocks.

Inevitably Meinike's body is uncovered in the forest. Rankin, of course, denies publicly that he knew Meinike; but he tells his new wife a different tale. Rankin fabricates a story, whereby Meinike was the brother of a girlfriend of his who drowned in a boating accident in Switzerland years before. Although Meinike was aware that the girl's death was accidental, he was blackmailing Rankin in compensation for his silence about the girl's death. When Rankin could not afford to pay Meinike anymore, he was forced to choke him to death. Mary agrees to guard Rankin's secret because, she says, "I'm already a part of it, because I'm a part of you."

Welles's *Stranger* anticipates Hitchcock's *Strangers on a Train*, writes James Welsh, "in the way an innocent person is drawn in to a web of guilt and complicity" in both movies.[16] In *Strangers on a Train*, Guy does not turn Bruno over to the police for murdering his wife, Miriam, since Guy subconsciously wanted to kill Miriam himself. In *The Stranger* Mary is a willing accessory to Rankin's slaying of Meinike because she firmly believes her new husband's phony story.

In order to finally convince Mary that Charles Rankin really is a war criminal, Wilson shows her some newsreels that illustrate the atrocities Rankin committed during the war. The flickering light of the movie projector is the only light in the room. This suggests that Wilson is shedding some partial light on Rankin's dark past for her.

The Stranger was the first Hollywood movie to incorporate actual footage of the Nazi death camps—this was the first time that American audiences viewed these brutal atrocities. "I do think that every time you can get the public to look at any footage of a concentration camp," it is a salutary experience for them, Welles commented. The Dachau footage happened to be filmed by Welles's fellow director George Stevens while he was a Signal Corps photographer during the war.[17]

Inspector Wilson eventually manages to convince the townspeople, including Mary, that Charles Rankin is indeed Franz Kindler. Shocked by Wilson's disclosures, Mary follows Rankin to the clock tower, where she knows he is hiding, in order to kill him herself. Mary resolutely climbs the ladder to the top of the clock tower.

Rankin looks down at the villagers gathered around the base of the tower. He tells Mary, "They searched the woods; I watched them, like God looking at little ants." In a parallel scene in Carol Reed's *The Third Man* (1949), Welles, as the evil black-market racketeer Harry Lime, surveys the people below him from the top of a Ferris wheel. The Welles character again sees himself as a God-like figure, superior to the ordinary rabble that are beneath him. Like Charles Rankin, Harry Lime is arrogant and defiant to the end.

Wilson joins Mary in confronting Rankin in the small room at the top of the clock tower. Meanwhile the tower clock ominously chimes the hour. The clock striking is an expressionist metaphor; it implies that time is running out for the fugitive and that his hour of doom is at hand. As Rankin struggles with Wilson, Rankin's gun falls to the floor. Mary picks it up and fires some shots at Rankin. One of the bullets hits the clock's mechanism, causing it to go into action: The mechanical figure of St. Michael the Archangel pursues the macabre figure of Satan beneath the clock face. St. Michael holds an extended sword on which Rankin is impaled. Rankin lurches forward, out onto the precarious ledge of the tower and falls to his death.

The expressionist symbolism recalls that Satan "was driven out of heaven and hurled down to earth," as described in the Apocalypse (or Book of Revelation), the last book of the New Testament.[18] Similarly, Rankin is a satanic demon who is cast down to earth by the avenging angel, St. Michael. Welles later termed Rankin's grotesque fate "pure Dick Tracy."[19] It brought to his mind his similar death fall in his amateur film *Hearts of Age*.

The Stranger, states Simon Callow, represents one of Welles's most pressing political concerns: the survival of fascism. Welles intended the movie to serve as a warning: "The evil that Hitler represented had by no means been expunged."[20] Indeed, Charles Higham thought that Welles's portrayal of Kindler was "one of the American cinema's few convincing portraits of a fascist."[21] Colin McArthur adds that "the underlying thread of violence" that is found in Kindler's characterization underscores the noir quality of *The Stranger*.[22]

The Stranger opened in July 1946, to mixed reviews, with some reviewers claiming it as a thriller right out of Hitchcock's top drawer, while others found that the film suffered by comparison with Hitchcock's *Notorious*, which opened shortly afterward and also dealt with Nazi war criminals hiding out in South America.

Although Welles did not remember *The Stranger* with much enthusiasm, it has the distinction of being the only film he ever directed that turned a profit on first release. The picture cost a little over $1 million, and it tripled that amount in revenues during its initial run. Yet *The Stranger* remains a sadly underrated movie in the Welles canon. This is because, in Welles's opinion, it "was his worst film and most critics have gone along with that view."[23]

Because Welles had to adhere to a strict schedule and budget, the movie turned out to be the most conventional of all of his commercial Hollywood pictures—bereft, in his opinion, of many of his trademark cinematic flourishes. "But any other director," Michael Barson rightly contends, "would have been proud to add this to his resumé."[24] The 2010 edition of Silver and Ursini's *Film Noir: The Encyclopedia* is one of the first studies of film noir to acknowledge that at long last *The Stranger* "has found a niche in the canon of film noir."[25]

After the success of *The Stranger* Welles had a poor track record as a director of commercial films. As a result, he was labeled "box office poison" by the major Hollywood studios. "Disenchanted with Hollywood," he therefore headed for an extended self-exile in Europe, where he acted in mainstream movies in order to raise money to finance his own independent projects. His performance as Harry Lime in the British movie *The Third Man* is widely acclaimed.[26]

After directing two independent films of his own, Welles returned to the United States to star in his own production of *King Lear* on Broadway in 1956. While in this country, a producer at Universal, Albert Zugsmith (*Tarnished Angels*), offered Welles the role of the crooked police detective in the screen version of Whit Masterson's crime novel, *Badge of Evil*. Zugsmith also suggested that Welles direct the picture. Welles replied, "Yes, if I can write the script and pay no attention to the book it comes from."[27]

Zugsmith gave Welles the preliminary adaptation of the novel by Paul Monasch, which Welles intended to completely overhaul while writing his own screenplay. Meanwhile the front office at Universal still had to endorse Welles as the film's director.

Touch of Evil (1958)

It was Charlton Heston's clout that enabled Orson Welles to direct as well as costar in the film. Welles played Hank Quinlan, a small-town police inspector who has taken to framing suspects when he fears he doesn't have enough evidence on them to get a conviction. He does this because his wife's murderer went free for lack of evidence when he was a rookie cop.

The studio phoned Heston to offer him the role of the hero, who would become in Welles's script Miguel "Mike" Vargas, a high-ranking

Mexican police official; he was offered the part because Universal wanted a bankable star for the picture.

In Heston's autobiography, he recalls that, when the studio called him about the part, they said, "We've got Welles to play the heavy." Heston wondered if they could really not have thought of the obvious: "Why not ask him to direct, too? He's a pretty good director, you know." Since the films that Welles had directed earlier in the 1950s had not been hits, the front office hired Welles as director as well as actor on the stipulation that he would be paid only for acting in the picture. "So Orson directed what turned out to be a classic film for nothing." Moreover, the parsimonious studio allocated a budget "of less than a million dollars for the whole film," Heston continued; "that left little money for the actors. Nevertheless, they all wanted to work for Orson, in the first film he'd directed in Hollywood in ten years."[28] Marlene Dietrich, Joseph Cotten, Mercedes McCambridge, and other stars appeared in cameos just to be in a Welles film.

Like Sam Spiegel before him, Universal production chief Edward Muhl kept Welles on a tight rein, to remind him that he was operating within the studio system and not as an independent. Muhl accordingly "restricted Welles to an $825,000 budget and a thirty-eight-day shooting schedule."[29]

While it is true that Welles would not have been familiar with the term *film noir* at that time, it seems undeniable that he would have been familiar with the concept; he was, after all, aiming to create a dark crime thriller, which is precisely what a film noir usually was. Moreover, *Touch of Evil* is now commonly regarded as the "epitaph" or "tombstone" of the classic noir period. Thus Foster Hirsch, as noted, regards the movie as the final statement of noir's conventions "and a convenient demarcation."[30]

The crime novel *Badge of Evil* was the basis of the film; it was a pulp novel by Whit Masterson, the joint pen name of Robert Wade and William Miller. Welles found the book routine, and the scenario Paul Monasch derived from it mediocre. He therefore completely reworked the script in less than a month, employing some dialogue from both the book and Monasch's draft.[31]

But Welles made some major changes in the story line while composing his screenplay. In the novel the character to be played by Heston was an Anglo-Saxon police officer with a Mexican wife. It was Welles who transformed the Heston character into Miguel Vargas, a Mexican police authority, and his wife into Susan, an Anglo girl from Philadelphia. In this manner Welles could position a corrupt American cop, Capt. Hank Quinlan, against an upright Mexican police detective, thereby making much more of the racial angle than had been the case either in the novel or the first script, which followed the novel fairly closely.

For the record, Welles did make use of Monasch's version of the script and hence Monasch should not have been denied a screen credit as coauthor of the screenplay.

At all events, for those who complained about a white actor playing a Hispanic, Heston declared to James Delson that he played Vargas as an intelligent, educated professional; his performance "doesn't contribute to the stereotype of the sombrero Mexican lazing around in the shade."[32]

One of the crucial departures that Welles made from the novel and the scenario was to relocate the setting from San Diego to Los Robles, a fictional Mexican-American border town patterned after Tijuana; in fact the tentative title of Welles's script was *Borderline*.[33]

Shooting began on February 18, 1957; Welles filmed the exteriors of the noir border town in Venice, a beach community south of Santa Monica. (Chaplin had made a silent short, "Kid Auto Race at Venice," there in 1914.) More than half the movie was shot at night in and around Venice, with its garbage-strewn alleys, stagnant canals, and pumping oil wells. Welles mostly filmed at night "in part to avoid studio interference, but also because the story demanded it."[34] Of course, "the enormous quantity of litter and debris" is an expressionistic metaphor for moral decay, which is rampant among the inhabitants of the squalid border town. As Vargas says in the film, border towns attract the dregs of the population on both sides of the border.

"Welles's most significant addition to the Monasch script," Thomson points out, "is the out-of-town motel," where a gang of Mexican hoodlums terrorizes Susan Vargas (Janet Leigh). "That motel is still one of the most frightening places in American film," along with the motel in which Marion Crane (Janet Leigh again) is murdered in Hitchcock's *Psycho*.[35]

Janet Leigh had appeared in Zinnemann's *Act of Violence* and was now a mature actress. She accidentally broke her arm two weeks before principal photography began, and had to wear her arm in a sling—except when she was on camera. Along with Heston and Leigh, Welles gathered a superior cast.

Akim Tamiroff had played in Welles's previous film, *Mr. Arkadin* (his brother-in-law, Konstantin Shayne, played Meinike in *The Stranger*). In the present film Tamiroff plays Uncle Joe Grandi, a petty Mexican gangster, to perfection. Uncle Joe is a "dumpy little man with an insecure scowl and an anxious snarl."[36] When he is agitated, which is often, Uncle Joe's toupee tends to slip. He is called "Uncle Joe" because he presides over a mob comprising mostly his nephews, a leather-jacketed gang of unruly delinquents.

Tamiroff made a specialty of playing repellant, disreputable characters, and Welles himself was playing an equally devious type in *Touch of Evil*. As Quinlan, "Welles builds up his own, already bulky figure with padding and then wears a rumpled, tent-like overcoat."[37] Pete Menzies, Quinlan's loyal partner, is enacted by Joseph Calleia (*The Glass Key*), who gives a peerless performance.

Marlene Dietrich was an old friend of Welles; he sawed her in half when he was entertaining the troops during World War II. Welles cast her as Tanya, the world-weary madam of the local brothel, a part tailor-made for Dietrich. For her part Dietrich donned the same black wig she had worn as a gypsy in *Golden Earrings* ten years earlier. She is able to wear a seductive costume and yet suggest a whiff of depravity. Although Dietrich completed her role in just one night, she gave a memorable performance.

Welles was fortunate enough to have not only an impressive cast but a first-rate production team as well. It was highlighted by production designer Alexander Golitzen (*Scarlet Street*) and cinematographer Russell Metty (*The Stranger*). Metty's black-and-white photography on both of his Welles pictures was outstanding. Metty was physically of Wellesian proportions, even like Welles chewing on a cigar; but, unlike Welles, he could be brusque to the point of rudeness.

Metty was renowned for his complicated crane shots, such as the one that opens *Touch of Evil*, in which the camera, mounted on a 22-foot crane, surveys the entire main street of a town on the Mexican border. Richard Chatten quotes Charlton Heston as saying that many cameramen would ask the director, "Do you want it fast or do you want it good?" Comments Heston, "With Russ, you got both."[38] Heston described this opening shot in detail for James Delson:

"Well, for the record, it begins on a close-up" of a man's hand clutching a time bomb, and the camera then "pans just enough to catch the unidentified figure dashing out of the frame." Then Metty's camera "pans down the alley" in the direction in which the figure holding the dynamite has fled, on the near side of the building, going in the same direction. You see the figure (and of course, now you can't possibly identify him) dart behind the building. He is followed by the camera, "but still too far away to tell who he is, he lifts the trunk of a car and puts what is obviously a bomb into the car, slams the lid and disappears into the shadows just as the camera, now lifting above the car, picks up the couple coming around the other side of the building and getting in the car. You establish him as a fat political type and she a floozy blond type. And they carry on—there's enough awareness of their dialogue to establish a kind of drunken nonchalance."

The camera zooms up on a Chapman boom as the car drives out of the parking lot and out into the street. The boom sinks down and picks up the car as it passes rundown buildings covered with peeling posters. "The camera then moves ahead of the car; the bomb is ticking all the while, and consequently the filmgoer wonders when it will explode. The car goes through the border station from Mexico into the United States. This extended take (3 minutes, 20 seconds in length), comes to a spectacular close as the bomb explodes."[39]

The laying out of this long take was incredibly complicated and was accomplished perfectly by Welles and Metty. In fact, Metty's camerawork serves Welles's intentions throughout the movie. At one point, the mobile camera pushes through the beaded curtains of a smoky Mexican dive, as Vargas roughs up an uncooperative suspect, inciting a barroom brawl. Metty's camera is like a whip in this scene, lashing the action into the viewer's face.

Furthermore, *Touch of Evil* was the first Hollywood film to use the handheld camera. This lightweight, portable camera enabled the cameraman to follow Grandi around a shabby motel room at close range as he frantically attempted to dodge the inebriated Quinlan, who was inexorably intent on killing him.

Welles insisted that Metty avoid using artificial light for the daytime scenes—unheard of technique in Hollywood films of the time; instead, Metty employed natural light in the daytime sequences, which contributed to the stark, newsreel-like quality of the cinematography, thereby helping to give the whole movie an air of spare, unvarnished realism. Welles favored Metty's use of natural light sources in the grim scenes that take place at night. This means that there is always an identifiable light source on the set, from which the light would ordinarily come in real life, such as a table lamp. This, too, makes the settings in the film look more like real buildings, and not just movie sets.

Metty was following Welles's very precise instructions during filming and added little to the conception of the shots. The actual idea of doing the opening scene in a single take, the avoidance of artificial light in the daytime scenes, the camera constantly on the move as it toured the shadowy streets and decaying buildings of the decadent border town—all of this came from Welles.

One reason the film had a tight budget, Heston explained, was that "Orson came on the picture dragging a reputation for extravagance like the chains clanking behind Marley's ghost. He didn't deserve it. He had his flaws as a filmmaker, but waste and inefficiency were not among them. I know directors who have wasted more money on one picture than Orson spent on the sum total of all the films he made in his career.

"Still, he knew he had to make the studio believe in him. He did this very resourcefully. The Sunday before shooting started, Orson called some of the actors to his house for an undercover rehearsal of the first day's work, a sound-stage interior of a tiny apartment. The next day, Orson began laying out a master shot that covered the whole scene. It was a very complicated setup, with walls pulling out of the way as the camera moved from room to room, and four principal actors, plus three or four bit players, working through the scene."[40]

The scene, which was twelve pages long, was scheduled for three days of shooting, which is about reasonable; that would be a little over four pages a day. Welles worked out the technical problems of shooting the complicated scene with director of photography Russell Metty. The scene depicts how Quinlan surreptitiously places dynamite in the motel room of Manelo Sanchez as spurious evidence that the suspect caused an explosion that killed two Americans.

On the first day of shooting, Heston recalls, "Lunch came and went and we were still rehearsing the shot; no camera had yet turned. Studio executives began to gather in uneasy little knots in corners, a bit daunted about approaching Orson while he was cueing an extra's move just as the tracking camera picked him up. They were also very worried. With most of the day gone, not a frame of film had passed through the gate yet.

"About four o'clock, Orson called for a take, the first of a good many. Just after six, he said silkily, 'Cut! Print the last three takes. That's a wrap on this set; we're two days ahead of schedule.' He'd designed his master to include all the coverage he needed in the twelve-page scene, scheduled for three shooting days: close-ups, two shots, over-shoulders, and inserts. All this was planned, of course, to astound Universal, which it surely did. It was also a fine way to shoot the scene."[41] This long, unbroken take (5 minutes, 23 seconds), in which Quinlan relentlessly interrogates Sanchez, creates an atmosphere of claustrophobia and tension, because the action is confined to the cramped, suffocating apartment.

Heston concluded, "The front-office people never came near the set again. They kept hoping for another miraculous twelve-page day. They never got one, but Orson had persuaded them that even if he did get into trouble, he could get out of it. As a matter of fact, they were dead right; he had a remarkably sure foot for tightropes."[42]

Welles later stated, "Everyone talks about the opening shot," when the bomb is planted in the trunk of the car. But he considered the interrogation scene, just described, to be one of "the greatest uses of the moving camera in the history of cinema."[43]

Delson commented to Heston that he handled himself well "when the famous Wellesian scene-stealing took place." For example, when Vargas

Hank Quinlan (Orson Welles) and Ramon Miguel Vargas (Charlton Heston) in Welles's *Touch of Evil*, generally thought to be the last "official" film noir of the classic period.

confronts Quinlan with his suspicion that Quinlan planted evidence in Sanchez's motel room, Quinlan raises his cane in anger. Its threatening shadow falls across Vargas's face, implying how Quinlan overshadows Vargas at this point—he still has power and influence in the town. In playing the scene Heston did not flinch in the face of Welles's threatening gaze, as Delson pointed out to him. "Well, I am happy to subscribe to the thesis that I can stand on equal ground with Orson in a scene," he answered.[44]

Principal photography wrapped in the wee hours of April 2, 1957. Welles was one night over the thirty-eight-day shooting schedule, and $31,000 over the $825,000 budget—a reasonable overage, considering the meagerness of the budget to begin with.[45] Welles spent two months supervising the editing and dubbing of the rough cut mainly with editor Virgil Vogel; another editor, Aaron Stell, also helped out.

After Welles delivered the rough cut to Universal, he decamped for Mexico, where he was engaged during the balance of the summer in preparing to direct a film about Don Quixote. It was extremely imprudent of Welles to fly the coop without discussing in detail his rough cut with the front office, a mistake he had made before.

While Welles was away from Hollywood, Edward Muhl, studio chief, screened Welles's rough cut. He and his fellow executives were baffled by it; they found it excessively dark and disturbing. They were unsure how to market it; it didn't seem to fit into any conventional genre or category. "The picture was just too dark and black and strange for them," Welles explained years later. "Movies weren't nearly that black" back then; those were different days.[46]

In Welles's absence, Muhl therefore asked Edward Nims, head of postproduction, who had edited *The Stranger*, to reedit certain scenes. Muhl further enlisted a young journeyman contract director named Harry Keller to shoot a few brief additional scenes to clarify the story line, with Cliff Stein as cinematographer. These scenes were shot on November 19, 1957, with Welles barred from the set on his return from Mexico. Keller accordingly shot "some bland and clichéd connecting footage."[47]

Welles dispatched a letter to Heston, cited in *This Is Orson Welles*, on November 17, implying that Heston should at the very least "insist on a certain standard of professional capacity and reputation in the choice of an alternate director. UNLESS THE STUDIO IS STOPPED THEY ARE GOING TO WRECK OUR PICTURE." (The caps are Welles's.) He refers to Heston's owning a piece of the film, saying, "You must realize that, if you have a financial interest in the picture, I have a professional one."[48]

"They did a half day's work without me," Welles told Peter Bogdanov-ich. "Heston kept phoning me to say what he was doing, and to ask if it was all right, because if I didn't approve he would walk off the set." When Heston reported to Welles that he was satisfied with Keller's work, Welles replied immediately in another letter: "The fact that your director is not, after all, a certifiable incompetent" seemed to be enough to satisfy Heston.[49]

Welles was reserving judgment until he saw Nims's cut of the film, and he did so on December 4, 1957. He fired off a fifty-eight-page memo to Muhl, suggesting some improvements, the following day, December 5.

"I find it hard to resist pointing out," Welles commented in his memo as diplomatically as he could, that Nims's cut "displays a much hastier craftsmanship" than his own cut of the film.[50] For his part, Muhl believed that Nims worked at a faster pace than Welles simply because he was more efficient.

Welles closed his memo "with a very earnest plea that you consent" to his suggestions to improve the final cut, "to which I gave so many long hard days of work."[51] Welles later sent a copy to Heston, with a cover let-ter, in which he stated that Muhl assured him that Nims was honoring many of Welles's suggestions. Welles only hoped that that was true. As a matter of fact, some of the modifications that Welles suggested were made by Nims, who saw himself more as Welles's ally than as his enemy.

In any case, Henry Mancini was commissioned to compose the score for the movie. Although Mancini became better known for his lighter scores for movies like *The Pink Panther*, he was equally adept at creating music for serious pictures. Welles had advised Mancini early on that he did not want "tempestuous, melodramatic, or operatic scoring."[52]

Mancini responded with an innovative score in which he adroitly integrated jazz, featuring a honky-tonk player piano (which appeared in the film in Tanya's brothel). Chuck Berg writes that Mancini's edgy, jazz-inflected score "accentuates the film's tension with Latin percus-sion," especially bongo drums. Moreover, Mancini brought his jazzy scoring just as effectively to the TV detective series *Peter Gunn* the following year. "Mancini acknowledged that his greatest contribution" to movie music was his incorporation of jazz "into the mainstream film scoring," beginning with *Touch of Evil*.[53] Preminger followed suit by having Duke Ellington compose a jazz score for *Anatomy of a Murder* the following year.

A sneak preview of *Touch of Evil* in Pacific Palisades in January 1958 drew a lukewarm reception from the audience. Consequently the front of-fice ultimately cut fifteen minutes from the film, from 108 minutes to 93 minutes, so it could run as the bottom half of a double bill—the same fate that befell Kubrick's *The Killing. Touch of Evil* was paired with *The Fe-male Animal*, a bargain basement version of *Sunset Boulevard*, with Hedy Lamarr as a has-been actress who falls for a beach bum. The picture, now forgotten, was directed by none other than Harry Keller and produced by Albert Zugsmith.

Most reviewers wrote *Touch of Evil* off as a sordid crime thriller. One of the exceptions was Howard Thompson, who wrote in the *New York Times* that Welles "succeeds in generating enough electricity for three such yarns and in general staging it as a wild, murky nightmare."[54]

Critical recognition of the film emerged when the movie was shown at the Brussels World Fair on June 8, 1958, where it received the grand prize. Two French critics, Francois Truffaut and Jean-Luc Godard, who were soon to become directors themselves, were on the jury and cham-pioned the movie. Furthermore, general audiences overseas by and large appreciated the picture; and it was acclaimed all over Europe.

In 1976 the fifteen minutes of missing footage, which had been ex-cised from the movie the first time around, was discovered by film archi-vist Robert Epstein at UCLA and restored to the film for release to the educational market.

In the mid-1990s Heston's copy of the Welles memo was unearthed, and producer Rick Schmidlin arranged to have the film painstakingly reconstructed in a version closely approximating Welles's suggestions in his memo. The restoration of the film was carried out in 1998 by Walter Murch, an Academy Award–winning film editor (*Apocalypse Now*). The fifteen minutes of Welles's footage that had originally been jettisoned was of course restored, while Keller's hokey explanatory scenes were eliminated whenever possible, bringing the reconstructed version to 111 minutes.

The studio had originally superimposed the film's credits on the pro-longed opening shot, which tracks the death car with the bomb planted in the trunk as it passes through an intersection, moving toward the border crossing. Murch removed the opening credits, and placed them at the end of the movie, as Welles had suggested in his memo. He also removed Henry Mancini's title music, which accompanied the opening credits.

Welles wanted overlapping fragments of source music during the extended opening shot, Murch explains.[55] Murch replaced Mancini's music with incidental music spilling onto the street from car radios, bars, and juke joints; and with location sounds, including the voices of pedestrians and even police sirens. As a result of these carefully compiled sounds, viewers are immediately plunged into the atmosphere of a noisy main street in a border town, as Welles intended.

In his memo Welles had offered fifty suggestions in all, with a view to fine-tuning the film. Granted, Nims had implemented a few of Welles's ideas, but the majority of his changes were ignored. I have described two of these modifications, in the film's opening scene. The other forty-eight are not all equally significant, but, as Murch states, they do have a powerful cumulative effect on the picture as a whole.

"The fifty changes that were made did not transform the film into something completely different," Murch emphasizes. "This *Touch of Evil* is simply a better version of the same film, which is to say, more in line with the director's vision."[56] Similarly, Michael Dawson, who restored Welles's *Othello*, told me that the aim of the reconstruction of a Welles film is not to "improve" on Welles's movie, but to present it as closely as possible to the version that he had intended.

In the light of the movie's status in Europe as a masterwork, *Touch of Evil* developed a cult following in America over the years, culminating in the release of Walter Murch's restored version in 1998. At that point the movie was heralded as a superb film noir in the United States as well as in Europe. Indeed, *Touch of Evil* was officially inducted into the Library of Congress's National Film Registry as a motion picture of lasting value, and is included in Eagan's book on the registry films.

Still, when Edward Muhl was asked his opinion of Welles at the time of the film's restoration, he answered that "Welles was a poseur who never made a film that earned any money."[57] The unrepentant Muhl was obviously not aware of the commercial success of *The Stranger*, not to mention that the restored version of *Touch of Evil* has done a land-office business for Universal on DVD.

As the movie gets rolling, Miguel Vargas is involved in two ongoing investigations: first, there is the death of millionaire Rudy Linnekar and his girlfriend, resulting from the explosion in the border town in the movie's first scene; second, Vargas is also bringing to trial in Mexico City the brother of Joe Grandi, the local crime boss in Los Robles, on drug charges. While Vargas pursues leads in his investigations, his wife, Susan, moves into the isolated Mirador Motel on the American side of the border, which—unknown to her—is owned by the Grandis.

Vargas suspects Quinlan, a blatant racist, of endeavoring to frame Manelo Sanchez, a Mexican shoe clerk who is engaged to Marcia Linnekar, for the death of her father, who opposed the marriage. When Vargas uncovers evidence that implies that Quinlan has framed Sanchez, Quinlan is apoplectic at being "caught" out of bounds.

Meanwhile, the conniving racketeer, Joe Grandi, decides to warn Vargas off the prosecution of his brother by victimizing his wife. He dispatches his mob of young thugs to the creepy, deserted motel. The gang includes a tough, muscular lesbian (Mercedes McCambridge), who sports a leather jacket like the guys. Susan is forced to take drugs to set her up as an apparent addict. As the hoodlums prepare to rape Susan, the leader of the pack instructs them gruffly, "Hold her legs." The lesbian says, "Let me stay; I wanna watch." A shadow falls across Susan's terrified face; and the door of her motel room slams, shutting out the viewer. "Nothing is really shown beyond terrible anticipation," Thomson writes, "but it is enough, and it is repellant."[58]

Assuming that Quinlan will endorse his badgering of Vargas through the persecution of his wife, Grandi moves Susan to El Rancho Grandi, a tawdry hotel in Los Robles, where he has a meeting with Quinlan who has been drinking heavily. Quinlan, who suspects that the devious Grandi might double-cross him somehow, intends to strangle Grandi with a silk stocking. The scene is lit only by a neon sign blinking on and off outside the window. The unsteady, eerie light suggests how unsteady and frightened Grandi feels. (Welles apparently borrowed the lighting effect from the scene in Chris's dingy hotel room in *Scarlet Street*.) After he kills Grandi, Quinlan, who walks with a cane, inadvertently leaves it behind in the hotel room.

A police physician (Joseph Cotten) subsequently advises Vargas that there is evidence that his wife had been involved in "a mixed party" (i.e., racially mixed) at the Mirador Motel, before she was transported in a drugged state to El Rancho Grandi. Vargas is outraged by the kidnapping of his wife; he has a conference with Quinlan's devoted partner, Pete

Menzies, about it. In the past Menzies had steadfastly supported Quinlan as a good cop, disregarding any evidence to the contrary. But Menzies himself discovers Quinlan's cane at the murder scene and realizes to his great consternation that he has been Quinlan's dupe and stooge for years.

The distraught Menzies agrees to wear a wire, attached to Vargas's tape recorder, to aid Vargas in trapping Quinlan into a confession. Menzies and Quinlan walk through a nighttime wasteland of oil derricks towering above a polluted river. Vargas clambers after them, even wading beneath a bridge to keep within range of the microphone concealed on Menzies.

Quinlan declares to Menzies self-righteously, "I never framed anyone who wasn't guilty!" When Quinlan's voice echoes from Vargas's recording device and ricochets back to him, he suddenly realizes that Menzies is involved in electronic eavesdropping at Vargas's behest. Aware that Menzies has betrayed him, Quinlan summarily guns down his erstwhile partner and friend.

Quinlan then prepares to open fire on Vargas, but the fatally wounded Menzies shoots Quinlan instead. Long ago Quinlan "saved Menzies's life by stopping a bullet meant for him, causing his game leg and necessitating his use of a cane."[59] Consequently, when Menzies shoots Quinlan, the latter says haltingly before he expires, "Pete, that's the second bullet I stopped for you." In the restored version of the film, Menzies had explained in an earlier scene about Quinlan taking a bullet intended for him. But his explanation was one of the passages deleted in the original release prints of the film, where Quinlan's remark about it is left unexplained.

The body of the corrupt cop falls backward into the slimy river, which is choked with trash. Quinlan's fate once again recalls Welles as Harry Lime in Reed's *Third Man*, just as Welles's Franz Kindler also evokes Harry Lime. In Reed's movie Lime dies in a foul, muddy sewer. In *Touch of Evil*, Quinlan ends by sinking into the depths of a filthy, stagnant river—an expressionistic symbol of his decline into moral degradation. Discussing this scene, Brian McDonnell observes that *Touch of Evil* certainly lays claim to being "the final great flourish of expressionistic style within the classic noir period."[60]

Filmmaker Curtis Hanson (*L.A. Confidential*) calls "the torturous relationship" between Quinlan and Menzies, his loyal sidekick, a heartfelt love story. Quinlan was "assisted, idolized, and loved by his heartsick deputy, who would rather die for him than betray him—and who ultimately does both."[61]

Tanya materializes on the bridge over the polluted river, in the wake of Quinlan's death. Earlier in the picture Quinlan had asked Tanya, who is a fortune teller, to foretell his future. "You haven't got any," she replied ruefully; "your future is all used up." How right she was. At film's end, Schwartz, a police detective, informs Tanya that Sanchez has confessed to the murder of Rudy Linnekar and his girl; Quinlan had been right all along about Sanchez. Tanya responds, "He was a great detective—and a lousy cop" (because he unlawfully took the law into his own hands).

Schwartz says, "You really liked him." Tanya sidesteps his observation, and answers instead laconically, "The cop did; the one who killed him; he loved him." Asked by Schwartz to sum up Quinlan's character, she responds, "He was some kind of man. What does it matter what you say about people?" Dietrich always believed that was "the best-delivered line of her life."[62] With that, Tanya murmurs, "Adios," and walks away, receding into the darkness.

Marlene Dietrich as Tanya, the fortune teller, in *Touch of Evil.*

Alastair Phillips reminds us that Paul Schrader rightly named *Touch of Evil* as the epitaph of the classic noir period: "The film's closing sequence, with Quinlan dead and Tanya disappearing into the darkness of the night, does indeed feel like the end of an era."[63]

Nonetheless, Foster Hirsch told the *New York Times*, we remember, "the impulse behind noir didn't suddenly stop after *Touch of Evil*."[64] Putting it another way, Alain Silver baldly states that "the cycle of noir films never did conclude." On the contrary, individual movies that bore the earmarks of film noir gradually began to accumulate in the 1960s and after. "Within a few years afterwards" a trend called "neo-noir began to appear."[65] They featured, for example, additional films inspired by the work of both Hammett and Highsmith. Neo-noir continues to serve as a reminder of how powerful and enduring the trend called film noir still is, and how it continues to influence American cinema.

Notes

1. André Bazin, Charles Bitsch, and Jean Domarchi, "Interview with Orson Welles," in *Orson Welles: Interviews*, ed. Mark Estrin (Jackson: University Press of Mississippi, 2002), 74.

2. James Harvey, "Sam Spiegel," *New York Times Book Review*, April 13, 2003, 29.

3. Clinton Heylin, *Despite the System: Orson Welles versus the Hollywood Studios* (Chicago: Chicago Review Press, 2005), 169.

4. Joseph McBride, *Orson Welles*, rev. ed. (New York: Da Capo, 1996), 99.

5. Biesen, *Blackout*, 207.

6. Simon Callow, *Orson Welles: Hello, America* (New York, Viking, 2006), 267.

7. Orson Welles and Peter Bogdanovich, *This Is Orson Welles*, rev. ed. (New York: Da Capo, 1995), 186.

8. David Thomson, *Rosebud: The Story of Orson Welles* (New York: Vintage, 1997), 268.

9. Heylin, *Despite the System*, 180.

10. Richard France, "Orson Welles's First Film," *Films in Review* 38, no. 9 (August–September, 1989): 403–7.

11. Peter Cowie, *The Cinema of Orson Welles*, rev. ed. (New York: Da Capo, 1989), 89.

12. Welles and Bogdanovich, *This Is Orson Welles*, 187.

13. Charles Higham, *Orson Welles: The Rise and Fall of an American Genius* (New York: St. Martin's Press, 1985), 225.

14. Heylin, *Despite the System*, 175.

15. Bret Wood, "Recognizing *The Stranger*," *Video Watchdog* (May–July, 1999): 23.

16. James Welsh, "*The Stranger*," in *Encyclopedia of Orson Welles*, ed. Chuck Berg and Tom Erskine (New York: Facts on File, 2003), 359.

17. Welles and Bogdanovich, *This Is Orson Welles*, 189. George Stevens (*Gunga Din*) filmed the gas ovens at Dachau and the liberation of the camp. See Max Hastings, *Victory in Europe: Photographed by George Stevens* (Boston: Little, Brown, 1985), 164–71.

18. Apocalypse, 12:7–9.

19. F. X. Feeney, *Welles* (Los Angeles: Taschen, 2007), 65.

20. Callow, *Orson Welles*, 276.

21. Charles Higham, *The Films of Orson Welles* (Los Angeles: University of California Press, 1973), 111.

22. Colin McArthur, "*The Stranger*," in *Film Noir: The Encyclopedia*, 283.

23. Thomson, *Rosebud*, 268.

24. Michael Barson, *Hollywood Directors* (New York: Noonday Press, 1995), 444.

25. McArthur, "*The Stranger*," 283.

26. Susan Doll, "Orson Welles," in *International Dictionary of Films and Filmmakers*, vol. 2, 551–56.

27. Chuck Berg, "Albert Zugsmith," in *Encyclopedia of Orson Welles*, 438.

28. Charlton Heston, *In the Arena: An Autobiography* (New York: Simon and Schuster, 1995), 153–55.

29. Eagan, *America's Film Legacy*, 545.

30. Everitt, "The New Noir: In the Daylight, but Still Deadly," sec. 2:28; see also Hirsch, *Detours and Lost Highways*, 1.

31. See McBride, *Orson Welles*, 145, ff.

32. James Delson, "Charlton Heston and Orson Welles," in *The Big Book of Noir*, 124.

33. Carl Richardson, *Autopsy: An Element of Realism in Film* (Metuchen, N.J.: Scarecrow Press, 1992), 141.

34. Eagan, *America's Film Legacy*, 545.

35. Thomson, *Rosebud*, 341.

36. Thomson, *New Biographical Dictionary of Film*, 952.

37. John Stubbs, "*Touch of Evil* from Novel to Film," in Orson Welles, *Touch of Evil: A Screenplay*, ed. Terry Comito (New Brunswick, N.J.: Rutgers University Press, 1998), 190.

38. Richard Chatten, "Russell Metty," in *International Dictionary of Films and Filmmakers*, vol. 4, 572.

39. Delson, "Charlton Heston and Orson Welles," 125–26.

40. Heston, *In the Arena*, 156.

41. Heston, *In the Arena*, 156.

42. Heston, *In the Arena*, 157.

43. McBride, *Orson Welles*, 150.

44. Delson, "Charlton Heston and Orson Welles," 124.

45. Heston, *In the Arena*, 160.

46. Welles and Bogdanovich, *This Is Orson Welles*, 322; see also McBride, *Orson Welles*, 146.

47. McBride, *Orson Welles*, 146.

48. Welles and Bogdanovich, *This Is Orson Welles*, 306.

49. Welles and Bogdanovich, *This Is Orson Welles*, 302, 303.

50. Orson Welles, "Notes on *Touch of Evil*," December 5, 1957, in the Universal Studios Archive, 11.

51. Welles, "Notes on *Touch of Evil*," 58.

52. Heylin, *Despite the System*, 301.

53. Chuck Berg, "Henry Mancini," in *Encyclopedia of Orson Welles*, 241.

54. Howard Thompson, "*Touch of Evil*," in *Touch of Evil: A Screenplay*, 225; Terry Comito reprints key reviews of the film in this volume.

55. Michael Ondaatje, *The Conversations: Walter Murch and the Art of Editing Film* (New York: Knopf, 2008), 186.

56. Walter Murch, "Restoring the Touch of Genius to *Touch of Evil*," *New York Times*, September 6, 1998, sec. 2:16.

57. Ondaatje, *The Conversations*, 186.

58. Thomson, *Rosebud*, 542.

59. McBride, *Orson Welles*, 157.

60. Brian McDonnell, "*Touch of Evil*," in *Encyclopedia of Film Noir*, 421.

61. Curtis Hanson, "The Dark Side," *Newsweek*, Special issue on movies, Summer 1998, 61.

62. Ean Wood, *Dietrich: A Biography* (London: Sanctuary, 2004), 297.

63. Phillips, "*Touch of Evil*," in *100 Film Noirs*, 252–53.

64. Everitt, "The New Noir," sec. 2:28.

65. Alain Silver, "Introduction: The Classic Period," in *Film Noir: The Encyclopedia*, 15.

Part Four

THE LOWER DEPTHS:
THE RISE OF NEO-NOIR

CHAPTER TWELVE

DASHIELL HAMMETT AND NEO-NOIR:
THE DAIN CURSE AND *HAMMETT*

After the heyday of film noir ended in the late 1950s, there were sporadic attempts to revive it in the 1960s with films like *The Spy Who Came in from the Cold* (1968). The 1970s ushered in a resurgence of interest in film noir with movies like *Chinatown* (1974), and the antihero took on a larger profile. This dark type of film, peopled with desperate and depraved characters, was christened neo-noir. This cycle of tough, cynical crime movies gained momentum in the 1980s with movies like *Body Heat* (1981) and in the 1990s with films like *L.A. Confidential* (1997). Moreover, "neo-noir continues to expand in the twenty-first century" with pictures like *The Ghost Writer* (2010).[1]

Contemporary audiences find the doomed protagonist of a neo-noir intriguing, writes David Everitt. "Almost always he damns himself by giving in to temptation—either a proposition from an alluring woman or a scheme to make easy money," often engineered by a femme fatale.[2] "The neo-noir spirit," comments Ronald Schwartz, boldly carries forward film noir's underlying cynicism and pessimism about "the moral bankruptcy of contemporary America."[3]

What's more, many detective movies made since the days of classic noir qualify as neo-noir, because they have the benchmarks of the noir films of yesteryear. Stephen Holden states that the noir formula demands that filmmakers create movies with strong story lines, "with hard-boiled dialogue and multifaceted, often duplicitous characters. Noir may be formula, but it is one with room for compelling flesh-and-blood characters."[4] So neo-noir films continue to be turned out in Hollywood, and, as

Richard Jameson puts it, "film noir is still possible, and has no apologies to make to anybody."[5]

Dashiell Hammett's name is inextricably linked with neo-noir since his influence on the detective film and on neo-noir remains strong. Neo-noir movies like *Chinatown* and *L.A. Confidential*, with their hard-boiled detectives, "draw strength from the honorable cinematic tradition" of the noir detective film dating back to *The Maltese Falcon*.[6]

Naremore declares that "neo-noirs are produced by Hollywood with increasing regularity. Consider such big-budget television productions" as *The Dain Curse* (1978), based on a Hammett novel. Both *The Dain Curse* and *Hammett* (1982), a theatrical film that features Dashiell Hammett himself as a private eye, have been rediscovered in recent years and belong to the trend in neo-noir. Naremore concludes that noir is never going to go away.[7]

Foster Hirsch, author of *Detours and Lost Highways: A Map of Neo-Noir*, has told the *New York Times* that "audiences remain intrigued by neo noir for essentially the same reasons they always were. There is the appeal of a story about characters who are thrown into a kind of nightmare scenario." There is a timeless attraction to characters who are dogged by cruel circumstances and fate.[8]

Hammett published his second novel, *The Dain Curse*, in 1929. It centered on the Continental Op, that is, an operative of the Continental Detective Agency. He works out of the agency's San Francisco office. The Op appears in Hammett's first two novels and most of the short fiction Hammett published in *Black Mask*. (The Op would be replaced by Sam Spade in *The Maltese Falcon*.)

Hammett scholar Robert Gale believes that the Op survives "because he is quick-witted, skillful at his job, cynically disillusioned, and consistently amoral"—he will bend the rules when he feels he has to in order to solve a case.[9]

Moreover, the Op shares with Sam Spade, who was to some extent modeled on the Op, the character of a lone wolf, who is driven by a personal sense of mission. Thus the role of the police force is marginal in *The Dain Curse*, as it is in *The Maltese Falcon*, because both the Op and Sam Spade sometimes question the competence of the police, not to mention their integrity. Just when the cops expect that the Op should cooperate with them in an investigation, he is apt to take over the entire case and solve it himself. As LeRoy Panek observes in *Reading Early*

Hammett, the police ultimately "don't make any difference to what goes on in *The Dain Curse*."[10]

In the novel, the Op is called upon to investigate the theft of some unset diamonds of negligible worth from the wealthy Leggett family. What starts out as a routine robbery case turns deeply serious when Edgar Leggett, head of the clan, is murdered; then his daughter Gabrielle becomes involved in a sinister religious cult centered at the Temple of the Holy Grail. What's more, her new husband, Eric Collison, is slain in due course by a hit man. In short, it becomes increasingly apparent that the Op moves in a threatening world of conniving clients, dead-end hoods, and crafty conspirators.

The Dain Curse was serialized before publication in book form in *Black Mask*, from November 1928 to February 1929. If *The Dain Curse* as a novel seems to lack sufficient narrative coherence at times, the reason is that Joseph Shaw, the editor of *Black Mask*, insisted that Hammett make "each of the four installments self-contained. . . . Although linking passages were provided," the shift from one installment to the next was awkward.[11] Hammett did make an effort to improve the story's narrative continuity when he revised it for publication as a book, but the complex plot is still difficult at times to follow.

While composing the novel's story line, he recalled the American fascination with spiritualism that had developed in the 1920s, and introduced it into the novel. Moreover, Arthur Conan Doyle late in life was "an avid believer in the spirit world." Conan Doyle even took to the lecture circuit to defend spiritualism and spoke in California in 1923. Hammett personally thought evangelists like Aimee Semple McPherson, with her Foursquare gospel, were charlatans.[12]

Hammett accordingly depicts in *The Dain Curse* Joseph and Aaronia Haldorn, who preside over the Temple of the Holy Grail in San Francisco, as con artists engaged in a spook racket. They employ technicians like Tom Fink to rig the ghostly gimmicks used in the services at the temple to impress their gullible clientele. The Haldorns' vulgar religious sideshow is, in the Op's estimation, just another example of the manner in which phoniness had penetrated almost every sector of modern life. Yet Gabrielle becomes one of the Haldorns' fervent followers. In fact, Gabrielle takes refuge in the Temple of the Holy Grail because she claims to experience bizarre spiritual apparitions.

Another topic of current interest that Hammett brought into the novel was drug addiction. Indeed, Gabrielle's "apparitions" turn out to be the result of nothing more "spiritual" than her addiction to morphine. Hammett had dealt with hopheads and their hallucinations firsthand while he was a Pinkerton agent, and hence he portrayed Gabrielle's addition very authentically.

The Op eventually cajoles Gabrielle into withdrawing from her dependence on drugs and supervises her rehabilitation. When Gabrielle inquires of the Op why he rather heroically helped her suffer through her horrendous withdrawal symptoms in order to be cured, he answers:

"I'm twice your age, sister; an old man. I'm damned if I'll make a chump of myself by telling you why I did it, . . . why I'd do it again and be glad for the chance."[13] This speech survives in the telefilm. The Op implies that he has developed an attachment to Gabrielle, but he chivalrously renounces the opportunity to admit his feelings for her, just as Sam Spade will renounce his emotional attachment to Brigid O'Shaughnessy (although the naive Gabrielle is quite different from Brigid, the femme fatale of *The Maltese Falcon*).

Hammett reworked the serialized version of *The Dain Curse* in preparing the story for book publication, dividing the novel into three parts, rather than four, as was the case of the serial version. Nevertheless, Harry Block, an editor for Hammett's publisher, Alfred Knopf, felt that the novel's plot was still too complicated, "and that there were too many characters" (102 by actual count).[14] Still Block ultimately accepted the manuscript for book publication. Withal, the reviews were mostly favorable, and the novel was a best seller.

The Dain Curse was never made into a feature film during Hammett's lifetime, because its sprawling plot and huge cast of characters simply defied compression into a two-hour movie. As a matter of fact, as early as 1928, before *The Dain Curse* was even published in *Black Mask*, Hammett had sought in vain to interest a Hollywood studio in the novel. In 1978 CBS-TV presented a five-hour miniseries that, in retrospect, surely qualifies as a neo-noir.[15]

None of Hammett's novels were adapted for television during his lifetime, but *The Adventures of Sam Spade*, starring Howard Duff (borrowing the private eye from *The Maltese Falcon*), had a five-year run on CBS radio (1946–1951). Hammett dissociated himself from the radio series and viewed it merely as a source of income. "I don't want to have anything to do with the radio," he said at the time; "it's a dizzy world—makes the movies seem highly intellectual."[16] Television also proved subsequently to be a source of income; Lillian Hellman, the executor of Hammett's estate, pocketed $175,000 for the TV rights to *The Dain Curse*.[17]

The Dain Curse (1978)

Hammett so patiently filled in all the details of the vast canvas he created for the novel that the book resists translation to another medium. Yet Robert Lenski's teleplay, as presented in three one-hundred-minute installments, by and large stays close to Hammett's original story. Lenski is credited in the opening credits, not only with the screenplay, but with developing the project for TV, which means that he was the executive producer of the miniseries. Little wonder that he received an Emmy nomination for his work on the production.

It was Lenski who decided that the miniseries would be set in the same period, the Roaring Twenties, as Hammett's novel, and not updated to the present. This gives the telefilm an authentic atmosphere. A surprising amount of the flavor of Hammett's original work has been preserved in Lenski's literate TV script. Lenski employs the novel's dialogue whenever possible; furthermore, Lenski was at pains to include material that pertained to the theme of the novel, as well as to the plot, such as one character's observations about the general erosion of traditional values in American society.

E. W. (Egbert) Swackhamer, who directed the miniseries, also received an Emmy nomination. He had worked mostly as a director of individual episodes of TV crime series such as *Murder She Wrote*, which proved to be good experience for directing *The Dain Curse*. Swackhamer had a first-rate cast to work with, starting with James Coburn, who played the Continental Op, renamed Hamilton Nash. Coburn had played a Bond-like spy in the film *Our Man Flint*. Hamilton Nash was addressed as "Ham" by his fellow operatives, which could be short for Hammett. As a matter of fact, with his moustache and his lean, lanky frame, Coburn did resemble Hammett. Coburn made a "stylish operative," according to David Thomson.[18]

Jean Simmons, who portrayed Sister Sharon Falconer in *Elmer Gantry*, plays Aaronia Haldorn, an evangelist modeled on Aimee Semple McPherson, in *The Dain Curse*. Oscar winner Beatrice Straight (*Network*) enacts a femme fatale, Alice Leggett, in the present miniseries.

Jason Miller (*The Exorcist*) is the neurotic, sly Owen Fitzstephan, a writer of exotic horror fiction. Paul Stewart (*Citizen Kane*) is Hamilton Nash's taciturn, imperturbable boss, known only at the detective agency as the Old Man. Finally, the miniseries included one TV star, Brent Spiner, who was cast as Tom Fink, a member of the nefarious Temple staff. Spiner was best known for his role as an android in the TV series *Star Trek: The Next Generation*.

The setting of the miniseries was transplanted from San Francisco in the novel to New York. The telefilm was shot entirely on location in New York City and its environs; rural scenes were filmed in the Pennsylvania countryside.

For the musical score, Charlie Gross (*The Group*) mainly utilized a jazz combo, featuring piano, clarinet, and trombone. He provided the type of jazzy score that one would have heard in a speakeasy in the Jazz Age.

The TV adaptation of *The Dain Curse* begins with Hamilton Nash being farmed out by the Old Man to a San Francisco insurance company to investigate the theft of some imperfect diamonds of no great value from the Leggett estate. But the stolen gems are small potatoes in the light of the lurid family history of the Leggett clan that Nash gradually uncovers.

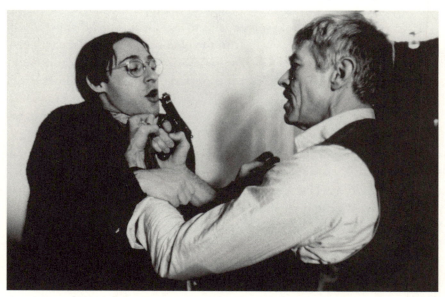

Tom Fink (Brent Spiner) is confronted by Hamilton Nash (James Coburn) in the neo-noir television adaptation of Dashiell Hammett's *Dain Curse*.

Nash investigates in turn Edgar Leggett, his daughter Gabrielle, and his second wife, Alice, with the help of his novelist friend Owen Fitzstephan, who knows the Leggetts. In brief, Edgar Leggett had initially been friends with the two sisters, Lily and Alice Dain.

While Nash is looking for the stolen diamonds, Gabrielle, a morphine addict, disappears. Nash traces her to the Temple of the Holy Grail, which is presided over by Joseph Haldorn and his wife Aaronia. Nash finds Gabrielle there and takes her home, only to learn that Edgar Leggett has apparently committed suicide. Edgar leaves behind a letter, confessing to the murder of his first wife, Lily—who is Alice's sister and Gabrielle's mother.

Nash decides in a powwow with the Leggetts that Edgar's letter was not a suicide note; he more than likely intended to flee the country for distant climes, not to kill himself. It seems that Edgar took the blame for Lily's murder because Alice had blamed Gabrielle, who—as a child of five—allegedly shot her mother while hypnotized by Alice. Nash rightly suspects that Alice herself shot Lily, so she could wed Edgar, a millionaire; and that Edgar, in turn, assumed the blame for Lily's demise to protect his daughter. Alice Leggett, Nash contends, then killed Edgar, in order to become a wealthy widow, eligible to pursue younger men like Owen Fitzstephan.

Alice, distraught over Nash's accusations, endeavors to escape; but she is shot by Owen Fitzstephan, as they struggle on the staircase, before she can make her getaway from the Leggett mansion. Alice, who exits the story at the close of the first of the miniseries's three installments, turns out to be a bona fide femme fatale, since Nash's accusations against her prove true. As LeRoy Panek comments, the narrative "characterizes Alice quite literally as a predator."[19]

In the miniseries's second installment, it is clear that Gabrielle is all too aware that the Leggetts are descendants of the Dain clan, which, legend has it, is accursed. She accordingly believes that she is marked by the Dain curse; that is, Gabrielle sees herself as a jinx and warns Nash not to get involved with her, "or the Dain curse will get you." In addition, she is convinced that her drug addiction is the result of the Dain curse.

Gabrielle moves into the Temple of the Holy Grail, a converted office building in downtown San Francisco. She is seeking spiritual solace from Joseph and Aaronia Haldorn, Nash notes, by way of their hocus-pocus.

Gabrielle's attorney, Madison Andrews, asks Nash to monitor Gabrielle's behavior while she is sojourning in the temple, a garish mausoleum, according to Nash. Now that Gabrielle has joined their cult, the Haldorns resent Nash's presence there as Gabrielle's guardian.

In an effort to discourage Nash from snooping around the temple, the Haldorns arrange to have a cloud of hallucinogenic vapor (courtesy of Tom Fink) pumped into his room while he is sleeping, in the hope that the fantasies he experiences will scare him into leaving. Swackhamer employs a distorting lens on the camera to produce Nash's delirious dream. In the best tradition of noirish expressionism, Nash's body is stretched out of shape, making him look grotesque indeed; he laughs maniacally all the while. But the bizarre vision does not prompt Nash to leave; he merely comes to, feeling woozy, and realizes that he has suffered a drug-induced nightmare.

Aaronia correctly suspects that Joseph suffers from delusions of grandeur and sees himself as a divine high priest, who is free to acquire a younger consort, Gabrielle. When the jealous Aaronia interferes in Joseph's plans to seduce Gabrielle, he is prepared to sacrifice her in a ritual slaying on the temple's altar. But Nash intervenes and shoots Joseph dead. Shortly after, Gabrielle and her devoted fiancé, Eric Collinson, elope; they rent a honeymoon hideaway near Quesada, a coastal town sixty miles from New York, for their honeymoon, as the second installment of the miniseries concludes.

Nash, who still sees himself as Gabrielle's protector, follows the newlyweds to Quesada. He soon discovers Eric's corpse floating offshore; and so he decides to search the house where Gabrielle and Eric were staying for possible clues to Eric's murder.

Swackhamer favors long, unbroken takes, like Welles did in *Touch of Evil*. There is, for example, a scene that depicts in purely visual terms how Nash ransacks the honeymoon house. In a single, uninterrupted tracking shot Swackhamer's camera glides around the premises, taking in the entire first floor with its panoramic gaze. The camera then climbs the stairs to the second floor and peers into each room. The viewer sees exactly what Nash sees while the shamus searches the house; Nash finds no clues.

Nash soon after finds Gabrielle cowering in the abandoned boathouse in a drug-addled daze. She is, of course, no help at all to Nash in unraveling the mystery of her husband's death. To Nash, Gabrielle looks like a department store dummy—an observation worthy of Hammett's acrid wit.

The slick, duplicitous Owen Fitzstephan arrives in Quesada, ostensibly to aid Nash in his investigation of Eric's murder. Owen is staying at the Sunset Hotel; it is appropriately named since while he is there the sun sets on his career when a bomb explodes near his room. Fitzstephan is seriously injured and is hospitalized. He is, in fact, permanently incapacitated, and his life begins to deteriorate from this point onward. That an attempt has been made on Fitzstephan's life tells Nash that Owen may be somehow implicated in the wicked schemes hatched at the Temple of the Holy Grail.

After he tracks down Gabrielle, Nash drives her to the house that she and Eric had rented for their honeymoon. With her complicity, he intends to wean her from morphine. Nash "stays with Gabrielle as she fights through withdrawal," managing her rehabilitation. Gabrielle kicks the morphine habit cold turkey in the telefilm's most harrowing sequence. Nash sequesters her in her bedroom, where she tosses and turns on her bed of pain, howling in anguish, until her acute withdrawal symptoms abate. After she is cured, she suggests that she and Nash might build a life together, but Nash graciously declines "to form a romantic relationship with her."[20]

Nash visits Fitzstephan in the hospital where he is recuperating from the bomb explosion and confronts him with all the evidence he has amassed against him as a result of his investigations. "Surprisingly, Nash gets him to admit his responsibility in committing or arranging all the murders" that have been committed.[21] Fitzstephan even acknowledges at one point that he is a Dain, since his mother and Gabrielle's maternal grandfather were brother and sister. Hence the Dain blood flows in him, and, he suggests, the Dain curse has forced him to do evil things—an assumption that Nash, of course, does not buy.

Be that as it may, Fitzstephan confesses to Nash that he was Alice's lover, then Aaronia's lover. Furthermore, the Temple of the Holy Grail, with its fake religious cult, was entirely his idea; he commandeered the Haldorns to run the operation for him.

Owen Fitzstephan in due course is judged by the authorities to have recuperated enough to stand trial. He appears in court in a wheelchair, hoping cleverly to gain the sympathy of the jury. In the course of the proceedings the redoubtable Tom Fink testifies that Owen instigated the temple racket and continued all along to supervise the Haldorns, who fronted for him, from behind the scenes. Fink then admits in open court that he planted the homemade bomb in Owen Fitzstephan's hotel. He did so because Owen owned the temple and Fink feared that Owen would turn state's evidence, thereby implicating him and the whole temple gang in his diabolical schemes. In short, Fink wanted to keep Owen from testifying against him and the others working at the temple.

District Attorney Jason McNally has built up an impressive case against Owen Fitzstephan, largely through the exhaustive investigations of the intrepid Hamilton Nash. To begin with, Nash maintains, Owen shot Alice on the staircase of the Leggett mansion, but not to keep her from eluding the long arm of the law from killing her sister Lily. His purpose was to ditch her as his mistress, since he now lusted for Gabrielle. As Gabrielle herself states in her testimony in court, "Owen Fitzstephan was the lover of my stepmother, Alice Leggett." After her death, "he switched his affections to me."

Owen then hired a contract killer to liquidate Eric Collinson, Gabrielle's young husband. He was determined to have Gabrielle as his exclusive property, but she consistently spurned his advances. LeRoy Panek, the best commentator on *The Dain Curse*, writes, "At the root of all of the evil in *The Dain Curse* lies Fitzstephan's appetite for Gabrielle and her rejection of him." In brief, Owen was driven by a dark "sexual ardor" for a woman he could not have.[22]

Fitzstephan during his trial enters a plea of "not guilty by reason of insanity." Nash testifies that Owen believes himself to be a sane man; but he wants the jury to declare him insane so that he will be sent to a mental institution and not executed for his crimes. "Yet," Nash concludes, "I believe he really *is* insane! He is mad as a hatter!!"

Nash adds in a voice-over on the sound track, "The jury took pity on Owen Fitzstephan and sent him to an asylum." Aaronia Haldorn, one of Owen's former mistresses, declared that she would take care of the disabled Owen when he got out; he was in fact discharged two years later. But Owen did not get off scot-free; as a result of Fink's makeshift bomb, Owen was a crippled wreck for the rest of his days. Dennis Dooley reflects, Fitzstephan "in some ways received a fitting punishment for his sins."[23] As I have had occasion to state before, in film noir there are no dispensations; one pays for his sins. Nash's final words are, "The Dain curse was over; I had done my job."

The makers of the miniseries derived from Hammett's novel likewise did their job. The TV version of *The Dain Curse*, an outstanding neo-noir, is available on DVD and will continue to be seen—and deservedly so. After all, the combination of an intelligent script, thoughtful direction, and a uniformly excellent cast, headed by James Coburn as Hammett's two-fisted private eye, make *The Dain Curse* a superb viewing experience. The Mystery Writers of America certainly thought so when they conferred the 1979 Edgar (for Edgar Allan Poe) on *The Dain Curse* as the outstanding television mystery drama of the year.

Dashiell Hammett has been impersonated on the screen in two films. He was first played by Jason Robards in Fred Zinnemann's *Julia* (1977), a biographical film about Lillian Hellman (Jane Fonda). The biopic "recalls her struggles to become a successful playwright, with the bemused encouragement of her close friend Dashiell Hammett."[24] Robards received an Oscar for his portrayal of Hammett. Dashiell Hammett was also played by Frederic Forrest in Wim Wenders's *Hammett*, derived from the novel by Joe Gores.

Hammett (1982)

Joe Gores, like Hammett himself, had been a private investigator before turning to crime fiction as a career. In *Hammett* (1975) Gores has "the father of modern detective fiction rise from his typewriter to hunt down a murderer."[25] Gores has won three Edgar Awards for his mystery novels; and his seventeenth detective novel, *Spade and Archer* (2009), is a prequel to *The Maltese Falcon*.

The murder case that Hammett solves in the novel *Hammett* was derived by Gores from Hammett's short story, "Dead Yellow Women," published in *Black Mask* in 1925. In the short story the Continental Op is assigned by the Old Man to Lillian Shan, a Chinese client living in a house on the shore on the outskirts of San Francisco. When Lillian, an expert in the occult, returned to her home unexpectedly from a research trip, she was met by the leader of a small band of Chinese thugs, who had her bound and gagged before he and his gang departed. When she finally broke free, she found that her maid and her cook had been slain.

The Op soon learns of the involvement of Chinatown overlord Chang Li Ching in the murder case, and that he is in cahoots with Neil

Conyers, a con man. Lillian in due course explains to the Op that Chang and Conyers are smuggling contraband guns to China for patriots who are preparing to resist the impending Japanese aggression in China. She confesses that the weapons are stored in her coastal home while awaiting transportation to China.

The Op counters that he has discovered that the cargo on the return trip to San Francisco is opium, smuggled into the United States by Conyers and his cohorts. Consequently, when Lillian arrived home prematurely, Conyers arranged to have Chinese hoodlums bind and gag her so that she would not find out that he was using her house for smuggling drugs into San Francisco, as well as to transport arms to China. The Op adds that Lillian's loyal servants were probably killed so that they could not tell Lillian that her house was involved in drug traffic. Soon after, Conyers is slain by a rival gang of drug dealers in Chinatown.

Lillian is not arrested for drug trafficking because she steadfastly claims that she knew nothing about Conyers's drug dealing; and the police believe her. The slick Chang is not charged with drug trafficking because he has effectively covered his tracks. What's more, neither Lillian nor Chang are prosecuted for sending contraband weapons to China for lack of evidence.

When Lillian Hellman included "Dead Yellow Women" in *The Big Knockover*, her collection of Hammett's short fiction, it was "praised for its careful construction, skillful plot, and accurate depiction of Chinatown's rabbit-warren layout."[26] Indeed, it was Hellman's resurrection of the story from *Black Mask* for her collection that very likely brought it to the attention of Gores, who made it the spine of his novel *Hammett*.

Francis Ford Coppola decided to produce a film version of Gores's novel, when the book was brought to his attention by one of his staff. Coppola had maintained his own independent production company, American Zoetrope, in San Francisco since 1969; he operated the facility as an independent production unit, producing films in partnership with major Hollywood studios. In 1978 Coppola invited the respected German filmmaker Wim Wenders to the United States to make his first American movie, an adaptation of Gores's novel *Hammett*, in which Dashiell Hammett, master of the penny dreadful, solves a real-life mystery. Coppola asked Wenders to direct the film, because Wenders was an internationally known German director who wanted to make a film in America.

After Gores himself failed to come up with a screenplay that Coppola, who was executive producer on the film, found acceptable, Gores left the project late in 1978. Wenders then collaborated on the script, first with Thomas Pope, then with Dennis O'Flaherty, both of whom complained that Wenders insisted on departing substantially from the original story line. Finally Coppola ordered Wenders to cease the multiple rewrites of the screenplay and to start principal photography. Joseph Biroc was chosen as director of photography; he was a distinguished cinematographer who had received an Academy Award for shooting *The Towering Inferno*.

On February 4, 1980, Wenders began filming, with Frederic Forrest in the title role. But Wenders continued revising the script nonstop throughout the production period. Coppola ultimately decided that Wenders had reworked the screenplay to the point where it involved an impenetrable mystery that was not adequately solved at the end. Wenders had not been shooting the approved screenplay, Coppola explains, "and I could not dissuade Wim from this path. . . . So I stopped production" and postponed the remainder of filming indefinitely.[27]

During the hiatus Coppola had the screenplay totally overhauled by mystery writer Ross Thomas, who attempted to steer the story back to the original plotline and provide a coherent ending. The new script entailed the reshooting of eighty percent of the picture. Coppola summoned Wenders back to finish the shoot in November 1981, using Thomas's shooting script. Wenders finished filming in a record twenty-three days. Coppola monitored the reshoot by regularly viewing the retakes done by Wenders and offering him suggestions. But Coppola did not reshoot any scenes himself, as some sources mistakenly assert.

"Wim shot very efficiently," Coppola recalls; he incorporated into the new version of the film the exterior scenes filmed around San Francisco from the original shoot.[28] The bulk of the scenes that had to be reshot were all filmed in the controlled conditions of the studio, where bad weather could not delay the filming.

Recalling the troubled production period of *Hammett*, Gregory Solomon observes, "Just ask Wim Wenders, who worked for Coppola, the executive producer on *Hammett*, how little the latter values a director's artistic freedom—unless he happens to be the director."[29] This statement is severely unfair to Coppola when one considers that he had to scrap much of what Wenders originally shot because it departed significantly from the official script—at a considerable financial loss to Coppola. In the end *Hammett* wound up costing $10 million, considerably over schedule and over budget.

Coppola brought together a top-notch cast and crew for the picture, most of whom stayed on for both shoots. Frederic Forrest, who had an uncanny resemblance to Dashiell Hammett, was a member of Coppola's "repertory company"—actors who appeared in several Coppola films such as *Apocalypse Now*. Peter Boyle, a bald, burly character actor, who had appeared in Scorsese's *Taxi Driver*, played Jimmy Ryan, Hammett's former employer at the Pinkerton detective agency in San Francisco. Ryan's character is modeled on "the Old Man," the boss at the agency where the Continental Op works in Hammett's fiction (he was played by Paul Stewart in the miniseries, *The Dain Curse)*. In the present film Ryan has left the agency and gone into business for himself as a private investigator.

The production designer was Dean Tavoularis, who won an Oscar for designing *Godfather II* and worked frequently on Coppola's films. Tavoularis's attention to historical detail gave *Hammett* the authentic look of the Roaring Twenties. Barry "Blackie" Malkin, another Coppola

Frederic Forrest as Dashiell Hammett in *Hammett*; he loads his gun as he sits at his typewriter. This is the only time the novelist was portrayed on the screen.

regular, had edited films like *Godfather II*; he served as supervising editor on *Hammett*. As an "in joke," one of the hoodlums in the film is called "Blackie" Malkin.

Philip Lathrop replaced the original director of photography, Joseph Biroc, who was not available for the reshoot. Lathrop was an impeccable craftsman, who had photographed *The Black Bird*, David Giler's 1975 send-up of *The Maltese Falcon*, with George Segal as Sam Spade. Inexplicably, Lathrop received no screen credit for his extensive work on *Hammett*.

Composer John Barry, best known for his scoring of several of the James Bond pictures, provided a jazzy score for *Hammett*, all wailing clarinets, sultry strings, and tinkling piano. The score was very appropriate for a film set during the Jazz Age.

The plot of *Hammett* was much simplified by Ross Thomas, in comparison to the scenario originally worked up by Wenders and his collaborators. Nevertheless, the story line still requires the sort of detailed exposition for the reader that I present here.

The film begins with this printed prologue: "This is an entirely imaginary story about the writer Dashiell Hammett, who, in the words of one of his most gifted contemporaries, helped get murder out of the Vicar's rose garden, and back to the people who were really good at it. The detective story has never been the same since."

The prologue paraphrases an observation by Raymond Chandler (who is unnamed), cited above, about Hammett's contribution to hard-boiled detective fiction. Chandler's point was that "Hammett gave murder back to the kind of people who commit it for a reason, not just to provide a corpse."[30] In sum, Hammett's tough, hard-edged crime fiction was a departure from the more refined, genteel detective stories of Doyle and Christie.

After the prologue, the camera roams around Hammett's cramped, cluttered flat in a seedy apartment building in a back street of San Francisco. Hammett is pounding away at his typewriter, as he finishes a short story for *Black Mask* that is already long overdue. Jimmy Ryan, his former boss at the local Pinkerton office, pays him a visit. Ryan quit the agency ("Long hours, short pay," is all he would say about his departure) and now works as a private eye.

Ryan asks Hammett's aid on his current case: he is attempting to locate Crystal Ling, a missing Chinese girl, whom Ryan has failed to find.

Crystal has fled from a notorious nightclub operated by Fong Wei Tau, an overlord in Chinatown; indeed, she has vanished without a trace.

While searching for Crystal, Hammett is driven around Chinatown by a cabbie named Eli, an old-timer played by Elisha Cook, Jr. (*The Maltese Falcon*). Gary Salt, who says he collects gossip for a local newspaper, stops Hammett on the street. Salt explains that he is familiar with Hammett's stories in *Black Mask* and thinks "Dead Yellow Women" (the story that inspired Joe Gores's novel *Hammett*) is one of his best. Salt ominously warns Hammett to give up desperately seeking Crystal, without saying why.

Undaunted, Hammett's investigation takes him to a refuge for stray waifs in Chinatown called the Mission. The venerable actress Sylvia Sidney (*Dead End*) does a cameo as Donaldina Cameron, the director of the Mission. She informs Hammett that Crystal had been staying at the Mission but has since disappeared once more. Unexpectedly Crystal Ling herself (Lydia Lei) shows up at Hammett's apartment; she insists that she is all right and entreats Hammett to convince Ryan to stop looking for her: "I am not lost!"

Crystal recounts that she was in the employ of Fong Wei Tau as a party girl at his Chinatown casino, where C. F. Callaghan, a prestigious local businessman, had become infatuated with her. But when his business failed, Callaghan took his own life and she took refuge in the Mission. In short, Crystal passes herself off to Hammett as a misunderstood young woman down on her luck. She then evaporates once more into the Frisco fog, leaving Hammett to ponder how much truth there was in her tale.

Hammett goes to see Fong at his gambling den, and Fong tells Hammett flatly that he wants Crystal back. Hammett encounters Ryan at the casino; in fact, Fong assumes that Hammett and Ryan are in cahoots and that they know Crystal's whereabouts. Fong accordingly threatens both of them with dire consequences if they fail to deliver Crystal to him. Hammett and Ryan escape from Lang's clutches by fleeing through the opium den in the basement of the casino, and Hammett and Ryan part company on the street. The hapless Hammett is then accosted by Lt. O'Mara, a crooked cop who warns him—somewhat belatedly—not to meddle in the Crystal Ling case.

Not to be dissuaded by threats, Hammett follows a lead to Gary Salt's lair, and searches the place in Salt's absence. Hammett learns that Salt is not a newspaperman of any stripe, but a purveyor of pornography, and that his featured attraction is Crystal Ling. Suddenly Hammett hears Salt coming into his studio, and Hammett quickly hides in Salt's dusty storeroom. Salt is accompanied by Funk, a henchman of mobster "English Eddie" Hagedorn. Funk demands at gunpoint that Salt hand over to him the negatives of some photographs that Salt took; Salt claims to no longer possess the negatives. Funk does not believe him and summarily shoots him dead on the spot. Funk escapes down a flight of stairs before Hammett can nail him.

In ransacking Salt's den of iniquity, Hammett had discovered individual photos of six rich and powerful business tycoons, each of whom is shown frolicking with Crystal. Hammett rightly infers that Funk wanted the original negatives of these photos and that Salt really did not have them. He decides to visit Funk's boss, "English Eddie" Hagedorn, played by Roy Kinnear, who patterned his performance after that of Sydney Greenstreet in *The Maltese Falcon* as a corpulent, refined criminal like Kasper Gutman.

Hagedorn, who is Fong's silent partner in Fong's vice ring, takes Hammett to a private conference presided over by Hagedorn himself. Fong is also in attendance—along with six prominent Frisco citizens, each of whom Salt had photographed in a sex romp with Crystal. Hammett confronts the six tycoons present with his interpretation of the information he has amassed. Someone stole the negatives of the compromising photos Salt had snapped. The blackmailer then demanded a total of $1 million from the six blackmail victims, in exchange for the negatives. Fong was involved in the blackmail plot and wanted his cut; hence he was bent on finding Crystal, who he assumed knew the whereabouts of the negatives.

Matters have come to a head on this night—which is why Hagedorn has brought Hammett to this meeting. The blackmailer wants the $1 million payoff this very night, and Hammett is delegated to meet the blackmailer on a deserted wharf to deliver the cash in exchange for the negatives. Hammett is driven to the wharf by his faithful taxi driver Eli, who is armed with an antique firearm that he is carrying to protect Hammett.

When Hammett arrives for the showdown on the pier, the blackmailer is revealed to be none other than Crystal herself. She materializes out of the swirling fog on the dock; but Hammett is not surprised to find out that Crystal Ling is behind the blackmail plot. After all, he never did quite buy her self-portrait as a pathetic refugee, more sinned against than sinning, that she had drawn for him the day she came to his apartment.

Crystal, who is a bona fide femme fatale, admits in her conversation with Hammett on the pier that Callaghan did not kill himself; his jealous wife shot him when she learned of his torrid romance with Crystal. The whole affair was hushed up by the Callaghan clan, who had the clout to have his death ruled a suicide, in order to spare his wife the scandal of a sensational murder trial. Meanwhile, Crystal took off for parts unknown.

Hammett may not have been shocked to learn of Crystal's duplicity, but he is genuinely stunned at this point to see Jimmy Ryan appear on the scene and identify himself as Crystal's partner in crime in the blackmail scheme. For Lt. O'Mara to be a crooked cop is one thing; for Jimmy Ryan, Hammett's old companion in arms, to be a corrupt private detective is quite another. Ryan obviously engaged Hammett to find Crystal because he wanted to get his share of the blackmail money. Lt. O'Mara, who is in the pay of Fong, is on hand on the wharf to see to it that Crystal surrenders the negatives of the porno pictures of the local tycoons.

But Crystal is not willing to share the loot with Ryan; she accordingly puts a bullet in him. Hammett's eulogy for his old buddy is terse: "In his heyday he was one of the best." Hammett then warns Crystal that the rich and powerful men she has blackmailed will spare no expense in having her tracked down and liquidated in reprisal for her endangering their reputations in Frisco's high society. Crystal shrugs off his threat; she is enveloped in the fog over Frisco as she walks away from the dock and vanishes.

As for Hammett, he heads back to his apartment and his typewriter to bat out this tale for *Black Mask*. He will, of course, change the names of the participants in the blackmail plot in his story in order to protect the guilty.

The film does not depend much on the source story, "Dead Yellow Women," for its plot; but Ross Thomas's screenplay does make good use of the short story's cast of characters, as they turn up in Gores's novel. Thus Lillian Shan in the short story and Crystal Ling in the film both mislead a private investigator about their illegal activities. Lillian in the story does not confess to the Op that she is helping to smuggle contraband weapons to Chinese loyalists who plan to resist Japanese imperialism when Japan endeavors to invade China. By the same token, Crystal in the movie does not divulge to Hammett that she is implicated in blackmail and murder.

Chang Li Ching in the short story is clearly the model for Fong Wei Tau in the film: both are crime lords in Chinatown; each of them operates a den of vice and is involved in a variety of sordid rackets. Moreover, neither of them is prosecuted for their criminal activities because they pay bribes to police officials who are on the take. It goes without saying that

Hammett in the film is based on the Continental Op in the short story. Hammett is, like the Op, a cynical but courageous private eye who will stop at nothing to get at the truth.

In the last analysis Ross Thomas was not so much concerned that his screenplay be faithful to Hammett's short story, "Dead Yellow Women," or to Gores's novel, as he was concerned in creating a story line based on key characters in the short story that would make the film script hang together as a consistent narrative. He did not totally succeed.

Hammett, which was to be distributed by Warner Bros., had its world premiere at the Cannes Film Festival on June 6, 1982, where it received poor press. Many of the press corps complained that *Hammett*'s plot yielded only a murky solution to the mystery about the missing Chinese call girl. In sum, the film was dismissed as an undistinguished detective yarn, mere "private eye-wash." Warner Bros. accordingly gave the film only a token release.

American film critics in the scattered cities where the movie played were more benign toward *Hammett* than the international press corps at Cannes. Warner Bros. released the film in November 1982, and it played in select cities like San Francisco and Chicago. Gene Siskel pointed out in his mildly favorable notice in the *Chicago Tribune* that the movie, like Gores's novel, tells two stories at once: "Hammett is writing a novel while at the same time he is trying to solve a genuine 1920s crime." Hammett's former Pinkerton boss enlists his help in solving an ostensibly routine case that, naturally, "turns out to be anything but routine."[31]

When the film failed to attract customers, Warner Bros. endeavored to give *Hammett* a shot in the arm with a new ad campaign in the summer of 1983, when the movie opened at last in New York. Vincent Canby was more positive in his review in the *New York Times* than Siskel had been. He singled out some of the cast for commendation: Frederic Forrest "is an attractive, easygoing Hammett"; Lydia Lei "is nicely wicked as a sort of Oriental Mary Astor"; and Roy Kinnear is fine as an "elegantly mannered, English-accented criminal." Canby concluded, "The best things about the film are the atmospheric, slightly stylized sets, which include . . . one old-fashioned opium den."[32] Indeed, Tavoularis's sets went a long way in giving the film an authentic Roaring Twenties feel.

When *Hammett* was ultimately released on DVD in 2005, some critics took a second look and praised the movie enthusiastically. Leonard

Maltin in his *Movie Guide* calls *Hammett* "a real treat for detective buffs." In his rave review Maltin declares, "You couldn't ask for a more faithful re-creation of the 1930s studio look, a magnificent looking (and sounding) film!"[33]

Admittedly, the plot of *Hammett* has some loose ends. After years of toiling as an honest private eye, Jimmy Ryan does a complete about-face and becomes a dishonest one. This dramatic change in his character is never adequately explained.

Seeing the film on DVD today, however, one notices an effective performance by Forrest as Dashiell Hammett. And the picture is further enhanced by Philip Lathrop's moody cinematography. With all its shortcomings, "*Hammett* is nonetheless a genuine contribution" to film noir, as Foster Hirsch emphasizes.[34]

Furthermore, it is heartening to see the favorable notice of *Hammett* in the 2010 *Film Noir Encyclopedia*: "Wenders pays homage to noir's hard-boiled literary roots," writes noir scholar Glenn Erickson. "*Hammett* is an affectionate homage that doesn't embarrass its origin" in the fiction of Dashiell Hammett.[35] A much earlier tribute to the writers of hard-boiled detective fiction like Hammett and Chandler came from Alistair Cooke, who stated, as early as 1949, that "they would be remembered when lots of what we now regard as our literary greats are buried in the school books."[36]

Notes

1. Alain Silver, "Introduction: Neo-Noir," in *Film Noir: The Encyclopedia*, 350.

2. Everitt, "The New Noir," sec. 2:29.

3. Schwartz, *Neo-Noir* (Lanham, Md.; Scarecrow Press, 2005), xii.

4. Holden, "Neo-Noir's a Fashion That Fits Only a Few," sec. 2:15.

5. Richard Jameson, "Son of Noir," *Film Comment* 10, no. 6 (November–December 1974): 33, Special film noir issue.

6. Jameson, "Son of Noir," 30.

7. Naremore, *More Than Night*, 10.

8. Everitt, "The New Noir," sec. 2:28.

9. Gale, *A Dashiell Hammett Companion*, 198.

10. LeRoy Panek, *Reading Early Hammett: The Fiction Prior to the Maltese Falcon* (Jefferson, N.C.: McFarland, 2004), 151.

11. Symons, *Dashiell Hammett*, 52.

12. Panek, *Reading Early Hammett.* 152–53.

13. Dashiell Hammett, *The Dain Curse* (New York: Vintage Books, 1989), 217.

14. Gale, *A Dashiell Hammett Companion*, 54.

15. Haut, *Heartbreak and Vine*, 10.

16. Mark Dawidziak, "Howard Duff and *The Adventures of Sam Spade*," in *The Big Book of Noir*, 359.

17. Gale, *A Dashiell Hammett Companion*, 54.

18. Thomson, *New Biographical Dictionary of Film*, 188.

19. Panek, *Reading Early Hammett*, 158.

20. Panek, *Reading Early Hammett*, 155, 159.

21. Gale, *A Dashiell Hammett Companion*, 53.

22. Panek, *Reading Early Hammett*, 167.

23. Dooley, *Dashiell Hammett*, 96.

24. Cecile Starr, "Fred Zinnemann and *Julia*," in *Fred Zinnemann: Interviews*, ed. Gabriel Miller (Jackson: University Press of Mississippi, 2005), 66.

25. Gates, "Becoming Sam Spade," 12.

26. Gale, *A Dashiell Hammett Companion*, 97.

27. Michael Schumacher, *Francis Ford Coppola: A Filmmaker's Life* (New York: Crown, 1998), 278.

28. See Schumacher, *Francis Ford Coppola*, 303–4, on Wenders reshooting *Hammett*.

29. Greg Solomon, "Walter Hill's *Supernova*," *Film Comment* 36, no. 4 (July–August, 2000): 22.

30. Chandler, "The Simple Art of Murder," in Raymond Chandler, *Later Novels and Other Writings*, 989.

31. Gene Siskel, "You Can't See the *Hammett* for the Forrest," *Chicago Tribune*, November 12, 1982, sec. C:5.

32. Vincent Canby, "Wim Wenders's *Hammett*," *New York Times*, July 1, 1983, sec. C:8.

33. Leonard Maltin, ed., *Movie Guide* (New York: Penguin, 2011), 575. For the record, the film is set in 1928.

34. Hirsch, *Detours and Lost Highways*, 102.

35. Glenn Erickson, "*Hammett*," in *Film Noir: The Encyclopedia*, 393.

36. Frank MacShane, *The Life of Raymond Chandler* (New York: Dutton, 1976), 214.

CHAPTER THIRTEEN

ANTHONY MINGHELLA:
THE TALENTED MR. RIPLEY
LILIANA CAVANI: *RIPLEY'S GAME*

Highsmith never got the breaks of the blue-chip authors of her time," writes *New York Times* columnist Frank Rich. Her first novel, *Strangers on a Train*, lays out the theme of *The Talented Mr. Ripley*, including class envy, the transference of guilt, and homoerotic infatuation. *Strangers on a Train* was made into a classic Hitchcock film. "But the screenplay's famous co-writer, Raymond Chandler, got more credit for what was on the screen than did the obscure author of the novel that was its source."[1] *Strangers on a Train* was dealt with above primarily as a Hitchcock film. In taking up the two films in this chapter, we shall focus more on their being adaptations of novels by Highsmith.

Patricia Highsmith was born in Fort Worth, Texas, in 1921, to parents who were soon divorced. Patricia's mother, Mary, later admitted that, since her first marriage was a total failure, she attempted to abort the pregnancy by drinking turpentine. Mary fared better with her second marriage to Stanley Highsmith; when Patricia was six years old, she moved, with her mother and stepfather, to New York City, where she grew up.

After publishing *Strangers on a Train*, Richard Corliss states, Highsmith left for Europe, "where she was welcomed as an important novelist, not just a thriller writer. From this pleasant remove," she wrote of a "ruthlessly imaginative expat, Tom Ripley," who has been called one of the great creations of American literature.[2]

Her novels continued to be more popular in Europe than in her native land. "Her amoral exploration of perverse behavior" did not endear her fiction to the American reading public, who often found it too gruesome.³ Not surprisingly, most of the movies made from her work were European films, made in France or Germany. Anthony Minghella's *The Talented Mr. Ripley* was the first Hollywood studio production derived from a Highsmith novel since *Strangers on a Train*.

Highsmith devoted five novels to Tom Ripley, her gentleman rogue and likeable psychopath, between 1955 and 1991. She always approached Ripley with an unblinking and nonjudgmental authorial stance, as she traced his "rake's progress from callow kid to elegant arriviste."⁴

In a rare TV interview she granted to Melvin Bragg on London's *South Bank Show*, Highsmith defended Tom Ripley, her favorite creation. "He could be called psychotic," she told Bragg; "I consider him a rather civilized person who kills when he absolutely has to," that is, when someone gets too close to his secrets. She continued, "There *are* people like Ripley and Bruno in *Strangers on a Train*, characters who succumb to temptation. But I don't look down on them for that reason."⁵ It is significant that Highsmith paired Tom and Bruno, since Bruno Antony was the prototype for Tom Ripley.

As for Tom being homosexual, Highsmith vacillated; to Bragg she conceded only that he was never queer. He was "a little bit homosexual, . . . not that he's ever done anything about it." Rich thought Highsmith somewhat disingenuous about Tom's homosexuality. He comments wryly about Tom: "In the later Ripley books, she none-too-convincingly marries him off."⁶ In *Ripley's Game* Tom and his French wife inhabit an elegant French country house, *Belle Ombre* (Beautiful Shadow, which is the title of Wilson's biography of Highsmith). Tom supports his affluent lifestyle by peddling forged paintings and by other equally shady activities. In essence, Tom is a refined con man and a fraud, an amoral individual who is convinced that he is entitled to his ill-gotten gains.

That Tom is a sociopath, without a conscience, who continues to thrive unpunished, did not unduly concern his creator: "I rather like criminals and find them extremely interesting, unless they are monstrously and stupidly brutal."⁷

When *The Talented Mr. Ripley* won the 1956 Edgar Allan Poe Award bestowed by the Mystery Writers of America, Highsmith believed that the prize really belonged to Tom Ripley, whom she considered her alter ego. What's more, she attributed the book's success to "the insolence and audacity of Ripley himself." She added, "I often had the feeling that Ripley was writing it, and that I was merely typing it."[8] There is no question that Highsmith identified with Ripley, whom she called her "favorite hero-criminal." Indeed, she sometimes signed letters to friends, "Pat H., alias Ripley."[9]

Tom Ripley survived his creator, who died February 4, 1995, in Locarno, Switzerland, where she lived the last fourteen years of her life. Although the five Ripley novels were written over a period of thirty-five years, Tom ages only ten years from the first book to the last. Presumably, he went on living at *Belle Ombre*. (Ripley seems to be eternal.)

Graham Greene celebrated Highsmith as "the poet of apprehension." She was "a writer who created a world of her own. . . . This is a world without moral endings." Even though Greene much admired Highsmith's novels, he still felt uneasy that some of her evildoers never pay for their crimes. "It makes the tension worse that we are never sure whether even the worst of them, like the talented Mr. Ripley, won't get away with it."[10] Considering some of the nasty villains in Highsmith's fiction, I think for Greene to call Tom the worst of them is going some.

Highsmith never made any bones about Tom Ripley's status as an unrepentant criminal. When she began her first Ripley novel, she wrote in her notes in capital letters that the subject was "EVIL." She further noted that the novel would show "the triumph of evil over good," because Tom's crimes did not lead to punishment.[11]

In the first Ripley novel, *The Talented Mr. Ripley*, Tom murders Dickie Greenleaf, with whom he has been obsessed, and assumes his identity. Then he must commit another murder to cover up the first one. He is never charged with either killing. (As a matter of fact, two possible titles for the book that Highsmith considered at that early stage were *The Pursuit of Evil* and *The Thrill Boys*.[12] Highsmith once said, "I find the public passion for justice quite boring and artificial, for neither life nor nature cares whether justice is ever done or not."[13]

The Talented Mr. Ripley was greeted with largely good reviews when it was published in 1955. In the United States the *New Yorker* termed the book "a *remarkably* immoral story very engagingly" told.[14] Anthony Boucher, in a notice entitled "Criminal at Large," in the *New York Times Book Review*, deemed the novel "a more solid essay in the creation and analysis" of character than *Strangers on a Train*.[15] Highsmith would never again garner glowing reviews like *that* in the American press. To most American literary critics Highsmith remained a cult figure.

Most movies made from Highsmith's novels were European in origin, since she was better appreciated there. Thus the first film of *The Talented Mr. Ripley* was made in France by René Clément as *Purple Noon* in 1960. Highsmith liked Alain Delon as Ripley, "but hated the film's altered ending."[16] In *Purple Noon* Tom is ultimately revealed as the murderer of the Dickie Greenleaf character when his corpse is discovered by the police. The moral ending that Clément grafted onto the narrative was antithetical to Highsmith's intentions.

The Talented Mr. Ripley (1999)

Anthony Minghella, a British film director who migrated to Hollywood in the early 1990s, was initially hired by Miramax to write the screenplay for *The Talented Mr. Ripley*. Miramax, an independent production company, was to produce the film and Paramount would release it. After he completed the script of what turned out to be a nifty neo-noir, Minghella was so captivated by the story that he asked Miramax to allow him to direct the movie as well. At that point Minghella had won an Academy Award for directing *The English Patient*, so the studio agreed.

Minghella's intelligent, witty, literate script introduced some intriguing alterations into the Highsmith book. There is, for example, Meredith Logue, who does not exist in the novel; she is a textile heiress. A New York socialite sojourning in Europe, Meredith is misled by Tom early in the film into believing that he is Dickie Greenleaf, with a view to becoming part of her affluent smart set. In addition, Minghella beefed up the role of Peter Smith-Kingsley, who is only mentioned in passing in the novel. Minghella calls Peter (Jack Davenport) a homosexual "who is centered and comfortable with himself," in a way that Tom is not; Peter loves Tom just as he is.[17]

In creating Tom Ripley, Highsmith may have been inspired by F. Scott Fitzgerald's 1925 novel *The Great Gatsby*. Ripley, like Gatsby, rises from his lowly origins through unlawful schemes, as he seeks to reinvent himself as a member of the upper crust. As Frank Rich puts it, in the best single essay on Minghella's film, Jay Gatsby might have been Tom Ripley's role model. For Gatsby was "a mythic charlatan who rubbed out his past, then built a fortune . . . , all in the mistaken faith that he could find happiness by being someone else."[18]

In the opening credit sequence, the movie's title is presented imaginatively, as Minghella explained. "The word *Talented*" evolves as the final adjective in a rosary of descriptions that have preceded Ripley's last name: mysterious, unhappy, lonely, and so on.[19] This is "an attempt to identify the contradictions surrounding this complex character."[20]

After the opening credits, Tom Ripley is seen sitting in his cabin aboard ship. The film returns to this shot of Tom at the close of the movie—we are to assume that the story unfolds on the screen as Tom remembers it.

The story begins in Manhattan in 1958, with Tom, a fastidious young man with Clark Kent glasses, borrowing a Princeton blazer to accompany a singer on the piano at a high society reception. Shipping magnate Herbert Greenleaf inquires if Tom knew his son Dickie at Princeton. Tom replies in the affirmative, although he never went to Princeton; at present he is a men's room attendant in a concert hall, a fact not in the novel. Herbert Greenleaf hires Tom on the spot to go to Mongibello, an Italian resort village, to persuade his son Dickie, who is living an aimless life there, to return to New York and the family business.

When Tom's ship docks in an Italian port, he meets Meredith Logue, an heiress, on the pier and, on a whim, introduces himself to her as Dickie Greenleaf. Tom moves on to Mongibello, where he meets up with Dickie Greenleaf on the sun-drenched beach. Tom is dazzled by Dickie, the blond-haired golden boy, and his "luscious indolence." He is also impressed by Dickie's rich American girlfriend, Marge Sherwood (Gwyneth Paltrow), an aspiring writer.[21] Dickie doubts that Tom ever knew him at Princeton, but Marge, at least for now, takes him at face value and welcomes him to their Ivy League clique.

In brief, Minghella's script follows Highsmith's novel rather closely from the outset. Once Minghella's shooting script was approved by the front office, he proved himself very adroit in choosing the actors. He cast Matt Damon, who had played romantic leads in films like Minghella's own *Mr. Wonderful* (1992), as Tom. Damon was cast against type as a furtive sociopath on the rise. Minghella picked Jude Law for the part of Dickie Greenleaf. Law gave a breakthrough performance as the bronzed, handsome, but somewhat malevolent Dickie. Philip Seymour Hoffman was perfect as the untidy, slightly overweight, yet well-bred Princeton pal of Dickie's, Freddie Miles.

Marge Sherwood (Gwyneth Paltrow) and Dickie Greenleaf (Jude Law) are not aware that Tom Ripley (Matt Damon) is a sociopath in Anthony Minghella's neo-noir film of Patricia Highsmith's *The Talented Mr. Ripley.*

As Don Siegel had demonstrated in his version of *The Killers*, mayhem can look just as brutal when it takes place in bright sunshine as when it is committed under cover of darkness. By the same token, *The Talented Mr. Ripley*, much of which was shot on location in Italy, is "awash in the sensual yellows and caramels of Naples, San Remo, Venice, and Rome."[22] Minghella's film is a lush, elegant thriller in the tradition of Hitchcock's *To Catch a Thief.*

Minghella was fortunate to obtain the services of the brilliant film editor Walter Murch, who had cut *The English Patient*, and had just finished restoring Welles's film noir *Touch of Evil* before going on to edit Minghella's neo-noir, *The Talented Mr. Ripley*. Minghella collaborated very closely with Murch during the editing period.

One of Minghella's departures from the novel is that he makes Tom's homosexuality much more pronounced in the film than Highsmith did in the book. The studio was concerned that the movie would be criticized in some quarters for depicting a homosexual who kills people. Minghella stuck to his guns. "It's a sorry state of affairs if you can only write about a homosexual character who behaves well," he declared. "It seems to me so much the fabric of the story—not so much that Tom was gay, but that he was in love with Dickie," and Dickie's lifestyle.[23]

Tom in due time reveals to Dickie that he is in the pay of Dickie's father; but he agrees to be a "double agent" by stringing Herbert Greenleaf along, despite the fact that Dickie is dead set against ever going home. Dickie accordingly invites Tom to share his bachelor flat in the village, since he views Tom as an ally in his tug of war with his father.

Tom and Dickie solemnize their friendship by spending an evening in the local jazz club, where Dickie plays his sax with a jazz combo. He invites Tom onstage to join in singing an Italian ditty, "Tu Wo Fa L'Americain," a hymn to American culture. The filmgoer resonates with Tom as he enjoys a sense of camaraderie with Dickie at this exhilarating moment.

The closest Tom and Dickie come to forging a deep personal relationship "is an early nocturnal scene in a smoky Naples jazz club, where Dickie's sultry sax" joins with Tom's tentative rendition of "My Funny Valentine." Tom vocalizes the bittersweet lyrics that express tragic longing. "By the time he takes a wrong turn in pursuit of his fantasy" to be part of Dickie's social circle, "we're already along for the ride," Rich writes; "to our extreme discomfort we find ourselves in our secret heart-of-hearts" rooting for Tom to succeed in his greedy and ambitious con game.[24]

Tom desires to model himself on Dickie, his golden boy, to the point where he can pass for someone to the manor born. As Tom expresses his personal creed, "It's better to be a fake somebody than a real nobody." One night Dickie comes back to his apartment to find that Tom has donned one of his jackets and bow ties. Dickie is miffed that Tom is wearing his clothes. For his part, Tom is embarrassed that Dickie has caught him impersonating him.

But Dickie gets over his irritation with Tom and invites him to go sailing with him, Marge, and Freddie. In the course of the excursion, Dickie takes Marge below deck so they can make love. Freddie catches Tom, who pretends to be reading a book on deck, peeking in a mirror at the foot of the stairs, which reflects the naked couple's gyrations. Freddie christens him "Peeping Tom" with a smirk. When Dickie hears about Tom's voyeurism, Tom attempts to mollify him by reaffirming the bond between them: "You are the brother I never had, and I am the brother you never had." Dickie is not impressed.

Eventually Herbert Greenleaf writes to Tom, terminating their financial arrangement, since Tom has failed to coax Dickie into returning to New York. Dickie comments that "the party is over," since Tom and Dickie had been splurging on the money Mr. Greenleaf was sending to Tom as a retainer. Dickie suggests that Tom join him in attending the San Remo Jazz Festival, "as one last trip together." During the railway journey to San Remo, Dickie falls asleep on the train; and Tom gently rests his head on Dickie's shoulder. Tom thus can display his unspoken affection and tenderness for Dickie only while Dickie is asleep.

For a while Dickie liked having an acolyte around, but the fickle Dickie is easily bored and grows tired of Tom. One afternoon, while Tom and Dickie are alone in a rowboat on the lake, Dickie begins taunting Tom as a freeloader; it is a prelude to his severing their relationship entirely. In a sudden burst of violence, Tom bashes Dickie's head in with an oar, to avoid being forsaken. Tom reflects in the novel at this point: "He had offered Dickie friendship, companionship, and respect, . . . and Dickie had replied with ingratitude."[25] Corliss comments, "The killing in the boat is less murder than the fatal flailing of a rejected suitor. Tom is crushed by Dickie's dismissal, so he crushes Dickie."[26]

Tom lies down next to Dickie's dead body on the floor of the rowboat, and nestles close to him, as he had done on the train. He even arranges Dickie's arms around him, as if they were embracing. Ironically, Tom can only embrace Dickie in death.

After Tom disposes of Dickie's corpse by sinking it in the lake, "he assumes Dickie's name, his appearance, his voice, his manner," writes Noel Mawer in his essay on the Ripley novels, "until it finally becomes easier for Tom to be Dickie than to be Tom Ripley."[27] Tom's impersonation of Dickie enables him to take over Dickie's apartment in Rome, where he manages to make everyone in the building assume that he *is* Dickie Greenleaf. Moreover, Tom socializes as Dickie with Meredith Logue and others who never knew him as Tom Ripley.

Tom attends Tchaikovsky's opera *Eugene Onegin* with Meredith. In the opera, based on the Pushkin poem, a young man kills his best friend in a duel, then embraces his corpse, just as Tom embraced Dickie's dead body. Tom is deeply moved by the scene, but Meredith does not notice.

Minghella manages to slip a bit of noirish German expressionism into his neo-noir at one point. Tom is shown rolling and tossing in bed, as he experiences a nightmare about Dickie. The camera photographs the room upside down, to indicate that Tom's world, since Dickie's murder, has turned topsy-turvy.

Freddie Miles shows up at Dickie's apartment, looking for Dickie. Tom informs him that he is sharing the flat with Dickie, who is away at the moment. Freddie, who has had misgivings about Tom from the start, is not taken in by Tom's ruse. Freddie sees Tom as a gate crasher in the world of privilege, to which he and Dickie belong. Panicked by Freddie's suspicions, Tom smashes Freddie's skull with a stone bust of the Emperor Hadrian, which is on the mantelpiece. Minghella explained that he chose a bust of Hadrian since "Hadrian suffered because of his love of a boy." Hadrian was enamored of a lad whom he worshipped. When the boy met an untimely death, Hadrian erected a shrine to his memory. Similarly, Tom idolized Dickie.[28]

Tom pretends that Freddie is drunk as he smuggles his corpse out of the apartment house, with Freddie slumped over and apparently leaning on him. He bundles the body into Freddie's sports car and deposits it in a cemetery. Subsequently, "Tom will lie, forge letters and documents, anything to keep on being Dickie, a role he feels he was born to play."[29]

Freddie's body is eventually discovered, and the police are suspicious of Tom's testimony about Freddie's death; but he is saved when a new, less experienced police inspector is assigned to the case. The police later inform Tom that they have witnesses that observed Dickie and Freddie getting into Freddie's car together on the night of the murder, and suspect Dickie of killing Freddie. The inspector shows Tom a "suicide note," which in fact Tom typed out and to which he forged Dickie's signature. The note says that Dickie was depressed by the death of Freddie Miles, among other things. The benighted inspector overlooks the fact that it is not customary for someone who is going to commit suicide to *type* one's suicide note, but to write it in one's own hand.

Herbert Greenleaf arrives in Rome to investigate his son's disappearance; he brings along Marge Sherwood and a private detective named Alvin MacCarron. The private investigator finds out that Dickie had almost killed another student at Princeton during a drunken brawl. MacCarron ultimately agrees with the police that Dickie murdered Freddie in a drunken rage and then took his own life in despair. Dickie's corpse is never found, so there is no evidence that he too was murdered. Mr.

Greenleaf is disappointed in his son's wayward life and gives up the search for him. He decides to disinherit his son and transfer the income from Dickie's trust fund to Tom's bank account, since Dickie is either dead or hiding out somewhere. So Herbert disowns Dickie.

Only Marge, who has known Tom since he arrived in Mongibello, puts two and two together and sees through "Ripley's game," and suspects him of killing Dickie. But Herbert Greenleaf and his private eye both disregard her suspicions and hustle Marge off to a ship bound for America. Fate seems to have conspired to cover up Tom's guilt for two murders.

By this time Tom has fallen in love with Peter Smith-Kingsley, who knows him as Tom Ripley, and they board a luxury yacht for a vacation cruise to Athens. On board Tom meets Meredith Logue, who knows him as Dickie Greenleaf. Because Peter would interfere with Tom's promising relationship with Meredith, who can give him an entrée to her elite social set, Tom determines to eliminate Peter. At film's end we return to Tom sitting alone in his cabin, as we saw him at the beginning of the movie. On the sound track we hear what Tom now recalls: his strangling Peter in this very same cabin.

Then we see Tom sitting in his cabin, staring blankly into space. He regrets having to kill the only person who has ever loved him for himself. But he could not risk Peter giving "Ripley's game" away. Minghella contended that, in killing Peter, Tom loses "the person who means the most to him." He is accordingly punished sufficiently for his crimes to satisfy the traditional standards of conventional morality.[30] At this point the camera photographs Tom through the cabin doorway, until the door swings shut and the screen fades to black.

My own reading of the film's ending differs from Minghella's. We recall that, for Highsmith, Tom is a confirmed sociopath. Hence he does not feel guilty about ending Peter's life. Minghella's diplomatic declaration that Tom is punished for slaying Peter by losing his true love appears to be designed to appease the industry censor by suggesting that Tom has not eluded justice after all.

In fact, some critics saw the movie's ending as indicating that "grisly crimes do not necessarily lead to punishment." What's more, in the final scene of *The Talented Mr. Ripley*, Tom has no more stirrings of conscience than mob boss Michael Corleone experiences at the close of *Godfather II*.[31]

THE TALENTED MR. RIPLEY AND RIPLEY'S GAME

In sum, *The Talented Mr. Ripley* is a neo-noir that is an exception to the dictum that in film noir a character pays for his sins.

Despite critical disagreement about the film's ending, *The Talented Mr. Ripley* was well received by reviewers. The *New York Times Magazine* heralded it with a cover story, and *Time* had a special section of three articles in its coverage of the movie. Moreover, in her review of the film, Janet Maslin wrote in the *Times*, "There are diabolically smart surprises wherever you care to look in this glittering thriller."[32]

In his survey of the Highsmith films, Andy Webster felt that Matt Damon was "overly cherubic" in his portrayal as Tom, who is, after all, a fraud, "stealing things he believes he's entitled to." On the other hand, Webster thought "Jude Law is spot on as Dickie Greenleaf," and Philip Seymour Hoffman "provided great color" as Freddie. In the same essay Webster states that John Malkovich makes a fine Tom Ripley in Liliana Cavani's *Ripley's Game*, adapted from Highsmith's novel of the same name.[33]

Ripley's Game, Highsmith's third Ripley novel, was published in 1974, nearly two decades after *The Talented Mr. Ripley*. Mawer notes that by this point in the series Tom has become "a malignant influence on those who are sucked into his orbit."[34] Tom is in cahoots with gangster Reeves Minot, operating a counterfeit painting racket. As Corliss explains, "He lives in a fine house near Paris with a handsome blonde wife, Heloise, who is blissfully indifferent to his shadier activities. From Dickie's estate and from his profits on his art-forgery racket, Tom has an income that gives him the leisure to paint, garden, and commit the odd homicide. His whole life is a consummate forgery."[35]

Withal, Tom sees himself as a fundamentally upright person, since he is involved in criminal activities in a "French society full of greedy, dishonest people, and crime is a way of life."[36] He is, in his own mind, as decent as the next fellow.

Tom is offended, therefore, when a picture restorer and framer, Jonathan Trevanny, who suspects him of being involved in art forgery, declines to shake hands with him at a party. Out of pique—a perverse whim—Tom suggests to Minot, who needs the services of an assassin to kill a Mafia boss, that Jonathan is the man for the job. Tom tricks Jonathan, who has leukemia, into thinking that his demise is only a few months away; he proposes that he commit a murder for hire, in order to have enough money to leave to his wife and his child, to provide for them. Jonathan takes the bait.

"Not surprisingly, Highsmith's latent amorality divided the literary critics."[37] Some reviewers thought Highsmith a superior crime writer; others, like British critic Tony Henderson, thought that *Ripley's Game* was "too much to stomach." Writing in *Books and Bookmen*, he urged Highsmith to put an end to Tom Ripley, "her horrible brain-child, for whom she appears to have conceived an inexplicable affection."[38]

When Highsmith had finished *Ripley's Game*, Wim Wenders, who later filmed *Hammett*, came to visit her at her home in Moncourt, France. He wanted to negotiate for a Highsmith novel that he could film. She handed him a copy of *Ripley's Game*, and he agreed to acquire the rights for filming.[39] As things turned out, Highsmith was disappointed with Wenders's film, *The American Friend* (*Der Amerikanische Freund*, 1979). She thought Dennis Hopper was woefully miscast as Tom Ripley, whom he played with a cowboy swagger. Pauline Kael agreed, writing that Hopper played Tom with a cowboy hat "and a decaying juvenile blandness." She further observed that Wenders's film version of the book lacked "the nasty cleverness of a good thriller."[40]

Still Wenders, a German, was willing to adapt a Highsmith novel, while Hollywood directors seemed wary of filming Highsmith's books—perhaps because the novels shared the criminal's perspective; and "she refused to judge them as others would." Consequently, her novels were filmed in France, Germany, and Italy, rather than in Hollywood, where a miscreant was usually expected to suffer or die "to supply a happy ending."[41] It comes as no surprise that the later film of *Ripley's Game* was an Italian-British coproduction (distributed by Fine Line Features, a subsidiary of New Line Cinema).

Ripley's Game (2003)

Ripley's Game was directed by an Italian filmmaker, Liliana Cavani, best known for *The Night Porter* (*Il Porture di Notte*, 1974), about a sadomasochistic relationship between an ex-Nazi and a former concentration camp inmate. Cavani cowrote the screenplay of *Ripley's Game*, a neo-noir, with Charles McKeown, with some uncredited assistance from John Malkovich, who plays Ripley. David Thomson felt that John Malkovich's taking the part of Ripley in the film was "sublime casting." He adds that Malkovich playing the assassin in *The Line of*

John Malkovich as Tom Ripley in *Ripley's Game*, based on a later Ripley novel by Patricia Highsmith.

Fire (1993), with "stealthy malice," was good preparation for his playing Ripley.[42]

Scottish actor Dougray Scott was selected to play Jonathan Trevanny in the wake of playing superbly a renegade spy in *Mission Impossible II* (2001). The present film was shot on location in Italy, France, and Germany.

Gary Indiana is pleasantly surprised that Cavani's script is so in tune with Highsmith's novel, hitting every story point with precision, so that "the many alterations she's made in the story seem perfectly unobtrusive, logical, and justified."[43] For example, Cavani, a native Italian, moved the story from the French village of Villeperce, where Tom lived in *Belle Ombre*, to the northeast region of Italy, where Tom has taken up residence in a Palladian villa with his wife, Luisa, a harpsichord virtuoso.

Cavani chose Ennio Morricone, the Italian film composer, to score *Ripley's Game*. The majority of his musical scores have been for Italian movies like *The Good, the Bad, and the Ugly* (*Il Guno, il Butto, il Cattivii*, 1966). But he had also written music for some Hollywood films like *The Untouchables* (1987), which the pulse-pounding score for *Ripley's Game* resembles.

From the moment Malkovich steps onto the screen there is little doubt that Tom Ripley is "a role he was born to play," a noir antihero,

a snide sociopath, and a high-class connoisseur.[44] Tom meets Jonathan
Trevanny, a local British picture framer, at a dinner party. "Bloody philis-
tine American," Jonathan mutters, and refuses to shake hands with Tom,
whom he believes has been involved in some shady transactions in the art
world. Tom is aware that Jonathan is suffering from leukemia and has
been given less than a decade to live.

Reeves Minot (Ray Winstone), a British racketeer and owner of a
Berlin nightery, arrives in town. An old acquaintance of Tom's, Reeves
asks him to assassinate a Russian Mafia boss, who is muscling in on
Reeves's turf. Tom declines, but suggests Jonathan as the man for the job.
As revenge for Jonathan's slight of him, Tom wishes to see the young
Englishman corrupted. *Ripley's Game* thus becomes a chilling parable of
Innocence corrupted by Evil.

Tom recommends Jonathan to Reeves because Jonathan has no connection with the Berlin underworld. Furthermore, Tom manages to convince Jonathan with the help of a spurious medical report that he has only
six months to live. Jonathan, who is beset by financial woes, is eager to
provide financial security for his wife, Sarah, and their child. "The essence
of Ripley's game is to see if financial desperation, combined with terminal illness, will incite a mild-mannered picture-framer to murder."[45] The
question is quickly answered when Jonathan accepts the lure of $50,000
from Reeves to perform the gruesome task.

Jonathan subsequently follows Leopold Belinsky, his prey, to the
Berlin Zoo and executes him in the insect room. But games have a way
of escalating. Reeves later explains to Jonathan that "even bastards have
friends." So Jonathan must "tidy up" the first murder by a second killing,
"if you value your life and that of your wife and son," Reeves ruefully
warns him. Hence Jonathan agrees to murder a Ukrainian Mafia boss on
the Berlin-Dusseldorf express train.

Tom, fearing that the mobster is too well protected by bodyguards
for Jonathan to liquidate on his own, shows up aboard the train just in
time to help the hapless Jonathan to fulfill his assignment. Tom strangles
Jonathan's intended victim for him, plus one of the Mafiosi's two hench-
men, in the train's cramped restroom. Jonathan shoots Gregor, the other
bodyguard, but Gregor is not fatally wounded.

Overwhelmed by Tom's talent for murder, Jonathan asks him, "Who
are you?" Tom replies, "I'm a gifted improviser. I lack your conscience,

and when I was young that troubled me. But it doesn't bother me anymore. I don't worry about being caught because I don't believe anyone is watching. The world is *not* a poorer place because these people are dead." After Tom expresses his self-righteous "philosophy" to Jonathan, they fly back to Italy together.

Members of the Russian Mafia, intent on revenge, inevitably track down Reeves and slay him. Realizing that he is now in danger, Tom, who is known to them, sends his wife away and, with Jonathan at his side, waits for the assailants to invade his home. Gregor and another gangster soon appear. Tom kills Gregor, and Jonathan murders the other mobster. Tom dumps the two corpses in the trunk of their car and sets it on fire in a nearby wood. Tom is euphoric while he watches the blaze. As Highsmith writes at this point, "Life afforded few pleasures tantamount to disposing of Mafiosi."[46]

Tom drives Jonathan back to his home and drops him off; before departing he notices a car outside Jonathan's house that is definitely not Jonathan's. He bursts into the house and finds Jonathan and his wife both held hostage by two Mafiosi, demanding to know Tom's whereabouts. When they recognize Tom, one of them draws a bead on him; Jonathan steps in front of Tom and takes the bullet aimed at him. Tom asks Jonathan, "Why did you do it?" But Jonathan expires before he can answer. Presumably Jonathan, who thought his days were numbered, died in Tom's place because he was grateful to Tom for helping him provide financial support for his wife and son.

Tom attends a harpsichord recital given by his wife, where he recalls images of Jonathan stopping the bullet intended for him. "With the corruption and death of an innocent, the transgressive deification—the transition of Ripley from self-invented man to amoral omniscient—is complete."[47]

Ripley's Game was not widely reviewed in the United States because it had no theatrical release; but the critics who did review it when it made its debut on DVD were mostly favorable. Andy Webster termed the movie "spare and largely true to the novel in story and tone, not the least because of Malkovich's exquisite detachment and understatement."[48] Gary Indiana states that "Cavani has crafted the most enjoyable and subtly textured Ripley film." He continues, "Cavani's film sets the bar for future Highsmith adaptations extremely high."[49]

Demetrios Matheou, who reviewed the film at the time of its European release, notes, "As casual about murder as he is about fine art,

Ripley—as he appears in Highsmith's novel—was the prototype" of the kinds of villains who populate current films. In fact, the film's Ripley is something of a "cultural monster" like the Hannibal Lector figure depicted by Thomas Harris in his novels, and the films made from them.[50] Because Cavani's *Ripley's Game* was reviewed rather enthusiastically by the relatively few American critics who gave it a notice when it surfaced on DVD, it seemed wise for me to quote some of these opinions to substantiate the movie's high critical reputation.

Highsmith biographer Andrew Wilson attributes the upsurge of interest in America for her novels to the popularity of Minghella's *Talented Mr. Ripley*, which prompted the reissuing of her novels in paperback. "It is only now, after her death," he writes, "that the power of her work is finally being appreciated, especially in America." Moreover, Cavani's film adaptation of *Ripley's Game* has found a larger audience in the United States as a result of its distribution on DVD. Perhaps Wilson said it all when he opined, "The mass market is now much more comfortable with literature and film that subverts genre expectations and disturbs popular notions of morality."[51]

"One of noir's defining elements," according to Foster Hirsch, is that "crimes are committed, not by hard-core gangsters, but by seemingly decent, hence 'innocent' middle-class citizens lured into antisocial behavior by greed, lust, or mischance."[52] Tom Ripley, who starts out in *The Talented Mr. Ripley* as a young man who goes to Europe to bring back an errant son, is led to commit crimes by all three: mischance, greed, and lust. Tom goes on in *Ripley's Game* to be a professional assassin, as well as a dealer in fraudulent paintings. Hence these two films are worthy additions to the ranks of neo-noir, with Tom Ripley as their noir antihero.

Notes

1. Frank Rich, "American Pseudo: *The Talented Mr. Ripley*," *New York Times Magazine*, December 12, 1999, 85.

2. Richard Corliss, "The Talented Ms. Highsmith," *Time*, December 27, 1999, 159.

3. Rich, "American Pseudo," 86.

4. Corliss, "The Talented Ms. Highsmith," 159.

5. Patricia Highsmith, interviewed by Melvin Bragg. *The South Bank Show*, March 1975.

6. Rich, "American Pseudo," 86.

7. David Blakesley, "*Strangers on a Train*," in *Encyclopedia of Novels into Film*, 429.

8. Highsmith, *Plotting and Writing Suspense Fiction*, 69.

9. Schenkar, *The Talented Miss Highsmith*, 164, 574.

10. Graham Greene, "Foreword," *Eleven: Short Stories*, by Patricia Highsmith (New York: Atlantic Monthly Press, 1984), ix, xi.

11. Wilson, *Beautiful Shadow*, 195.

12. Schenkar, *The Talented Miss Highsmith*, 573.

13. Leonard Cassuto, "Bound for Perdition: *Strangers on a Train*, the Novel," *Wall St. Journal*, November 23, 2008, sec. W:17.

14. "Books in Brief," *New Yorker*, January 14, 1956, 100.

15. Anthony Boucher, "Criminal at Large," *New York Times Book Review*, December 25, 1955, 1.

16. Andy Webster, "Patricia Highsmith: DVD Filmography," *Premiere* 18, no. 1 (September 2004): 116.

17. Rich, "American Pseudo," 87.

18. Rich, "American Pseudo," 98.

19. Richard Corliss, "Can Matt Play Ripley's Game?," *Time*, December 27, 1999, 155.

20. Ondaatje, *The Conversations*, 275.

21. Corliss, "Can Matt Play Ripley's Game?," 156.

22. Peter Rainer, "*The Talented Mr. Ripley*," *New York Magazine*, January 3, 2000, 84.

23. Rich, "American Pseudo," 86.

24. Rich, "American Pseudo," 86, 82.

25. Patricia Highsmith, *The Talented Mr. Ripley* (New York: Norton, 2008), 97.

26. Corliss, "Can Matt Play Ripley's Game?," 161.

27. Noel Mawer, "Highsmith's Ripley," *The Big Book of Noir*, 292.

28. Minghella's remarks are from his audio commentary track included on the DVD of *The Talented Mr. Ripley* (released by Paramount in 2000).

29. Corliss, "Can Matt Play Ripley's Game?," 156.

30. Michael Bronski, "*The Talented Mr. Ripley*," *Cineaste* 35, no. 3 (January 2000): 91.

31. Rich, "American Pseudo," 82; see also Gene Seymour, "*The Talented Mr. Ripley*," *Newsday*, December 24, 1999, sec. B:2.

32. Janett Maslin, "Stealing a New Life," *New York Times*, December 24, 1999, sec. E:1.

33. Webster, "Patricia Highsmith," 116.

34. Mawer, "Highsmith's Ripley," 292.

35. Corliss, "The Talented Ms. Highsmith," 159.

36. Mawer, "Highsmith's Ripley," 293.

37. Wilson, *Beautiful Shadow*, 330.

38. Tony Henderson, "*Ripley's Game*," *Books and Bookmen*, May 1974, 84.

39. Schenkar, *The Talented Miss Highsmith*, 485.

40. Pauline Kael, *When the Lights Go Down* (New York: Holt, Rinehart, and Winston, 1980). 314–15; see also James Campbell, "Happy Birthday, Mr. Ripley," *New York Times Book Review*, February 8, 2009, 25.

41. Sayre, "In the Shoes of a Scary Stalker," sec. 2:12.

42. Thomson, *New Biographical Dictionary of Film*, 616.

43. Gary Indiana, "*Ripley's Game*," *Film Comment* 39, no. 6 (November–December 2003): 75.

44. Nathan Lee, "The Game That Ripley Couldn't Win," *New York Times*, April 4, 2004, sec. 2:26.

45. Demetrios Matheou, "*Ripley's Game*," *Sight and Sound* 13 (ns) no. 7 (July 2003): 52.

46. Patricia Highsmith, *Ripley's Game* (New York: Norton, 2008), 226.

47. Wilson, *Beautiful Shadow*, 330.

48. Webster, "Patricia Highsmith," 116.

49. Indiana, "*Ripley's Game*," 75.

50. Matheou, "*Ripley's Game*," 56.

51. Wilson, *Beautiful Shadow*, 463.

52. Hirsch, *The Dark Side of the Screen*, 216.

AFTERWORD

OUT OF THE SHADOWS, BACK TO THE FUTURE, NOIR MARCHES ON

"*Ignotum est pro magnifico*" ("We fear what we do not know")

—Tacitus

"Forget it, Jake. It's Chinatown."

—Robert Towne

And now, for something different, involving, perhaps, an awkward shift in voice and tone, for which, we, of course, apologize. Father Phillips originally intended to conclude this volume with an epilogue entitled "The Dark Mirror," but events conspired otherwise and he was interrupted by a medical intervention. Not wanting in any way to delay production of this book, Father Phillips asked me to complete in this "afterword" what he would have put into his epilogue. In order that I might do so effectively, we corresponded closely over several weeks, to the extent that I believe that I have been able to conclude the book much as Father Phillips might have done himself. I do know he *liked* the above title I conjured up to introduce these observations. Meanwhile, I am grateful to be able to share these observations about neo-noir and honored to be included in these pages.

Readers might reasonably wonder why America needs yet another book dealing with film noir, that murky, pseudogenre of crime films that emerged "out of the shadows" both before and after World War II and became a dominant visual style thereafter. Film noir, unlike the western or science fiction, is more a question of style than of content, though in general, of course, noir films also tend to be crime films. But not necessarily, and not always. The noir style has been known to cross genre boundaries, intruding on science fiction, for example, in such films as *Dark City* and *Blade Runner*, with its futuristic mean streets. Because noir is reflective of the darker, cynical side of American society, we do not believe that it dissipated or disappeared, or that it ceased to be influential at the beginning of the 1960s. It simply became more colorful, and even, arguably, more stylish as evidenced by Lawrence Kasdan's *Body Heat* (1981), a later, colorful noir featuring a career-defining role for Kathleen Turner as an astonishing femme fatale. But some nine years earlier, Roman Polanski had already broken new ground for film noir with *Chinatown* (1974), in which the genre resurfaced and then peaked, with Jack Nicholson as a world-weary private eye adrift in a vile world of perversion and corruption. Polanski gave the genre a new definition, a new nastiness, and a colorful new sheen. And other filmmakers besides Lawrence Kasdan would eventually follow his lead.

John Huston (director of *The Maltese Falcon*) as Noah Cross and Jack Nicholson as private eye Jake Gittes in Roman Polanski's neo-noir *Chinatown*.

In fact, *Chinatown* is an excellent example to demonstrate the legacy of noir. Father Phillips, who gave much consideration about exactly how far to extend his study into neo-noir territory, remarked to me that Polanski had the good sense to bring John Huston into his project, and John Huston, no stranger to noir himself on the directing side of his career, had the good sense to accept such a shockingly wicked and cynical role. *Chinatown* appeared at just the right time, as the classic film noirs were beginning to recede from view, reminding audiences of the noir style and sensibility, reasserting and demonstrating its power. Father Phillips considered including *Chinatown* at the far end of his survey, but, after all, it's a "classic" by now, and readers don't need to be reminded of the punch it packs. Hence the author turned to less well-known examples, such as the five-hour adaptation of *The Dain Curse*, a good novel that had fallen by the wayside, a novel with over a hundred characters, written as an exposé of the evangelistic craze that was sweeping Southern California at the time the novel was written. Father Phillips was drawn to this adaptation both because it was well done and because it had not been much covered by other noir critics.

So many neo-noirs could be mentioned here. One in particular that Father Phillips is especially fond of, for example, is *Hammett* (1982), produced by Francis Ford Coppola, directed by Wim Wenders, and adapted from the Joe Gores novel published in 1975 in which former Pinkerton detective and mystery writer Dashiell Hammett becomes involved in a 1928 murder case in San Francisco. Joe Gores (1931–2011), himself a prizewinning novelist who, like Hammett, specialized in hard-boiled mysteries, was a former San Francisco private investigator who knew the same territory that Hammett had also inhabited. For Gores, writing actual investigative case reports was not so different from writing mystery novels (or so he claimed). The three major writers who created the literary foundation for film noirs were Dashiell Hammett, Raymond Chandler, and James M. Cain. Though Father Phillips claims in his book *Creatures of Darkness* (2000) that Chandler might have been the better craftsman, Hammett did it first. As is pointed out in chapter 1 of this book, Raymond Chandler wrote that "Hammett deserves most or all of the credit" for having invented the "hard-boiled murder story," or, as the crime novelist Ross Macdonald put it so well: "We all came from under Hammett's black mask." Of course Hammett's most famous hard-boiled novel turned into a film noir classic was *The Maltese Falcon*.

So, just as in *Creatures of Darkness* (2000) Father Phillips focused on the hard-boiled fiction of Raymond Chandler, so in the current book he surveys the larger noir universe. Determined to give Dashiell Hammett his due, from the actual Hammett of the *Black Mask* stories to the imagined Hammett as conceived by Joe Gores and filmed by director Wim Wenders, at the urging of producer Francis Coppola, Phillips would argue that *Hammett*, despite its troubled production history, was an overlooked and neglected film. In his entry for the film in *The Francis Ford Coppola Encyclopedia* (2010), Phillips wrote that "with all its shortcomings, *Hammett* is a treat for mystery fans." When the composer John Barry died in February 2011, moreover, the obituary in *Time* magazine said his score for the movie *Hammett* was one of his finest achievements.

The third member of this literary noir triumvirate, along with Hammett and Chandler, is another Marylander, like Hammett. Ultimately drawn westward after an East Coast career in journalism, to the moral sinkhole that was Los Angeles, James M. Cain is covered in some detail in Father Phillips's recent book *Some Like It Wilder* (2010), where the classic *Double Indemnity* (1944) is in fact discussed in considerable detail. The story was, of course, adapted from the James M. Cain source by writer-director Billy Wilder, working in tandem in this instance with Raymond Chandler in near perfect synchronization to create that benchmark noir classic. Phillips gives Chandler credit for being the first to understand that Cain's snappy dialogue first needed to be shaped and could not simply be transferred unchanged from page to screen. The legacy of film noir rested, in brief, upon the achievements of Hammett and Chandler and Cain, standing behind such films as *The Maltese Falcon* and *Double Indemnity*.

Following *Chinatown* and *Hammett*, director John Dahl would build his career upon this noir legacy, creating several clever-but-nasty neo-noir thrillers, notably *Kill Me Again* (his feature-film debut picture in 1989), followed by *Red Rock West* (1993) and *The Last Seduction* (1994), starring Linda Fiorentino as an extraordinary and unforgettable femme fatale (later to be rendered forgettable, unfortunately, in the oddly mistitled film, *Unforgettable* in 1996, which, sadly, was not). Then, in 1997, Oliver Stone framed his noir genre send-up, *U-Turn*, derived from a demented, over-the-top script by John Ridley (and featuring Jennifer Lopez as would-be femme fatale Grace McKenna), as follows: "In *U-Turn*, we deal with all those good old things from film noir and thrillers of the past, like money and sex, dreams, betrayal, love, lust. What your moral code is or isn't. How far you will go to achieve your desires. Some people may say this is the real truth of human behavior. Some people may say this is very perverse, that it's not the way most people think or behave. *You* be the judge," Stone concluded defiantly. Stewart Klawans, usually a stern judge and critic for the *Nation* magazine, found *U-Turn* "*really* out of control," but also "outrageously entertaining." In fact, it had him "laughing out loud in the movie house and chuckling all the way home." *New York Times* critic Janet Maslin called it "A Darker Shade of Noir," a "steamy film noir anomaly in the never dull, ever-checkered career of Oliver Stone," who had transcended boundaries before, alienating audiences fiercely and fearlessly in *Natural Born Killers*.

Another film noir appearing in 1997 was intended to be taken more seriously. *L.A. Confidential*, directed by Curtis Hanson and adapted from James Ellroy's 1990 novel, is set in Los Angeles in 1953, described by critic John C. Tibbetts as a city "with one foot gently planted in fairyland and the other jammed in the muck." In keeping with the noir tradition it offered a convoluted plot of murder and betrayal and corruption. No one is to be trusted in this murky world, least of all the police, who plant evidence and brutalize confessions out of likely suspects. One young cop appears to be an idealist. He believes in justice and is willing to snitch on his fellow officers, who hate him for playing by the rules; but he ultimately finds out that the game is fixed. When a Mafia drug runner is murdered, a power vacuum is created that sucks in all kinds of riffraff, including some decidedly dirty cops; but the plot keeps the identity of the ringmaster a secret until the final shoot-out. A prime suspect is a wealthy playboy who runs a prostitution ring of whores "cut" by plastic surgeons to resemble movie stars, one of whom, a Veronica Lake look-alike (Kim Basinger) gets romantically involved with two "good" detectives, the idealist and his evil twin, who hates him but in the end must work with him, not only to solve the mystery, to plumb the heart of the corruption, but simply to survive. A third cop, Jack (Kevin Spacey) joins forces with them and also with a sleazy publisher (Danny DeVito), who dishes dirt and specializes in celebrity blackmail. Jack sees himself as a celebrity, who serves as advisor to a television police drama that would seem to resemble *Dragnet*.

Kevin Spacey could pass for Jack Webb (namesake for the film character, it would seem), even if he were not an actor.

The characters all seem to be genre prototypes, but they are developed counter to expectations. Basinger's femme fatale, for example, turns into a call girl with a heart of gold, seeking to redeem herself. The "good" cop is as much a manipulator as his evil twin, a hero twice over, who can survive only if he betrays his principles. A sleazy judge is at heart a pervert who will look the other way when his homosexual lover's throat is slit after the boy hears too much and becomes a threat. The cynicism and the casting, moreover, bring the film very much into the present time. Director Curtis Hanson used several actors from Australia (Guy Pearce, for example, later to play King Edward VII in the 2010 Academy Award–nominated *The King's Speech*) and New Zealand (Russell Crowe, later to become a really major Hollywood star), because, Hanson told the *New York Times*: "I wanted actors about whom the audience has no preconceived notion. I wanted the audience to accept these two characters at face value and not to make assumptions about them based on roles the actors had played before." That same logic applied to the casting of Australian actor Simon Baker Denny as Matt Reynolds, a sympathetic bisexual, who is caught in bed with Kim Basinger before he is later murdered. That same actor, now known as Simon Baker, went on to become quite popular, starring as an ironic sleuth-hypnotist in the CBS television series, *The Mentalist* (first aired in 2008 but still going strong in 2011).

A nasty noir resurgence that began in the 1970s overflowed into the 1990s, and involved many of the talents of the so-called new Hollywood. *Blood Simple* (1984), for example, the first inkling of genius from the Coen brothers, developed from noir characters and concepts, and *Miller's Crossing* (1990) demonstrated the Coens' mastery of the crime films of the 1930s and their style and the legacy of such "classics" as *The Glass Key* (1931) and *Red Harvest* (1929). Noir accents also helped to catapult Quentin Tarantino to success in his first feature, *Reservoir Dogs*, which was much admired in Britain, to be followed by *Pulp Fiction*, a sort of minor masterpiece of stylish noir nastiness.

Yet another earlier paradigm neo-noir was *The Usual Suspects* (1995), one of the most accomplished film noir "caper" films ever made, written by Christopher McQuarrie and directed by Bryan Singer. *The Usual Suspects* follows the lead of Quentin Tarantino's *Reservoir Dogs* and *Pulp*

Fiction. The plot is brilliantly constructed, complicated, convoluted, and challenging, and so paranoid as to be archetypically noir. As *Newsweek* critic Jack Kroll described it, the collision of these five felons sets off a story line that is the most convoluted since Humphrey Bogart's classic *The Big Sleep.* The plot is not easily summarized. At the opening five criminals are rounded up for a police lineup: Todd Hockney (Kevin Pollak), a "hardware specialist"; Fred Fenster (Benicio del Toro), an "entry man"; Michael McManus (Stephen Baldwin), a break-in artist; Dean Keaton (Gabriel Byrne), once a corrupt cop, now apparently wanting to go straight; and Roger "Verbal" Kint (Kevin Spacey), a crippled con man who is apparently mentally handicapped but who in fact is devious and quite probably the brains behind the caper to come.

After meeting in the lineup, these five felons plan a jewel heist that not only nets them $3 million in jewels but also exposes fifty dirty New York cops. This heist and exposé was brilliantly engineered by Dean Keaton, who seems to be the group's criminal mastermind. But later, in Los Angeles, fencing the gems, Keaton gets involved in more dangerous dealings involving a brutal Hungarian drug ring. One of the "usual suspects" is interrogated by U.S. Customs Special Agent David Kujan (Chazz Palminteri), investigating a smuggling operation believed to be organized by a legendary European crime lord named Keyser Söze, after a ship has been bombed in San Pedro, south of Los Angeles. All of the "usual suspects" were involved in the explosion onboard this ship, believed to have as its cargo a $91-million stash of cocaine. Twenty-seven Euro-thugs died, including four of the "usual suspects."

The story evolves further as Agent Kujan questions the remaining suspect, Roger "Verbal" Kint, one of the two survivors. The other, a Hungarian gangster named Kobayashi (the late Pete Postlethwaite), a lawyer and enforcer for the enigmatic criminal mastermind Keyser Söze, is hospitalized in an intensive-care burn unit. So the story is told by a "Verbal" narrator whom Agent Kujan considers "stupid." It becomes all too clear at the end, however, that Verbal is anything but stupid, and that he is making up the story as he goes along. Hence, this con artist proves to be not only an unreliable narrator, but quite possibly the ringleader of the whole operation. The turning point of this dodgy and deceptive story comes when Kujan berates Verbal by telling him that he is smarter than his prisoner. At this point, the camera shoots Verbal from below, in profile, and Kujan cannot see the smile that crosses Verbal's face. Later on Verbal plays into Kujan's perception by describing himself as a "stupid cripple."

What is most impressive about *The Usual Suspects* is the fact that the filmmakers give their audience credit for being able to follow a highly textured and difficult story. Nothing is dumbed down in a plot that is both challenging and interesting. Much of the story is obviously fabricated by the "Verbal" narrator, but even if the truth remains veiled, Verbal is an excellent storyteller. Most importantly, however, *The Usual Suspects* created an impressive talent pool of noir actors. Steven Spielberg, who cast Pete Postlethwaite as a racist prosecutor for *Amistad* (1997), called Postlethwaite "probably the best actor in the world," for example. He also played the philosopher-hunter Roland Tembo in Spielberg's *The Lost World: Jurassic Park* (1997), but the actor's obituary singled out only two key roles: *The Usual Suspects* and *In the Name of the Father* (starring with his stage-acting colleague Daniel Day-Lewis in 1993 and earning an Academy Award nomination for his performance as Giuseppe Conlon).

Now, even as important though Postlethwaite may be to the criminal ensemble of *The Usual Suspects*, he is overshadowed by the other suspects, genre stars in their own right. Gabriel Byrne, for example, had swaggered through *Miller's Crossing* (1990) before being picked for the lineup in *The Usual Suspects*, and Kevin Spacey, a natural actor and a very "Verbal" Kint, would move on to a starring stint in *L.A. Confidential*.

"In an age when all movie genres are being subverted, postmodernized, [and] deconstructed," Jack Kroll wrote of *The Usual Suspects*, film noir "is *the* key American movie type, and the most fun when it's done right." If Tarantino's *Reservoir Dogs* was "out to deconstruct the film noir, to create the ultimate parody of the metaphysical gangster film," Kroll continued, director Bryan Singer "wants to respect its classic form." Kroll concluded by calling *The Usual Suspects* "the best, most stylish crime movie since Stephen Frears's 1990 *The Grifters*. But Frears was British, born in Leicester in the Midlands, educated at Cambridge, and trained at London's Royal Court Theatre. It would be up to American-born directors like Quentin Tarantino, Curtis Hanson, the Coen brothers, and Bryan Singer, trained at the University of Southern California, to reclaim noir and to bring it home. Bravo!

Readers may wonder why a Roman Catholic priest, a Jesuit no less, would be so fascinated by the morally messy stories and often corrupted characters usually captured by film noirs. But, then, who better to understand the failed and the fallen than one who has presided inside the confessional booth? When I asked Father Phillips about this, he responded as follows: "I think that the searchlight film noir turns on the underside of American culture reveals moral issues that good and decent people should well consider seriously. The reader or viewer will bring their own moral values to bear when evaluating what they have read or seen." Phillips went on to reiterate that Dashiell Hammett came from a strong Roman Catholic tradition in Maryland, where he had grown up as a Roman Catholic and had therefore developed a traditional Catholic moral compass. James M. Cain was also born of Irish-Catholic stock and raised in Maryland, first in Annapolis, where his father taught at St. John's College, then to the northern Eastern Shore, where his father, James William Cain, served as president of Washington College in Chestertown. Gene Phillips has always been drawn to Catholic talents, starting with the acclaimed British novelist Graham Greene, whom he interviewed for his first book, and, later, no less than Alfred Hitchcock, whom he interviewed in London, while Hitchcock was making *Frenzy*, perhaps his nastiest film, about a psychopathic serial killer, and also noirish in its own way.

In short, then, this book begins with discussions of "classic" film noirs, and ends with discussions of later effusions from the noir font. Film noir certainly did not die in 1960; it merely turned the corner and adapted to color cinematography and, I believe, to a wider and wilder, even more interesting sensibility. "Overlooked Noir"? But of course! It was bound to happen, as noir elements gradually insinuated themselves into mainstream American cinema. After all, it's *dark* in there, in the ultimate universe of noir cinema. This book, therefore, memorializes the persistence of noir, producing increasingly more effective and interesting movies about the underside of American life, from *Chinatown* to *L.A. Confidential*, and beyond.

Jim Welsh, cofounding editor emeritus
Literature/Film Quarterly
Salisbury University
Salisbury, Maryland (USA)

Sources Cited

Klawans, Stuart. "Stone vs. Formaldehyde." *Nation,* October 27, 1997, 34–35.

Kroll, Jack. "Crooks, Creeps and Cons." *Newsweek,* August 28, 1995, 58.

Maslin, Janet. "A Darker Shade of Noir from Oliver Stone." *New York Times,* October 3, 1997, B18.

Phillips, Gene D. *Creatures of Darkness: Raymond Chandler, Detective Fiction, and Film Noir.* Lexington: University Press of Kentucky, 2000.

———. *Some Like It Wilder: The Life and Controversial Films of Billy Wilder.* Lexington: University Press of Kentucky, 2010.

Shapiro, T. Rees. "Pete Postlethwaite, 64: Gifted British Actor in 'The Usual Suspects,' 'Name of the Father.'" *Washington Post,* January 4, 2011, B4.

Skenazy, Paul. *James M. Cain.* New York: Continuum, 1989.

Tibbetts, John C. "Dark and Compelling." *New Times* (Kansas City), September 18, 1997, 14.

Weinraub, Bernard. "Between Image and Reality in Los Angeles." *New York Times,* September 7, 1997, sec. II: 52–54.

Welsh, James M., Gene D. Phillips, and Rodney F. Hill, eds. *The Francis Ford Coppola Encyclopedia.* Lanham, Md.: Scarecrow Press, 2010.

FILMOGRAPHY

Only the key films highlighted in the text are listed below. The films are listed in chronological order.

Stranger on the Third Floor (RKO, 1940)
Director: Boris Ingster
Producer: Lee Marcus
Screenplay: Frank Partos, and Nathanael West (uncredited)
Cinematographer: Nicholas Musuraca
Production Design: Van Nest Polglase, Albert D'Agostino
Music: Roy Webb
Editor: Harry Marker
Cast: Peter Lorre (Stranger), John McGuire (Michael Ward), Margaret Tallichet (Jane), Charles Waldron (District Attorney), Elisha Cook, Jr. (Joe Briggs), Charles Halton (Albert Meng), Ethel Griffes (Mrs. Kane)
Running Time: 67 minutes
Premiere: September 1940

The Maltese Falcon (Warner Bros., 1941)
Director: John Huston
Producer: Hal Wallis
Screenplay: John Huston and Allen Rivkin (uncredited), from the novel by Dashiell Hammett

Cinematographer: Arthur Edeson
Production Design: Robert Haas
Music: Adolph Deutsch
Editor: Thomas Richards
Cast: Humphrey Bogart (Sam Spade), Mary Astor (Brigid O'Shaughnessy), Peter Lorre (Joel Cairo), Sydney Greenstreet (Kasper Gutman), Elisha Cook, Jr. (Wilmer Cook), Gladys George (Iva Archer), Effie Perine (Lee Patrick)
Running Time: 100 minutes
Premiere: October 1941

The Glass Key (Paramount, 1942)
Director: Stuart Heisler
Producer: Fred Kohlmar
Screenplay: Jonathan Latimer, from the novel by Dashiell Hammett
Cinematographer: Theodor Sparkuhl
Production Design: Hans Dreier and Haldane Douglas
Music: Victor Young
Editor: Archie Marshek
Cast: Brian Donlevy (Paul Madvig), Veronica Lake (Janet Henry), Alan Ladd (Ed Beaumont), Richard Denning (Taylor Henry), Joseph Calleia (Nick Varna), William Bendix (Jeff), Moroni Olsen (Ralph Henry)
Running Time: 85 minutes
Premiere: September 1942

Laura (Twentieth Century-Fox, 1944)
Director: Otto Preminger
Producer: Otto Preminger
Screenplay: Jay Dratler, Samuel Hoffenstein, and Betty Reinhardt, from the novel by Vera Caspary
Cinematographer: Joseph LaShelle
Production Design: Lyle Wheeler and Leland Fuller
Music: David Raksin
Editor: Louis Loeffler
Cast: Gene Tierney (Laura Hunt), Dana Andrews (Mark McPherson), Clifton Webb (Waldo Lydecker), Vincent Price (Shelby

Carpenter), Judith Anderson (Ann Treadwell), Dorothy Adams (Bessie Clary)
Running Time: 88 minutes
Premiere: October 1944

Ministry of Fear (Paramount, 1944)
Director: Fritz Lang
Producer: Seton I. Miller
Screenplay: Seton I. Miller, from the novel by Graham Greene
Cinematographer: Henry Sharp
Production Design: Hans Dreier and Hal Pereira
Music: Victor Young
Editor: Archie Marshek
Cast: Ray Milland (Stephen Neale), Marjorie Reynolds (Carla Hilfe), Carl Esmond (Willi Hilfe), Dan Duryea (Cost / Travers), Hillary Brooke (Mrs. Bellane), Percy Waram (Inspector Prentice)
Running Time: 84 minutes
Premiere: October 1944; general release: February 1945

Spellbound (Selznick, United Artists, 1945)
Director: Alfred Hitchcock
Producer: David O. Selznick
Screenplay: Ben Hecht and Angus MacPhail, from the novel *The House of Dr. Edwardes*, by Francis Beeding
Cinematographer: George Barnes
Dream Sequence: Salvador Dali
Production Design: James Basevi and John Ewing
Music: Miklos Rozsa
Editors: William Ziegler and Hal Kern
Cast: Ingrid Bergman (Dr. Constance Petersen), Gregory Peck (John Ballantyne), Leo G. Carroll (Dr. Murchison), Michael Chekhov (Dr. Brulov), Norman Lloyd (Garmes), Rhonda Fleming (Mary)
Running Time: 111 minutes
Premiere: October 1945

Scarlet Street (Diana Productions, Universal, 1945)
Director: Fritz Lang
Producer: Fritz Lang

Screenplay: Dudley Nichols, from the novel *La Chienne* (*The Bitch*) by
    Georges de la Fouchardiere
Cinematographer: Milton Krasner
Production Design: Alexander Golitzen
Music: Hans Salter
Editor: Arthur Hilton
Cast: Edward G. Robinson (Chris Cross), Joan Bennett (Kitty
    March), Dan Duryea (Johnny), Margaret Lindsay (Millie), Rosa-
    lind Ivan (Adele), Jess Barker (Janeway), Arthur Loft (Dellarowe)
Running Time: 98 minutes
Premiere: December 1945; general release: February 1946

The Stranger (International Pictures, RKO, 1946)
Director: Orson Welles
Producer: S. P. Eagle (Sam Spiegel)
Screenplay: Anthony Veiller, Orson Welles, and John Huston (un-
    credited); from the story by Victor Trivas, Decla Dunning
Cinematographer: Russell Metty
Production Design: Perry Ferguson
Music: Bronislaw Kaper
Editor: Ernest Nims
Cast: Orson Welles (Franz Kindler, alias Charles Rankin), Loretta
    Young (Mary Longstreet), Edward G. Robinson (Inspector Wil-
    son), Philip Merivale (Judge Longstreet), Richard Long (Noah
    Longstreet), Billy House (Mr. Potter)
Running Time: 95 minutes
Premiere: July 1946

The Killers (Universal, 1946)
Director: Robert Siodmak
Producer: Mark Hellinger
Screenplay: Anthony Veiller and John Huston (uncredited), from the
    short story by Ernest Hemingway
Cinematographer: Woody Bredell
Production Design: Jack Otterson and Martin Obzina
Music: Miklos Rozsa
Editor: Arthur Hilton

Cast: Burt Lancaster (Swede), Ava Gardner (Kitty Collins), Edmond O'Brien (Jim Reardon), Albert Dekker (Big Jim Colfax), Sam Levene (Sam Lubinsky), Charles McGraw (Al), William Conrad (Max)
Running Time: 105 minutes
Premiere: August 1946

Song of the Thin Man (Metro-Goldwyn-Mayer, 1947)
Director: Edward Buzzell
Producer: Nat Perrin
Screenplay: Nat Perrin, Steve Fisher, from a story by Stanley Roberts, based on characters created by Dashiell Hammett
Cinematographer: Charles Rosher
Production Design: Cedric Gibbons, Randall Duell
Music: David Snell
Editor: Gene Ruggiero
Cast: William Powell (Nick Charles), Myrna Loy (Nora Charles), Keenan Wynn (Clarence "Clinker" Krause), Dean Stockwell (Nick Charles, Jr.), Gloria Grahame (Fran Page), Don Taylor (Buddy Hollis)
Running Time: 86 minutes
Premiere: July 1947

A Double Life (Universal-International, 1947)
Director: George Cukor
Producer: Michael Kanin
Screenplay: Ruth Gordon, Garson Kanin
Cinematographer: Milton Krasner
Production Design: Bernard Herzbrun, Harvey Gillette
Music: Miklos Rozsa
Editor: Robert Parrish
Cast: Ronald Colman (Anthony John), Signe Hasso (Brita), Edmond O'Brien (Bill Friend), Shelley Winters (Pat Kroll), Ray Collins (Victor Donlan), Philip Loeb (Max Lasker), Millard Mitchell (Al Cooley)
Running Time: 105 minutes
Premiere: December 1947

Act of Violence (Metro-Goldwyn-Mayer, 1948)
Director: Fred Zinnemann
Producer: William Wright
Screenplay: Robert Richards, from a story by Collier Young
Cinematographer: Robert Surtees
Production Design: Cedric Gibbons and Hans Peters
Music: Bronislau Kaper
Editor: Conrad Nervig
Cast: Van Heflin (Frank Enley), Robert Ryan (Joe Parkson), Janet
    Leigh (Edith Enley), Mary Astor (Pat), Phyllis Thaxter (Ann
    Sturges), Berry Kroeger (Johnny), Taylor Holmes (Gavery)
Running Time: 82 minutes
Premiere: December 1948

Sunset Boulevard (Paramount, 1950)
Director: Billy Wilder
Producer: Charles Brackett
Screenplay: Charles Brackett, Billy Wilder, and D. M. Marshman, Jr.
Cinematographer: John F. Seitz
Production Design: Hans Dreier, John Meehan
Music: Franz Waxman
Editor: Arthur Schmidt
Cast: Gloria Swanson (Norma Desmond), William Holden (Joe
    Gillis), Erich von Stroheim (Max von Mayerling), Nancy Olson
    (Betty Schaefer), Fred Clark (Sheldrake), Cecil B. DeMille,
    Hedda Hopper (themselves)
Running Time: 111 minutes
Premiere: August 1950

Strangers on a Train (Warner Bros., 1951)
Director: Alfred Hitchcock
Producer: Alfred Hitchcock
Screenplay: Raymond Chandler, Czenzi Ormonde, from the novel by
    Patricia Highsmith
Adaptation: Whitfield Cook
Cinematographer: Robert Burks
Production Design: Ted Haworth

Music: Dimitri Tiomkin
Editor: William Ziegler
Cast: Robert Walker (Bruno Antony), Farley Granger (Guy Haines), Ruth Roman (Anne Morton), Patricia Hitchcock (Barbara Morton), Leo G. Carroll (Senator Morton), Laura Elliot (Miriam Haines)
Running Time: 100 minutes
Premiere: June 1951

The Killing (United Artists, 1956)
Director: Stanley Kubrick
Producer: James B. Harris
Screenplay: Stanley Kubrick and Jim Thompson, from the novel *Clean Break* by Lionel White
Cinematographer: Lucien Ballard
Production Design: Ruth Sobotka
Music: Gerald Fried
Editor: Betty Steinberg
Cast: Sterling Hayden (Johnny Clay), Coleen Gray (Fay), Jay C. Flippen (Marvin Unger), Marie Windsor (Sherry Peatty), Elisha Cook, Jr. (George Peatty), Vince Edwards (Val), Joe Sawyer (Mike O'Reilly)
Running Time: 83 minutes
Premiere: May 1956

Touch of Evil (Universal-International, 1958)
Director: Orson Welles
Producer: Albert Zugsmith
Screenplay: Orson Welles from the novel *Badge of Evil* by Whit Masterson
Adaptation: Paul Monasch (uncredited)
Cinematographer: Russell Metty
Production Design: Alexander Golitzen, Robert Clatworthy
Music: Henry Mancini
Editor: Virgil Vogel, Aaron Stell; and Ernest Nims (uncredited)
Cast: Orson Welles (Hank Quinlan), Charlton Heston (Ramon Miguel Vargas), Janet Leigh (Susan Vargas), Akim Tamiroff (Joe Grandi), Joseph Calleia (Pete Menzies), Marlene Dietrich (Tanya)

Running Time: 93 minutes (premiere); 111 minutes (1998 restored version)
Premiere: February 1958

Anatomy of a Murder (Columbia Pictures, 1959)
Director: Otto Preminger
Producer: Otto Preminger
Screenplay: Wendell Mayes, from the novel by Robert Traver
Cinematographer: Sam Leavitt
Production Design: Boris Leven
Music: Duke Ellington
Editor: Louis Loeffler
Cast: James Stewart (Paul Biegler), Lee Remick (Laura Manion), Ben Gazzara (Lt. Frederick Manion), Joseph N. Welch (Judge Weaver), Kathryn Grant (Mary Pilant), Arthur O'Connell (Parnell McCarthy)
Running Time: 160 minutes
Premiere: July 1959

The Killers (Universal-International, 1964)
Director: Don Siegel
Producer: Don Siegel
Screenplay: Gene Coon, from the short story by Ernest Hemingway
Cinematographer: Richard Rawlings (color)
Production Design: Frank Arrigo and George Chan
Music: John Williams
Editor: Richard Belding
Cast: Lee Marvin (Charlie), Angie Dickinson (Sheila Farr), John Cassavetes (Johnny North), Ronald Reagan (Browning), Clu Gulager (Lee), Virginia Christine (Mae Watson), Norman Fell (Mickey)
Running Time: 95 minutes
Premiere: May 1964

Chinatown (Paramount Pictures, 1974)
Director: Roman Polanski
Producer: Robert Evans

Screenplay: Robert Towne
Cinematographer: John Alonzo
Production Design: Richard Sylbert
Music: Jerry Goldsmith
Editor: Sam O'Steen
Cast: Jack Nicholson (J. J. "Jake" Gittes), Faye Dunaway (Evelyn Cross Mulwray), John Huston (Noah Cross), John Hillerman (Russ Yelburton), Diane Ladd (Ida Sessions)
Running Time: 131 minutes
Premiere: June 1974

The Dain Curse (CBS-TV, 1978)
Director: E. W. Swackhamer
Producer: Martin Poll
Screenplay: Robert Lenski, from the novel by Dashiell Hammett
Cinematographer: Andrew Laszlo (color)
Production Design: John Lloyd, Gene Rudolf
Music: Charles Gross
Editor: Murray Solomon
Cast: James Coburn (Hamilton Nash), Jean Simmons (Aaronia Haldorn), Hector Elizondo (Sheriff), Beatrice Straight (Alice Leggett), Paul Stewart (The Old Man), Jason Miller (Owen Fitzstephan), Brent Spiner (Tom Fink), Roland Winters (Hubert Collinson)
Running Time: 300 minutes
Premiere: First telecast May 22, 23, and 24, 1978

Hammett (Warner Bros., American Zoetrope, 1982)
Director: Wim Wenders
Executive Producer: Francis Ford Coppola
Producers: Fred Roos, Ronald Colby, Don Guest
Screenplay: Ross Thomas, Dennis O'Flaherty, from the novel by Joe Gores
Adaptation: Thomas Pope
Cinematographers: Joseph Biroc, Philip Lathrop (uncredited) (Widescreen, color)
Production Design: Dean Tavoularis

Music: John Barry
Editors: Marc Laub, Robert Lovett, Randy Roberts, Janice Hampton
Supervising editor: Barry Malkin
Cast: Frederic Forrest (Hammett), Peter Boyle (Jimmy Ryan), Marilu Henner (Kit Conger), Roy Kinnear (Eddie Hagedorn), Elisha Cook, Jr. (Eli), Sylvia Sidney (Donaldina Cameron)
Running Time: 97 minutes
Premiere: November 1982

L.A. Confidential (Warner Bros./Regency, 1997)
Director: Curtis Hanson
Producers: Curtis Hanson, Arnon Milchan, Michael Nathanson
Screenplay: Curtis Hanson, Brian Helgeland, based on the novel by James Ellroy
Cinematographer: Dante Spinotti
Production Design: Jeannine Oppewall
Music: Jerry Goldsmith
Editor: Peter Honess
Cast: Russell Crowe (Bud White), Kevin Spacey (Jack Vincennes), Guy Pearce (Ed Exley), Kim Basinger (Lynn Bracken), Danny DeVito (Sid Hudgens), James Cromwell (Dudley Smith)
Running Time: 138 minutes
Premiere: September 1997

The Talented Mr. Ripley (Paramount, Miramax Films, 1999)
Director: Anthony Minghella
Producer: William Horberg and Tom Sternberg
Screenplay: Anthony Minghella, from the novel by Patricia Highsmith
Cinematographer: John Seale (Widescreen, color)
Production Design: Roy Walker
Music: Gabriel Yared
Editor: Walter Murch
Cast: Matt Damon (Tom Ripley), Gwyneth Paltrow (Marge Sherwood), Jude Law (Dickie Greenleaf), Cate Blanchett (Meredith Logue), Philip Seymour Hoffman (Freddie Miles), Jack Davenport (Peter Smith-Kingsley)

Running Time: 139 minutes
Premiere: December 1999

Ripley's Game (Fine Line Features, Cattleya, Baby Films, 2003)
Director: Liliana Cavani
Producers: Ileen Maisel, Simon Bosanquet, Ricardo Tozzi, Russell
    Smith
Screenplay: Charles McKeown and Liliana Cavani, from the novel by
    Patricia Highsmith
Cinematographer: Alfio Contini (Widescreen, color)
Production Design: Francesco Frigeri
Music: Ennio Morricone
Editor: Jon Harris
Cast: John Malkovich (Tom Ripley), Dougray Scott (Jonathan Trev-
    anny), Ray Winstone (Reeves), Lena Headey (Sarah Trevanny),
    Chiara Caselli (Luisa Ripley), Sam Blitz (Matthew Trevanny),
    Luis Wende (Ernst)
Running Time: 110 minutes
Premiere: December 2003

SELECTED BIBLIOGRAPHY

Agee, James, *Film Writing and Selected Journalism*. Edited by Michael Sragow. New York: Library of America, 2001.

Alleva, Richard. "Hitchcock: A Director's Sense of Good and Evil." *Commonweal*, July 16, 2010, 14–19.

Alpi, Deborah. *Robert Siodmak: A Biography with Critical Analyses of His Film Noirs*. Jefferson, N.C.: McFarland, 1998.

Armour, Robert. *Fritz Lang*. Boston: Twayne, 1977.

Arthur, Paul. "Noir Happens: *Act of Violence*." *Film Comment* 35, no. 4 (July–August 1999): 56–58.

Berg, Chuck, and Tom Erskine, eds. *The Encyclopedia of Orson Welles*. New York: Facts on File, 2003.

Bergman, Paul, and Michael Asimow. *Reel Justice: The Courtroom Goes to the Movies*. Kansas City, Mo.: Andrews and McMeel, 1996.

Bogdanovich, Peter. *Who the Devil Made It?: Conversations with Film Directors*. New York: Ballantine Books, 1998.

———. *Who the Hell's in It?: Hollywood's Legendary Actors*. New York: Ballantine Books, 2006.

Booth, Philip. "Hemingway's 'The Killers' and Heroic Fatalism." *Literature/Film Quarterly* 38, no. 1 (Winter 2007): 404–11.

Borde, Raymond, and Etienne Chaumeton. *A Panorama of American Film Noir, 1941–53*. Trans. Paul Hammond. San Francisco: City Lights Books, 2002.

Bould, Mark. *Film Noir: From Berlin to Sin City*. New York: Columbia University Press, 2005.

Brill, Lesley. *John Huston's Filmmaking*. New York: Cambridge University Press, 1997.

Buckley, Michael. "Fred Zinnemann: An Interview." *Films in Review* 33, no. 1 (January 1983): 25–40.

Callow, Simon. *Orson Welles: Hello, America*. New York: Viking, 2006.

Cameron, Ian. *The Book of Film Noir*. New York: Continuum, 1992.

———, ed. *Movie Reader*. New York: Praeger, 1972. Includes a special section of six articles on Preminger's work.

Campbell, James. "Happy Birthday, Mr. Ripley." *New York Times Book Review*, February 8, 2009, 23.

Caspary, Vera. *Laura, Bedelia, and Evvie: 3 Novels*. New York: Houghton Mifflin, 1992.

Chandler, Charlotte. *Nobody's Perfect: Billy Wilder*. New York: Applause Books, 2004.

Chandler, Raymond. *Later Novels and Other Writings*. Edited by Frank Mac-Shane. New York: Library of America, 1995.

———. *Strangers on a Train: Unpublished Screenplay*. Los Angeles: Warner Bros., 1950. Extensive revisions of the screenplay by Czenzi Ormonde are not included in this draft of the script.

Combs, Richard. "Anatomy of a Director." *Sight and Sound* 10 (ns), no. 4 (April 2009): 38–41.

Conley, Tom. *Film Hieroglyphs: Ruptures in Classical Cinema*. Minneapolis: University of Minnesota Press, 1991.

Conrad, Mark, ed. *The Philosophy of Film Noir*. Lexington: University Press of Kentucky, 2006.

———, ed. *The Philosophy of Neo-Noir*. Lexington: University Press of Kentucky, 2007.

Cooper, Stephen, ed. *Perspective on John Huston*. New York: G. K. Hall, 1994.

Corliss, Richard. "The Talented Ms. Highsmith." *Time*, December 27, 1999, 159.

Dellolio, Peter. "Expressionist Themes in *Strangers on a Train*." *Literature/Film Quarterly* 31, no. 4 (Fall 2003): 260–69.

Desowitz, Bill. "Strangers on Which Train? The Alternate Version of *Strangers on a Train*." *Film Comment* 28, no. 3 (May–June 1992): 4–5.

Dick, Bernard, ed. *Columbia Pictures*. Lexington: University Press of Kentucky, 1992.

Dickos, Andrew. *Street with No Name: A History of Classic Film Noir*. Lexington: University Press of Kentucky, 2007.

Doherty, Thomas. *Hollywood's Censor: Joseph Breen*. New York: Columbia University Press, 2007.

Dooley, Dennis. *Dashiell Hammett*. New York: Ungar, 1984.

Duncan, Paul. *Alfred Hitchcock*. Los Angeles: Taschen, 2003.

Eagan, Daniel. *America's Film Legacy: Landmark Movies in the National Film Registry.* New York: Continuum, 2010.

Ebert, Roger. *The Great Movies I.* New York: Broadway Books, 2003.

———. *The Great Movies II.* New York: Broadway Books, 2005.

Eisner, Lotte. *Fritz Lang.* New York: Oxford University Press, 1977.

Elert, Nicolet, Andrew Sarris, and Grace Jeromski, eds. *International Dictionary of Films and Filmmakers.* Rev. ed. 4 vols. New York: St. James, 2000.

Eliot, Marc. *Jimmy Stewart: A Biography.* New York: Random House, 2006.

Estrin, Mark, ed. *Orson Welles: Interviews.* Jackson: University Press of Mississippi, 2006.

Falk, Quentin. *Travels in Greeneland: The Cinema of Graham Greene.* Rev. ed. New York: Quartet Books, 1984.

Farber, Manny. *Farber on Film: The Complete Film Writings of Manny Farber.* Edited by Robert Polito. New York: Library of America, 2009.

Film Comment 10, no. 6 (November–December 1974). Special film noir issue.

Fine, David. "From Berlin to Hollywood: Fritz Lang's *The Woman in the Window* and *Scarlet Street.*" *Literature/Film Quarterly* 35, no. 4 (Fall 2007): 282–93.

Frank, Sam. *Ronald Colman: A Bio-Bibliography.* Westport, Conn.: Greenwich Press, 1997.

Freedman, Jonathan, and Richard Millington, eds. *Hitchcock's America.* New York: Oxford University Press, 1999.

Fujiwara, Chris. *The World and Its Double: Otto Preminger.* New York: Faber and Faber, 2008.

Gale, Robert. *A Dashiell Hammett Companion.* Westport, Conn.: Greenwood Press, 2000.

Garis, Robert. *The Films of Orson Welles.* New York: Cambridge University Press, 2004.

Gemunden, Gerd. *A Foreign Affair: Billy Wilder's American Films.* New York: Berghahn, 2008.

Giannetti, Louis, and Scott Eyman. *Flashback: A Brief History of Film.* Rev. ed. Boston: Allyn and Bacon, 2010.

Gorman, Ed, Lee Server, and Martin Greenberg, eds. *The Big Book of Noir.* New York: Carroll and Graf, 1998.

Gottlieb, Sidney, ed. *Alfred Hitchcock: Interviews.* Jackson: University Press of Mississippi, 2003.

Grant, Barry, ed. *Fritz Lang: Interviews.* Jackson: University Press of Mississippi, 2003.

Greene, Graham. "Foreword." In Patricia Highsmith, *Eleven: Short Stories.* New York: Atlantic Monthly Press, 1989, ix–xi.

———. *The Ministry of Fear*. With an Introduction by Alan Furst. New York: Penguin Books, 2005.

Griffith, Richard. *Anatomy of a Motion Picture: The Making of Anatomy of a Murder*. New York: St. Martin's Press, 1959.

Gunning, Tom. *The Films of Fritz Lang*. London: British Film Institute, 2000.

Halliwell, Leslie. *Film Guide*. Edited by David Critten. Rev. ed. New York: HarperCollins, 2008.

Hammen, Scott. *John Huston*. Boston: Twayne, 1985.

Hammett, Dashiell. *The Big Knockover: Selected Stories and Short Novels*. Edited with an Introduction by Lillian Hellman. New York: Vintage Books, 1989.

———. *The Dain Curse*. New York: Vintage Books, 1989.

———. *The Glass Key*. New York: Vintage Books, 1989.

———. *The Maltese Falcon*. New York: Vintage Books, 1992.

———. *Nightmare Town: Stories*. Edited by Kirby McCauley, Martin Greenberg, and Ed Gorman. With an Introduction by William Nolan. New York: Vintage Books, 2000. Includes the first draft of *The Thin Man*. (See next item.)

———. *The Thin Man*. New York: Vintage Books, 1992.

Hanson, Helen. *Hollywood Heroines: Women in Film Noir*. New York: Tauris, 2007.

Hare, William. *Early Film Noir*. Jefferson, N.C.: McFarland, 2003.

———. *L. A. Noir: Dark Versions of the City of Angels*. Jefferson, N.C.: McFarland, 2004.

Haut, Woody. *Heartbreak and Vine: Hard-Boiled Writers in Hollywood*. London: Serpent's Tail, 2002.

Hemingway, Ernest. "The Killers." In *The Short Stories of Ernest Hemingway*. With a Preface by the Author. New York: Scribner, 2003, 279–89.

Heston, Charlton. *In the Arena: An Autobiography*. New York: Simon and Schuster, 1995.

Heylin, Clinton. *Despite the Studio System: Orson Welles*. Chicago: Chicago Review Press, 2005.

Hibbs, Thomas. *Art of Darkness: American Noir*. Dallas: Spence, 2008.

Higham, Charles. *Orson Welles: The Rise and Fall of an American Genius*. New York: St. Martin's Press, 1985.

Highsmith, Patricia. *Ripley's Game*. New York: Norton, 2008.

———. *Strangers on a Train*. New York: Norton, 2001.

———. *The Talented Mr. Ripley*. New York: Norton, 2008.

Hillier, Jim, and Alastair Phillips. *100 Film Noirs*. London: British Film Institute, 2009.

Hirsch, Foster. *The Dark Side of the Screen: Film Noir*. Rev. ed. New York: Da Capo, 2009.

——. *Detours and Lost Highways: A Map of Neo-Noir*. New York: Limelight, 1994.

——. *Otto Preminger*. New York: Knopf, 2007.

Hopp, Glenn. *Billy Wilder*. Los Angeles: Taschen, 2003.

Horton, Robert, ed. *Billy Wilder: Interviews*. Jackson: University Press of Mississippi, 2001.

——. "Day of the Craftsman: Fred Zinnemann." *Film Comment* 33, no. 5 (September–October, 1997): 60–67.

Huston, John. *The Maltese Falcon: A Screenplay*. Edited by William Luhr. New Brunswick, N.J.: Rutgers University Press, 1998.

——. *An Open Book*. New York: Knopf, 1980.

Irwin, John. *Unless the Threat of Death Is behind Them: Hard-Boiled Fiction and Film Noir*. Baltimore: Johns Hopkins University Press, 2006.

Iyer, Pico. "Private Eye and Public Conscience." *Time*, December 12, 1998, 98.

Johnson, Diane. *Dashiell Hammett: A Life*. New York: Random House, 1983.

Kiszely, Philip. *Hollywood through Private Eyes: The Hard-Boiled Novel in the Studio Era*. New York: Peter Lang, 2006.

Kracauer, Siegfried. *From Caligari to Hitler: A Psychological Study of the German Film*. Princeton, N.J.: Princeton University Press, 1974.

Krutnick, Frank. *In a Lonely Street: Film Noir and Genre*. New York: Routledge, 1991.

Lambert, Gavin. *On Cukor*. New York: Putnam, 1972.

Lane, Anthony. "Killing Time: *Mr. Ripley*." *New Yorker*, January 3, 2000, 128–30.

Lawrence, Frank. *Hemingway and the Movies*. Jackson: University Press of Mississippi, 1981.

Layman, Richard, and Julie Rivett, eds. *Selected Letters of Dashiell Hammett*. Washington, D.C.: Counterpoint, 2001.

Leitch, Thomas. *Encyclopedia of Alfred Hitchcock*. New York: Facts on File, 2002.

Lennig, Arthur. *Stroheim*. Lexington: University Press of Kentucky, 2000.

Levy, Emmanuel. *George Cukor: Master of Elegance*. New York: William Morrow, 1994.

Literature/Film Quarterly 2, no. 4 (Fall 1974). Special Graham Greene issue.

Long, Robert Emmett, ed. *George Cukor: Interviews*. Jackson: University Press of Mississippi, 2001.

——, ed. *John Huston: Interviews*. Jackson: University Press of Mississippi, 2001.

Luhr, William. *Raymond Chandler and Film*. Rev. ed. Tallahassee: Florida State University Press, 1991.

Lyons, Barry, "Fritz Lang and Film Noir." *Mise-en-Scene*, 1980, no. 1, 11–15.

MacShane, Frank. "Stranger at the Studio: Raymond Chandler in Hollywood." *American Film*, May 1976, 57–59.

Maltin, Leonard, ed. *Movie Guide*. New York: Penguin, 2011.

Marling, William. *The American Roman Noir: Hammett, Cain, and Chandler*. Athens: University of Georgia Press, 1995.

Mayer, Geoff, and Brian McDonnell. *Encyclopedia of Film Noir*. Westport, Conn.: Greenwood Press, 2007.

McBride, Joseph. *Orson Welles*. Rev. ed. New York: Da Capo Press, 1996.

McGilligan, Patrick. *Alfred Hitchcock: A Life in Darkness and Light*. New York: HarperCollins, 2004.

———. *Fritz Lang: The Nature of the Beast*. New York: St. Martin's Press, 1997.

———. *George Cukor: A Double Life*. New York: St. Martin's Press, 1991.

Metress, Christopher, ed. *Critical Response to Dashiell Hammett*. New York: Greenwood Press, 1994.

Meyers, Jeffrey. *Bogart: A Life in Hollywood*. New York: Houghton Mifflin, 1997.

Miller, Gabriel, ed. *Fred Zinnemann: Interviews*. Jackson: University Press of Mississippi, 2005.

Muller, Jurgen, ed. *Movies of the Forties*. Los Angeles: Taschen/BFI, 2005.

———, ed. *Movies of the Fifties*. Los Angeles: Taschen/BFI, 2005.

———, ed. *Movies of the Sixties*. Los Angeles: Taschen/BFI, 2005.

———, ed. *Movies of the Seventies*. Los Angeles: Taschen/BFI, 2005.

Naremore, James. *More Than Night: Film Noir in Its Contexts*. Rev. ed. Los Angeles: University Press of California, 2008.

———. *On Kubrick*. London: British Film Institute, 2007.

Nash, Jay, and Stanley Ross, eds. *Motion Picture Guide*. 12 vols. Chicago: Cinebooks, 1985. Pagination is consecutive throughout all twelve volumes.

New York Times Film Reviews. 20 vols. New York: New York Times, 1996. This collection of reviews is unpaginated.

Noletti, Arthur, ed. *The Films of Fred Zinnemann: Critical Perspectives*. Albany: State University of New York Press, 1999.

Oliver, Charles, ed. *A Moving Picture Feast: The Filmgoer's Hemingway*. New York: Praeger, 1989.

Oliver, Kelly. *Noir Anxiety*. Minneapolis: University of Minnesota Press, 2003.

Ondaatje, Michael. *The Conversations: Walter Murch and the Art of Editing Film*. New York: Knopf, 2008.

Ozer, Jerome, ed. *Film Review Annual*. Englewood, N.J.: Film Review Publications, 2000.

Palmer, Barton, ed. *Perspectives on Film Noir*. New York: G.K. Hall, 1996.

Panek, LeRoy. *Reading Early Hammett: The Fiction Prior to* The Maltese Falcon. Jefferson, N.C.: McFarland, 2004.

Perry, George. *Bogie: The Life and Films of Humphrey Bogart*. With "An Appreciation" by Richard Schickel. New York: St. Martin's Press, 2006.

Petrie, Graham. "Transfer of Guilt: *Strangers on a Train*." *Sight and Sound* 19 (ns), no. 7 (July 2009): 46–49.

Phelps, Donald. "*La Chienne* and *Scarlet Street*," *Film Comment*, 32, no. 1 (January–February, 1996): 67–71.

Phillips, Gene, ed. *Stanley Kubrick: Interviews*. Jackson: University Press of Mississippi, 2001.

Preminger, Otto. *Preminger: An Autobiography*. Garden City, N.Y.: Doubleday, 1977.

Price, Theodore. *Hitchcock and Homosexuality: A Psychoanalytic View*. Metuchen, N.J.: Scarecrow Press, 1992.

Rich, Frank. "American Pseudo: *The Talented Mr. Ripley*." *New York Times Magazine*, December 12, 1999, 80–86, 98–114.

Richardson, Carl. *Autopsy: An Element of Realism in Film*. Metuchen, N.J.: Scarecrow Press, 1998.

Sarris, Andrew, ed. *Film Directors Encyclopedia*. New York: St. James Press, 1998.

———. *You Ain't Heard Nothin' Yet: The American Talking Film, 1927–49*. New York: Oxford University Press, 1998.

Sayre, Nora. "In the Shoes of a Scary Stalker: *Strangers on a Train*." *New York Times*, April 12, 1998, sec. 2:11, 12.

Schenkar, Joan. *The Talented Miss Highsmith: The Secret Life and Serious Art of Patricia Highsmith*. New York: St. Martin's Press, 2009.

Schrader, Paul. "Notes on Film Noir," in *American Movie Critics*, ed. Phillip Lopate. Rev. ed. New York: Library of America, 2008.

Schwartz, Ronald. *Neo-Noir*. Lanham, Md.: Scarecrow Press, 2005.

Siegel, Don. *A Siegel Film*. London: Faber, 2003.

Sikov, Ed. *On Sunset Boulevard: The Life and Times of Billy Wilder*. New York: Hyperion, 1998.

Silver, Alain, and James Ursini, eds. *The Film Noir Reader*. New York: Limelight, 1996.

———. *Film Noir Reader 2*. New York: Limelight, 1999.

———. *Film Noir Reader 4*. New York: Limelight, 2004.

———. *The Noir Style*. Woodstock, N.Y.: Overlook Press, 2003.

Silver, Alain, James Ursini, and Paul Duncan. *Film Noir*. Los Angeles: Taschen, 2004.

Silver, Alain, James Ursini, and Robert Porfirio, eds. *The Film Noir Reader 3*, New York: Limelight, 2002.

Silver, Alain, James Ursini, Robert Porfirio, and Elizabeth Ward, *Film Noir: The Encyclopedia*. New York: Overlook Duckworth, 2010.

Spoto, Donald. *Spellbound by Beauty: Alfred Hitchcock and His Leading Ladies*. New York: Harmony Books, 2008.

Staggs, Sam. *Close-Up on Sunset Boulevard*. New York: St. Martin's Press, 2003.

Stevens, George, Jr., ed. *Conversations with the Great Moviemakers*. New York: Knopf, 2006.

Symons, Julian. *Dashiell Hammett* (New York: Harcourt, Brace, Jovanovich, 1985.

Telotte, J. P. *Voices in the Dark: Narrative Patterns of Film Noir*. Chicago: University of Illinois Press, 1989.

Thomson, David. *Have You Seen . . . ?: 1,000 Films*. New York: Knopf, 2008.

———. "Impulse: Otto Preminger." *Sight and Sound* 15 (ns), no. 5 (May 2005): 30–33.

———. *New Biographical Dictionary of Film*. Rev. ed. New York: Knopf, 2010.

———. *Rosebud: The Story of Orson Welles*. New York: Vintage Books, 1997.

Tibbetts, John, and James Welsh, eds. *The Encyclopedia of Novels into Film*. Rev. ed. New York: Facts on File, 2005.

Truffaut, Francois. *Hitchcock*. With the collaboration of Helen Scott. Rev. ed. New York: Simon and Schuster, 1985.

Variety Film Reviews. 24 vols. New Providence, N.J.: Bowker, 1997. This collection of reviews is unpaginated.

Vogel, Amos. "You Have to Survive Even If It Kills You." (Austrian Filmmakers in Hollywood.) *Film Comment* 30, no. 2 (March–April, 1994): 31–36.

Wagner-Martin, Linda, ed. *Hemingway: Eight Decades of Criticism*. East Lansing: Michigan State University Press, 2009.

Walker, Alexander. *Stanley Kubrick, Director*. Rev. ed. New York: Norton, 1999.

Welles, Orson. *Touch of Evil: A Screenplay*. Edited by Terry Comito. New Brunswick, N.J.: Rutgers University Press, 1998.

Welles, Orson, and Peter Bogdanovich. *This Is Orson Welles*. Rev. ed. New York: Da Capo, 1998.

Wessells, Henry. "Raymond Chandler and the Origins of Film Noir." *AB Weekly*, December 8, 1997, 1501–06.

Wexman, Virginia. *A History of Film*. Rev. ed. Boston: Allyn and Bacon, 2010.

Wilder, Billy, Charles Brackett, and D. M. Marshman, Jr. *Sunset Boulevard*. Edited by Jeffrey Meyers. Los Angeles: University of California Press, 1999.

Wilson, Andrew. *Beautiful Shadow: A Life of Patricia Highsmith*. New York: Bloomsbury, 2003.

Youngkin, Stephen. *The Lost One: Peter Lorre*. Lexington: University Press of Kentucky, 2005.

Zinnemann, Fred. *A Life in the Movies: An Autobiography*. New York: Scribner's, 1992.

INDEX

Note: Page numbers in italics refer to photographs.

Academy Awards, 127, 160, 171
Act of Violence, 178–84, *182,* 198, 280
adultery, 31
After the Thin Man, 57
Agee, James, 87, 127, 141, 179
Alpi, Deborah, 134
ambiguous endings, 171
The American Friend, 258
America's Film Legacy (Eagan), 42
Anatomy of a Murder, 159, 160, 161–72, 178, 214–15, 282
Andrews, Dana, 153, 160
Angel Face, 160
Another Thin Man, 57–58
Archer, Eugene, 159
Arnold, Edward, 47
Arthur, Paul, 178, 179
Asimow, Michael, 167, 169
Asphalt Jungle, 187
Astor, Mary, 34, *37,* 38, 181
awards: Academy Awards, 127, 160, 171; Brussels World Fair grand prize, 215; Edgar Awards, 235, 248; Emmys, 229

Babener, Liahna, 160
Badge of Evil (Masterson), 206, 207
Baker, Simon, 270
Ballard, Lucien, 188
Barnes, George, 89
Barry, John, 239, 268
Barson, Michael, 206
Basinger, Jeanine, 163, 168
Bazin, André, 18
Beeding, Francis, 88
Bendix, William, 51, 55
Bennett, Joan, 77
Berg, Charles, 36, 41
Bergman, Ingrid, 88, *91*
Bergman, Paul, 167, 169
Biesen, Sheri, 198
Bigwood, James, 92
Biroc, Joseph, 237
Black Mask, 7–10, 30, 227, 235–36
Block, Harry, 228

Blood Simple, 270
Body Heat, 266
Bogart, Humphrey, 34, 36, *37,* 40–41
Booth, Philip, 132
Boucher, Anthony, 249
Boudu Saved from Drowning, 19
Bould, Mark, 80
Brackett, Charles, 118
Bredell, Elwood "Woody," 137, 139
Breen, Joseph, 13, 31–32, 47, 50–51, 78, 105
Brussels World Fair grand prize, 215
Buckley, Michael, 58
budgets, 14, 34, 38
Buscombe, Edward, 186
Buzzell, Edward, 58–59, 62
Byrne, Gabriel, 271, 272

The Cabinet of Dr. Caligari, 17, 23
Cain, James M., 6–7, 10, 268, 273
Calleia, Joseph, 52, 55, 209
Callow, Simon, 205
Canby, Vincent, 243
Caps, John, 120
Caspary, Vera, 152–53
Cassavetes, John, 144
Catholic themes, 5
Cavani, Liliana, 258–62
Censorship Code, 105
censorship issues: homosexuality, 31–32, 34–35, 38, 96, 105, 154, 186–87; language, 163–64, 166; moral objections, 78–79; political corruption, 47, 50; profanity, 50; resisting, 161, 167; violence, 50–51, 147. *See also* Breen, Joseph
chance meetings, 100
Chandler, Raymond: background, 4–6; on censorship, 13; Cooke's tribute to, 244; on Hammett, 4,
10, 62, 239, 267; *Strangers on a Train,* 94–96, 98
Chatten, Richard, 209
Chekhov, Michael, 88–89, *91*
Chinatown, 225, 226, *266,* 266–67, 282–83
Christie, Dame Agatha, 3–4
Christine, Virginia, *136,* 143
Clash by Night, 23
Clean Break (White), 185–86, 189
Coburn, James, 229, *230,* 235
Coen brothers, 270
cold war, 15
Colman, Ronald, 111, 112, *114,* 117
Conan Doyle, Sir Arthur, 3, 4, 227
Conley, Tom, 80
Conroe, Irwin, 79
Cook, Elisha, Jr., 35, 187, *188,* 240
Cooke, Alistair, 244
Coppola, Francis Ford, 236–39
Corber, Robert, 99
Corliss, Richard, 247, 254, 257
Cortez, Ricardo, 31
Coursodon, Jean Pierre, 131
courtroom drama. *See Anatomy of a Murder*
Creatures of Darkness (Phillips), 267
Crispin, Edmund, 102–4
Cristofer, Michael, 189
Crowther, Bruce, 113
Cukor, George, 111–18, 120, 128

Dahl, John, 268
The Dain Curse (novel), 226–29
The Dain Curse (television adaptation), 229–35, *230,* 267, 283
Dalgliesh, Adam, 4
Dali, Salvador, 92
Damon, Matt, 251, *252, 257*
Daniels, Bebe, 31

Dark Memory (Latimer), 49
Das Kabinett des Dr. Caligari (The Cabinet of Dr. Caligari), 17, 23
Davenport, Jack, 250
Davis, Bette, 32
Dawson, Michael, 216
"Dead Yellow Women" (Hammett), 235–36, 240, 242–43
De Corsia, Ted, 187
Dekker, Albert, 137
de la Fouchardiere, Georges, 76
Dellolio, Peter, 101
Del Ruth, Roy, 31–32, 33
Delson, James, 209
DeMille, Cecil B., 119, 122–23, *123*
Derry, Charles, 151
Desowitz, Bill, 105
De Sylva, B. G. "Buddy," 49–50
Dickinson, Angie, 144
Dickos, Andrew, 16, 194
Dickstein, Morris, 123
Dieterle, William, 32
Dietrich, Marlene, 209, *219*
disillusionment, 15, 178
Dixon, Wheeler, 181
documentary-like approach: *Anatomy of a Murder,* 161; *A Double Life,* 112; as film noir convention, 15–16; *The Killers* (1946), 137; *The Killing,* 189; Zinnemann films, 177
docu-noirs, 178–79
Dodd, Clare, 47
Doherty, Thomas, 105
Donlevy, Brian, 51, 55
Dooley, Dennis, 234
Double Indemnity, 13, 14, 18, 20, 268
A Double Life, 111–18, *114,* 120, 128, 279
downbeat endings, 184
dream sequences, 91–93

drug addiction, portrayals of, 228, 231, 233
Dunning, Decla, 198
Duryea, Dan, 71, 77

Eagan, Daniel, 42, 127, 141, 160
Ebert, Roger, 36, 96, 159
Edeson, Arthur, 35, 37–38
Edgar Allan Poe Awards, 235, 248
Edwards, Vince, 190
Eisner, Lotte, 17, 69, 75–76
Eliot, Marc, 164
Ellis, Jack, 177
Ellroy, James, 269
Emmy nominations, 229
Epstein, Robert, 215
Erickson, Glenn, 244
Esmond, Carl, 72, *73*
European directors, 151. *See also specific directors*
Everitt, David, 225
evil, 260, 262
expressionism, 16–18, 22–23, 114–15, 167–68, 205
extended takes, 169–70
Eyman, Scott, 83

Falk, Quentin, 74
Farber, Manny, 94, 106, 127, 139, 159–60, 184
fascism, 205
fatalism, 184
The Female Animal, 215
femme fatales, 16, 225; *The Dain Curse,* 229, 231; *A Double Life,* 112–13; *Hammett,* 241–42; *The Killers* films, 136, 144, 146–47; "The Killers" short story, 140–41; *L.A. Confidential,* 270; *The Maltese Falcon* films, 30, 31–32, 34; *Scarlet*

Street, 77; *The Song of the Thin Man,* 58–59, 61; *U-Turn,* 268–69
Ferguson, Perry, 201
film noir: epitaph of, 207; genre boundaries, 266; proto-noir, 21; terminology, 14–15. *See also* neo-noir
Film Noir (Kirgo), 81
Film Noir (Silver and Ursini), 206
Film Noir Encyclopedia (Erickson), 244
Fiorentino, Linda, 268
Fisher, Steve, 58–59, 62
Fitzgerald, F. Scott, 250–51
Fleishman, Avram, 121
Flippen, Jay C., 187, *188*
Flora, Joseph, 132
Fonseca, M. S., 38
Forrest, Frederic, 235, *238, 243,* 244
Foy, Bryan, 153
Frank, Nino, 14, 41–42, 156
Frank, Sam, 117
Frears, Stephen, 272
Freeman, David, 122–23
French naturalism, 18–21, 135
French reviewers, 14
Fried, Gerard, 188

Gale, Robert, 226
Gale, Steven, 40
gangster pictures, 138, 148
gangsters' dialogue, 132
Gardner, Ava, *136*
Gates, David, 42
Gazzara, Ben, 165
German expressionism, 16–18; *Anatomy of a Murder,* 167–68; *The Glass Key,* 51; *The Killers* (1946), 135, 137; *The Maltese Falcon,* 37; *The Ministry of Fear,* 71; *Song of the Thin Man,* 58–59; *Spellbound,* 92; *Stranger on the Third Floor,* 22–23; *Strangers on a Train,* 101; *The Talented Mr. Ripley,* 254–55
German fatalism, 184
The Ghost Writer, 225
Giannetti, Louis, 83
Gilmore, Art, 189
The Glass Key (1935 film), 42, 47–49
The Glass Key (1942 film), *48,* 49–55, 276
The Glass Key (Hammett novel), 42, 45–46
Goetz, William, 152, 198
Going Steady (Kael), 187
Golden Age of British detective fiction, 3–4
Golitzen, Alexander, 77, 209
Goodrich, Frances, 57
Gordon, Ruth, 111, 117
Gores, Joe, 42, 235–37, 267
Grahame, Gloria, 58–59
Granger, Farley, 96–98, *103*
Grant, Kathryn, 168, *169*
Gray, Coleen, 190
The Great Gatsby (Fitzgerald), 250–51
Greene, Graham, 69–70, 249
Greenstreet, Sydney, 34–35
Gross, Charlie, 230
Gulager, Clu, 146
Gunning, Tom, 76
"The Gutting of Couffignal" (Hammett), 30

Hackett, Albert, 57
Hammett, Dashiell, 8; *After the Thin Man,* 57; *Another Thin Man,* 57–58; background, 4–7, 273; *Black Mask* stories, 7–10, 30, 227, 235–36, 240, 242–43; Cooke's

tribute to, 244; "Dead Yellow Women," 235–36, 240, 242–43; as friend of Nathanael West, 21; *The Glass Key* (novel), 42, 45–46; on *The Maltese Falcon* (film), 41; *The Maltese Falcon* (novel), 6, 7–10, 13–14, 29–31, 33–35, 41–42, 226, 228; Ned Beaumont character as, 45–46; on-screen portrayal, 235–44; radio series, 228–29; *Red Harvest*, 9, 45; self-assessment, 64; significance of, 4, 64, 267–68; *Strangers on a Train* screenplay, 94; television adaptations, 228–35; *The Thin Man*, 55–56, 62

Hammett (film), 235–44, *238, 267*, 268, 283–84

Hanson, Curtis, 218–19, 269

Hanson, Philip, 13

happy endings, 125

hard-boiled detective fiction, 4–7, 13–15, 132

Harmon, Melissa, 141

Hass, Robert, 35

Hasso, Signe, *114,* 115, 117

Haubner, Steffen, 125

The Haunted Screen (Eisner), 17

Hawks, Howard, 33, 142

Hayden, Sterling, 187, *188*

Hays Office (Will Hays), 47

Hearts of Age, 205

Hecht, Ben, 88, 89–90

Heflin, Van, 180–81, *182*

Heisler, Stuart, 49–55

Hellinger, Mark, 135–36

Hellman, Lillian, 9, 56, 64, 94, 229, 236

Hemingway, Ernest, 6–7, 131–34, 139, 141, 142

Henderson, Tony, 258

Henry, Catherine, 158–59

Heston, Charlton, 206–7, 209–10, *212, 212–14*

Heylin, Clinton, 198, 199–200

Highsmith, Patricia: background, 247–48; increased interest in, 262; *Ripley's Game* (novel), 257–58; *Strangers on a Train* (novel), 94–95, 98, 101, 106, 247; *The Talented Mr. Ripley* (novel), 248–50

Hirsch, Foster, 6, 20, 87, 138, 141–42, 155, 179, 185, 220, 226, 244, 262

Hitchcock, Alfred, *97; Spellbound,* 87–94, *91; Strangers on a Train,* 94–106, *97,* 204, 247

Hitler, Adolf, 16

Hoffenstein, Samuel, 152

Hoffman, Philip Seymour, 251, 257

Holden, Stephen, 15, 225

Holden, William, 127

Holmes, Sherlock, 3

Holt, Jason, 24

homosexuality: censorship and, 31–32, 34–35, 38, 96, 154, 186–87; *The Killing,* 186–87; *Laura,* 154–55, 161; *Maltese Falcon* films, 31–32, 34–35, 38; *Strangers on a Train,* 95–98, 105; *The Talented Mr. Ripley,* 252–53

Hopper, Dennis, 258

Horton, Robert, 184

The House of Dr. Edwardes (Beeding), 88

Houston, Penelope, 190

Human Desire, 20

Huston, John, *266; Asphalt Jungle,* 187; *Chinatown, 266,* 267; Hammett on, 41; *The Killers* (1946), 132–35,

138, 199; *The Stranger*, 199. *See also*
The Maltese Falcon (1941 film)
Huston, Walter, 39

illusion and reality. *See A Double Life*
Indiana, Gary, 261
Ingster, Boris, 21, 24

James, P. D., 4
Jameson, Richard, 226
jazz, 214–15, 230, 239
Jensen, Paul, 72, 99
Johnson, Diane, 46
Jones, Malcolm, 106
Judeo-Christian environment, 5

Kael, Pauline, 76, 94, 99, 187, 194,
   258
Kalat, David, 79
Kanin, Garson, 111, 112, 117
Kaper, Bronislau, 181, 202
Keaton, Buster, 122
Kehr, Dave, 112–13
Keller, Harry, 213–14
Kennedy assassination, 147–48
The Killer Inside Me (Thompson), 186
The Killers (1946 film), 132–42, *136*,
   148, 195, 199, 278–79
The Killers (1964 film), 132, 142–48,
   145, 282
"The Killers" (Hemingway), 131–34
Killer's Kiss, 185
The Killing, 184, 185–95, *188*, 281
Kinnear, Roy, 241, 243
Kirgo, Julie, 81
Kiszely, Philip, 34
Klawans, Stewart, 269
Krasner, Milton, 77, 113
Kroll, Jack, 271, 272
Kubrick, Stanley, 184, 185–95

L.A. Confidential, 225, 226, 269, 284
La Bete Humaine, 20
La Chienne, 18–20, 76
Ladd, Alan, *48*, 48–49, 55
Lake, Veronica, *48*, 48–49, 55
Lancaster, Burt, *136*
Lang, Fritz: background, 16–19;
   Clash by Night, 23; *Human Desire*,
   20; *M*, 71, 75; *Ministry of Fear*,
   69–76, *73*, 198, 277; *Scarlet Street*,
   17, 18, 19, 76–83, 277–78; *Spione*
   (Spies), 117
The Last Seduction, 268
Latimer, Jonathan, 49–50, 55
Laura, 152–61, *155*, 162–63, 276–77
Laurents, Arthur, 96
Law, Jude, 251, *252*, 257
Leavitt, Sam, 165
Legion of Decency, 78–79, 166
Lehman, Ernest, 104
Lei, Lydia, 240, 243
Leigh, Janet, 208
Lenski, Robert, 229
Lethem, Jonathan, 134–35
Levene, Sam, 137
lighting: *Act of Violence*, 179–80, 181;
   Anatomy of a Murder, 163; *The*
   Killers (1946), 137; *The Killers*
   (1964), 143; *The Maltese Falcon*,
   37; *Ministry of Fear*, 71; *Scarlet*
   Street, 17; *The Song of the Thin*
   Man, 58–59; *Spellbound*, 89; *Touch*
   of Evil, 210
The Lineup, 144
locations, 162
Loeffler, Louis, 165–66
Lorre, Peter, 21–24, *22*, 34, *37*
Loy, Myrna, 56–57, 62, *63*
Lubitsch, Ernst, 76
Lyons, Arthur, 185

M, 71, 75

Macdonald, Ross, 10, 267–68

Malkin, Barry "Blackie," 238–39

Malkovich, John, 257, 258–60, *259*

The Maltese Falcon (early films), 31–33

The Maltese Falcon (1941 film), 33–42, *37*; character types, 16, 187; filmography, 275–76; as first film noir, 13–14, 21, 24; *The Killers* compared to, 134–35

The Maltese Falcon (Hammett novel), 6, 7–10, 13–14, 29–31, 33–35, 41–42, 226, 228

Maltin, Leonard, 243–44

Mamoulian, Rouben, 153–54

Mancini, Henry, 214, 216

Marshman, D. M., Jr., 118

Marvin, Lee, 144–46, *145,* 148

Maslin, Janet, 257, 269

Masterson, Whit, 206, 207

Matheou, Demetrios, 261–62

Maugham, Somerset, 9

Mawer, Noel, 254, 257

Mayer, Louis B., 126

Mayersberg, Paul, 171

Mayes, Wendell, 163

McArthur, Colin, 133

McCarter, Jeremy, 3

McCarthy, Joseph, 15, 165

McDonnell, Brian, 69, 118, 218

McGilligan, Patrick, 96

McKeon, Barbara, 101–2

McPherson, Mark, 158

McQuarrie, Christopher, 270

mental illness, 112

Menzies, William Cameron, 92

Metty, Russell, 201, 209–11

Milland, Ray, 71, *73*

Miller, Jason, 230

Miller, Seton, 70–71

Miller's Crossing, 270

Minghella, Anthony, 106, 250–57, 262

Ministry of Fear (film), 69–76, *73,* 198, 277

The Ministry of Fear (Greene), 69–70

Monasch, Paul, 207–8

Moorhead, Agnes, 201

moral issues, 78–79, 273

Morricone, Ennio, 259

Movie Guide (Maltin), 244

The Moving Toyshop (Crispin), 102–4

Muhl, Edward, 207, 213–14, 216

Murch, Walter, 215–16, 252

musical score: *Act of Violence,* 181; *The Dain Curse,* 230; *A Double Life,* 114–15, 120; *The Glass Key,* 55; *Hammett,* 239, 268; *The Killers* (1946), 138; *The Killers* (1964), 146; *The Killing,* 188; *Laura,* 156, 158–59; *Ripley's Game,* 259; *Scarlet Street,* 78, 83; *The Stranger,* 202; *Touch of Evil,* 214, 216

Musuraca, Nicholas, 22–23, 24

Naremore, James, 33, 143, 190, 226

Narrative Films (Fleishman), 121

Narrow Margin, 187

Nash, Jay Robert, 172

National Film Registry, 42, 127, 141, 216

naturalism, 18–21, 177

neo-noir, 21, 220; *The Dain Curse,* 229–35, *230,* 267, 283; *The Talented Mr. Ripley,* 21, 106, 250–57, *252,* 262, 284–85

Ness, Richard, 89

New York State Board of Censors, 79

Nichols, Dudley, 76–77

Nicholson, Jack, *266*

Nilsson, Anna Q., 122
Nims, Ernest, 203, 213–14
Nolan, William, 4–5, 64
Norman, Barry, 122, 158

O'Brien, Edmond, 117, 136–37
Ormonde, Czenzi, 101–4
Orr, Christopher, 15
Oscars. *See* Academy Awards
Othello, 111, 115–16
O'Toole, Lawrence, 46

Palmer, Barton, 156
Paltrow, Gwyneth, 251, *252*
Panek, LeRoy, 226–27, 231, 234
Partos, Frank, 21
Patrick, Lee, 39
Peck, Gregory, 88, *91*
Perkins, V. F., 167
Perrin, Nat, 58–59
*A Personal Journey through American
    Movies*, 185
The Phantom Lady, 60
Phelps, Donald, 82
Phillips, Alastair, 220
Pinkerton Agency, 7–8
Polanski, Roman, 266–67
Portrait of a Sinner, 141
Postlethwaite, Pete, 272
Powell, William, 56–57, 62, *63*
pre-Code period, 31
Preminger, Otto: *Anatomy of a
    Murder*, 159, 160, 161–72, 178,
    214–15, 282; background, 151–52;
    Laura, 152–61, *155*, 162–63,
    276–77
Previn, André, 181
Price, Vincent, 153–55
profanity, 50
protagonists, 34

proto-noir, 21
psychoanalysis, 87–90, 94
pulp fiction, 7
Pulp Fiction, 270
Purple Moon, 250

Queen Kelly, 119–20

Rafferty, Terrence, 77, 121
Raft, George, 34, 47
Raksin, David, 156
Reading Early Hammett (Panek),
    226–27
Reagan, Ronald, 144–45
realism, 15–16, 137, 162, 210
Red Harvest (Hammett), 9, 45
Reed, Carol, 204
Relling, William, 118
Remick, Lee, 164
Renoir, Jean, 18–20, 76
Reservoir Dogs, 270, 272
Reynolds, Marjorie, 72, *73*
Rich, Frank, 250–51
Ridley, John, 268–69
Ripley's Game (film), 258–62, 285
Ripley's Game (Highsmith novel),
    257–58
Rivkin, Allen, 33
Robards, Jason, 235
robbery movies, 187
Robinson, Edward G., 77, 201
Rosher, Charles, 58–59, 62
Ross, Stanley Ralph, 172
The Rough and the Smooth, 141
Rozsa, Miklos, 114–15, 138
Russell, Ken, 160
Ryan, Robert, 181, *182*, 184

Sadoul, George, 34
Salter, Hans, 78

Sarris, Andrew, 75, 142, 156
Satan Met a Lady, 32
Sayre, Nora, 95
Scarlet Street, 17, 18, 19, 76–83, 277–78
Schenck, Joseph, 151
Schenkar, Joan, 94, 98
Schmidlin, Rick, 215
Schrader, Paul, 10, 14–15, 20, 185, 220
Schroeder, Barbet, 161
Schwartz, Ronald, 225
Scorsese, Martin, 185
Scott, Dougray, 259
Selznick, David O., 88
Sennewald, Andre, 50–51
settings of film noir: *A Double Life,* 112; *The Killers* (1946), 137; *The Maltese Falcon,* 34, 37; *Ministry of Fear,* 71; *Scarlet Street,* 77; *The Stranger,* 201
Shadoian, Jack, 139
Sharp, Henry, 71
Shaw, Joseph "Captain," 7, 227
Shayne, Konstantin, 203
shooting schedules, 14
Shurlock, Geoffrey, 163–64, 186
Sidney, Sylvia, 240
Siegel, Don, 142–48
Silver, Alain, 62, 144, 206, 220
Simmons, Jean, 229
Simon, Michel, 19–20
"The Simple Art of Murder" (Chandler), 6
Sinclair, Ian, 71
Singer, Bryan, 270, 272
Siodmak, Robert: background, 16–17, 135; *The Killers* (1946), 132–42, 136, 148, 195, 199, 278–79; *The Phantom Lady,* 60; *The Rough and the Smooth,* 141

Siskel, Gene, 243
Sklar, Robert, 151
Sloan, Jane, 96
Smith, Murray, 171
sociopaths. *See Ripley's Game* (film); *The Talented Mr. Ripley* (film); *The Talented Mr. Ripley* (Highsmith novel)
Some Like It Wilder (Phillips), 268
Song of the Thin Man, 58–62, 63, 187, 279
sound use, 116. *See also* musical score
Spacey, Kevin, 271, 272
Spade and Archer (Gores), 42
Sparkuhl, Theodor, 19
Spellbound, 87–94, 91, 277
Spiegel, Sam, 197–98, 199
Spies, 117
Spiner, Brent, 230
Spione (Spies), 117
Spoto, Donald, 94
The Spy Who Came in from the Cold, 225
Sragow, Michael, 165
Stanley Kubrick, Director (Walker), 189
Stark, Ray, 98
Stell, Aaron, 213
Stewart, James, 164, 169, 171
Stewart, Paul, 230
Stone, Oliver, 268–69
storyboarding, 36–37
Straight, Beatrice, 229
The Stranger, 197–206, 202, 278
Stranger on the Third Floor, 21–24, 275
Strangers on a Train, 94–106, 97, 103, 204, 247, 280–81
Stroheim, Erich von, 119, 120, 126, 127

Sturges, Ann, 184
Sunset Boulevard, 118–28, *123, 126,* 280
Surtees, Robert, 179, 180, 181
Swackhamer, E. W. (Egbert), 229, 232
Swanson, Gloria, 118–19, *123, 126,* 127

The Talented Mr. Ripley (film), 21, 106, 250–57, *252,* 262, 284–85
The Talented Mr. Ripley (Highsmith novel), 247–50
Tamiroff, Akim, 208–9
Tarantino, Quentin, 270, 272
Tavoularis, Dean, 238, 243
Taylor, John Russell, 75, 104
television adaptations, 228–29
temporary insanity plea, 170–71
theremin, 89
The Thin Man (film), 56–58
The Thin Man (Hammett novel), 55–56, 62
The Third Man, 204, 218
This Gun for Hire, 48–49
Thomas, Ross, 237, 239, 242–43
Thomas, Tony, 16, 117, 159
Thompson, Howard, 215
Thompson, Jim, 186, 190
Thomson, David, 48, 76, 148, 159, 180, 229, 258–59
Thurber, James, 64
Tibbetts, John C., 269
Tierney, Gene, 153, *155,* 159–60
Timm, Larry, 138
Touch of Evil, 20, 197, 206–20, *212, 219,* 281–82
Traver, Robert (aka John Voelker), 161–62
Travis, Victor, 198
trial scenes, 165

Tudor, Andrew, 148
Turner, Kathleen, 266
Turner, Lana, 164
Tuttle, Frank, 47–48, 48

Ursini, James, 62, 144, 206
The Usual Suspects, 270–72
U-Turn, 268–69

Van Dyke, W. S. "Woody," 56–58
Veiller, Anthony, 132–33, 199, 200–201
violence, 53, 147
violence and censorship, 50–51
Voelker, John, 161–62
Vogel, Virgil, 213

Walker, Alexander, 189
Walker, Robert, 95, *97, 103,* 106
Wallis, Hal, 32
Wanger, Walter, 76, 79
war criminals, 199
Warner, H. B., 122
Warner, Jack, 38
Waxman, Franz, 120
Webb, Clifton, 153–55, *155*
Webster, Andy, 257, 261
Welch, Joseph N., 165, 168, 170
Welles, Orson: *Hearts of Age,* 200, 205; *The Stranger,* 197–206, *202; Touch of Evil,* 20, 197, 206–20, *212*
Welsh, James, 204, 265–73
Wenders, Wim, 236–38, 244, 258
West, Nathanael, 21
White, Lionel, 185–86, 189
"The Whosis Kid" (Hammett), 30
Wiene, Robert, 17
Wilder, Billy: background, 16–19; *Double Indemnity,* 13, 14, 18, 20,

268; Farber on, 184; Hirsch on, 141–42; *Sunset Boulevard,* 118–28, *123, 126,* 280

Williams, John, 146

Williamson, Judith, 59

Wilson, Andrew, 262

Wilson, Edmund, 4, 6

Winchell, Walter, 157

Windsor, Marie, 187, 193

Winstone, Ray, 260

Winters, Shelley, 112–14, 117

Wishart, David, 188

witty dialogue, 57

World War II, 15

Young, Loretta, 201

Young, Victor, 55

Younger, Richard, 83

Zanuck, Darryl, 152, 153–57

Zinnemann, Fred, 16–17, 142, 177–84, 198

Zola, Emile, 18

Zugsmith, Albert, 206

ABOUT THE AUTHOR

Gene D. Phillips is the author of over twenty books dealing with literature, drama, and film, including *Beyond the Epic: The Life and Films of David Lean* (2006), *Some Like It Wilder: The Life and Controversial Films of Billy Wilder* (2009), and *The Francis Ford Coppola Encyclopedia* (2010), coauthored with Jim Welsh and Rodney Hill.